The Measure of Life

THE MEASURE OF LIFE

Virginia Woolf's Last Years

❧

HERBERT MARDER

Cornell University Press

ITHACA AND LONDON

Excerpt from *Letters of Leonard Woolf*, copyright © 1989 by the Estate of Leonard Woolf, reprinted by permission of Harcourt, Inc.

First published 2000 by Cornell University Press

Printed in the United States of America

Library of Congress Cataloging-in-Publication Data

Marder, Herbert
    The measure of life : Virginia Woolf's last years / Herbert Marder.
      p. cm.
    Includes bibliographical references and index.
    ISBN 0-8014-3729-6
    1. Woolf, Virginia, 1882–1941—Last years.   2. Novelists, English—20th century—Biography. I. Title.
    PR6045.072 Z8152   2000
    823'.912—dc21
    [B]

                                              00-020957

Cornell University Press strives to use environmentally responsible suppliers and materials to the fullest extent possible in the publishing of its books. Such materials include vegetable-based, low-VOC inks and acid-free papers that are recycled, totally chlorine-free, or partly composed of nonwood fibers. Books that bear the logo of the FSC (Forest Stewardship Council) use paper taken from forests that have been inspected and certified as meeting the highest standards for environmental and social responsibility. For further information, visit our website at www.cornellpress.cornell.edu.

Cloth printing   10 9 8 7 6 5 4 3 2 1

for Norma
Michael and Yuri
and Eric

who make my circle just

.

The waves on the beach, which for the most part beat a measured and soothing tattoo and seemed consolingly to repeat over and over again as she sat with the children the words of some old cradle song murmured by nature, "I am guarding you—I am your support," but at other times suddenly and unexpectedly . . . had no such kindly meaning, but like a ghostly roll of drums remorselessly beat the measure of life, made one think of the destruction of the island and its engulfment in the sea, and warned her whose day had slipped past in one quick doing after another that it was all ephemeral as a rainbow— this sound which had been obscured and concealed under the other sounds suddenly thundered hollow in her ears and made her look up with an impulse of terror.

Virginia Woolf, *To the Lighthouse*

&

Perfection, any kind of perfection, always demands some kind of concealment. Without something hiding itself, or remaining hidden, there is no perfection. But how can the writer conceal the obviousness of the word and its figures of speech? With the light. . . . To conceal with light: the Greek specialty. Zeus never stopped using the light to conceal. Which is why the light that comes after the Greek light is of another kind, and much less intense. That other light aims to winkle out what has been hidden. While the Greek light protects it. Allows it to show itself as hidden even in the light of day.

Roberto Calasso, *The Marriage of Cadmus and Harmony*

Contents

Illustrations

Editorial Note

Virginia Woolf wrote diary entries and letters at breakneck speed. In publishing posthumous collections of these works, her editors wisely reproduced her words as she wrote them, keeping irregularities of punctuation and spelling intact. These uncensored and nonregularized writings give a vivid impression of the writer's personality, and I quote them without any editorial changes throughout this book. Similarly, I use Woolf's provisional titles for works-in-progress. *The Years*, for example, is initially referred to as "The Pargiters" and "Here and Now" in accordance with Woolf's usage, and *Between the Acts* is referred to as "Pointz Hall."

The Measure of Life

Figure 1. Julia and Leslie Stephen, with Virginia behind them, at Talland House, St. Ives, 1893.

Prelude: The Shapes a Mind Holds

> But the dead, thought Lily, encountering some obstacle in her design
> which made her pause and ponder, stepping back a foot or so, oh,
> the dead! she murmured, one pitied them, one brushed them aside,
> one had even a little contempt for them. They are at our mercy.
>
> Virginia Woolf, *To the Lighthouse*

In one of Virginia Woolf's family photos her parents, Julia and Leslie
Stephen, are reading while the future novelist, eleven years old, sits
at the back of the room and looks right past them into the camera's
lens. Thirty-four years later, in *To the Lighthouse*, Woolf dramatizes
the photo and tells us what the characters are thinking. On a quiet
summer evening Mr. and Mrs. Ramsay sit side by side, apparently
concentrating on their books, but in fact carrying on an unspoken argument, each having heard the other side so often that speech is superfluous. He silently reproaches her for refusing to say that she loves
him, thus withholding her full allegiance. She silently replies there
must be boundaries, he must leave her some room in which to breathe
and revive her spirits. Though their differences are deeply rooted, for
the most part they are evenly matched, and the scene ends with an uneasy but loving truce that will go on indefinitely.

Both the snapshot and the fictional scene are attuned to the complexities of human relationships. Each is subversive in its own way, focusing on the tensions beneath the surface of domestic life, the crucial
moments "between the acts." The parents in the photo are defined by
their social and intellectual position—her dress, his beard, the books
and pictures and painted screen—while their watchful daughter looks
beyond them, as if they already belonged to the past. *To the Lighthouse* echoes this theme, describing a seemingly stable family life that
proves to be fragile and impermanent. The central section of the novel,
entitled "Time Passes," which comes right after Mr. and Mrs. Ramsay's silent argument, displays a relentless cycle of growth and decay,

the passing seasons and vast natural forces that threaten to obliterate all human values.

The contrast between these different views of the same domestic scene influenced the shape of this biography. *To the Lighthouse* diverges from the photo in one major way: Virginia is absent from the fictional version; that is, there is no child in the room with Mr. and Mrs. Ramsay. Woolf tried to achieve a special kind of impersonality, to be fully engaged and invisible at the same time, or, as she wrote about Shakespeare, to be "serenely absent-present." I have followed her lead, as far as the biographical genre permits, by combining an unobtrusive style with an attempt to convey the emotional as well as historical truths about people and events. In the process I have had to examine my assumptions about the nature of biography and the role of the biographer.

§

The questions are often general, and taken up at the table after dinner: Why does any one write biographies and why do people read them? We consider some common answers, say it's a search for identity, remembering one's cultural parents. Or it's having an imaginary playmate—the biographer, a lonely and isolated person, gets involved in another world, living and breathing it; a novelist does that too, in a sense. But, I say, the difference between them resembles the difference between a child and a parent. A fictional character is largely a child of the writer's imagination, while a biographical subject is more of a lawgiver, like a parent.

In this age of psychobiography, when everything has been mapped and opened to inspection, from Luther's identity crisis to Joyce's coprophilia, the biographer has remained relatively unknown, using objectivity as a cover, blending, like a nesting quail, into the dense underbrush of documents, transcripts, and commentaries. Winnowing these millions of words, so it seems, the writer must dismiss personal motives and efface himself or herself in order to survive. Although the biographer's feelings about the subject are decisive, his work is often treated as if it involved no more than refining raw information and elaborating a style—the messenger's self merging silently, unobtrusively, with the message. But as Virginia Woolf reminded her readers, we inevitably endow others with our own feelings and intentions. Especially so when the subject is no longer there to contradict us. The dead are at our mercy, Lily says in *To the Lighthouse*, a point Woolf elaborated in her essay on Christina Rossetti.

Seeking to imagine the past, she remarked, we shall arrange the inhabitants "in all sorts of patterns of which they were ignorant, for they thought when they were alive that they could go where they liked; and as they speak we shall read into their sayings all kinds of meaning which never struck them, for they believed when they were alive that they said straight off whatever came into their heads. But once you are in a biography all is different."

In a biography all is different. The person has become a subject in more than one sense, existing on terms she never imagined, a subject whose acts may be rationalized and whose words may be reinterpreted (biographers love unconscious motives) to mean exactly the opposite of what they say.

And still one reads lives, and people aspire to write them. In my case the biographical impulse has come at a late stage, after years of preoccupation with Virginia Woolf's work—a way of refocusing my attention, perhaps, after long exposure. Knowing how writers project their own feelings and motives onto their subjects, I hope to offset that tendency by reminding the reader that though the style may be unobtrusive and the sequence of key events well established, one's way of reading and the facts one selects are deeply influenced by personal history. Here, then, is a sketch of this biographer's origins followed by an account of how this book came to be written.

I was born in Vienna a few years before World War II and grew up in New York City. My childhood experience as a refugee taught me that most things, aside from personal loyalties, are transitory and unreliable. When I was thirteen my mother grew seriously ill, leaving me on my own for extended periods until her death from stomach cancer five years later; I was a student at City College then, and the idea of a degree and a career seemed meaningless. I passed my classes without trying and devoured large quantities of poetry and fiction, including the works of Virginia Woolf.

I married and enrolled in graduate school, keeping up an interest in the unfashionable Woolf. A friend egged me on to write a thesis on her novels. "Come on," she said, "no one spins a sentence the way she can—I mean, tell us what's happening in that room of one's own." Whereupon my eyes were opened. Virginia Woolf's reputation then, in the early sixties, was at a low point and perhaps due to make a comeback, although conventional wisdom held that three or four existing studies covered the subject more than adequately. My friend's suggestion took root. Woolf appealed to me because she was somewhat offbeat and outside the standard syllabus. I had read her purely for pleasure—she was one of my favorite writers—and naturally I had overlooked the possibility of mining her books for a thesis topic. Women and fiction—it was then an uncluttered field, without the sludge that encrusted Yeats and Eliot.

My adviser at Columbia said: "Not much mileage in feminism these days. Virginia Woolf was not a political animal. She was a lady, you know—disliked workingmen, Negroes, and Jews."

"There are subversive, radical ideas all over her books," I said.

He puffed decisively on his unlit pipe. "E. M. Forster says she was a snob and proud of it—a true Brit. Could generate some heat. I think you should go ahead."

So it was settled. The thesis, which described Woolf's war against her conditioning as an upper-middle-class lady, was published in the late sixties, at the very beginning of the Bloomsbury revival. Then, in 1972, Quentin Bell's biography of Virginia Woolf transformed the portrait of the artist I had carried in my mind. Aside from brief excerpts, I hadn't known her letters and diaries, which confirmed the subversiveness of the novels. There was now a dense penumbra of previously unpublished writings offering a richness of detail one couldn't guess at, an unknown Virginia. At the same time a new wave of feminism gave her work much greater visibility, turning her into an iconic figure, a major precursor; feminist critics, probing her political and psychological insights, showed how subtly she had anticipated later discussions of gender, cultural constructs, and the social order. Through the years her portrait gained in complexity, became stranger and more familiar, more like a person one had actually known, still remaining elusive, staying two steps ahead of me, in spite of the critical essays I wrote trying to keep up with her. I sometimes thought my interest in Virginia Woolf had something to do with my mother, who picked up after her sons and never asked them to do housework, who had been so radical politically and so conservative domestically—savoring the coming revolution while she kept the family going by sewing necks on cashmere sweaters in a sweatshop. The refrain of my mother's sacrifices—she would give anything for her children, she declared, so that they lived well and didn't suffer as she had suffered; all she expected in return was a little gratitude—brings to mind Virginia Woolf's discussion of the self-sacrificing wife and mother in Victorian England.

※

In January 1931, at the age of forty-nine, Woolf spoke to a gathering of professional women about her career as a writer and her attempts to kill the Angel in the House. The Angelic ideal, described in a well-known Victorian sequence of poems, was synonymous with sexual stereotypes that were still dominant in the thirties. Virtuous women, according to the myth, lived in an almost disembodied state, ethereally rising above animal lusts and dedicating their lives to the welfare of the family. During her youth, Virginia said, in the last days of Victoria's reign, every middle-class household had a resident Angel—she was as much a fixture as drapes and sideboard. In spite of her moral radiance, she was a practical body and did her domestic chores with great efficiency, which was most convenient for the Master of the House. Virginia's verdict on this character was scathing and compassionate. The Angel, she maintained, "was intensely sympathetic. She was immensely charming. She was utterly unselfish. She excelled in the difficult arts of family life. She sacrificed herself daily. If there was chicken, she took the leg; if there was a draught she sat in it—in short she was so constituted that she never had a mind or a wish of her own, but preferred to sympathize always with the minds and wishes of others. Above all—need I say it—she was pure."

Humor softens the indictment, but Virginia's anger pervades this sad catalogue of virtues. The spurious ideal had haunted her youth, for it was her parents' Angel. They had adopted its values and accepted the unequal roles it prescribed because "a real relationship between men and women was then unattainable." The Angel had infected their lives with unreality. In some ways the falseness grew worse after her mother's death, in the first year of Virginia's adolescence. Behind the myth of domestic virtue lurked the ugly reality that Virginia's older half brother, George, came into her room at night to kiss and fondle her. There was no one for her to turn to for help or guidance, no escape from sexual guilt and confusion. The aging Leslie Stephen was too wrapped up in his grief to notice her distress. More and more deaf and irascible, he subjected his daughters to emotional blackmail, insisting that there should always be an Angel in the house and one of them must inherit the job. Virginia was appalled by the self-pity that turned this man, who could be so sensitive, into a crude bully, blind to other people's feelings. After her father's death the Angel grew even more insidious, trying to smother her with its conventional wisdom, to prevent her from thinking and writing freely—an outrage against which she violently rebelled. "I turned upon her and caught her by the throat," she told her listeners. "I did my best to kill her. My excuse, if I were to be had up in a court of law, would be that I acted in self-defense."

This ironic vignette hardly suggests the length and bitterness of her struggle, which persisted well into midlife and culminated with her effort to re-create the past in *To the Lighthouse*. There she reconstructed the world of her childhood and drew vivid portraits of her parents in order to loosen the hold they still had on her. "I used to think of him & mother daily," she noted in her diary. "I was obsessed by them both unhealthily; & writing of them was a necessary act." The novel helped dispel nostalgia, but the Angel, being ectoplasmic, kept coming back to life, for "it is far harder to kill a phantom than a reality." And the phantom put on subtle disguises, still exploiting her need for parental approval. Virginia's next book, *Orlando*, a fantastic biography of her friend Vita Sackville-West, was a kind of ghost sonata in which her new love for Vita merged with her old desire to please her father. The story of Orlando, who lives for three hundred years and goes through a sex change halfway through, is simultaneously a chronicle of English literature and a love token. The hero/heroine's transformation from man to woman reflects the infusion of Virginia's father's ghost into the body of her lesbian lover. The book's inner dream logic says: my father (represented by the English classics, which I learned to love from him) and my lover (the aristocratic writer descended from Elizabethan nobles) inhabit one body, happily joined in the androgynous figure of Orlando.

Three years later, looking ahead to a new decade after completing *The Waves*, an austere novel depicting her own circle of friends and their collective ethos, Virginia announced with some confidence that the Angel was dead at last. She would now enter a phase in which she created chronicles without nostalgia—juxtaposing Victorian and modern times, observing that the domestic tyranny of the former led to the political fanaticism of the latter. She would respond to the changed political climate of the 1930s, writing to defend freedom in an age of concentration camps.

The Waves was a transitional work, a severely intellectual novel in the form of "soliloquies" by six friends. Taken together, the group portrait presents them not as conventional characters but as distinct phases of a single "complete human being"; the book's vision of overlapping personalities suggests a renunciation of the personal self, a desire for egoless anonymity. At times Virginia harnessed a Swiftian contempt for the human race, adopting the lupine, predatory style suggested by her married surname—the two opposing sides of her—Woolf/Anon—escaping at last like genies from a bottle. Strains of anger and renunciation run through all her work of the 1930s—the wolfish satire and the absolute vision no longer softened by charm, no longer linking her to the adolescent "Ginny," her father's daughter. With *The Waves* behind her, Virginia expressed some qualified optimism about the future. "Oh yes, between 50 & 60 I think I shall write out some very singular books, if I live. I mean I think I am about to embody, at last, the exact shapes my brain holds. What a long toil to reach this beginning—if *The Waves* is my first work in my own style!"

⚶

Virginia Woolf's last decade forms a coherent and distinct stage of her development. As Carolyn Heilbrun has pointed out, she "became a different person in her fifties." Her angry treatment of the Angel in the House may serve as one sign of her increasing concentration on social realities. While preparing her speech she had an inspiration for a new book about women and work, a book to confirm women's rebellion against patriarchal authority and to show how they had used their new freedoms. These subjects occupied her for several years and ultimately formed the basis of *The Years* and *Three Guineas*. But the Victorian legacy had another aspect. Behind the ministering Angel lurked its stunted double, a bitter spirit that emerged at unguarded moments to proclaim the inferiority of blacks, Jews, and colonials. Disdain for the poor and uneducated was in the air in the upper-middle-class society of Virginia's youth, and she inherited many of its prejudices. Her sense of superiority as a "lady" was deeply ingrained; like most of her friends she occasionally let drop a casual "nigger" or (her Jewish husband notwithstanding) an anti-Semitic remark. She had a sharp tongue and a gift for satire that could produce flashes of memorable cruelty. The early diaries sometimes sound as if they were the work of a holdover from the *ancien régime*. One of the earliest entries describes her feelings on seeing "a long line of imbeciles" during a walk in the country; their demented looks and ungainly bodies repelled her—she had herself recently suffered a mental breakdown and protested that the sight of these misshapen figures "was perfectly horrible. They should all be killed." On another occasion, recording her dealings with one of her servants, she noted the hopelessness of the poor, who "have no chance; no manners or self control to protect themselves with; we have a monopoly of all generous feelings— (I daresay this isn't quite true; but there's some meaning [in] it.)" The facile judgment and retraction reflect the rigidity of the class-conscious vision. Similar myopic and class-bound attitudes colored her mature work of the 1920s. The heroine of her "society novel," *Mrs. Dalloway*, will not let reports of distant atrocities disrupt the

pleasant routines of her day. She admits she is spoilt; she knows innocent people are being "hunted out of existence, maimed, frozen. . . .
She could feel nothing for the Albanians, or was it the Armenians?
but she loved her roses (didn't that help the Armenians?)—the only
flowers she could bear to see cut." Woolf's narrator apparently en-
dorses this appeal to private sensations, seeming to accept, if not endorse, her heroine's vision of roses as humanitarian aid. It's not merely
that the genocide is very remote; Clarissa is equally callous in her
treatment of a poor cousin whom she resents having to invite to her
party. Virginia deplored the disagreeable side of the fashionable lady,
but identified with her nonetheless, observing that her attitudes were
merely representative of those held by many members of her class.

This bias is only one side of the picture. Woolf's political sympathies, though she rarely expressed them in her early years, were firmly
with the democratic left and the Labour Party, to which Leonard
Woolf was a high-level adviser. As a young woman she had volunteered to lecture at Morley College for working-class men and
women, and later she participated in the grassroots activities of the
Women's Cooperative Guild, a network of working-class consumers.
Furthermore, as an artist and intellectual she had an unladylike commitment to highbrow ideas and modernist aesthetics. Her upper-class
reflexes and socialist politics coexisted without noticeable friction,
absorbed or obscured by the richness of her artistic personality. Virginia sometimes oscillated between the extremes of callousness and
sensitivity, and in this respect she resembled the fictional Clarissa
Dalloway, whom Alex Zwerdling has aptly described as a "laminated
personality made up of layers that do not interpenetrate." Real life,
of course, is not nearly so neat, and the various layers of Virginia
Woolf's personality merged and shifted noticeably over the years.

By 1929, when she published her feminist critique, *A Room of
One's Own*, the egalitarian impulse had grown more dominant; she
looked forward to a time when writers would examine the lives of ordinary women who remained unknown, condemned to obscurity—
"for all the dinners are cooked; the plates and cups washed; the children set to school and gone out into the world. Nothing remains of it
all. . . . No biography or history has a word to say about it." Some
adventurous future novelist would perhaps penetrate "without kindness or condescension . . . into those small, scented rooms where sit
the courtesan, the harlot and the lady with the pug dog." Her tone
betrayed a fair amount of condescension, but later in the 1930s that,
too, changed—no more racial slurs or disparaging remarks about the

poor in that charged atmosphere. As the dictators consolidated their hold on the Continent and storm troopers arrested and killed their opponents, Virginia increasingly identified with the rebels and victims of oppression, declaring herself an "outsider," a pacifist, and (by virtue of her marriage) a Jew. This new posture formed another layer, further complicating the mix of her social, intellectual, and artistic identities. The complexity of her outlook in the 1930s contrasted sharply with the prevailing calls for ideological purity and the simple taking of sides.

It is still hard to reconcile the multiple layers of Virginia's personality and tempting to solve the problem by making her merely one thing or another. Two decades ago Jane Marcus described her as "a guerrilla fighter in a Victorian skirt," a revolutionary and a "Marxist" (Marcus's quotes), and the labels have been influential, setting the tone for much subsequent criticism. They have tended to obscure Woolf's conservatism, which persisted right through the 1930s. Her training as a lady left its mark on the radical program of *Three Guineas*, which she addressed to privileged upper-middle-class women, and it emerged in the disdain she felt for her village neighbors when the war exiled her to Sussex. A most unusual guerrilla fighter who was a dedicated pacifist; a "Marxist" who never referred to Marx, either in her diary or in her extensive reading notes. Heilbrun in her essay "Virginia Woolf in Her Fifties" describes her in a simpler, less restrictive way as a writer of genius who discovered the full extent of her anger and expressed it in terms that were relevant to the crises of her time.

❧

With the threat of war constantly present and growing, the atmosphere of the 1930s disturbed many of Virginia's former assumptions; not only her class consciousness but also the artistic aims that produced *Mrs. Dalloway* and *To the Lighthouse* had become superfluous. The crisis tested her values and character, forcing her to place a new emphasis on mundane facts and the external world, to set new goals in response to the pressures of political events. As she said while writing her next book, *The Years*, she had forced herself "to break every mould" and to find a new form of expression more nearly in tune with the social consciousness of the day.

My decision to write this biography grew out of a fascination with the way people change under stress. I set out to describe the changes Virginia went through in the 1930s, her efforts to oppose the collective insanity without making things worse. The barbarians were winning everywhere, and their victory would mean the end of civilization as she knew it. She believed that a sane person should refuse to imitate the enemy, responding to violence with passive resistance and passionate "indifference." Resisting the prevailing mood, she stressed the importance of tolerance, reason, and gaiety, reaffirming these civilized attitudes while strident voices tried to drown her and one another out. Looking at her struggle, I felt that the enlightened Virginia of the 1930s, who displayed great sanity and courage under fire (her decision to choose the time and manner of her death did not diminish that), required a biography of her own. The challenge would be to chart the intersection between her personal evolution and historical events. Furthermore, the biographer would have to convey the intricate interpenetrating layers that grow around a personality in the course of change, presenting not only the reformed Virginia but also the reversions to an earlier Virginia who harbored ancient prejudices and still at times yielded to them.

She herself gave some hints of how the job might be done. In 1939 she stated her dissatisfaction with the standard biographical form (she was in the midst of writing an authorized life of Roger Fry) and noted the elusiveness of the truth, even about events that one knows from firsthand experience. Nevertheless, one can arrive at an understanding; she believed that there is a pattern hidden behind the apparently random "cotton wool" of daily life and that one can define the basic themes or motifs that connect one's life to that underlying pattern. Such core motifs calibrate us, they are the "background [measuring] rods or conceptions" that give our lives shape and meaning. Drawn to that vision, I observed the interplay of motifs all through Virginia's diaries and letters, tracing their variations, images folded and overlaid on each other—her constant references to water, for example— the meanings refracted from a single core, as in an early draft of *The Waves*, where she pictured "many mothers, like one wave succeeding another," and went on to evoke the pulsing rise and fall of ancient civilizations, Egypt, Greece, and Rome. That novel, Virginia told a friend, was "completely opposed to the tradition of fiction. . . . I am writing to a rhythm and not to a plot." All writing, she said, is "nothing but putting words on the backs of rhythm."

So the act of giving birth, the rise and fall of civilizations, and the flow of words in a sentence are threaded together by a common rhythm, and they are connected to other motifs: Virginia's revolt against the "masculine" sentence and Victorian conventions; her habit of composing sentences on long daily walks (her loping stride inherited from her alpinist father); and her use of the walking motif in her fiction. These images and their associations, backed by the breaking waves and the flowing river, form a symbolic fabric that brings Virginia herself closer, not by explaining but by establishing her presence, inviting us to see things as she saw them.

Keeping in mind the limits of biography, the meagerness of what one can know about any other human being, and the vast areas that remain in darkness, I vowed to respect the otherness of my subject, to listen to what Virginia Woolf actually said rather than what one expected her to say. In short, to believe her, resisting the temptation to impose any single paradigm—repression, sexual abuse, bipolarity—but rather to rely on her own testimony and to trace the self-creating motifs, the core of identity, defined by her own words. She distrusted psychological formulas and insisted that we err in "perpetually narrowing and naming these immensely composite and wide-flung passions." I followed her lead in another way by placing special emphasis on the offbeat rhythms and variegated textures of everyday life. Such a style, which concentrates on the effort to recover the subject's own point of view—what Virginia called "the background rods or conceptions"—shaping the story so as to display those leading motifs, constitutes "allobiography": a kind of writing that adopts the position of the *other*, who is the biographical subject.

In keeping with this style, I resolved not to speculate about facts but to rely on the evidence of letters, diaries, and other contemporary sources, limiting myself to what could be fully substantiated in the documentary record. I used the word "perhaps" very rarely and only after careful consideration. Staying as close as possible to Virginia Woolf's point of view, I also resolved not to anticipate events any more than necessary, to remember that time flows in one direction and that the biographer's foreknowledge, though a powerful lens, can easily distort the outlook.

She was a difficult writer, an ironist who made up stories and led her readers along obscure byways. She was often playful, sometimes malicious, and she enjoyed embellishing the facts about people, which has caused some critics to doubt her reliability as a witness. But like any good satirist she was adept at drawing clear lines between fact and fantasy and generally did so. As her friend William Plomer observed, she "was really devoted to the facts themselves." Although her poetic gifts were most evident, another side of her, the social being, was "a sort of scientist" with an interest in "anthropological truth." An astute observer of people and events, Virginia Woolf used her fanciful revisions of drab reality to delight and raise consciousness, not to manipulate or mislead. At the same time, her life was shadowed by the mysterious affinity between art and suffering. She spoke simply and movingly about important matters like her love of her husband and sister, her hatred of tyrants and dictators, her rebellious nervous system. Particularly during the 1930s she lived up to her ironic description of herself as "the truthfullest of people." When reviewers praised the beauty of her writing, ignoring its substance, she protested that she would rather be known as an ugly writer but an honest one, a serious artist who was only trying to say, as exactly as possible, something that had never been said before.

I   *Human Nature Undressed*

Is there a ratio between art and life, between the refined forms of a writer's work and the daily litter of papers and bills, head colds, dirty dishes, uninvited guests?

As Virginia Woolf said after finishing *The Waves*, "My ship has sailed on. I toss among empty bottles & bits of toilet paper. O & the servants." Her history reflects a constant struggle against banal interruptions, against the random daily events that interfered with her literary work. She was relatively poor after her father's death and had to earn her living. Sir Leslie Stephen, though distinguished, was only a man of letters, and he didn't leave enough capital for Virginia to live on, at least by upper-middle-class standards. She and Leonard (whom she called her "penniless Jew") worked hard as writers and publishers, putting in long hours six or seven days a week. For many years, till her novels began to sell and the Hogarth Press became profitable, the Woolfs' income was as modest as their way of life. They were intellectuals who had no desire for luxury or grand possessions. Their left-wing politics placed them on the fringes of the privileged upper middle class, but they kept up easy relations with members of the establishment. Virginia's family and friends were the kind of people who had dominated the senior levels of the English civil service, armed forces, and professions since the nineteenth century. According to a 1930 estimate, the governing class was remarkably small—no more than 100,000 people from the higher bourgeoisie, plus a few hundred aristocratic families—out of a total population of 45 million. Virginia belonged to this elite by birth and training. She voted Labour and held heretical opinions, but her cousins were pillars of the establishment—

eminent professionals, knighted civil servants, an admiral, a former cabinet minister. Connections. She spoke their language, she was a lady, and her way of life grew out of that soil and reflected the values of her class.

A very exceptional lady, nevertheless. By the late 1920s her outlook had been tempered by long years of intellectual and artistic activity. She had an established reputation as a novelist and critic. Two major novels in the modernist mode, *Mrs. Dalloway* and *To the Lighthouse*, had brought her some fame and even notoriety, but they were too original and complex to attract a large readership. This began to change in October 1928, after the publication of her biographical fantasy, *Orlando*, a more accessible book that sold surprisingly well. She followed it with her long essay on women and fiction, *A Room of One's Own*, which also introduced her writing to a wider public.

Virginia Woolf habitually used odd moments at the end of work or before guests arrived to write in her diary. She wrote whatever came into her head, as if she could never get her fill of writing, as if she hoped to get through the artistic barricades to some more essential state. The whole work, with its constant shifts in mood and perspective, has a shimmering unity that often seems to baffle as it enlightens. On March 28, 1929, she wrote in her diary after six weeks of silence. An illness had prevented her from working, and for half the time she had lain in bed, making up the ending of *A Room of One's Own* in her head—she saw things with startling clarity during her enforced idleness—so that she was able to write it all down in a single excited outpouring when she recovered. A fertile illness, then. She had run into Vanessa that afternoon, she wrote, while shopping on Tottenham Court Road. Holding on to her bundles, she felt her deep kinship with her sister—how they mirrored each other, both "sunk fathoms deep in that wash of reflection in which we both swim about." Vanessa was preparing to leave for four months in the south of France, but the passing of time, Virginia thought, drew them closer together. It was a "potent" spring day, a day when everything was heightened by the bustle and excitement of the streets.

Her mind was exploring "a thousand things as I carried my teapot, gramophone records & stockings under my arm." She thought about her next novel; she would go far out beyond the fanciful satire of *Orlando* and let herself sink down to unconscious depths. "I am going to face certain things. It is going to be a time of adventure & attack, rather lonely & painful." The new novel would convey a mystical sense of living on several different planes at once. She had been fascinated by a story Vanessa told about a giant moth, literally "half a foot, across," that tapped loudly at her window one night. For Virginia the moth's instinctive action was linked to some hidden dayspring behind the visible world. She imagined that her new book would connect at every point to that mythic realm, so that every object, no matter how ordinary—the pull cord on the window shade and the bowl on the table—would be "saturated" with its light. "Why admit any thing to literature that is not poetry—by which I mean saturated. . . . The poets succeed by simplifying: practically everything is left out. I want to put practically everything in; yet to saturate." A program that might well have been approved by Proust or Kafka, Lawrence or Joyce.

She went on to ask whether there was something too facile about these literary plans. When she was younger her books "were so many sentences absolutely struck with an axe out of crystal: & now my mind is so impatient, so quick, in some ways so desperate." Desperate perhaps because she was aging, like some of her friends, who seemed increasingly "wrinkled & dusty." Had she deteriorated? No, she was not like the others, she still felt the rush of ideas within her. "Only in myself, I say, forever bubbles this impetuous torrent. . . . I am more full of shape & colour than ever. I think I am bolder as a writer. I am alarmed by my own cruelty with my friends. Clive, I say, is intolerably dull. Francis is a runaway milk lorry." A sudden confession that preserves her exacting standards while apologizing for them. The exaggerated claim—"only in myself, I say, forever"—hints at some desperation, as well as defiance.

But on this spring day she saw an opening, a doorway, through which she could pass in pursuit of some "strenuous adventure." Sometimes, when she woke in the small hours of the night, she had to brace herself against her terrors by reminding herself that she had been able to conquer them in the past. The decision to write *Orlando* had come out of these struggles with her demons. "All this money-making," she noted in December 1928, "originated in a spasm of black despair one night at Rodmell." She had vowed to find a way out—and since part of her misery was caused by "the perpetual limitation of everything; no chairs, or beds, no comfort, no beauty; & no freedom to move," she decided there and then to acquire these things. And now in March she could boast that she had made "£1000 all from willing it early one morning. No more poverty I said; & poverty has ceased." Her strengths appeared most clearly at times when she seemed most vulnerable. She deplored her shaky nerves, but she knew her own importance as a writer. She was proud of making money and contributing to the prosperity of the Hogarth Press. Her work was not just scribbling, but had the tangible effect of "keeping 7 people fed & housed. . . . They live on my words"—these seven distinct, idiosyncratic personalities. Next year, she predicted, they would be living off *A Room of One's Own*. After that came the new novel, with its metaphysical theme that would demand great concentration; she would "enter a nunnery," banishing worldly interests. The din of the traffic all around her seemed to dismantle these plans, even as she made them. Yes, she would continue as she had been, going out into society and meeting people while she wrestled with her very abstruse theme. She lived on incongruity, and thrived on contrasts—a trait that emerged strikingly in her diary on another March 28, exactly a year later, when she was close to completing a draft of the new novel. "Home from tea with Vanessa and Angelica," she wrote. "A fine spring day. I walked along Oxford St. The buses are strung on a chain. People fight & struggle. Knocking each other off the pavement. Old bareheaded men; a motor car accident; &c. To walk alone in London is the greatest rest." Seemingly a detached observer and also perversely implicated, she saw the random aggression, the accident, the poverty-stricken old men, as if these scenes revealed something she wanted, some truth, some confirmation of a reality she felt within herself.

♃

Virginia loaded her diary with curious details and particulars of daily life, having concluded that the most commonplace facts often bring one up against essential questions. In 1930 she recorded a tour of the greenhouses at Waddesdon, one of the Rothschild estates. Taken round by Mr. Johnson, the head gardener, she was repelled by the display of showy flowers. "Cyclamen by the hundred gross. Azaleas massed like military bands. . . . One flower wd. have given more pleasure than those dozens of grosses." The observation inspired some further reflections about human pursuits and cultivated gardens.

> [Virginia's diary, April 13, 1930]
> There were rows of hydrangeas, mostly a deep blue. Yes, said Mr Johnson, Lord Kitchener came here & asked how we blued them . . . I said you put things in the earth. He said he did too. But sometimes with all one's care, they shot a bit pink. Miss Alice [de Rothschild] wouldn't have that. If there was a trace of pink there, it wouldnt do. And he showed us a metallic petalled hydrangea.

Figure 2. Oxford Street, London, 1930.

No that wouldnt do for Miss Alice. It struck me, what madness, & how easy to pin ones mind down to the blueness of hydrangeas, & to hypnotise Mr Johnson into thinking only of the blueness of hydrangeas. He used to go to her every evening, for she scarcely saw anyone, & they would talk for two hours about the plants & politics. How easy to go mad over the blueness of hydrangeas & think of nothing else.

Virginia's satirical treatment of the gardener and his obsession—he reminded her of "a nectarine, hard, red, ripe"—is coupled with a sense of familiarity, an awareness of how easy it is "to go mad" over one's garden—or the form of a novel or a political program. How easy, she says with consternation and sympathy, how human, to fall into a hypnotic trance and so pass one's life going round and round one narrow track.

She could poke merciless fun at the gardener's obsession and treat her friends' private lives with irreverent glee. But she had her own domestic compulsions—modest problems she could not treat with her usual humor—for example, the servant question, which harked back to her Victorian childhood and was therefore a serious matter. In spite of their socialist principles, the Woolfs could not do without a cook in residence, though they employed her with mixed feelings. During the years immediately following World War I, Virginia and Leonard had two live-in maids to do their cooking, washing, and cleaning. Paid help was a necessity at a time when there were few labor-saving devices. According to the social historians Noreen Branson and Margot Heinemann, upper-class English social life "depended on the almost unlimited supply of low-paid domestic servants. . . . Dependence on servants was not confined to the great houses or the very rich; the pattern repeated itself, albeit on a more modest scale, right throughout the upper middle class. You did not normally invite people to a meal at a restaurant, you invited them to lunch or dinner in your home, and the meal would be cooked and served by your domestic staff. You did not normally spend your holidays in hotels; you either owned or rented a house, and stayed there with a staff of servants to look after you while you invited other friends to stay."

This description fits the Woolfs' case precisely. They had two houses—one in London, where they lived most of the year and which also contained the offices of the Hogarth Press; the other a country cottage, where they went during summers and on weekends. Both places were homely and unpretentious. Monk's House in Sussex had belonged to a pub-keeper and at first lacked an indoor toilet, though it had a fine garden. But both houses supported a way of life centered on the giving and receiving of hospitality—frequent invitations to lunch, dinner, weekends in the country—and they were maintained by "low-paid domestic servants."

For Virginia and Leonard, as for most people of their class, problems with servants were one of the irritants of daily life, a minor evil that occasionally blew up into a major disturbance. Domestic help was a staple of polite conversation, like garden pests and the weather. There were long stretches when Virginia's letters to her sister, Vanessa, contained a daily digest of visits to employment agencies and negotations about hours and wages. The problem subsided at times but always recurred. By the mid-1920s the Woolfs, hoping to simplify their lives, were down to one live-in maid, with two or three others coming in as needed to help with the cleaning and the garden. But in the summer of 1929 the servant problem got worse.

Relations between Virginia and Nelly Boxall, who had been with them since the early years of their marriage, were strained. Nelly's moods varied unpredictably, shifting from friendliness to open hostility without warning. She was good-hearted, passionate, mean—and altogether "the most faithful and enraging of her kind." Her presence in the house was a constant distraction; there was no escaping her. Virginia, who was now in her late forties, was deeply immersed in the new novel, her fictional "autobiography," which was proving even more difficult than she had expected. It presented six friends summing up their lives in a series of impersonal soliloquies. The story, she noted, was not about individual selves but about "something in the universe that one's left with." And all through this time she was embroiled in a series of violent quarrels with her cook. It was the sort of ironic contrast that Virginia loved to expose in the lives of others. Nelly Boxall tried her spirit and entered into her emotional life; she tricked her into sympathy and resentment. Virginia's diary, where she had often recorded her anger and frustration with the servants, also reflected her desire to understand their lives. "If I were reading this diary," she noted in December 1929, "if it were a book that came my way, I think I should seize with greed upon the portrait of Nelly, & make a story—perhaps make the whole story revolve round that—it would amuse me. Her character—our efforts to be rid of her—our reconciliations."

A garrulous person with a "funny rather mulish face," Nellie had come to the Woolfs as a young woman in 1916 and was growing middle-aged in their service. In the late 1920s she played the twin roles of trusted old servant and shrewish dependent, alternately pampering Virginia and baiting her. She was an excellent cook, who could be relied on to serve appetizing food when the Woolfs had three dinner parties and two tea parties in eight days. She was also a hypochondriac—constantly preoccupied with her own internal organs and, as Virginia noted, childishly demanding. "Nelly has vacillated between tears & laughter, life & death for the past 10 days; can't feel an ache anywhere without sending for me or L. to assure her that aches are not certainly fatal. Then she cries. Never, never, never will she get over it. . . . And nothing the matter save what one of us would call an upset inside." Nellie was a natural manipulator who knew how to disarm her mistress, first getting under her skin and then exploiting her guilt. "Oh ma'am I never meant to tire you—dont go on talking now if it tires you—but you wouldnt give me any help. Now Grace had all the help she wants. . . . For 3 years I've been ill."

Virginia endured Nelly's cantankerous temper and observed her character with curiosity, but there were times when her ironic detachment failed her. During the summer of 1929 the tension at Monk's House, where the rooms were small, grew unbearable. Nelly was sullen, slowly working herself up to a display of temper, in the course of which she would give notice. It was her way of letting off steam, and it had happened so often in the past that Virginia had vowed never, never to believe her again. But this year, when the complaints and threats began, when working days were disrupted by bitter scenes, Virginia was closer than ever before to letting Nelly go permanently. After a violent quarrel, she did ask her to leave the house, to which Nelly replied stridently that nothing could please her more. Virginia was tormented by mixed feelings. She was sickened by the quarrel— it was sordid and ridiculous. It would be "stupendous" to free herself from this degrading relationship, although she hardly knew how to accomplish it after so many years. But if she didn't act now she would be condemned to keep Nelly on forever, and the thought appalled her: "I looked into her little shifting greedy eyes, & saw nothing but malice & spite there . . . she doesn't care for me, or for anything." During recent years the Woolfs had spent countless hours pacing up and down, discussing Nelly's ultimatums, her complaints about coal scuttles and working hours. She resented their having guests and let them know it. She felt overworked and unappreciated. She was jealous. Virginia remarked that these imbroglios were "worse than operations for cancer." And yet, two days after ordering Nelly out of the house, she noted with relief that they had made peace again, she was staying. "Heaven be praised; it is all over & calm & settled." The thought of Nelly being cast out, with nowhere to go and jobs hard to find, was too painful.

Both women were highly emotional, but in different ways, divided as much by temperamental as by class differences—and living side by side in such close quarters—the mistress, all speed and remoteness, vainly trying to penetrate the maid's stubborn immovability, and both of them baffled by a certain mutual fascination. After one of their quarrels Nelly had said: "I am too fond of you ever to be happy with anyone else," which was the greatest compliment possible. This relationship gave Virginia her most intimate contact with a member of the lower classes since her youth, when the family cook, Sophia Farrell, had been a powerful presence in her life. The relationship allowed her to imagine her own prehistory. Nelly represented the self "in a state of nature; untrained; uneducated, to me almost incredibly without the power of analysis or logic; so that one sees a human mind wriggling undressed—which is interesting; & then, in the midst of one's horror at the loathesome spectacle, one is surprised by the goodness of human nature, undressed; & it is more impressive because of its undress." Nelly's psychology baffled her; she was appallingly spiteful one moment and then, ignoring the fact that she had been fired, bicycled miles to fetch cream for their dinner, acting out of genuine good nature, because Mr. and Mrs. Woolf must not suffer.

Their irrational quarrels were rooted in something beyond personal differences. Virginia thought that the fault lay in the system, which allowed the uneducated Nelly to let herself into their lives, to become dependent on them as if she were part of the family, when they were culturally so different. It was a version of the colonial dilemma. Like the Europeanized "native," Nelly had lost her identity; she had become a "mongrel," a displaced person without roots anywhere. Virginia and Leonard were paying for the sins of previous generations, sweeping up a "rubbish heap" left by their Victorian parents. Unfortunately, Virginia's analysis didn't make it any easier when she went into the kitchen and found Nelly sulking. She longed to be treated as an employer, not a friend. The spiteful scenes would happen again, the cycle of quarrels and reconciliations. But their ties were strong, and she suspected that they would last a lifetime, feeling half pleased that parting was so much harder than she had expected it to be.

Virginia's uneasy bonding with Nelly and her other servants took place against a background of economic inequality and hardship for the working classes. Having for a long time spent part of each year in Rodmell, Virginia knew something about rural poverty, and at times the ugliness came close. One day in June 1929, after visiting a sad-eyed young mother in the village, she lamented that "incubus of injustice," the struggle to survive when there was barely enough money for food. It was intolerable—she understood the desire to rebel, imagined wanting to do something violent if she were in the young woman's place. "Annie Thompsett & her baby live on 15/ a week. I throw away 13/- on cigarettes, chocolates, & bus fares. She was eating rice pudding by the baby's cradle when I came in." Virginia hired Annie to help her with occasional cleaning and cooking. A year later, when Annie was evicted from her home on short notice, the Woolfs bought a nearby cottage and let her live there in return for doing their housework on a regular basis.

Ironically, the crash of 1929, which caused massive unemployment and hunger in the north of England, hardly touched well-to-do upper-class people in London. In that year Virginia and Leonard were becoming affluent for the first time in their lives, and she had earned almost a cabinet minister's salary. The Hogarth Press prospered; Virginia joked that they were "hauling in money like pilchards from a net." The appearance of *Orlando* and *A Room of One's Own* had secured her position. From here on she was pretty sure of being well paid for anything she wrote. This was the context in which she had boasted about making £1,000 merely by willing it early one morning. The yearly wage of a skilled worker at this time was about £150.

Virginia's grudging indulgence of Nelly grew out of her guilty conscience. As she wrote her new friend, Ethel Smyth, in 1930, she was infuriated by servants and quite unable to be ruthless when dealing with them face to face: "They are so weakly and devoid of all support, and one sees their poor fluttering lives as one talks." The thought of Nelly made her savage with rage against her own class for their ineptitude as governors—for "having let grow on our shoulders such a cancer, such a growth, such a disease as the poor are." The shrillness of her tone suggests she was aware of being on morally questionable ground—blaming the system while enjoying its benefits. It was a burden that she resented and expiated daily.

In addition to her moral distaste, Virginia's vehemence had another, less obvious cause. She lived very close to a psychological borderline; she was a manic-depressive who had kept her illness in check for years but always knew it could return. When she was well, her energy was remarkable, but she had recurring minor breakdowns—

intense headaches combined with fits of gloom, which sent her to bed for days and sometimes weeks. Shortly after her marriage, in 1913, she had swallowed a huge dose of Veronal and lain in a coma all night, coming within a hairsbreadth of dying.

Her fame as a novelist and a woman of letters had partly eclipsed the memory of her suicide attempt—it was an old story, sixteen years had gone by since then. But she still lived close to the edge; she could blunder into an emotional whirlpool and be sucked under for good. That possibility, which was often on her mind, influenced her attitude toward practical matters like money and servants. She had written *Orlando* with the conscious aim of ending her financial insecurity and making domestic life more gracious, hoping by those means to resist depression. In spite of her book's success, she still found herself fighting off suicidal thoughts at three in the morning. She had described her terrors in 1926, while she was writing the last pages of *To the Lighthouse*. She woke with the sensation of being on a rack: "physically like a painful wave swelling about the heart—tossing me up. I'm unhappy unhappy! Down—God, I wish I were dead." Comparing herself to Vanessa, whose life was so full, who had her children to justify her, she felt worthless—a vain, incompetent chatterer whom people laughed at. "Failure failure. (The wave rises). Oh they laughed at my taste in green paint! Wave crashes. I wish I were dead! I've only a few years to live I hope." The urgency of the waves passing through her body, draining her like a physical seizure, is partly undercut by the absurd reference to her taste in green paint—a typical, though perhaps unintended, note of satire. But the pain is dominant. The episode left Virginia with a vision of the sea and waves breaking on the shore, supplying a major motif of the new novel, which she ultimately called *The Waves*. In June 1929 some doubts about her writing made her reflect again that she lived at the edge of a "great lake of melancholy" into which she might pitch and be drowned at any moment; only her work kept her afloat. "Lord, how deep it is. . . . Directly I stop working I feel that I am sinking down, down. And as usual, I feel that if I sink further I shall reach the truth. That is the only mitigation; a kind of nobility. Solemnity. I shall make myself face the fact that there is nothing—nothing for any of us. Work, reading, writing are all disguises; & relations with people. Yes, even having children would be useless." The seductiveness of those depths, which made them all the more terrifying, is clear from the qualities she encounters there: "nobility," "solemnity." She did not know whether she really wished to escape her "glooms"—they offered a sterner truth, a desolate reward that tempted her, and she re-solved to defend herself by bringing along more work than she could possibly get done when she left for her summer holiday in July.

❧

Work was her lifeline; she concentrated on the difficulty of writing, screwing her brain, as she worded it, "tight into a ball," until she came to the verge of extinction (again, her own word)—it took a desperate need, or a masochistic obsession, to drive her on. Sometimes she wondered why she inflicted so much pain on herself. An appetite for the highs?—release of sunbursts in her brain, a flare in which she saw colors separate and run together, till the brilliance overloaded? Recurring struggles to maintain her balance, reversals—black "caverns of gloom and horror open round me"—and then bursts of intoxicating euphoria.

"What is called a reason for living," says Camus, "is also an excellent reason for dying." Virginia tested herself every morning with a dose of strenuous reality. She could have made money by writing popular fiction, but she wanted to be used up by a morning's writing, consumed by her work, so that, as she said of Mrs. Ramsay in *To the Lighthouse*, there would be "scarcely a shell of herself left for her to know herself by." It was a daily trial—many small deaths to deflect her interest in the big one, trading one obsession for another. As long as she accepted the self-prescribed "effort and anguish," she tricked the wild other self that could fasten really dangerous screws on her. She survived by absorbing regular doses of pain.

There was the ordeal of bringing herself to the highest tension, the screw of creation, every morning, keeping the devil down, the terrors, keeping this balance for almost forty years—a mental economy dating back to her youth. When she finished a book she suffered. When the reviews came in she suffered again, naked. A hostile review was dangerous, threatening her belief in the work and her system for survival. After each book she figured a mental balance sheet of favorable and unfavorable judgments, and began it all over again—the grind, the marshaling of ideas.

A high level of daily pain, then, combined with creative excitement and occasional ecstasy—which can leave one depleted, but also, as Virginia said, open to gaiety and recklessness. "I always remember the saying that at one's lowest ebb one is nearest a true vision. I think perhaps 9 people out of ten never get a day in the year of such happiness as I have almost constantly"—joy that she shared with her friends and loved ones, who knew her as the most delightful of companions, "a creature of laughter and movement," the novelist Elizabeth Bowen called her. When she emerged into the light of common day she often felt elated just to be there—a vigorous woman at the height of her powers, who was fascinated by the sights and sounds she encountered on her long, rambling walks through London, the scenes at every corner, which yielded "the greatest rest." The same visceral response to the city fills the opening episode of *Mrs. Dalloway*, where Clarissa Dalloway walks across St. James's Park to buy flowers, drinking in the atmosphere, musing on a hundred and one things, and confessing as she stands at the curb while the taxicabs pass, that she has a perpetual sense "of being out, far out to sea and alone"—which, if anything, heightens the pleasure of walking toward crowded Bond Street on this sunny morning.

2   *A Taste of Salt*

By the late 1920s many political observers in England had grasped the fact that the treaty imposed at Versailles in 1919 had not resolved anything. Europe was lurching toward the next great war; governments were ruled by inexorable forces, national leaders were hollow men, pretending to shape events that were in fact beyond their control. Absorbed in her work, Virginia heard the warning signals faintly at first. But she was in touch with the younger generation of writers and aware of their pessimism about the future. After *The Waves*, her most ambitious variation on the lyrical style, she became increasingly engaged, struggling to decipher political realities while the politicians subsisted on fantasy and self-deception. Her life story during the thirties composes itself around the debate about social responsibility, around her efforts as a writer and social critic to work against the use of force.

Virginia's friendship with the composer Ethel Smyth, whom she met in 1930, reflected a desire to broaden her outlook beyond her own exclusive circle. Though Ethel had fought for women's rights, she still kept the outlook of the sporting and hunting set from which she came. Hers was a red-blooded English kind of eccentricity, a spirit of enterprise and daring, which made her feel quite at home with the ordinary man or woman in the street. "I belong to the crowd," she told Virginia. Previous generations of Smyths, including her father, who was a major general in the Royal Artillery, had endowed her with a strong grasp of facts and a desire to get things done. Ethel's unabashed egotism sprang from ancestors whose energies had never been sapped by deep thought; this had its advantages, as she said in the first volume of her memoirs: "Though it must be pleasant to have brilliant ancestors, the possible legacy of an exhausted nervous system is perhaps not worth the glory of a flaming pedigree." Her family had been resolutely philistine, never rising above decent mediocrity, to which fact she owed her own extraordinary good health and high spirits. Ethel's outspoken autobiographical writings, and her quarrels with male conductors on behalf of female musicians, had made her somewhat notorious. Edward Sackville-West summed up her personality as an amalgam of contradictory elements: intense loyalty and shameless egoism, violent spite and incorruptible integrity. "Whatever she felt at the moment she went all out for, like a bull released into the glare of the arena."

During the height of the women's suffrage campaign before World War I, Ethel had interrupted her musical career for two years to give full time to political action. She volunteered to commit civil disobedience and smashed the windows of a cabinet minister who opposed votes for women. She was sent to jail, where she taught fellow suffragists to sing her music and was observed by Sir Thomas Beecham conducting a chorus of prisoners, beating time "in almost Bacchic frenzy with a toothbrush." Sylvia Pankhurst, the leader of the movement, who was in the cell next to hers, described Ethel as "a being only these islands could have produced"—a true original—rugged, astute, a striking figure dressed in a battered, mannish hat and country clothes, which were offset by a dazzling purple, white, and green tie. For Virginia, who had always belonged to an intellectual coterie, Ethel played the Dickensian role of the wild child of nature, like the uninhibited Mrs. Manresa in *Between the Acts*, "whose nature was somehow 'just human nature.'" Her friendship with Ethel coincided with Virginia's growing desire to address social problems, the crisis of European civilization, in a language that would appeal to the ordinary educated reader.

Ethel had read *A Room of One's Own*, Virginia's essay on women in the literary profession, and pronounced it the most lucid account she had ever read of the obstacles women writers have to overcome and the odds against their doing so—an artful book, combining powerful logic, humor, and poetry. She wrote Virginia at once, asking to see her—they had so much in common, Ethel insisted, and would certainly become intimate friends.

The Woolfs' house at 52 Tavistock Square stood in a row of four-story houses that had been built on the duke of Bedford's London estate after the Napoleonic wars. In Virginia's time the neighborhood

Figure 3. Ethel Smyth in the upstairs sitting room at Monk's House, c. 1931.

was pleasantly residential, the square forming a kind of "Bloomsbury village" in the midst of the city. Her drawing-room windows looked out on the trees and lawns of the square itself, which formed a private garden fenced off from nonresident passersby by iron railings. Identical stone steps flanked by iron railings ran up and down along the block. At number 52, steps into the areaway also gave access to the basement offices of the Hogarth Press. But a visitor would climb the stoop and then one flight up to the Woolfs' flat, which occupied the top two floors of the building.

When Ethel Smyth climbed those stairs on February 20, 1930, she was seventy-one years old. Virginia, who met her at the door, was forty-eight, tall and lean, with graying hair and an inscrutable look, the corners of her mouth pulled down, slightly sardonic, reserved—a woman who often seemed to inhabit another world. Virginia's niece, Angelica Garnett [née Bell], gives the best picture of what she was like in her later years. Even at rest, she gave an impression of intense activity—her "attitude was far from sitting, it was striding; long narrow thighs and shins in long tweed skirts, loping over the Downs . . . or through the London traffic. . . . She was never placid, never quite at rest. Even when, knees angular under the lamp and cigarette in holder, she sat with a friend after tea, she quivered with interest in the doings of other people." This keen alertness combined with an air of vulnerability. Mrs. Garnett remembered her "shadowy temples over which stretched a transparent skin showing threads of blue; the wrinkled waves of her high, narrow forehead; the tautness of those sardonic lips pulled downwards at the corner; her bladed nose, like the breastbone of a bird or the wing of a bat, surmounted by deeply hooded melancholy grey-green eyes. She had the worn beauty of a hare's paw."

An elusive figure into whose presence Ethel plunged like an athlete quick off the mark. Her first words were, "Let me look at you." As a child she had heard the legend of Virginia's great-grandfather, who drank himself to death in India. He was embalmed in a cask that exploded, ejecting the corpse in front of his widow's eyes and driving her mad. Ethel demanded to know precise details of Virginia's family tree, whipping out a notebook and pencil to jot down the answers. Virginia found her a "bluff military old woman," older than she expected, cross-dressed in a tailor-made suit, wisps of iron-gray hair peeping out from under her Napoleonic three-cornered hat.

In the hours that followed, Ethel offered a thorough digest of her life and interests. People called her an egoist, she said, but she had always fought for the underdog, bullied and badgered to get women players into the orchestra, invited the director of the Royal College of Music to lunch and harangued him about the unfair practices of his male colleagues. She talked about her new choral work, based on a philosphical dialogue by Harry Brewster, who had been the love of her life. Writing music was like writing novels, and orchestration provided the coloring. She wanted her music to be heard, it had not received the recognition it deserved—but perhaps that was a blessing in disguise, for she was free to write as she pleased, undistracted by worldly success. Virginia noted another characteristic: her need to live in the country because of her passion for games. Ethel praised the pleasures of golf, bicycling, the hunt—she had been thrown by a horse two years before and had broken her arm, an accident that left her undaunted. But now a new phase of her life had begun, a new romance—Virginia herself: "I've thought of nothing but seeing you for ten days."

The talk went on vivaciously from four until seven when Leonard came in. Ethel was the sort of character Virginia found most interesting. She had seen everything—studied in Germany and Italy, climbed the Alps, known Brahms and Tchaikovsky. During the early years of this century Ethel had visited the opera houses of Europe—Prague, Berlin, Vienna, Munich—playing her opera scores for any conductor who would listen. She accompanied herself and sang all the vocal roles with great relish, impressing people like the great conductor Bruno Walter, who became her lifelong friend and often praised the music, though he seldom performed it.

Ethel had great self-confidence, speaking in a commanding voice and dropping her soup spoon on her plate with a clatter. She was masterful in love as in everything else. Harry Brewster, a wealthy American married to a woman older than himself, had been the grand passion of her youth. After his wife's death, he followed her around Europe and even trimmed his beard to please her, but she declined to marry him, explaining that it was too late—her talent for matrimony had atrophied. She despised the "tendril-like instinct" of most women, and had taught herself to say, "Let me stand alone." Besides, marriage was hostile to genius; George Eliot, whom she had observed once at a concert with her "repulsive" husband, had spoiled her work by sacrificing her freedom.

Jotting down her impressions after this first meeting, Virginia admired Ethel's shrewdness, found her sincere and impulsive, but suspected that she might eventually display a streak of fanaticism—there was "a vein, like a large worm, in her temple which swells." On the whole, she liked her—the abruptness, the demands for immediate intimacy, the passionate temper—and she found the way they went on together quite entertaining. Within a few minutes of Ethel's arrival they had agreed to use one another's first names—"all was settled; the basis of an undying friendship made in 15 minutes:—how sensible; how rapid." Virginia took Ethel with a good many grains of salt, but she accepted her as one accepts a force of nature. With any luck their friendship might avoid the usual "expansive fluff" and produce something "gritty" and lasting.

That spring Ethel bombarded her with letters, numbered lists of questions, parcels of books, telegrams, flowers. She dropped in unexpectedly at the Hogarth Press, looking like an "old char in her white alpaca coat." Virginia grew increasingly fond of her and found her extremely irritating. Ethel was transformed into a termagant whenever she touched the subject of her musical grievances—out poured floods of words, stories, arguments, delivered with frantic haste; she rushed on, hardly stopping for breath. The volume of words was astonishing. On one occasion she spoke for a full twenty minutes without a break, driving the silent Leonard, who had joined them, nearly frantic.

On July 3 the Woolfs went to a party at Ethel's house in Woking, a short drive to the southwest of London. It was a lovely summer day, the roses were blazing against the walls. The small whitewashed cottage, which Ethel had built on a plot of land given her by an American heiress, was beautiful in its simplicity. The entertainment was ordered and graceful. Ethel had orchestrated the whole day—several of her friends had gathered to meet Virginia and Leonard. After a while they strolled to a nearby golf course for some rounds of Ethel's favoite game, then returned to the house for supper, followed by an evening party—champagne was served in the garden, the guests raising their glasses as light drained from the flower beds. It was planned like a piece of chamber music, formal and varied, to encourage easy give-and-take among friends and neighbors. Surprisingly, Ethel showed herself to be a gracious and skillful hostess, managing the entertainment with "delicious ease." Her intimate banter with her old friends revealed an Ethel whom Virginia had not seen before, evoking largeness and space and good breeding.

Toward the end of August, Virginia in her turn asked Ethel to stay overnight at Monk's House, her country retreat, where they could let their hair down. During that visit she observed the split between the two Ethels—the one, who couldn't get over her own ill-treatment, whose grievances had become a refrain, and the other, who showed great insight and generosity. Comfortably settled in front of the fire that evening, Virginia had an odd sensation, as if veils were lifted, revealing layers of Ethel's personality, selves arising from the depths of the past, an iridescence surrounding her old, broad forehead. Virginia glimpsed her image as a sturdy blond girl of eighteen, a vigorous young countrywoman. The apparition vanished, and she saw Ethel looking starkly granitic, defiant, like "an old crag that has been beaten on by the waves." Then she observed still another face, the woman of the world who had lived in many different societies, campaigning for her music in a mannish shirt and tie. These shifting presences tantalized Virginia, who felt her emotions stirred, "like so many strange guests: as if chapter after chapter of [Ethel's] life, panel after panel of [her] psychology were opening and shutting in the twilight."

At times during the weekend the tone of their conversation became slightly operatic; there were "some interesting moments." Ethel had cast Virginia in the role of the one true friend she had been waiting for, the grand passion of her old age, and she admitted to feeling jealous: "I don't like other women being fond of you"—a confession on which Virginia pounced instantly: "Then you must be in love with me Ethel." "I have never loved anyone so much. . . . Ever since I saw you I have thought of nothing else." Perhaps she was unwise to admit it? Virginia felt not in the least put out by her words, assuring Ethel that she craved affection. Privately, she was skeptical; her comments had a satirical edge. She had been impressed by Ethel's manner, but she noted that her exaggerations might be a sign of approaching senility. Ethel's avowals grew still more operatic after that visit: having known Virginia, she could face death serenely and sing her "Nunc dimittis"; she no longer minded how long she lived and had no wish to prolong the time, now that her "last barren years" had been fructified.

Three years later, Ethel jotted some reflections on the friendship into her diary: "How far V. is human I don't know. She is very incalculable, and has never been known to admit that she can be in the wrong. And yet you love her, love her. . . . She is arrogant, intellectually, beyond words yet absolutely humble about her own great gift. Her integrity fascinates me. To save your life, or her own, she could not doctor what she thinks to be the truth." Virginia, for her part, was ironically aware of forming a rather outlandish figure in Ethel's imagination.

[Virginia to Ethel, December 29, 1931]

No, I think you grossly underrate the strength of my feelings — so strong are they — such caverns of gloom and horror open round me I daren't look in. . . . Do you know how I cared for Katherine Mansfield, for Charlie Sanger — to mention friends only? No, you dont. But then, for months on first knowing you, I said to myself here's one of these talkers. They dont know what feeling is, happily for them. Because everyone I most honour is silent — Nessa, Lytton, Leonard, Maynard: all silent; and so I have trained myself to silence; induced to it also by the terror I have of my own unlimited capacity for feeling — when Lytton seemed to be dying — well yes: I cant go into that, even now. But to my surprise, as time went on, I found that you are perhaps the only person I know who shows feeling and feels. Still I cant imagine talking about my love for people, as you do. Is it training? Is it the perpetual fear I have of the unknown force that lurks just under the floor? I never cease to feel that I must step very lightly on top of that volcano. No Ethel, there's a mint of things about me, I say egotistically, you've no notion of; the strength of my feelings is only one.

Here Virginia followed a typical pattern, telling Ethel the unvarnished truth about herself and at the same time fending her off. The letter uses self-explanation as a screen, evading Ethel's grasp by giving her more than she bargained for, suggesting the mysterious rapport she had with the biographer Lytton Strachey, and the celebrated economist John Maynard Keynes. Virginia was playing her role as a brilliant purveyor of confidences, answering questions that had never been asked, cannily insisting that "a mint of things" had been left out of the picture. The confidences were true, moreover, Virginia having seen that only the truth could deceive Ethel.

Her letters, during the first year of their friendship, contained many such disarming sketches of her inner life and feelings. Written at breakneck speed, spewed forth together with invitations, gossip, news that Pinka had given birth to six black puppies, they composed an intimate self-portrait. There's more of Virginia in these letters, more of the unadorned Virginia, than in any others she wrote during this decade. Why? Because Ethel intensely, vehemently demanded to know, because she wouldn't be put off, because Virginia respected her courage and was herself, as she said ironically, "the truthfullest of people." It was a quality people rarely gave her credit for. She was often cavalier about facts, and her jokes misfired, but she didn't lie about her feelings if she could help it.

Her letters aimed to satisfy Ethel and keep her from encroaching beyond a certain point, but they did more than that. They became an end in themselves, a venture into self-examination, into tracing the outlines of her own psychology, which Virginia hadn't tried before. The human mind undressed. She could confide in Ethel, who had so few inhibitions, and open a window on some hidden crannies and recesses of her own personality.

The influence of Virginia's family and roots came into it, too. She relished the idea of drawing her self-portrait for the major general's daughter. Through Ethel she addressed her own ancestors; she too came from a hardy and practical clan. They were Scottish farmers and French aristocrats, men of action, merchants who traded in contraband, women who deployed good looks and strong minds. Her father had climbed the Matterhorn and been a struggling journalist before writing his shelf of biographies and tomes on English literature. Her mother, a famous beauty with a passion for nursing, had left her family for weeks at a time to haunt sick rooms and attend invalids.

Virginia's world was more rarefied than her parents' world, let alone that of her grandparents. Ethel had accused her of being a "damned intellectual," and her reply was somewhat acerbic—yes, she belonged to that "narrow, ascetic, puritanical breed." Coming to tea one afternoon, Ethel had met one of Virginia's Cambridge friends, the young literary critic F. L. Lucas, and later condemned him as a prig. Virginia, whose education had consisted mainly of reading the books in her father's library, confessed to being enthralled by bookish academics like Lucas—"their integrity always makes me their slave." A spirit of open-mindedness and freedom from cant shone through his frosty and glittering exterior, earning her admiration.

But intellectual interests reflected only the surface of her mind. She had to describe something more profound—that she entered a world of her own when she wrote her novels, which was the one thing that gave meaning to her life: the discipline of descending into those depths and staying there. All her other activities, keeping house, seeing friends, choosing manuscripts for the Hogarth Press, were colored by that privileged state.

On April 22, 1930, a typical day at Monk's House, Virginia wrote

Ethel a rambling letter full of homely domestic incidents and ideas about fiction, a complete blend of artistic and mundane interests. After spending the morning writing her novel, she had cooked lunch and baked bread, she said, and went on to grumble about her social obligations. People constantly dropped in and interrupted her work, which was one of her crosses, especially because it exploited her love of good company and conversation. The previous day her sister, together with Clive Bell, her husband, and Duncan Grant, the homosexual painter with whom Vanessa shared her life, had dropped in on Virginia and spent three hours there talking without a break. But she had a bone to pick with Ethel, who had criticized her friends, charging that they were prudish—and the very opposite was true. "Everything is possible. . . . Our society is one of the freest I have ever met." Even its most cloistered members—she was defending her Cambridge friends again—were capable of breaking out and overcoming middle-class reticence. "Even with little Don Lucas . . . I would discuss, and have discussed, the most intimate details of sexual life. He and his wife are separated."

Virginia inserted some more mundane news. She and Leonard were planning a trip around England to place Hogarth Press books at bookstores. Soon she would go out her back gate and take a brisk walk across the marshes while Leonard planted hollyhocks in the garden. Annie, the part-time servant, would come in and "dish up two grilled herrings"—their dinners were frugal; cost seven pence. They would spend the evening reading in front of the fire. Behind these ordinary events there was intense excitement. Her writing had begun to take fire that morning. She just looked forward now to a few days without people dropping in, because much as she loved family and friends, she needed silence. If she could sit in one place, observing her routine, doing the same things every day, some few pages of her book would be "solidly written in the end." She longed to submerge and live for three months in her writing only—"I am like one of Leonard's fish (we have a pond) which is off at the shadow of a leaf." But that would not happen. Visitors came daily. She would go back to London with her ideas still unrealized. So the letter flitted back and forth between surface and depth.

Another time she described her quiet morning ritual—breakfast, some village gossip with Leonard, a slow walk to her garden lodge, where she would prepare to write, letting herself down, "like a diver, very cautiously into the last sentence I wrote yesterday. Then perhaps after 20 minutes, or it may be more, I shall see a light in the depths of the sea, and stealthily approach—for one's sentences are only an approximation, a net one flings over some sea pearl which may vanish; and if one brings it up it wont be anything like what it was when I saw it, under the sea." She used this image of diving again and again to refer to that otherworldly state. She wanted to "drift into some obscure pool and be shaded by weeds." Her submarine imagery was attuned to her changing moods, the fanciful and the poetic. Writing to praise Duncan Grant after receiving a figured rug he had designed for her, she reported that it gave her "the sensation of being a tropical fish afloat in warm waves over submerged forests of emerald and ruby. . . . As you know, it is the dream of my life to be a tropical fish swimming in a submerged forest." Virginia's aura was so strong, her concentration on the watery depths so palpable, that others seemed to feel it in her presence. Her niece Angelica recalled the atmosphere in the dining room at Rodmell, which was "sunk below the level of the garden and dimly green like a fish-pond." In that filtered light Virginia presided like "the Queen of a translucent underwater world." Monk's House left Angelica with the impression of "a sea shell through which the water flows, leaving behind it a taste of salt."

In her letters to Ethel, Virginia mischievously emphasized her strangeness, which fit with spending every morning in limbo, trying to find words for things no one ever had written about. That was only part of the strangeness. She would try to give Ethel, who had such a strong hold on reality, a glimpse of the time when she went mad. The years preceding that event could be distilled into a kind of fable, which began when she was Virginia Stephen, meeting her brother's friend Leonard Woolf. He found her an "odd fish," and the next day went off for seven years to Ceylon, to run a colonial district, taking with him a romantic image of the two Stephen sisters. In England those were the years of rebellion against Victorian morality; her friends were staunch believers in sexual freedom; Virginia behaved unconventionally like the others, sitting up into the small hours, earnestly talking to young men. There were petty intrigues and violent rows—she "stormed Hampstead heights at night"—a lot of sound and fury, but no sexual adventures for her. (Not surprisingly, since most of her male friends were homosexual and her love of women still Platonic.) "My terror of real life has always kept me in a nunnery." At the back of her mind all this time lurked an image of her brother's friend in Ceylon, who was something of a wild man. People said that "he had bit his thumb through in a rage." She thought the figure romantic—"Woolf in a jungle." They met again after he returned and were married. Then she went mad. It was a shattering event, her "brains went up in a shower of fire works," and she was prostrate, locked up in a rest home and forced to lie in bed completely idle, without reading or writing, for six months, learning "a good deal about what is called oneself." She recovered, feeling emotionally flayed by the doctor's tyranny, but having stored up myriads of ideas and images, from which she still drew most of the things she wrote about; her novels all came from that source. The inventions of madness shoot out under intense pressure, she said, more fully shaped than the "mere driblets" of sanity. "As an experience, madness is terrific, I can assure you." Virginia still received daily aftershocks of her breakdown, living on top of a "volcano."

Her account left out the grizzly details of her illness—the self-starvation, the voices telling her to do "all kinds of wild things," the sudden violent outbursts, when she had to be forcibly restrained by three nurses. She had drawn on those experiences in *Mrs. Dalloway* for her portrait of the shell-shocked Septimus Smith, who heard voices spewing hate and ordering him to kill himself. Subsequently she rendered the feeling tone of "madness" in the "Time Passes" section of *To the Lighthouse*, which described a deserted summerhouse where the family, absent for years, had left combs and brushes on the dresser and things rotting in the drawers. The narrator's report of swallows fluttering in the drawing room and thorned briars tapping at the windows on stormy nights presents the obliteration of human life and meaning with complete indifference.

Virginia's diaries and letters link her mental breakdowns and her creative visions by applying the same imagery to both states. Often she pictured a descent into watery depths, a process of diving or plunging into the oceanic abyss; sometimes she invoked volcanic fires. The forces of destruction and creation interpenetrated, and she speculated that her illnesses served a "mystic purpose," possibly even had "some religious cause at the back of them," which explained why her physical ordeals so often inspired her with "a tremendous sense of life beginning."

❧

Virginia noticed that her presence had a disconcerting effect on strangers, who stared and sometimes laughed as she passed in the street. Her friends, too, found her odd, incalculable. So Ethel must make allowances for her, she said derisively, since her understanding of human nature was limited, and her mind resembled "a cracked looking-glass at a fair. Only, as I write this, it strikes me that as usual I am romancing." She came back repeatedly to the idea that she saw the world through special optics, that her mind followed laws of its own—all sorts of people told her so, which made her feel like a laboratory specimen: "I'm so odd, and I'm so limited, and I'm so different from the ordinary human being." But even if her own romancing sometimes fueled the myths about her, Ethel must realize that they were based on distortions. Perhaps what baffled others was just her dazzling transparency. "I don't think I ever feel anything but the most ordinary emotions. . . . Virginia is so simple, so simple . . . just give her things to play with, like a child."

Sexually, too, her inclinations were transparent enough. Sometimes Clive or Vita, using the license of old friends, called her a "fish," but she didn't feel in the least bit cold. She got exquisite pleasure from a touch; physical proximity to either sex had the power "to make the world dance" for her. The most casual contacts stimulated her with a constant "fanning and drumming," a tattoo of sensations; she was sensually alive to other people, and tremendously responsive to Leonard, though she couldn't find any conventional phrase for the attraction. Her ideas of artistic form "and all that makes me wish to write the Lighthouse etc" depended on constant stimulation of this kind. These pleasures, as she implied, didn't include going to bed with men. Sex with Leonard had been a failure, and they slept in separate bedrooms, though she loved him in every other way. She had been tempted by men two or three times, she told Ethel, but the impulse was always abortive and misdirected. Generally, when she liked a man, her feelings were "all of the spiritual, intellectual, emotional kind." But it was wrong to define and dictate people's sexual behavior. "Lord Lord how many things I want—how many different flowers I visit—and often I plunge into London, between tea and dinner, and walk and walk, reviving my fires, in the city, in some wretched slum, where I peep in at the doors of public houses. Where people mistake, as I think, is in perpetually narrowing and naming these immensely composite and wide-flung passions."

Virginia's sexual feelings, when she had them, were directed toward women friends, though she joked about her passion for Tom Eliot. She had had a love affair with Vita Sackville-West in the mid-1920s, but even then her vulnerability had kept her from straying far from her "nunnery." Vita assured her husband at the time that the physical side of the affair was very limited—yes, they had gone to bed together twice, but that was incidental, since "Virginia is *not* the sort of person one thinks of in that way; there is something incongruous and almost indecent in the idea." In spite of the unreliability of such statements, Vita's account was probably true. She felt somewhat out of her depth with Virginia, and concerned, as she also told Harold, that the affair "might get beyond my control before I knew where I was." She promised to be "sagacious," which was not difficult, since she had hardly been tempted. Virginia inspired a different kind of attachment.

She could be touchingly affectionate and demonstrative with close friends and family. As her niece reported, she regularly embarrassed Vanessa by demanding "her rights, a kiss in the nape of the neck or on the eyelid, or a whole flutter of kisses from the inner wrist to the elbow." She resisted all labels, assuring Ethel that she got "exquisite pleasure from contact with either male or female body." Still, she had an aura of remoteness, and was always brewing her special compound of truth and fantasy.

She did some romancing about Ethel, portraying that old soldier as a woman who had dared everything—lived in the glare of her own healthy appetites and "walked over Mountains with Counts." After attending a concert of Ethel's music, Virginia wrote that she had an image of a red rose in a thicket, which stood for the many loves and ages her friend had been through. By comparison she pictured herelf as "furtive and sidelong . . . a flat fish with eyes not in the usual place." Again Virginia had her tongue in her cheek, but a deposit of truth clung to these images. Her tone had become playful rather than indignant. No doubt she was an "odd fish," or some other form of marine animal—an alligator or a whale. Writing novels for her was always a matter of diving to the bottom and staying there till the pressure drove her gasping to the surface. She could endure those depths for only two hours a day, but her emotional equilibrium depended on that sunken life, which was very full and absorbing and rocked by obscure currents of its own.

[Virginia to Ethel, October 16, 1930]

One of these days I will write out some phases of my writer's life; and expound what I now merely say in short—After being ill and suffering every form and variety of nightmare and extravagant intensity of perception—for I used to make up poems, stories, profound and to me inspired phrases all day long as I lay in bed, and thus sketched, I think, all that I now, by the light of reason, try to put into prose . . . after all this, when I came to, I was so tremblingly afraid of my own insanity that I wrote Night and

Day mainly to prove to my own satisfaction that I could keep entirely off that dangerous ground. I wrote it, lying in bed, allowed to write only for one half hour a day. . . . These little pieces [her short stories] were written by way of diversion; they were the treats I allowed myself when I had done my exercise in the conventional style. I shall never forget the day I wrote The Mark on the Wall—all in a flash, as if flying, after being kept stone breaking for months. . . . How I trembled with excitement; and then Leonard came in, and I drank my milk, and concealed my excitement, and wrote I suppose another page of that interminable Night and Day (which some say is my best book). All this I will tell you one day.

Virginia examined and shaped her ideas, as she said here, "by the light of reason." Thus she came back to a theme she had started with—that she was an intellectual working in obedience to high standards of clarity and coherence. As an artist she believed in a golden mean, valued harmony and proportion. The scale of things was important. Ethel in her enthusiasm sometimes confused great things with small, ignoring the difference between King Lear and the latest best-seller. The writers Virginia admired most joined discrimination and enthusiasm, achieving a rare and happy union of thought and feeling. She admitted that the austere, intellectual side of her nature had been born in "the Polar region of Cambridge." For that very reason Ethel's impulsiveness sometimes brought her back to a more central and temperate position. As the old woman had announced at their first meeting, her name was legion: "I'm in the street. I belong to the crowd. I say the crowd is right."

❧

The Woolfs spent August and September at their cottage in Rodmell every year. Virginia looked forward to writing without constant interruptions, and the summer of 1930 began well. For the first time, they were alone in the house—that is, Nelly Boxall, who would ordinarily have been sleeping under their roof, had developed a kidney ailment that spring and been rushed to the hospital by Virginia, who had consulted doctors and arranged for her care, losing a fortnight's writing in the confusion. Nelly was now away recuperating, and their domestic work was being done by the young widow, Annie Thompsett, who came half a day and then went home. No more daily encounters with the volatile Nelly, who had to be handled with so much care. Virginia felt as one does after freeing her swollen feet from a pair of tight boots—the atmosphere in the house was "occasionally sublime"; as for her health, she assured Ethel that she was feeling "steady as a cab horse."

But at the end of August, shortly after Ethel's overnight visit, the weather turned very hot; Virginia's mood darkened and the specter of mental disorder swam to the surface.

Every morning after writing her daily portion, she read a canto of Dante's Inferno. It was a bracing and painful exercise—putting her own page into the crucible by comparing it to the supreme poetry that made all other writing unnecessary. The heat was oppressive, there were several "sulphurous" days, and on the hottest one of the summer she sketched a brief memorial of a classics master from Eton who had tutored Vita Sackville-West's children—clean-cut, an attractive young man, he had died climbing in the Alps, fallen into a crevasse with his fiancée just a week before. There the two bodies now lay, frozen for all time, while she sweated in the heat. She imagined how the landscape had fractured, saw them scaling the rock face, and then falling, "whirled, like hoops; battered; senseless, after the first horror of feeling out of control." Her days recently had resounded with dogs barking and men hammering on the neighboring church spire, making her feel a threat of violence hanging over the village. Her personal artistic struggles echoed something in the air. Behind the economic crisis, which was in full swing, there were signs of a political breakdown—tremors of an England and Europe slipping "out of control."

The heat was brutal the next day, flies and bees swarming outside the door of her garden lodge, where she sat writing. In the afternoon old friends, Maynard Keynes and his wife, Lydia, came for tea. They talked politics around the table and then went to look at the greenhouse. Walking with Lydia in the garden, Virginia felt the heat suddenly descend on her head "like a wire cage of sound," a viselike pressure, a blow, and the thought ran through her head: "then I am ill: yes, very likely I am destroyed, diseased, dead. Damn it! Here I fell down—saying 'How strange—flowers.'" Someone carried her into the house—she saw Leonard looking frightened—and she fainted again trying to go upstairs.

The doctors diagnosed it as a mild sunstroke—not as serious as she had thought, though jangled nerves kept her in bed for almost two weeks. But this seizure, this minor brush with death, taught her something about herself; she was surprised and pleased that her first response had been a strong gesture of defiance. She had absorbed the pounding in her head and turned its violent aftershock into resistance. Reserves of strength, anger, throbbed in her veins—if she had really died it would have been like someone killed in battle, one of Dante's impenitent sinners. She would have approached the divine presence "with fists clenched and fury on my lips." The possibility of annihilation was always present—only her friends saved her from it, she had told Ethel. What would happen to her without them? Like an animal whose organs have been sucked out of its body, like a cast-off shell, a husk, she would be thrown on the dust heap, she would be "blown into the first puddle and drown."

This incident brought on an immediate flying visit from Ethel, followed by the usual telegrams, letters, and tokens of affection. Virginia recovered. A stretch of sunny, cool weather set in, lifting her spirits, as if the mishap had unloaded some burden of anxiety, making her forget the heat of August; her emotional state reversed itself. All things considered, what with being free of live-in servants, it had been a liberating summer—in spite of her sunstroke, the happiest time she and Leonard had ever spent at Monk's House. Her defiance of death, as she called it, had braced her—and left "one new picture" in her mind. Even the enforced days of rest and silence had been "fertilising." She was longing for new experiences, and decided that she "would like to have another life, & live it in action."

Back in London later that fall, she let Ethel lure her to a concert at the Austrian embassy. As she wrote her nephew before the event, she didn't much care for musical soirées, but she was sure that Ethel would "commit some rape" among the princes and dukes—it was too good to miss. The event fully satisfied her craving for satire. The mansion in Belgrave Square was crowded with dapper diplomats and members of the smart set. Ethel stunned the flunkies at the door by peeling off her moth-eaten coat and sweater and extracting dubious black leather shoes from a cardboard box held together by paper fasteners. These she put on, because, as she said, "I'm a damned snob, and like to be smart." Then, while the quartet played, she whispered loudly: "Isn't this slow movement sublime—natural and heavy and irresistible like the movement of one's own bowels." Whereupon an attaché sitting beside them jumped.

3 Lady Rosebery's Party

Virginia wrote her mystical "playpoem," *The Waves*, in the two-year period between the 1929 Wall Street crash, which began the worldwide Great Depression, and the financial crisis that forced England off the gold standard in September 1931. There were 2 million unemployed workers in England in April 1930, when she finished her preliminary draft, and the number had increased to 2.7 million, 20 percent of the workforce, by the time she finished her second draft in February 1931. From May to August of that year, while she prepared typescripts and corrected proofs, a run on the pound threatened to destroy the British banking system and caused the fall of the Labour government. The crisis, which Sidney Webb described at the time as "the most remarkable happening in British political history," gave only a hint of the international disorder that lay ahead.

The political and economic uncertainties increasingly affected Virginia's mood, though her responses were not primarily political at first. A diary entry of August 15, 1931, written in the last days of the Labour government, reflects her attitude, which blended serious concern and ironic detachment. Her old friend and neighbor Maynard Keynes, who returned from visits to Downing Street and spread "sensational rumours," provided her with an insider's view of the crisis. More important, Leonard, from his perspective as a political editor and adviser to the Labor Party, gave her frequent glimpses of the clashing interests within the government. Anticipating that the political situation would deteriorate further, Virginia asked herself whether her work—she was then revising *The Waves*—should be dismissed as mere fiddling while Rome burned. Would future ages look back on their present predicament with horror? "Sometimes I feel the world desperate," she wrote; "then walk among the downs. Last night [after a visit from the political hostess, Sybil Colefax], after thunder & rain . . . I stood by the gate and watched Asheham hill cloud & kindle like the emerald it is. And all round the hills lay low, in cloud." The downs offered a refuge, and Rodmell seemed peaceful enough, but her relief was only temporary.

The Waves, with its echoes of Swiftian rage and contempt, reflects a heightened awareness of destructive forces. Virginia had little interest in economic policies or political jockeying as such, but she was highly sensitive to atmosphere—and her fiction at this time presents human life against a chaotic, essentially amoral background. The novel places its characters within an inscrutable and indifferent natural cycle, a cosmic realm where human values and meanings diminish toward the vanishing point. It was as if the country peace at Monk's House, free of traffic noise, enabled her to hear the wider ambient sound, the anger smoldering in the world's capitals, amplified through the pulse of her own inner violence.

She had reached a beginning, crossed a historical dividing line, and sensed that the Depression, and the cultural climate that came with it, created an environment that would be less congenial and harder to work in than that of the 1920s. Previous successes were useless, and she was afflicted by an exaggerated fear that *The Waves* was a failure, declaring that she must chart her path into the future through this book. Writing to thank one early reader, George Rylands, who had worked briefly at the Hogarth Press, for praising it, she observed that the style of *To the Lighthouse* and *Mrs. Dalloway* belonged to the past and was no longer available to her. "I'm full of ideas for further books, but they all develop from The Waves." If he had thought it "a barren and frigid experiment—merely Virginia hanging to a trapeze by her toe nails—then I should have felt, Why go on? . . . and have probably taken a vow of silence for ever."

⚶

On January 21, 1931, a few days before finishing the second draft of *The Waves*, Virginia spoke about her experiences as a writer to the National Society for Women's Service in London. She rarely made public appearances, but did so this time in order to show her support for struggling professional women, sharing the platform with Ethel Smyth, who told "rollicking" stories about her musical career. For Virginia the event was important because in preparing her discussion of the Angel in the House she had hit on an idea for a new book "about the sexual life of women." The conception had come to her while she was in her bath and excited her so much that she spent the next few days mulling it over, and incidentally resting her mind before writing the last pages of *The Waves*. The new book would take up the account of sexual oppression from where she had left off in *A Room of One's Own*, with particular emphasis on Victorian women, whose sufferings were embodied in the tragedy of Antigone, buried alive by the tyrant Creon for defying patriarchal law. She would focus on elusive realities of her parents' generation and then bring the discussion up to the present day, asking whether women in the thirties had acquired the will or the power to unbury themselves. The emphasis would be on liberation, as she implied in her first working titles: "The Open Door" or "Opening the Door."

The picture of Virginia in her bath, taking a cue from her lecture on professions for women to plan a new book while still absorbed in *The Waves*, suggests her habitual way of working. The Woolfs' Rodmell servant, Louie Everest [later Louie Mayer], remembered hearing her talking to herself in the bath every morning, so loquaciously that she "thought there must be two or three people up there with her." Leonard explained that Virginia was speaking aloud the sentences she had composed during the previous night to see if they sounded right, "and the bath was a good, resonant place for trying them out." Virginia's room, Everest recalled, was littered with scraps of paper on which she had written her ideas during odd moments.

On the whole, in spite of brief interruptions such as this one, *The Waves* crowded out everything else, absorbing all her creative energies between October 1930 and February 1931. It was exhausting to screw her brain so tight, as she put it, and she looked forward to the end of the novel, when her mind could be playful and free again. She reached that point on the morning of February 7 and wrote the date in her diary in a state of exaltation. She had "reeled across the last ten pages with some moments of such intensity & intoxication that I seemed only to stumble after my own voice, or almost, after some sort of speaker (as when I was mad). I was almost afraid, remembering the voices that used to fly ahead." In doing its work, she said, her imagination had discarded the set pieces that she had prepared in advance, the well-defined images and symbols that she had planned to join coherently in a set order. But no—her imagination had refused to follow that predetermined plan, playing with the images and boldly tossing them aside, "never making them work out; only suggest." She hoped by these means to make the novel's primal scene vivid to the reader, keeping "the sound of the sea & the birds, dawn, & garden subconsciously present, doing their work under ground." The design would be plotted against this refrain of the elements. The thought of evocative images, taking their own course and breeding in the reader's mind, exhilarated Virginia, giving her a sense of freedom in spite of the growing social disorder. Her mind was very much on the present crisis, however, when she made the prediction quoted above, that between the ages of fifty and sixty she would "write out some very singular books, if I live. I mean I think I am about to embody, at last, the exact shapes my brain holds. What a long toil to reach this beginning—if The Waves is my first work in my own style!"

✑

Like other modernist works, *The Waves* follows a model of spatial or organic form in a sense described more than a hundred years earlier by Schopenhauer. In his preface to *The World as Will and Representation* he declared that his book presents the elaboration of a single idea, a work in which all the parts are interdependent as in an organism, every part supporting the whole, and supported by it, so that though one encounters them in succession, they echo the unity of a living creature. Such works, he adds, should be read with the understanding that the end is already implicit in the beginning, forming "a connexion in which no part is first and no part is last . . . and even the smallest point cannot be fully understood until the whole has been first understood." Similarly, in its presentation of a single cosmic day in which the whole cycle of human life unfolds, *The Waves* places its characters against an ever-present, timeless reality.

The central idea grew out of Virginia's meditations on her brother Thoby's death, which had happened in 1906, when she was twenty-four. It had been a shockingly senseless death—a vigorous young man in the bloom of health, killed by typhoid fever, which the doctors failed to diagnose till it was too late. He had shown great promise. His friends had expected that he would be one of the leaders of his generation. He drank contaminated water while touring Greece, grew ill and died. A quarter of a century later Virginia returned to that event, seeking to come to terms with its apparent arbitrariness. It was part of an inexorable cycle, the "many mothers, like one wave succeeding another," she wrote in her first draft of *The Waves*, "wave after wave, endlessly sinking and falling." She observed the cycle through the eyes of six friends, all of whom had been shaken by the early death of Percival (her idealized image of Thoby). The novel implicitly asks how one can or should live in a world in which such things happen.

The six characters explain their experiences and themselves, beginning in childhood and bringing the life stories up to late middle age, when a spokesman for them all offers a summing up of their collective wisdom. The friends have known each other intimately since childhood, and sometimes feel that they are parts of one another, forming a single complex organism—as if the separate soliloquies in which they tell the novel's events all compose a larger collective consciousness. Framing the nine groups of soliloquies, each standing for a different stage of life, from childhood to the eve of death, Woolf placed italicized interludes that describe the play of light over a seaside landscape at nine moments during a single day, from an hour before the sun rises to after it sets.

The Waves is still less conventional in its form than this summary suggests. The alternating soliloquies that compose the novel are only secondarily about external events. Woolf's emphasis is on the elemental beings of the characters, or what she called on the original manuscript's title page "the life of anybody . . . life in general." The speakers anticipate the elusive or unknowable narrators of postmodern fiction since Samuel Beckett. Although there is a chronological order, these characters are outside time, speaking, even in childhood, with fully adult voices. Percival, the hero who dies, is associated with absence and negation, the void that is always there at the center and is too painful to be looked at directly. All memories imply this unspeakable thing and the speakers must make room, allow for this fact without allowing it to eclipse daily life.

We are are part of one another, Virginia Woolf believed, our selves overlap, and *The Waves* portrays six parts of Virginia, partly drawn from her friends, those intimate others closest to her, where they converged and their selves merged with hers. The novel was "autobiography" in this sense—a calling forth of her selves. Of all the complementary roles, Rhoda's was the most inward, mysterious and detached from mundane events, the image of a poetic visionary looking beyond society, which appalls her, toward ethereal pools "on the other side of the world . . . where the swallow dips her wings." The others were more attached to outer things, implicated in worldly affairs. Jinny was related to Leslie Stephen's "poor little Ginny," a lovename for Virginia. She was the girl child responding to a formidable father, and later the young woman entranced by her body's dance of desirability. Susan represented a domestic self whom Virginia identified with her sister, Vanessa—calm earthiness, enfolding close-held passions—a body leaning on a gate in sunlight, the weight in her side foretelling the children she would bear. The three women form a three-sided figure, each face looking in a different direction—Jinny within her billowing dress aware of her sexuality; Rhoda, longing to be faceless and bodiless; Susan absorbed in the routines of kitchen, farmyard, and nursery.

The male characters form a complementary triad. Louis derived many of his traits from her husband Leonard's austere and sensitive character. He was the thin-skinned outsider, surviving among strangers, seeking justice and haunted by deep racial memories—an innocent who felt shocked by his own sensuality, as by a blow on the nape of the neck. Neville was related to the homosexual Lytton Strachey, famous for his scathing wit—fastidious and lewd, part scholar and part sensualist. Finally, Bernard was the chronicler, a male storytelling self that Virginia Woolf the novelist associated with the literary tradition, a supple companion whose voice echoed the voices of Bloomsbury writers like Desmond MacCarthy and E.M. Forster. The male figures can be paired with members of the female triad: Bernard and Susan are absorbed in the natural world; Neville and Jinny are impelled by sensuality; and Louis and Rhoda pursue transcendental visions.

Taken together, the two three-sided figures describe a state of wholeness, "a six-sided flower," as Bernard calls it, "made of six lives." In their hexagram Virginia imagined "the complete human being whom we have failed to be, but at the same time, cannot forget."

❧

The defensive quality of the Woolfs' marriage, their outsiders' alliance against the rest of the world, provides an important motif in *The Waves*. The novel describes their fictional counterparts, Rhoda and Louis, as "conspirators" who never can think and feel like other people, though they do their best to mask their singularities. Louis's severely critical attitude, his rational and businesslike manner, conceals his awareness of not fitting into English society and also his contempt for those who mindlessly conform. He is the son of a banker in Brisbane, his Australian accent corresponding to Leonard's Jewishness, which Virginia had once, at the beginning of their courtship, thought might come between them. "You seem so foreign," she had told him. Her account of Louis in *The Waves* stresses his racial memory, his insistence, even as a boy, that he has already lived many

Figure 4. Virginia at Monk's House, 1932; the chair fabric was designed by Vanessa Bell.

Figure 5. Leonard holding Pinka, Clive Bell, Julian Bell, Virginia, Quentin Bell kneeling, Auberon Duckworth, and Duncan Grant at Charleston, 1930.

thousands of years and heard "rumors of wars [and] seen women carrying red pitchers to the banks of the Nile." All this, that his roots go down deep, and into such darkness, he conceals behind his methodical, businesslike exterior.

Rhoda's singularity, on the other hand, is immediately apparent. Ordinary existence shocks and disorients her. Although she performs the expected social rituals, meets her friends and frequents drawing rooms, she is always turning toward the window with eyes fixed on something beyond the visible horizon.

The novel's two "conspirators" know the violence lurking near the surface of daily life and are attracted and repelled by it, feeling, like the heroine of *Mrs. Dalloway*, that it is "very, very dangerous to live even one day." Their speeches invoke elemental forces. Plain, uneventful days open into chaos for them; habit and routine conceal something monstrous. "I see wild birds," says Louis, "and impulses wilder than the wildest birds strike from my wild heart. . . . I hear always the sullen thud of the waves; and the chained beast stamps on the beach. It stamps and stamps." Rhoda's inner language, the tale she tells herself, reflects a similar sense of wild, uncontrollable energy, some monstrous form of life that "emerges heaving its dark crest from the sea. It is to this we are attached; it is to this we are bound, as bodies to wild horses." Louis and Rhoda's language, their vision of wildness and a rough beast from the sea, echoes the tone of the Romantic poets, from Shelley worshiping the west wind to Yeats declaring that great writers own "nothing but their blind stupefied hearts."

The Waves, in accord with the Romantic tradition, shows that artworks enable one to live in a world where Percival's death has happened. This knowledge is elaborated by Rhoda in an episode that progresses from Swiftian rage to aesthetic release. Having learned that Percival died after being thrown by his horse in India, she goes out walking along crowded Oxford Street, where she finds that "the human face is hideous" and that roaring motorcars "hunt us to death like bloodhounds." This knowledge of destructiveness is a "gift," she reflects, a shock of extreme reality. After a while Rhoda turns aside and buys a ticket for an afternoon concert. In the concert hall she merges with the sleek crowd, who have gorged themselves on beef and pudding enough to sustain them for a week and now "cluster like maggots," seeking to appease a different hunger, swarming "on the back of something that will carry us on." The music begins. She hears it differently than ever before. Percival's death is the gift, enabling her to delve beneath mere semblances, to feel, while the music lasts, the permanence and clarity of pure forms and know their geometric rigor. "There is a square; there is an oblong. The players take the square and place it upon the oblong. They place it very accurately; they make a perfect dwelling-place. Very little is left outside. The structure is now visible; what is inchoate is here stated; we are not so various or so mean; we have made oblongs and stood them upon squares. This is our triumph; this is our consolation." Rhoda leaves the concert hall and throws a bunch of violets into the Thames as an "offering" to her dead friend, a romantic gesture, inspired by Shelley's poem "The Question," that invokes the consolation of art.

These scenes suggest a basic premise governing the novel's form. Its soliloquies do not render the characters' speech or even thought but represent neo-Romantic artworks, formal and stylized compositions, like Rhoda's "perfect dwelling-place." The selves of the speakers are conceived as artistic creations in their own right, each one a summing up, a fusion of indispensable elements. *The Waves* is a complaint against indifferent nature, as represented by the italicized progress of the primal day, an appeal for an aesthetically ordered world. Like the Romantic poetry it echoes, the novel encloses intensely personal feelings within patterned forms.

Destructive impulses can be temporarily checked, as Rhoda found in her lament for Percival. But the novel's interludes reflect the inevitable cycle of growth and decay, the putrefaction that follows all blossoming. From a panoramic view of the seashore, the narrator brings us down to ground level, observing oozing matter from rotten fruit and yellow excretions exuded by slugs. The corruption is coupled with glimpses of beauty. "The gold-eyed birds darting in between the leaves observed that purulence, that wetness, quizzically. Now and then they plunged the tips of their beaks savagely into the sticky mixture." The mood of formal elegance and romantic desolation climaxes with Rhoda's suicide, an event seen only indirectly, and tersely, almost casually, reported by Bernard. He ponders her extreme loneliness and constant search for "some pillar in the desert, to find which she had gone; she had killed herself." That is all, except for an equally terse suggestion that she had stepped in front of an oncoming vehicle in the street. Bernard's self-identification with Rhoda and his implicit approval of her act admit no special emphasis or explanation.

Virginia presented her idea of the composite self most fully in a long monologue spoken by Bernard at the novel's end. Shaping his memories into a complete artwork, he becomes a medium through whom all the other voices speak. In his summing up he is no longer certain whether he is a man or woman, poet or businessman. He has charted all the stages of despair, absorbed all the nihilism that flowed from Percival's death. He has lived through Rhoda's suicide and that too has entered the composite self. He cannot separate himself from his friends—living and dead. "Am I all of them? Am I one and distinct? I do not know. . . . There is no division between me and them. . . . Here on my brow is the blow I got when Percival fell. . . . I see far away, quivering like a gold thread, the pillar Rhoda saw, and feel the rush of the wind of her flight when she leapt." Bernard resists the extremes of cynicism and nostalgia, returning us, in the heightened language of his final soliloquy, to the ordered space where players place an oblong upon a square. He strikes a final romantic pose, makes a last ironically self-conscious gesture—that of the solitary horseman riding out to defy death, the lance-bearing champion (Percival's double) who does all he can, knowing it is not enough, but constructing out of inevitable defeat some shelter, some accommodation in the "perfect dwelling-place" of art.

✧

The Waves was Virginia's densest, most intricately wrought novel, and its power was reflected by the length and severity of the depression that set in a few days after she finished the second draft. She was outside herself, "outside life," she told Ethel, "fluttering like a leaf in a gale." She felt oppressed by the narrowness of her routine, the drudgery of being a writer, bound to a desk, deprived of adventure and distant horizons—and her work on *The Waves* was far from finished. She continued through the stages of revising, polishing, and getting the typescript ready for the printer during that spring and summer, with recurring intervals of depression and feelings of anticlimax, her reactions corresponding in intensity to her involvement during the original composition. As she said on February 17, she was caught in the backwash, tossed in the track of *The Waves*, "among empty bottles and bits of toilet paper." Reflecting about this period, Leonard remarked that Virginia's mental state generally became shaky when she was completing a novel. The act of creation was accompanied by feverish excitement, and publication, with its more mundane cares, was a form of torture for her. Echoing Virginia's own imagery, her habit of identifying the creative act with natural forces, Leonard said that at such times feeling and imagination took complete control of her, producing a "volcanic eruption" that slowed the conscious mind and left it following a step behind. The creative act formed a privileged category, different from normal activities—distinguishable from madness but close to it. The difference was that the creations of "genius," however hectic the process might be, were subject to the artist's rational control and judgment. Like any professional writer, Leonard added, Virginia revised her work meticulously in order to bring it up to a high level of polish and coherence. There were two times in the course of writing a book when she seemed to be carried away, possessed by artistic euphoria or its opposite. She was in an inspired state when she wrote out a novel, as she had been in 1930 and 1931 while composing *The Waves*. And she was again overcome by artistic furor when the time came to send a major work out into the world—while correcting proofs and waiting for reviews. The wild impulsiveness driving the act of creation would then take hold and drive her toward madness. "It was a kind of passion of despair, and it was emotionally so violent and exhausting that each time she became ill with the symptoms threatening a breakdown."

Her compositions achieved their own luminous order, still figures on a ground of wildness.

Fear that *The Waves* was a failure preyed on Virginia's mind, and she defended herself against it by anticipating the worst things her critics were likely to say. On February 21 she mentioned the just-finished book in a chatty letter to her brother-in-law, Clive Bell, deploring its obscurity and naming its weaknesses—"too difficult: too jerky: too inchoate altogether. But what's the point of writing if one doesn't make a fool of oneself?" Bold words masking anxiety and written to blunt the edge of Clive's cutting tongue. Making a fool of herself in public was just what Virginia dreaded most of all—her nightmare. Later that year, the suspicion that her friends didn't like the book distressed her so much she fled to her sitting room, trembling with mortification. She was particularly vexed, she wrote, by a vision of the popular novelist Hugh Walpole, with whom she liked to gossip, going about London saying her work was "all about nothing" and damning it with faint praise for its exquisite writing. Her reaction to these imagined slights was exaggerated, but she couldn't help it—intolerable to think of her work being dismissed, her ideas derided. At the same time she was aware of her own extravagance. "I mean L. accuses me of sensibility verging on insanity," she confessed.

This plunge into despair after the pride of creation was an old story; she connected it with her great capacity for feeling—a condition she wouldn't willingly give up, in spite of the pain it caused her. The letdown was inseparable from the craving that made her screw her brain so tight as a writer. A fertile disorder. In spite of her complaints, she had reasons to be grateful and even to rejoice: "If I werent so miserable I could not be happy," she wrote in her diary. Driven by creative dread, she was enriched by constant stimulation, finding "immense satisfaction" in the life of an ordinary Monday or Tuesday. From that she took comfort when she compared herself to Aldous Huxley, a writer who freely traveled around the world, or when she envied her sister with her children and domestic life. Virginia's baldly oxymoronic statement—"If I werent so miserable I could not be happy"—also might mean, If I weren't tied down I couldn't fly. And more ominously, if I weren't on a lethal course, I couldn't find the still center.

Still in the grip of her forebodings about the reception of *The Waves*, Virginia attended the premiere of Ethel Smyth's "masterpiece," "The Prison," a Harry Brewster poem set for chorus and orchestra, and subsequently she had a row with Ethel that threatened to end their friendship. The old campaigner had persuaded a fashionable hostess, Lady Rosebery, to sponsor a supper after the concert, at which time fashion and art were to join hands. In spite of Ethel's eccentricities, she wished the approval of the smart set, having a suburban dislike of Bohemianism and a jealous concern about her social standing as an artist.

Virginia loved parties and usually looked forward with enthusiasm to a good party, any party, the bigger the better. She enjoyed the chance meetings and social jousting immensely. But she suffered acutely when the party failed, when she felt slighted, or the festivities masked falseness or insincerity. "She would leave a boring party," Leonard wrote, "as if it were the last scene of Wagner's Götterdämerung with Hogarth House and the universe falling in flames and ruin about her ears."

In her sensitive state Virginia found the atmosphere of Lady Rosebery's party intolerable—a *danse macabre* of false good cheer, compliments, bland chitchat that seemed to mock everything she cared about—not a congenial face to be seen—only strained politeness where she had expected laughter and spontaneity. She felt that there was no meaning, that cynics abused her, that she and the other guests were "pinioned there and betrayed and made to smile at our damnation." She was reminded of the days when, as a young debutante, she had been dragged off to society parties by her conventional half brothers and felt appalled by her own "posturing and insincerity." Those scenes were inseparable from the disturbing memory of George's incestuous embraces, a shadow that seemed to envelop Lady Rosebery's bland guests. Waves of anger and humiliation out of all proportion to the event reduced her, when she got home, to a state of nervous exhaustion. Her harshest judgment fell on Ethel, who had put her through this ordeal among elderly butlers and peers of the realm; Ethel, who ought to have known how the party would distress her, had sacrificed friendship in order to feed her own "irresistible vanity." So Virginia concluded, making no allowances for poor Ethel, who was only a guest herself—no, she was a false friend. Virginia could not fall asleep and finally took chloral, a sedative that turned the screw further, leaving her the next day "in a state of horror and disillusion." She began to feel suicidal. "If you weren't here," she said to Leonard, "I should kill myself—so much do I suffer." The confession helped her to calm herself; for the next few days she canceled her engagements and spent most of her time resting in bed.

She kept silent about this episode and two weeks later, in an angry and artful letter, finally told Ethel how much she had hated the party, though without describing the dreary aftermath. She recognized that there were causes other than the event itself for her extreme revulsion—she had been "reeling and shocked, as I see now . . . by my own struggle with The Waves." The party had provided a pretext, an outlet for her feelings, but they should not be written off as a mere temper tantrum. Virginia was aware that her reaction seemed overwrought, but she insisted that Ethel's insensitivity concealed a streak of cruelty. In this letter, as in her moments of inspiration, a voice flew ahead, leaving the writer herself behind—a pitiless voice declaring her complete disillusionment with Ethel, who had organized the party.

[Virginia to Ethel, March 11, 1931]
    "Ethel likes this sort of thing," I said. . . . And I felt betrayed—I who have spoken to you so freely of all my weaknesses—I to whom this chatter and clatter on top of any art, music, pictures, which I dont understand,—is an abomination. . . .

This [revulsion] no doubt seems to you wantonly exaggerated. . . . But it is not. I see of course that it is morbid, that it is through this even to me inexplicable susceptibility to some impressions suddenly that I approach madness and that end of a drainpipe with a gibbering old man. But this is me; and you cant know me and merely brush this aside and disregard it as a fit of temper. I dont attempt to rationalize; but I can now, after 2 weeks, see how selfish, cold and indeed brutal I may have seemed to you, when in fact I felt more strongly about you and therefore about your betrayal of me to wolves and vultures than ever before. Excuse this; and continue whatever your scheme may be. I dont suppose I shall understand your explanation, if you give one, or you mine.

An obsessive voice breaks through Virginia's measured phrases—"I see of course . . . this even to me inexplicable susceptibility"—from which she suddenly confronts madness and the image of the sinister "drainpipe with a gibbering old man." And again, resuming her reasonable tone—"but this is me"—she moves point by point toward the angry outburst about her friend's "betrayal of me to wolves and vultures." Wolves and vultures, predators and scavengers—her imagery suggests the wolf's head colophon of the Hogarth Press, with which she identified. One glimpses a vindictive, wolflike Virginia—her anger against Ethel hardening into haughty remoteness—"continue whatever your scheme may be." In the long run the anger threatened to turn back against herself—it had left her feeling "more jangled and dazed and out of touch with reality than I have been in years." The flying voice that inspired fiction also could mock and abandon her in a wilderness of wolves and vultures.

The bitterness of her accusations briefly persuaded Ethel that their friendship was over, but Virginia's anger subsided and a few days later she dismissed the quarrel in her diary as a mere histrionic display: "one fine blaze about Lady Rosebery's party with Ethel—that valiant truculent old moss-trooper of a woman. . . . Her strength of feeling is her power over one." The rift closed for the time being, but the incident cast a shadow, and it was still on Virginia's mind a month later, when the Woolfs spent a Sunday visiting Beatrice and Sidney Webb, Leonard's old colleagues from the socialist Fabian Society. When the conversation touched on suicide, Virginia vigorously defended the right to end one's life under certain circumstances. Afterward, in her bread-and-butter note, she thanked her hostess particularly for supporting her views about suicide and explained her own personal stake in the matter. "Having made the attempt myself, from the best of motives as I thought—not to be a burden on my husband—the conventional accusation of cowardice and sin has always rather rankled. So I was glad of what you said." The scientific Mrs. Webb, who recorded the encounter in her diary, found her visitor impressive, but not very sympathetic—"fastidiously intellectual . . . a consummate craftsman. (She is beautiful to look at.) Coldly analytical, we felt she was observing us with a certain hostility; she is also extremely sensitive—apt, I think to take offense at unintentional rudeness." Beatrice Webb, the social investigator, finding herself being observed, and responding in kind. . . . Her note suggests Virginia's touchiness, her barely concealed irritability during the troubled months preceding the publication of *The Waves*.

Shortly after returning home from the visit, which had somewhat flustered her, Virginia wrote to Ethel, bringing up Lady Rosebery's party again and confessing that her reaction had been even more violent than she had admitted at the time—she had turned to Leonard and said, "If you weren't here, I should kill myself." She mentioned this example of her violent moods not so much for its own sake but because Ethel, with her psychological insight, might find it "amusing" to try deciphering the states of mind leading up to it. In her next letter she added a further conciliatory note, remarking that Ethel's example often gave her courage, for if the old soldier could be "so downright and plain spoken . . . I need not fear instant dismemberment by wild horses." Her language still retained traces of the former outrage, but savage wolves and vultures had been replaced by semi-satirical wild horses. Subsequently she created a permanent place for Ethel in her private mythology. Once she had owned a white tailless cat, Virginia wrote early in May, a "superb brute" that spent most of its nights fighting and eventually got so covered with wounds that it had to be destroyed. She respected Ethel, the fighter, as she had respected that tailless cat—they were both indomitable. From then on, when Ethel's pugnacity grew annoying, Virginia would remind herself that the uncastrated cat, as she often called Ethel, could not change her nature. The fable made it easier for Virginia to respond charitably, to curb the restless, predatory side of herself, which lashed out from time to time against her unruly friend.

❧

Virginia's domestic routine controlled a certain wildness by means of strict discipline. This balancing act, which they had transformed into a way of life, cemented the Woolfs' relationship. They had damped the violence, cushioned the danger, with layers of domesticity, and Virginia felt easy enough to mention her suicide attempt in a casual thank-you note. She would not have to kill herself, since Leonard was there and would be there to sustain her.

But the early months of 1931 strained her confidence. Hoping to ease the tension, the Woolfs set off on April 14 for a two-week motor tour in France and ran into cold, wet weather that dogged them throughout the holiday. The tour included two stops that carried important literary associations. They visited Montaigne's tower and surveyed the fine views of the countryside that the great humanist had enjoyed while writing his essays, and touched the very steps he climbed, "worn into deep waves, up to the tower." From there they drove on to the castle at Chinon, made famous by Joan of Arc, and heard, as Virginia noted in her diary, a clock ringing, which "has rung since the 13th Century: wh. J. heard. Rusty toned. What did she think? Was she mad? a visionary coinciding with the right moment." Two nicely appropriate emblems of transparency and mystery—the skeptic, Montaigne, who wanted to give the reader an uncensored glimpse of his innermost thoughts, and the visionary girl who heard voices.

After their return to England, Virginia took pleasure in the memory of her closeness with Leonard during the long days on the road with their physical discomforts. She was grateful to feel such keen interest after nineteen years of marriage. "How moving to find this warmth, curiosity, attachment in being alone with L. If I dared I would investigate my own sensations with regard to him, but out of laziness, humility, pride, I dont know what reticence—refrain. I who am not reticent." She was just aware of her self-censorship. She couldn't infringe Leonard's sense of privacy, even in the privacy of her journal. Accepting him, she accepted his reticence—and incorporated it into her own code of behavior. She "dared" not break through that privacy, or say to herself that Leonard's reticence produced her own. Moreover it was dangerous to unleash her critical faculties, which could be merciless, at such short range. The survival instinct that cemented their union was too necessary, too charged, to be subjected to analysis.

In her lighter moods Virginia gave thanks for material things—newly acquired luxuries like electric lights and a Frigidaire and the bright, airy room in which she slept at Monk's House—debunking the moralists who said these pleasures were hollow. She enjoyed "material blessings" and found them good for the soul, things that anchored one to earth. Graced with these comforts, their country weekends eased the strain caused by retyping and correcting *The Waves*, which she did through May and June, then correcting a professionally typed copy, preparatory to showing the manuscript to Leonard. What with their intimacy at Rodmell and the improvements and the joy of cutting fresh asparagus from the garden, Virginia found their way of life "almost divine."

Her nerves were jangled by Ethel's relentless egoism, however, and she had to invoke the steadfastness of Leonard and recall the hot rolls they had enjoyed at breakfast and savor the fact that "the cat had eaten the chicken" in order to calm herself. Since the Rosebery party the tough old woman had been on her best behavior, but toward the end of May, after they had spent a morning traipsing round the Chelsea flower show, she started one of her tirades, nailing Virginia to her chair with the story of her ill-treatment by the conductor Adrian Boult and "the history of her persecution for the past 50 years." After this encounter Virginia felt the light rays fanning around her eyes, foreshadowing a dangerous headache, and the pain was only relieved by two days of rest at Monk's House. Then she basked again in the security of her attachment to Leonard: "If it were not for the divine goodness of L. how many times I should be thinking of death," she declared, and found herself soberly repeating, "This is happiness."

She had said: "If I werent so miserable I could not be happy."

⚜

Living with her emotions on a hair trigger, Virginia was drawn to silent, undemonstrative people. As she had told Ethel, her most intimate friends displayed their feelings most sparingly. Leonard's autobiography is true to type, presenting the features of a blunt moralist who said little about his private life and personal feelings, emphasizing objective facts and relating them to general truths—a dry, rather monolithic character. In 1931 he impressed his niece with his rocklike austerity and discipline. The adolescent Angelica Bell regarded him with mixed feelings as representing the father figure who was missing from her life. Unlike the two charming, artistic men, Clive Bell and Duncan Grant, who shared her mother's ménage at Charleston, Leonard was often irritable and overbearing, but there was a "refreshing purity" in his nature, which she appreciated more and more. To Angelica, who sensed that something was wrong and later learned that her real father was not Clive Bell, as she had always believed, but Duncan Grant, her aunt and uncle offered an alternative model of adult life, one that was emotionally honest and responsible without tameness.

Leonard had his unpredictable side. Behind the craggy mask of the fifty-year-old writer, editor, and political observer still survived the passionate suitor who had once written love letters to Virginia enumerating all his faults—selfishness, lust, cruelty, and unspeakable beastliness—flaying himself because, as he believed, she would immediately have detected a lie and spurned him. He was a passionate moralist and like his fictional counterpart, Louis, in *The Waves*, his practical manner concealed an "infinitely young and unprotected soul."

Leonard's essential character emerged decisively in that earlier self, the man who courted and married Virginia Stephen. He was then thirty-one and had just returned for a year's leave in England after seven years as a government officer in Ceylon, feeling disillusioned and uncertain about his future. He had good prospects in the colonial service, but climbing the ladder and eventually governing a colony, as he might have done, was not the sort of success that appealed to Leonard. He determined, if Virginia would marry him, to quit his job and start afresh as a writer. He had no clear idea how he would earn his living, but Virginia's beauty and intelligence made the risks seem insignificant. This was the romance of Leonard's life. He decided in advance that if she refused him he would return to Ceylon and bury himself in his work, a romantic exile stoically bearing his burden in solitude. But Virginia, finding that they could spend whole days talking without growing bored or tired, began to return his feelings and said that very possibly she would marry him. Her qualified acceptance was enough for Leonard, who quit his job, seizing the opportunity to escape from a prosaic career and to follow a seductive path that might lead anywhere.

He traded the role of colonialist, about which he had moral qualms, for another that proved to be equally demanding. During their courtship Leonard and Virginia created a fable that defined their roles, an Aesopian parody of courtly love. Lyndall Gordon has pointed out how the fable, and the private language that went with it, enabled Virginia to accept the proposed intimacy. In it she was an exotic creature, sometimes a bird with brilliant plumage but most often "a Mandrill, a large, fierce West African baboon, whom they also called 'the great brute.' This Brute took into her service an insignificant mouse or Mongoose (Leonard). . . . The imposing creature then conceived a ridiculous passion for her unattractive servant with his thin, flea-ridden body." She accepted him into her service; he embraced her as his mistress and patron, swearing allegiance. From that time on, as long as she lived, he acted as the loyal preserver of her health and well-being.

Angelica Garnett said that Leonard always remained in some ways "the administrator of the Hambantota District in Ceylon." In any case, his years in the Orient had shaped his outlook, taking him to villages in the jungle, where he encountered the extremes of wildness in human nature and in the natural environment. He found the "beauty, ugliness and danger of the jungle" fascinating, and, in spite of his innate caution, couldn't keep away from it. The lushness and solitude of that primal world drew him again and again. There he was alone in another sense, as the sole European in that district, and he immersed himself in the task of running it efficiently. His strict business habits and concept of justice were formed there.

Leonard and Virginia were married in August 1912. Less than a year afterward she had the mental breakdown that nearly caused her death, turning their idyll into a "nightmare." The onset of illness caught Leonard by surprise. He had had a glimpse of the danger in February 1912, before their marriage, when Virginia suffered nervous exhaustion and went to a nursing home for two weeks. "A touch of my usual disease, in the head, you know," she wrote to a friend. Furthermore, Virginia had warned him that she was unstable and passed "from hot to cold in an instant, without any reason." Leonard went ahead with his eyes open, sensing that trials lay ahead, but he was unprepared for their severity. He had to learn how to care for a desperate wife who was sometimes catatonic and at other times so overstimulated that she became violent and had to be physically restrained. When she refused to eat, and was in danger of starving, he fed her a spoonful at a time, taking an hour or two over each meal. After her suicide attempt he moved with her to a country house and arranged for treatment by shifts of private nurses in order to keep the doctors from committing her. All in all, with periods of remission, the illness consumed two years, from summer 1913 to autumn 1915.

Leonard had his romance, and thereafter realized the full burden of responsibility that came with it. The determination to nurture Virginia and restrain her violent impulses, to serve and control her, satisfied his psychological needs. But he was shocked by the violence of his own feelings. A month after their marriage he began writing a novel about those feelings, *The Wise Virgins*, which he completed toward the end of 1913 and published the following year. In it he implicitly justified his devotion to Virginia by describing what might have happened if he had not married her.

In the novel the autobiographical character, Harry Davis, is in love with Camilla, a gifted, enigmatic painter. Like Leonard, Harry is extremely self-critical, contrasting his own "coarseness" with Camilla's refined "purity of beauty." Camilla is virginal and austere, evoking images of distant "hills and snow," and behind that concealing some destructive force that might at any moment break out against others or against herself. When she rejects him, Harry makes love to Gwen, a pretty suburban girl in a white dress, and allows himself to seduce her in his room at night. He knows that her attractions are mainly physical, but he has "ruined" Gwen and he must do the honorable thing by marrying her, aware of having fallen into a banal trap. The childish Gwen willingly falls into her new role. "Already she was the woman, his wife, trusting, timid, submissive, unseeing, loving. He watched her coldly, saw her already *his*, his chattel, his wife, his dog. He did not hate her; he hated himself." The novel ends on a note of self-disgust, as Harry realizes his failure and imagines the life he might have led with Camilla. The mood of *The Wise Virgins*, with its echo of Virginia's name, is bitterly ironic, invoking the parable of the wise and foolish virgins from the Gospel According to Matthew. The "wisdom" of Camilla and her sister contrasts with the double folly of Harry and Gwen, who yield to sexual passion and then obey the demands of conventional morality. The novel reflects Leonard's rebellion against the tyranny of sex and, indirectly, his commitment to Virginia, whose chastening influence saved him from making the same mistake as Harry.

Leonard's romance demanded all his gifts of spontaneity and willingness to serve. The lure of uncertainty and occasional wildness still had power over him as he and Virginia grew toward middle age. In 1931, Angelica Garnett observed, they were "deeply affectionate and indivisibly united." Leonard was extremely active that year, having just taken on the job of editing a new socialist periodical, *The Political Quarterly*, for which he also wrote occasional essays. In addition to this, and his responsibilities directing the Hogarth Press, he was completing *After the Deluge*, a book about the forms of democratic government since the French Revolution. His first responsibility, however, was to protect Virginia's health and well-being. He, the Fabian intellectual, journalist, and publisher, the meticulous balancer of books, who had once welcomed the romantic solitude of the jungle, had preserved this corner of dangerous beauty, this wildness enclosed among the agendas of his professional life.

4 *God's Fist*

The dramatic realignment in British politics during the summer and fall of 1931, when the financial crisis came to a head, was accompanied by widespread disillusionment—an awareness, particularly among the young, that the world was moving toward war again. The somber national mood had by this time impressed even the *Times*. The *Times*'s New Year's Day leader, in its usual opaque style, noted the public's distrust of "the uses and futilities to which Parliament is being turned" and the tendency to compare the present emergency to that of 1914. Speaking for the left in Leonard Woolf's *Political Quarterly*, C. E. M. Joad detected general contempt for the "rule of old men" and a longing for a strong man to enforce new policies. The fascist tendency was noticeable even among socialists, said Joad, and it made the country vulnerable to an authoritarian movement that could be the prelude to English fascism. His fears were partially validated by events later that year.

Maynard Keynes's dire warnings about the state of the British monetary system resounded in the background as Virginia struggled to put the finishing touches on *The Waves*. On July 17 the typescript was ready for Leonard to read. She felt "a rather unpleasant little lift in my heart" when she thought of him rendering an opinion on this extremely personal, difficult book. Leonard read it during the weekend at Rodmell and on Sunday morning came to her garden lodge to say that it was a masterpiece, the best of her novels. He had one reservation, dealing not with the quality of the writing but with the extreme difficulty of the first hundred pages, which would discourage a great many readers. She should "simplify and clarify a little" for their sake, though he doubted that such changes could make much difference. At that moment the response of other readers meant very little in comparison to Leonard's approval. Virginia's heart lifted in joy, and she dashed off a note to Ethel, saying that she felt so relieved she was "like a girl with an engagement ring." She set out for a stroll, ignoring the rain and even the fact that developers were spoiling her favorite views of the downs. Her elation continued for a few days and then subsided as the ordeal of correcting proofs and seeing her writing in cold print loomed ahead.

The financial crisis kept brewing throughout the summer and came to a head in mid-August, while government officials and members of Parliament were away on their long holidays. The Labour government, led by the formidable Ramsay MacDonald, was divided against itself. Leonard had worked with MacDonald on Labour Party committees and found him to be treacherous and unpredictable. MacDonald was a man of the people, a handsome, mustachioed Scotsman "with a golden bell-like bull-like voice," who had the gift of saying nothing so persuasively and at such length that he enchanted the voters. According to Leonard, MacDonald's skills as an orator were combined with a love of dissembling and an "instinct to double-cross." The prime minister, who had come up through the ranks of the working classes, was fascinated by high society and cut an imposing figure in white tie at elegant receptions. As Virginia had noticed when she met him at a dinner party, he was enthralled by the fashionable Lady Londonderry and ignored everyone else. Beatrice Webb reported that he shunned his less-polished political colleagues and that his open "avoidance of all Labour M.P.s [had] become one of the standing jokes of British political life." As head of the government, he seemed to love tortuous maneuvers for their own sake. No one was ever sure what he intended—not even those who knew him best. "If you ever got a glimpse of what was really in his mind," Leonard wrote, "it was so convoluted and equivocal that you felt you had got inside a mental maze." These qualities were much in evidence during 1931.

On August 22 the cabinet ministers, who had been urgently recalled to London from their summer haunts in Scotland and the French Riviera, assembled in emergency session. All month there had been a secret run on the banks, concealed by the press, and the treasury was about to run out of money. The Labour government, whose aim thus far had been to stay in power by balancing the conflicting interests of the trade unions and the other constituencies, now wrestled with spending cuts. The deficit, they were told, had destroyed faith in the monetary system, and foreign bankers refused to provide any more loans unless strict economies were imposed. The world's largest financial center was on the brink of collapse. Moved by these dire warnings, the ministers resolved to economize, but could not agree on how to do it. Some wanted higher taxes on the rich, some wanted a tax on imports. The majority favored some cut in the dole, the monthly benefit paid to 2.7 million unemployed workers, but a substantial minority held out against it. In the meantime, Ramsay MacDonald had consulted the opposition leaders, who favored "drastic economies" and opposed any new taxes. MacDonald and Snowden, his chancellor of the exchequer, urged a 10 percent cut in the dole, which nine ministers adamantly opposed as a betrayal of working-class interests.

This impasse came during the weekend of August 23–24, and it left no alternative but for the cabinet to resign. They did so, expecting that the Conservative opposition would form a new government, but MacDonald had a different sequel in mind. He accepted the king's invitation to head a national coalition, including Conservatives and Liberals, for the purpose of making the drastic cuts in social services that the Labour ministers found so unpalatable. On Monday morning a glowing editorial in the *Times*, headed UNITED FOR ACTION, launched a chorus of praise for the men who had taken "their political lives in their hands," putting their country ahead of their own political interests. Those who refused to cut services for the poor, said the *Times*, had surrendered to party political pressures—and their "rebellion [was] nothing less than ignominious." Arthur Henderson, the leader of the dissenting ministers, had "chosen to aim at the leadership of folly rather than to preserve the loyalty of a follower of wisdom." MacDonald was the darling of the Conservatives, who had nothing but praise for his courage and public-spiritedness. MacDonald paid for this maneuver. The majority of his followers regarded it as a betrayal and he was subsequently drummed out of the Labour Party. Reporting the crisis in her diary, Beatrice Webb summed up the indignation felt by those on the left. She noted that the cuts in social services were made at the expense of the poor, who were politically too weak to defend their interests. The rich remained completely unscathed and continued to enjoy all their pleasures and privileges: "Luxury hotels and luxury flats, Bond street shopping, racing and high living in all its forms to go unchecked; but the babies are not to have milk and the very poor are not to have homes. The private luxury of the rich is apparently not wasteful expenditure."

Bypassing the normal parliamentary system, the new "national government" reflected a wish to muddle through without clearly defining policies or examining what hardships the poor might suffer as a result of them. Left-wing intellectuals warned that the "group of self-appointed leaders, asking for a free hand in the name of patriotism" were undermining constitutional government by creating a "Party Dictatorship." Many others were beginning to share Joad's concern that the country was on the road to fascism. John Lehmann, a young poet who worked for the Woolfs at the Hogarth Press, recalled the feelings of "consternation and gloom that settled on all our circle" as they contemplated these events.

Ramsay MacDonald, that eminent model of the politician as actor, had been unable to resist top billing in a new role as the man who saved his country. In the process he had reversed his political direction and changed his allegiances, heading a government of those who had bitterly opposed him and earning the opprobrium of those who originally voted him into power. His new government went ahead to cut social services. A month later, finding the crisis still unabated, it turned around and suspended the gold standard, a symbol of financial stability dear to conservative hearts. To the surprise of most people this act, which relieved the pressure on the pound, had almost no effect on the day-to-day course of business. Having come this far, Mac-Donald called a general election for the end of October, asking the public to approve the coalition's policies by voting for "national" candidates. What they wanted was a "doctor's mandate." Their shrewd slogan addressed the majority who feared social revolution and were looking for painless, or at least orthodox, remedies. MacDonald and his allies would not specify the treatment in advance, but they were honest doctors and would cure the ailing economy.

⚬✦⚬

Virginia's adjustment to the heightened tensions of the thirties combined skepticism, suppleness, and tenacity. Her comment on the general election of October 1931—"I shall try to make myself believe in that reality; and then fail; and try again; and fail again"—was aimed not at politics in general but at sham politicians, and it anticipated the future government's futility and ineptness. Her judgment about the election's unreality was shrewdly attuned to the drift of things, more tough-minded than escapist. Leonard Woolf's account of her political outlook, which has been quoted out of context to prove her detachment from the "real world," suggests a distinction between allegiance to a particular party and political awareness in a more global sense.

Ever since 1914 in the background of our lives and thoughts has loomed the menace of politics, the canker of public events. (One has ceased to believe that a public event can be anything other than a horror or a disaster.) Virginia was the least political animal that has lived since Aristotle invented the definition, though she was not a bit like the Virginia Woolf who appears in many books written by literary critics or autobiographers who did not know her, a frail invalidish lady living in an ivory tower in Bloomsbury and worshipped by a little clique of aesthetes. She was intensely interested in things, people, and events, and . . . highly sensitive to the atmosphere which surrounded her, whether it was personal, social, or historical. She was therefore the last person who could ignore the political menaces under which we all lived.

A bit further on, Leonard qualified this picture of Virginia as the least political animal since antiquity by adding that, in addition to her important work as a political pamphleteer, she was interested in grassroots politics in the village where she lived—actively supported the Women's Cooperative Guild, a union of working-class women, and was involved in the Rodmell branch of the Labour Party, which met regularly at their house. What Leonard meant was that Virginia shunned national committee work and campaigning of the sort in which he himself engaged. But she was extremely shrewd in her assessment of the "atmosphere which surrounded her," including "the political menaces under which we all lived."

Both *The Waves* and Leonard's *After the Deluge*, a study of communal psychology and politics, were published early in October 1931, in the midst of the election campaign. Virginia's novel received puzzled but respectful reviews in the national press, while Leonard's book was ignored, its message drowned out by the political clamor, and he felt that his labor on it had been wasted. His pessimism about the state of the country, aggravated by this disappointment, reflected "something deeper than reason, strangling, many coiled," Virginia said, a bitter mood that she detected in all members of the Woolf family and connected with ancestral memories of oppression.

Three days before the election, Virginia received a letter from Goldsworthy Lowes Dickinson or "Goldie," the influential Cambridge humanist and political thinker, praising *The Waves* as "a great poem," a work wedded to the here and now and attuned to the universal. It was unlike any other book and could only have been written at the present moment. For Dickinson *The Waves* illuminated recent history and the present crisis, revealing a continuity between poetic vision and political events. His letter described the vision he had had after reading it. Absorbed in thought, he had taken a walk by the River Cam, passing groups of young men in boats and clustered on the riverbanks. Among them was one who advised the rowers firmly and kindly about the right way, the best way, to handle their oars. Dickinson saw him as an incarnation of Virginia's Percival, a cultural ideal, a friend who lives in our memories of youth and is colored by them. In his mind's eye Dickinson saw another young man piloting an airplane, a fighter who dropped bombs on this young athlete and "all the Percivals," till the pilot in his turn was shot down. He fell "with the proud sense that he [was] 'doing his bit' for the dear old country." Goldie returned home, reflecting that there was a "fraudulent election" on and asking himself how he should vote. He saw the idealized Percival, who died far from his friends, as a reminder of lost generations. The tens of thousands who had died in the Great War were victims of fraudulent politics, and a new wave of young men would soon follow them. It was a thought that could unhinge the world, but Virginia's novel-poem had shown him the underlying element in which we all move, waves in the sea, sharing the knowledge "that the other waves have their life too and . . . we are somehow they."

In her answer, written on election day, Virginia reported that she and Leonard had set out in the morning, driving toward Cambridge to take voters to the polls, and got as far as North London, before being forced to turn back by a dense, impassable fog, which was perhaps fitting. That evening they would listen to the results on the wireless. She still could not believe in the reality of the election. But Goldie's reading of *The Waves* had moved and pleased her. He had understood what she meant—that "we are the same person and not separate people. The six characters were supposed to be one." *The Waves* was her attempt to set down "a reason for things" in the face of her brother's early death. She was still struggling with that event. Behind the novel, she told Vanessa, lay her "dumb rage" that Thoby was not there with them always. Those feelings were amplified, as Goldie's response suggests, by memories of the slaughter in the last war.

Virginia's occasional illnesses and brittle moods continued through the autumn, her highs and lows often paralleling readers' reactions to *The Waves*. In September, convinced that Hugh Walpole and John Lehmann both hated the book, she retreated to her room in a state of acute depression. "I have come up here," she wrote in her diary, "trembling under the sense of complete failure . . . & already feeling

rising the hard and horny back of my old friend Fight fight." The next
morning she swung to the opposite extreme, trembling with elation,
because Lehmann had written, saying that her new method thinned
the walls between the novel and poetry almost to the vanishing
point. She also received a shock of pleasure from E. M. Forster, who
wrote that he felt on reading it the sort of excitement one feels on en-
countering a classic—praise that confirmed her own artistic reality.
Grounded in that opinion, she looked ahead to the coming decade, in
which she would at last embody "the exact shapes my brain holds."
Still, conflicting opinions swirled around her like a "dust dance," renewing her sense of isolation. The consequences could be devastating,
as she explained to Ethel during a bout of illness. Ethel, who in spite
of her eccentricities was conventionally religious and belonged to the
Church of England, had tried to tempt her with the consolations of
Christianity. To which Virginia, feeling tense and malicious, fired
back her own account of what Ethel's God had done to her. "I was
struck with a brilliant idea; wrote and wrote; he smashed his fist on
my head. Lord, I said, I will write. Then he altogether took from me
the power of adding word to word. So I went to bed. A head like wood
instead of one like fire—thats your God. What he likes is to take
away, to destroy, to give pain for pleasure." Virginia's God was a jealous God who concealed monstrousness in ordinary things and allowed his creatures to enjoy some happiness on condition that they
were properly miserable.

The unreality of politics rasped her—its deceptions always there in
the background. Her days since the summer had been punctuated by
political arguments—Maynard Keynes still carrying on about "the
great financial crisis." How elated he had been, she recalled, announcing the abandonment of the gold standard, which confirmed his
theories. He and his secretary had hardly been able to contain their
excitement, "like people in the war." On that occasion she had found
all the talk about money, coming on top of MacDonald's chicanery,
intolerable, and had finally retired to her room, where she calmed her
rage by reading Donne's poems, perversely concluding that the world
would be better off if people abandoned all doctrines and causes.

There was no comfort for her in the election results. The majority
of the electorate believed that MacDonald had saved the country. The
popular Conservative leader, Stanley Baldwin, went around warning voters that if the Socialists regained power "the pound would be
smashed and the poor starve." And they believed that too. Many ordinary voters were stampeded by the unsupported charge that the pre-

vious Labour government had risked the loss of savings deposited in the Post Office Savings Bank. On October 28 they gave the National government the largest majority ever recorded in British history — 551 parliamentary seats as against Labour's 52. Having smashed his own party, MacDonald seemed to run out of ideas, basing his new government on inertia and committing himself to do as little as possible. Virginia felt burdened by the national decadence and her judgment of the nation's leaders echoed the disillusionment of the young. Though she did not believe in the use of force, her contempt for the current government aligned her in spirit with her nephew, Julian Bell, whose long satirical poem, "Arms and the Man," appeared in *New Signatures*, a Hogarth Press anthology that introduced left-wing poets like W. H. Auden, Stephen Spender, and C. Day-Lewis. Bell expressed his desire for revolutionary change in oddly old-fashioned couplets.

> Strike then, and swiftly; if the end must come
> May war, like charity, begin at home . . .
> Nor leave the politicians to their trade
> To spread the idiot tangle they have made.

⚶

On the morning of December 10 Virginia woke from a dream of her old friend, Lytton Strachey, feeling that she had to write him a letter. She was again in the midst of an enforced period of rest, and had been battling severe pain in her head since the end of November — an unusually long siege, much of it spent in bed. The dream of Lytton, which was "more vivid than real life," went back to the time when they were both very young, though he had his beard: "I was at a play, in the pit and suddenly you, who were sitting across a gangway in a row in front, turned and looked at me, and we both went into fits of laughter." She wrote for old times' sake and because she had heard that he was about to set out on a journey to Malaga and might be away for months. When he received her "dream letter" Lytton was on another sort of journey, as she learned a few days later from his friend, Ralph Partridge. He was seriously ill and steadily declining; the doctors could not agree on diagnosis or treatment. A curtain seemed to fall, a shadow darkened Virginia's daily life. Lytton might die. They were intimate friends, and he retained his place in Virginia's affections, even though the circles in which they moved no longer overlapped and they saw each other only a few times a year. They rarely corresponded; this letter had been her first in four years, aside from a brief note. But they often had laughed together in the past, and her prescient dream reminded her of how much she depended on his being there in the audience, on seeing her thoughts reflected in his eyes. She still engaged him in imaginary dialogues.

Lytton's influence and personality had been on her mind for months before this dream. She was writing a parody of his Victorian biographies, an "escapade" that she had planned in order to distract herself after finishing *The Waves*. In *Eminent Victorians* and *Queen Victoria*, Strachey, a famous iconoclast, had displayed the murky truth about legendary figures such as Florence Nightingale, General Gordon, and the great queen herself. Virginia set to work on a canine biography, a send-up of Strachey's biographical style, lightening the satire with fantasy. Her subject was an eminent Victorian dog, Flush, who came from a long line of well-bred spaniels and had belonged to Elizabeth Barrett and Robert Browning. Virginia focused the spotlight on her four-footed hero, keeping the famous lovers in the background, giving tantalizing glimpses of their romance. She satirized the typical English love of dogs and their sentimental cult of the great Victorians. Strachey had wittily defaced his readers' idols. Virginia, detecting smugness, aimed her spoof at iconoclasm itself.

Her ties to Lytton, who had been one of her brother Thoby's closest friends, were deeply rooted. He had known her and Leonard separately, before they knew each other, and had helped to bring them together. He was one of the selves whom she had characterized in *The Waves*—Neville, the austere homosexual scholar who loves Percival. Much earlier he had provided the inspiration for Jacob's friend, Bonamy, in *Jacob's Room*. "He's in all my past—my youth," she told Ethel. He was a permanent presence in her life, a part of her, one of the six intimate friends without whom she would not care to survive. There was no one, she said, except Leonard, that she cared for more.

The "bearded serpent" was a tall, ungainly man who knotted his long, loose limbs into arabesques, and sat silent, ready to slice through the talk with some biting witticism. Since the day her brother first introduced her to "the Strache" she had valued his passion for literature and art, his shy impertinence, his languid and polished sentences spoken in a low baritone or a falsetto of astonishment. Behind his icy blue eyes she had detected an echo of her own sensibility—they thought alike about most things. Then Lytton had come to the house after Thoby's death and shared their grief more than anyone else outside the family. He had loved Thoby's monumental Englishness, the charm and intelligence that seemed to belong to another age.

"If it were not for his extraordinary sense of humor," he had told a friend, "he would hardly be of this world. . . . When you see him I'm sure you'll agree he's a survival of barbaric grandeur." Thoby, who was six feet two and had a "face hewn out of the living rock," represented for Lytton a forever unattainable ideal, "the perfect human specimen."

A few years after Thoby's death, while Lytton was undergoing one of his emotional crises, he had proposed marriage to Virginia and she had momentarily accepted. The serpent, tempting her through their common feelings for a dead brother, a ghost of forbidden fruit. Lytton realized almost at once that he could not marry anyone, certainly not Virginia. He was a little in awe of that formidable virgin. "She is her name," he wrote to Leonard Woolf, relaying the whole adventure in a letter to Ceylon. By their next meeting Virginia, too, had had second thoughts. She assured Lytton that no harm had been done, she was not in love with him and their friendship should continue as before. In a subsequent letter to Ceylon he observed that Virginia was "young, wild, inquisitive, discontented and longing to be in love," and urged Leonard to come back and marry her before he lost his chance. "If you came and proposed she'd accept. She really would," he announced, carried away by the matchmaking instinct. Leonard, who had met Virginia once or twice, playfully replied that he was ready to "take the next boat home" if she would have him.

Virginia began writing *Flush* as a joke on Lytton, the ironist, who held so many keys to her past. But *Flush* also had other meanings, since Elizabeth Barrett and Robert Browning, who had rebelled against repression and lived and worked as equals, set a precedent for her own partnership with Leonard. *Flush* indirectly referred to the fable of their marriage. As with Ethel, fable and fantasy helped Virginia free herself from obsessions and high seriousness. *Flush* satisfied her need for lightness, the humor of a parodic form that helped her cheat the destroyer God who gives pain for pleasure. Considering the pain now connected with Lytton's illness, her choice of the mock biography had its ironic side.

He had grown weak from loss of weight and a crisis came on; the end of December was consumed by alarm over Lytton's condition. His doctors still could not agree on a diagnosis—was it an ulcerated colon or a form of typhoid, the disease that had killed Thoby? Virginia, who had been ill herself, felt awkward about intruding at the bedside, where a watch was being mounted by several brothers and sisters and by members of his household, consisting of present and former lovers.

She borrowed her neighbor's phone daily to call for news. She had lived through about twenty years in a single week, she wrote Ethel on December 23. Everything was colored by the illness—she talked to him constantly in her mind, shared all her thoughts with him. Two days later, when Lytton seemed to take a turn for the better, Virginia said that she was "past feeling" and welcomed a release from the simplified emotions produced by the crisis. Picking up the telephone in her neighbor's bedroom to call the inn where Lytton's family was assembled, she stared with great intensity at the objects on Miss Dixey's table, and the wineglasses, the tea caddy, the Victorian photograph in an ornate frame were welcome signals of returning complexity—"annoyance, humour, the desire to laugh with him"—after the crushing single-mindedness of the past week.

Virginia lived in her friends, as did her fictional Mrs. Dalloway, who imagined herself "being laid out like a mist between the people she knew best." It was impossible to return to her ordinary routine as long as Lytton's illness dragged on. She kept busy by revising and polishing "A Letter to a Young Poet," an essay, begun the previous autumn, on the state of contemporary poetry. Was it true, as some people feared, that poetry was dead? Many recent books of poetry had been deformed by impurities, by the pressure of nonpoetic ideas, and by the search for political relevance. These clotted lines were preferable to the smooth, meaningless phrases of poetic "necrophiles . . . who much prefer death to life," who imitate Keats, Shelley, or Byron and avoid the living struggle. She urged her "young poet" to experiment freely and forget fame, to remember "that the greatest poets were anonymous . . . Shakespeare cared nothing for fame . . . Donne tossed his poems into the waste-paper basket." Lytton's illness made her long to efface herself, to attain the lightness of anonymity. Her life was simplified more and more in the new year. She comforted herself with the thought that he came from tough Anglo-Indian stock and had showed a calm tenacity that would carry him through. During the first days of 1932 he seemed to get better; then another crisis impelled Virginia and Leonard to drive to his country house in Wiltshire, Ham Spray, on January 14. They did not see Lytton, whose strength would have been overtaxed by visitors; instead, they visited the nearby inn where his family and intimate friends were keeping watch. Pippa Strachey sobbed on Virginia's shoulder after lunch: "Hopeless almost—he is so ill—how can he get better?" But before leaving they heard that his temperature suddenly had gone down to 99 and the family, though worn down, felt hopeful again. Another hint of complexity leaked into Virginia's diary here. She envied the rural setting of Ham Spray, the silence and remoteness from traffic and vacationing crowds, the stillness of villages in the heart of "solid England," which made Rodmell seem almost suburban. She recorded these feelings four days later, when Lytton was rallying yet again, but her tone was guarded; all the ups and downs resolved themselves into a general decline. Her muted voice reflected the strain of living with imminent death, attached to the telephone, numbed by the alternation of hope and gloom—a flattened life, without the usual densities and contours.

❧

Virginia was moved by the intense suffering of Lytton's companion, Dora Carrington, with whom her relations had always been complicated. Carrington (as she liked to be called) had lived with Lytton since 1918, managing his household and tending to his comforts. She painted and worked as a graphic artist, but her art came second. Years before, when she feared he would leave her, Carrington had assured Lytton of her complete devotion. "You are the only person who I have ever had an all absorbing passion for. I shall never have another." She had frankly acknowledged her masochism, claiming that hers was "one of the most self abasing loves that a person can have." Her only desire, she said, was to make him "happier than any person could be." Since then her life had revolved around Lytton's.

Carrington's story too had elements of romance and fable. In 1915, when she was a young art student, she had spent a weekend as Vanessa Bell's guest in Sussex. They were staying at Asheham, then Virginia's country house, which she had lent to her sister. One of the other guests was Strachey, a luxuriantly bearded, waspish writer, thirteen years older than Carrington, who accompanied her on a stroll across the downs. Momentarily attracted by her impish china-blue eyes and boyish figure, he impulsively stopped and kissed her. Carrington broke away and on returning home complained to her fellow art student, Barbara Hiles: "That horrid old man with a beard kissed me." No need to worry, Barbara replied, because Strachey was a homosexual. "What's that?" asked Carrington, to whom the word was unknown, and Barbara's explanation failed to mollify her. Early the following morning she crept into his bedroom with scissors, intending to cut off his beard. As she bent over the sleeper, he opened his eyes and looked directly into her eyes, giving her the speculative look of a penetrating observer—ironic and undemanding, sensitive and dispassionate. Carrington was fascinated, so the legend ran, and at once fell deeply in love.

A romantic moment, which began a long, obsessive attachment. Carrington, who hated her body and felt she betrayed her deepest self when she took pleasure in having sex with a man, found deep satisfaction in guarding Lytton's health, serving him as Leonard served Virginia. He was her revered "Papa," her naughty mentor, his wit masking serious artistic ambitions. They were united by every tie except sexual intercourse, which they had attempted only once. Carrington had occasionally taken lovers without disturbing this attachment, and finally married Ralph Partridge, an ex-army officer with literary interests, mainly because Lytton had grown fond of him. The three lived together and remained devoted to each other, in spite of the "dangerous complexity" of their ménage. Carrington insisted that Lytton alone made her life worth living, and this too became part of her legend. Once, during the early days, Arthur Waley, the sinologist, had asked her what she could possibly see in the cranky, ungainly man of letters, and Carrington had replied impishly: "Oh, it's his *knees*." Lyrical absurdity, combined with sly derision. Lytton's knees were the sign under which she defended her embattled selfhood.

In this time of illness, more than ever, he was her "all-absorbing passion." She had built her life on that passion, and it haunted the domestic objects surrounding her at Ham Spray—a pair of Lytton's spectacles, a favorite cracked teapot, the shelves of books they had arranged together—but there was a wildness in Carrington. She was a stranger, like Rhoda in *The Waves*, who knew another, deeper day, where the sun rises and sets once only. Her friends were afraid that if Lytton died, she would kill herself. It was all but taken for granted. On January 1 Virginia noted in her diary that a friend had been "summoned to be with Carrington, who will commit suicide they think."

Virginia liked Carrington's vivacity, but she had mixed feelings about her influence on Lytton, blaming her for the shallowness of his last book, *Elizabeth and Essex*. The idea that the painter might commit suicide stirred crosscurrents of guilt, confusing echoes of her own self-destructive acts. She remembered also that time when Ralph Partridge had pressured Carrington to marry him. He had been working then as a manager at the Hogarth Press, and Virginia had encouraged him to persist, secretly hoping to detach Lytton from the uneducated girl. Ironically, the marriage had had the opposite effect, but Carrington had detected Virginia's censorious attitude and been hurt by it. His friends did not think her good enough for him, she had complained, but it was unfair of Virginia to say that she and Lytton had nothing in common, considering how much she loved Donne, Macaulay, and Lytton's own essays. Furthermore, Virginia had told friends that Lytton was bored with Carrington, and this too had been reported back to her. Now, though it was too late, Virginia spoke and wrote consolingly, assuring Carrington that her companionship had brightened Lytton's life and her devotion lengthened it.

On January 20, having learned from a nurse that Lytton's case was hopeless, Carrington tried to kill herself by breathing exhaust fumes in her garage; she was found unconscious in the backseat of the car by Ralph and revived. On January 21, for the last time, Virginia reported a reprieve: "much better again." She felt a kind of vertigo, seeming to see "the globe of the future perpetually smashed—without Lytton & then, behold, it fills again." The following day she corrected herself: "Much better was much weaker. Lytton died yesterday morning."

[Virginia to Carrington, January 31, 1932]

One hates so the feeling that things begin again here in London without him. I find I cant write without suddenly thinking Oh but Lytton wont read this, and it takes all the point out of it. . . . And what it must be for you—I wish some time I could see you and tell you about the time, after Thoby's death, before you knew [Lytton], when I used to see him. But I could never give him what you did. I used to laugh at him for having grown so mellow and good tempered (you know how I loved laughing at him) and he said, "Oh but you know, it is rather wonderful—Ham Spray and all that—and it's all Carrington's doing. . . ." Before he knew you, he was so depressed and restless—and all that changed.

5 *Ghosts: The Empty Room*

The Sussex downs, where Virginia had had a country home since 1912, offered a quick escape from London and a promise, as she wrote in 1932, of "untrodden grass; wild birds flying; hills whose smooth uprise continue that wild flight." She spent two months of every summer at Monk's House and came down from the city during long weekends and holidays through the year, rambling around the countryside and over the downs in all kinds of weather. There was no greater pleasure in her life, she said, than walking alone in the country. The village of Rodmell, composed of a single street off a country road—a blacksmith shop at the crossing; a pub, a church, and a small cluster of houses—grounded her in England. From her back garden, which bordered on the churchyard, she glimpsed a five-hundred-year-old steeple with its black cross outlined against distant Asheham Hill and noted in her diary that the scene combined "all the elements of the English brought together accidentally." The water meadows began a few paces beyond her garden—houses and countryside running together harmoniously into an ageless pastoral landscape.

The downs, bare and treeless because of their chalky soil, frame the vista on both sides of the River Ouse: "whale-backed" hills that are never out of sight in this corner of Sussex, they rise around Rodmell like waves of turf on the horizon, their massive banks dotted with sheep and crossed by ancient footpaths. The green, round slopes can seem stark at times, but the weather here is moderated by breezes from the nearby Channel, and the low ground is covered with luxuriant shrubs and grasses. Leonard Woolf observed that their benign influence "can make one's happiness exquisite and assuage one's misery." The landscape was celebrated by the eighteenth-century naturalist Gilbert White, who found a maternal sweetness and humor "in the shapely figured aspect of chalk hills, in preference to those of stone. . . . I perceive somewhat analogous to growth in the gentle swellings and smooth fungus-like protuberances, their fluted sides, and regular hollows and slopes, that carry at one the air of vegetative dilation and expansion."

Coming back after one of her long, rambling walks, Virginia observed that the countryside contained enough beauty to "float a whole population in happiness," if only people would learn to use their eyes. She spent an hour or two walking every afternoon, sometimes skirting the mires and wildflowers along the river, sometimes covering seven or eight miles, scrambling over stiles, climbing the downs. Her loping stride affected the rhythm of her prose, for, as she explained while composing *The Waves*, "Writing is nothing but putting words on the backs of rhythm." Her attention moved back and forth between a bird-filled hedge and the page of the novel she was making up in her head. For Virginia the pleasures of walking were intertwined with the pleasures of writing; the combination of physical activity and imaginative freedom put her into something like a trance. After a stretch of open-air composition, she felt herself "swimming, flying through the air," as she said in her diary. She enjoyed the "current of sensations & ideas; and the slow, but fresh change of down, of road, of colour; all this churned up into a fine thin sheet of perfect calm happiness." On that sheet she painted some of her "brightest pictures," talking out loud to herself, chattering shamelessly, while the downs seemed to soar above her "like birds wings sweeping up & up."

This half-wild rolling landscape was fragile and endangered. Rodmell is only forty miles from London, and barely five miles over the downs from the crowded seaside resort of Brighton from whose outskirts ugly holiday villas were advancing along the coast. In April 1931 Virginia had been enraged when a local politician put up a hideous new house on the hillside overlooking the village; in September of that year the rumor that a developer planned to cover the same hill with cottages caused her sleepless nights. In her most despondent moods she imagined the rural culture of Sussex being obliterated and a rash of mean houses, shops, dog kennels creeping over the downs, turning the whole district into a suburb of Brighton. At the end of the year, while she was preoccupied with Lytton's illness, an even greater eyesore appeared in the neighborhood. Workmen began putting up a framework of steel girders across the River Ouse from Monk's House:

three galvanized iron sheds, "literally the size of St. Paul's and West-minster Abbey." She was condemned to look at these monuments of progress all through the three weeks of her 1931 Christmas holidays. The structures, built to house a cement factory, dominated the view from Virginia's garden terrace, and she saw them as omens. When the Alpha Cement Company had completed construction, it would begin stripping chalk and clay from the surrounding downs, leaving gashes on the slopes that are visible to this day, although the factory is gone. Writing to Ethel a week after Lytton's death, Virginia surprised her-self with the vehemence of her baffled anger: she would rather live in any "suburban slum," she said, than watch the downs and marsh be-ing "murdered inch by inch by these damnable buggers. Only I gen-erally like buggers; I cant think of a word to fit them—thats all." Her outrage against the builders and her bitterness about Lytton, who had been Bloomsbury's arch bugger, merged with a vision of the wild downs caged by girders. Virginia woke in the small hours of the night oppressed by an awful sense of "being in an empty hall. Lytton dead & those factories building."

⚜

Lytton and Carrington's relationship preserved a remnant of patriar-chal destructiveness; behind the Bohemian facade of their ménage à trois they had created their own equivalent of the Victorian house-hold—he playing the dominant role of paterfamilias, Carrington running the house and providing domestic stability, Ralph Partridge acting as emotional moderator. Carrington had revered Lytton, as a proper Victorian wife was supposed to revere her lord and master, completely subordinating her personality to his. She had lost the abil-ity or desire to stand on her own. Ironically, her emotional bondage nullified all of Lytton's advanced ideas about personal freedom, turn-ing Carrington into the equivalent of a love slave. Virginia, who had defined the Victorian ideal woman, the Angel in the House, in her scathing speech of January 1931, felt threatened by Carrington's self-abasement and blamed her for exerting a bad influence on Lytton. But now she was forced to ask whether the bad influence might have gone the other way. The question arose a week after Lytton's death when his brother, Oliver, dined with her at Tavistock Square—an old codger whose garrulous talk Virginia transcribed into her diary at length. He reported that Lytton's mysterious stomach ailment had been an incurable cancer. Oliver was a hardheaded rationalist who confessed that he was cold and indifferent to his own children. He gossiped fluently about a reading party before the war, his former wife's infidelities (she had borne five children, "never by the same man") and went on to discuss the nature of civilization; then, almost in the same breath, he stated the prevailing view that Carrington would kill herself; she had tried it before; her friends were now afraid to leave her alone. He pronounced such an act "quite reasonable," as long as one did it deliberately, allowing time for the first shock of grief to subside. "Suicide seems to me quite sensible." Virginia noted the opinion and crisply summed up Oliver as "a tough old buffer: with one flame inside him." She, too, had argued for the right to end one's life, though not in such cold, detached terms. The sensibleness of suicide in Carrington's case was far from self-evident, and furthermore, Virginia knew the difference between having such a theory and acting on it. Oliver Strachey could be casual, almost indifferent, but she had suffered in a similar way and wished to save Carrington from herself. In the following weeks she did as much as their long and ambivalent relationship permitted her to do—sending letters and requests to illustrate books for the Hogarth Press and twice visiting Carrington at Ham Spray. Carrington's depressed state merged in her mind with other symptoms of post-Victorian pathology.

Carrington's diary reveals the self-immolating logic behind her mourner's mask. Lytton was unique, she insisted, a companion to whom she never had to lie, who never expected her to be different from what she was, and who "could do no wrong." Like a good father, he loved her unconditionally, comforting her at times of sadness and enlivening her successes by sharing them. Her whole life had revolved round her desire to please him; without that motive she saw no reason to live. "What point is there now in what I see every day [she wrote], in conversations, jokes, beautiful visions, pains, even nightmares? Who can I tell them to? Who will understand? . . . I write in an empty book. I cry in an empty room." The last words, written on February 17, 1932, parallel the tone of Virginia's own diary, in which, on February 8, she had noted her insomniac vision of "being in an empty hall. Lytton dead & those factories building." The verbal coincidence between Virginia's "empty hall" and Carrington's "empty room" suggests the intuitive connection between them. Carrington took the victim's emotional logic to its conclusion, claiming that suicide is rational and permissible, and citing Hume's essay "Of Suicide," which argues that ending a life of misery is often the lesser of two evils. She copied into her diary his judgment that the suicidal person "does no harm to society. He only ceases to do good. I am not obliged to do a small good to society at the expense of a great harm to myself." Behind this argument lay the feeling that her life had no meaning except in relation to Lytton. He conferred the self-esteem that permitted her to go on living, and his death made her feel worthless.

Carrington engaged in a kind of magical thinking; she had the artist's need to create her own legend. Her friend Julia Strachey's memoir, "Carrington: A Study of a Modern Witch," described the subtle spell she laid on her friends. She had the shy spontaneity of the child-woman and evoked people's protective instincts. But without her "Papa" she could not imagine the future or go on working her special magic. Carrington had had a premonition of Lytton's death just before the onset of his illness, when she entered a contest sponsored by the *Weekend Review*, which had published a list of well-known writers, including Lytton, and challenged their readers to submit obituaries in the selected writer's own style. The idea appealed to Carrington's love of black comedy; she submitted a whimsical portrait of the great biographer at the age of ninety-nine, "knitting a coatee for his favorite cat." The venerable man saw a loose button lying on the grass. Vexed by this "unspeakable" disorder, he stooped to pick it up, and instantly expired under the ilex tree. She signed the entry with her nickname, "Mopsa," and when she heard that she had won first prize, wrote Lytton in mock terror that her two guineas would be withheld when they discovered who she was; they would say he wrote it for her. But afterward she found herself overcome by tears. During Lytton's illness the memory of this prank caused her great distress as a sign that she had not appreciated or loved him enough.

"What is to happen now to Carrington?" Virginia asked right after Lytton's death. Having worked very hard to kill the Angel in the House within herself, she was sensitive to its insidious power and aware of its hold on Carrington. Virginia's decision the previous year to write a spoof on Stracheyan biography reflected her skeptical judgment of Lytton's iconoclasm. His writing glamorized the Victorians, even as it deflated their pretensions, and by inverting the old pieties gave them a new nostalgic afterlife. He was intellectually emancipated, but his strenuous, discriminating tone owed something to the influence of General Strachey, his domineering father. Although Virginia's *Flush* was a minor satire, it represented another effort to undo the knot of reverence that still tied her to the Victorians. It aided the clarification of her political thought. We should do away with public statues, she implied, and have neither saints nor anti-saints, neither the staid eminences of Leslie Stephen's *Dictionary of National Biography*, nor the clay-footed egoists of Strachey's *Eminent Victorians*. Her little canine biography, written for relief after *The Waves*, opened a new stage of Virginia's career, which would be marked by progressively more radical positions, and by a further effort to demystify the Victorians once and for all. Looking ahead ten years in 1931, she had predicted: "I shall write out some very singular books, if I live."

By keeping her eyes on Flush, Virginia dissolved the spell of those powerful ancestral figures. A small dog filled the foreground; the Brownings and their antagonists flitted by safely on the margins of the picture. She outlined her anti-Victorian critique without the emotional involvement that exhausted her a few years later when she developed the subject at length in *The Years* and *Three Guineas*. *Flush* skirted complexities; it presented glimpses of the staid middle-class household at Wimpole Street ruled over by the tyrannical Mr. Barrett—dark, upholstered rooms where nothing was itself; "everything was something else." Beyond that unreal fortress, separated from it by only a few streets, lay London's rookeries, a jungle of slums where, as Elizabeth Barrett found when she paid off the dognappers who stole Flush, "wild beasts prowled and venomous snakes coiled." Probing psychologically, Virginia hinted at the fierce sexual repression of the dwellers in that middle-class fortress, but the story ended happily for Flush, who eloped to Italy with the Brownings and there found a freedom that humans never know, love "that has no shame; no remorse . . . so carelessly Flush embraced the spotted spaniel down the alley, and the brindled dog and the yellow dog—it did not matter which." In this warmer, clearer Mediterranean light Flush escaped imprisoning distinctions of rank and breeding. Being infested with fleas, he was shorn and saw himself naked in the mirror, stripped of his thoroughbred insignias, discovering the joys of anonymity. Flush had lost his glossy coat and gained something immensely more valuable, as Mrs. Browning noticed, remarking that his manner suggested wisdom. "She was thinking perhaps of the Greek saying that happiness is only to be reached through suffering. The true philosopher is he who has lost his coat but is free from fleas."

Virginia's satirical "escapade" coincided with a more serious intention. She had been planning to write a book about "the sexual lives of women" ever since her Angel-in-the-House speech and at various times while writing *Flush* she made mental sketches for that book, perhaps to be called "Knock on the Door." She aimed to explore the varieties of "love," which she had treated so lightly in *Flush*.

⁘

Thoughts of Carrington receded into the background during February 1932 while Virginia worked hard revising her critical essays for a new collection, *The Common Reader: Second Series*. She was leading a very active social life as well, seeing many old friends and quarreling again with her maid, Nelly. Word filtered through from Ham Spray that Carrington's mental state was still precarious and Virginia wrote from time to time, offering consolation and memories of Lytton's youth. Her awkward appeals to Carrington—"We have to live and be ourselves . . . it is more for you to live than for any one"—carried the burden of her own suicidal history. "We are all thanking you for what you gave Lytton," she said in her condolence note of January 21. "Please Carrington, think of this, and let us bless you for it." A week later she wrote the letter quoted at the end of the previous chapter, stressing how much Carrington had done for Lytton—"I could never give him what you did"—and admitting the futility of her attempts at consolation. "This is no help to you now," she said, "but it is for us." Later in February, after a visit to Ham Spray, she thought she might write a memoir about her youthful friendship with Lytton. She regretted that she had seen too little of him in recent years, but the bond between them remained constant.

Virginia was also involved during February in two public matters of very different kinds. The Potocki affair, which surfaced at the beginning of the month, concerned a Polish count who was being prosecuted for privately trying to publish a book of obscene poems. The poems bore a dedication to "John Penis in the Mount of Venus," and as Virginia described them in an arch letter to Clive Bell, included such memorable lines as "O what luck to sit and fuck: and Come and Hunt in Pegg's Cunt." Leonard had agreed to organize the count's defense, and Virginia was drawn into the whirl of activity surrounding the case—so distracted by it, she wrote Ethel, that she had "not had time to buy suspenders: my stockings sag down; nor nibs: I've none left to write with—nor boots—oh nothing, and all because of the Polish Counts male organ sticking in the Mount of Venus." At the end of February she and Leonard went to court to hear their barrister friend Jack Hutchinson plead the case, and saw the silly count sentenced to prison for six months. A day after the trial, which displayed the sort of lewd absurdity Lytton would have relished, Virginia wrote

Carrington another consolatory letter, thanking her for sending photographs of Lytton and saying that she dreamed about him constantly. She had "the oddest sense of seeing him coming in the street." The letter echoes with regret over past misunderstandings and missed opportunities. "I cant describe to you the sense I have of wanting to tell Lytton something. I never read a book even with the same pleasure now. He was part of all I did." And she again urged that Carrington must live in order to keep that memory and influence alive. "As long as you are there," she said, "something of the best part of his life still goes on." Virginia conceded, however, that there is no defense against suffering, and she returned to this theme on March 10, after again visiting Carrington at Ham Spray: "So go on, dearest, devilish though it is for you." In a sense she was continuing a deferred argument with herself. Her lame words of sympathy—"something of the best part of his life still goes on"—reflect real compassion that goes beyond their conventional form. Responding to this feeling, Carrington thanked Virginia for writing, saying that her letter was one of the very few that had helped her, "yours most of all because you understand."

At the same time Virginia made a decision that reflected her increasing dislike of all official cultural activities. On February 29 she received an invitation from Cambridge University to deliver six lectures on English literature. She was moved by the knowledge that her father had delivered the first series of the same Clark Lectures in 1883, and that she was the only woman ever to receive such an invitation. Writing to Clive Bell on the same day she gleefully vowed to "tell as many people as I can in a casual sort of way"; nevertheless, she refused to lecture. As her diary shows, she defined herself increasingly as a political outsider, a cultural tribune whose duty is to preserve her independence. No, she didn't want to spend a year on criticism rather than fiction, and in addition she wouldn't become a "functionary" and so be silenced when it came to attacking the establishment; how could she write her "Knock at the Door," the antipatriarchal book that she had been planning, if she played that scholarly charade? She refused for both artistic and political reasons, pleased to be able to refuse, though it was a bittersweet thought that her father "would have blushed with pleasure could I have told him 30 years ago, that his daughter—my poor little Ginny—was to be asked to succeed him: the sort of compliment he would have liked."

⁂

By early March Carrington's friends began to think that their attempts to restore her interest in life were succeeding. They believed she had resigned herself. She was busy putting things in order in the house and working in the garden. She planted snowdrops and daffodils in a grove she had cleared overlooking the downs. Ralph observed, though, that she was doing "too much tidying" among the shrubbery, particularly of a favorite spot under the ilex, where she had hoped to bury Lytton's ashes. She said repeatedly that she wanted to be left alone to commune with her thoughts, but the requests worried him. "She declares she just wants solitude," he said, "but I find that unbelievable." Still, she seemed better, and his surveillance could not go on indefinitely. On March 10 Ralph went up to London, leaving her at Ham Spray. Since their cook was away with the flu, she would be alone in the house, so he took the precaution of asking the Woolfs to visit her that day. "The only chance," Virginia later explained, "seemed to be to give her some interruption."

During that visit Virginia was intensely aware of Carrington's suffering, which performed a silent accompaniment to the ordinary social routine. They were late for lunch, arriving at one-thirty, and Carrington, who generally thought she did everything wrong, welcomed them apologetically, assuming she had bungled the invitation. She gave them a "succulent" lunch, bowls of hot soup in the freezing-cold dining room. They gossiped haltingly about Mrs. Keppel, once King Edward VII's mistress, whom Virginia had met the previous day—a brazen, likable old courtesan, "whose fists have been in the money bags these 50 years," still bustling about and just leaving for Berlin to hear Hitler speak. After lunch they went into Lytton's study to warm up. A pleasant fire in the fireplace and the glow of the books, neat files of fine editions, the shelves in perfect order, just as Lytton had liked them. Collecting and arranging this library had been one of their favorite pastimes. Afterward Carrington showed them her newly planted grove and left them to potter round the garden while she returned to the house to write some letters. Eventually Leonard settled down to work on the car and Virginia wandered back into the house, where Carrington found her looking at a book. Thus far they had not gone beyond ordinary chitchat. Years later Leonard remembered the day as "one of the most painful days I have ever slowly suffered." Its grimness contrasted with the crisp beauty of the weather, which was incongruously sunny and sparkling.

Alone with Carrington, Virginia asked to see the view, and they stood at an upstairs window looking at the garden and downs. Carrington said, "I want to keep Lytton's rooms as he had them. But the Stracheys say this is morbid. Am I romantic about it, d'you think?" Virginia assured her, "Oh no, I'm romantic too." Carrington burst into tears and Virginia took her in her arms, the barriers breaking down between them. They stood entwined and Carrington spoke about her feelings of failure. "There is nothing left for me to do. I did everything for Lytton. But I've failed in everything else. People say he was very selfish to me. But he gave me everything. I was devoted to my father. I hated my mother. Lytton was like a father to me. He taught me everything I know." It was a powerful appeal, and Virginia responded directly to the unspoken meaning of Carrington's words, breaking through another layer of reserve. She recognized, without judging it, the urge to self-destruction, sensing, as she said later, "that she could not go on much longer." "I did not want to lie to her—I could not pretend that there was not truth in what she said. I said life seemed to me sometimes hopeless, useless, when I woke in the night & thought of Lytton's death." These words, echoing Carrington's own state of mind, touched and consoled her as much as any words could, though Virginia later wondered whether they had also reinforced her despairing mood.

Carrington had settled back into her domestic life and seemed to be recovering; she was scheduled to leave for a holiday in the south of France the following week, but her suicidal intentions moved ahead on their own separate track. "I held her hand," Virginia remembered. "Her wrists were very small. She seemed helpless, deserted, like some small animal left." Carrington had become ghostlike, pale, looking inward, as if ready to disappear into the interior of herself, leaving only a childlike, compliant creature in view. The impression was reinforced later, after tea, when the Woolfs were about to leave. Carrington gave Virginia a small French box with the Arc de Triomphe painted on it as a memento of Lytton. She was not supposed to give Lytton's things away, she said, but this was all right, since she had originally given it to him herself. Virginia noticed again "how frightened she seemed of doing wrong—like a child who has been scolded."

The Woolfs had been prepared to stay the night if they were asked, but Carrington gave no sign of wanting to prolong the visit. She kissed Virginia, who guardedly asked her to remember them when she was in London. "Then you will come & see us next week—or not—just as you like?" To which Carrington replied, "Yes, I will come, or not." Carrington stood at the front door and waved, her loneliness emphasized by the country quiet, and then disappeared into the house. Virginia and Leonard drove away. That same evening Virginia sent Carrington a note by the last mail—she couldn't help writing, she said, just to thank her for keeping Lytton's memory alive, and the house "so lovely—the rooms, the carpets, the trees outside. . . . I felt consoled walking under the trees." She repeated the exhausted arguments in favor of life—"You do what no one else can do"—and signed herself, "your attached old friend who would do anything if she could."

The next evening, March 11, Stephen Tomlin brought the news that Carrington was dead. She had shot herself early that morning after eating breakfast and reading her letters. She stood near a window, having replaced a favorite rug that usually lay there with another inferior one and fired a shot that tore open her thigh. The gardener found her bleeding on the floor. She was still conscious when Ralph arrived and insisted, with just the hint of a pun on Ralph's surname, that she had picked up the gun to fire at two partridges on the lawn, and it went off by accident. She had carefully planned the act, however, smuggling the gun, borrowed from an acquaintance in the neighborhood, into the house without anyone suspecting it was there. She left a letter, perhaps written while Virginia and Leonard walked in the garden, stating her hope that Ralph would remarry, listing presents for her friends, and asking them to bury her ashes next to Lytton's in the "graveyard" she had cleared under the ilex.

Virginia and Leonard were the last people she spoke to before the "accident." Virginia's note, which arrived in the morning mail, was among the last letters she read. The Woolfs were baffled by the event, as if they had stumbled into an invisible wall. Walking in London that night, Leonard groped for words to express their own and the general failure: "Things have gone wrong somehow." Virginia later remembered that they were passing a silent blue street with scaffolding above. "I saw all the violence & unreason crossing in the air: ourselves small; a tumult outside: something terrifying: unreason." The memory of Carrington as they had last seen her—"very gentle and affectionate"—conflicted with that impulsive outburst of violence. There was no way to reconcile them. But death itself changed the way one thought about things. For Virginia it fixed the memory of her final intimacy with Carrington; they had been closer on that day than at any time in the years they had known each other. They had stood entwined at the window and looked at the view.

[Carrington's diary, March 1932]
Advice to Oneself

Turn down the wick!
Your night is done
There rises up another sun
Another day is now begun
Turn down your wick.

Turn down the lamp!
Time to expire
"Body and soul" end your tune
Retreat my pale moon,
And turn out your lamp.

6   *Ghosts: From the Acropolis*

For weeks afterward Virginia was haunted by Carrington's solitary figure, waving, and turning back into the house. She replayed it again and again, like a film loop, imagining Carrington waking in the morning, fetching her letters and shooting herself. Reexamining her own acts during that last afternoon, she wondered whether she "could have said more in praise of life. . . . Only I couldn't lie to her." Well-meaning lies were worse than useless, she knew, but the event itself reproached her. She felt uneasy about Lytton. He had been part of her personal mythology—her dead brother's loving friend—but now that image was coupled with another, tyrannical one, and she wondered whether Lytton's control of Carrington had been too despotic, causing this misplaced act of filial obedience. "I sometimes dislike him for it," she wrote. "He absorbed her[,] made her kill herself." At times she was swayed by friends who thought the act tragic and beautiful, a heroic authentication of the Carrington/Lytton legend. Lytton's old friend, Mary Hutchinson, was deeply affected by the "romantic completeness" of Carrington's suicide. "A beautiful gesture," she said, "her life & her death." Her attitude repelled Leonard, who curtly dismissed Mary's words as nonsense. "It was histrionic," he said. "The real thing is that we shall never see Lytton again. This is unreal." Carrington's death was a pure waste, and besides he was afraid of the effect all this suicide talk might have on Virginia. She recorded the argument noncommittally in her diary, refusing to endorse either side. She was jarred by the unstable images of her dead friends. It puzzled and disoriented her that the dead changed so oddly in her mind, their ghosts blundering on "like people who live & are changed by what one hears of them."

Carrington's other friends insisted that nothing could have stopped her, but Virginia continued to feel "hemmed in and depressed and haunted," as she told Ethel—haunted by the possibility that something she said or did not say during that last hour with Carrington had made a difference. Her mood brightened on March 24, a beautiful day at Rodmell, where the Woolfs had gone for the Easter holidays. After her guilt and self-doubt the relief was intense; she felt acutely conscious of her surroundings, the soft air caressing her like "a blue veil in the air torn by birds voices. I am glad to be alive & sorry for the dead: cant think why Carrington killed herself & put an end to all this." Defying death, enjoying the blooming meadows, she resolved to follow Vanessa's and Duncan's ironic advice, to think of the elephant-gray industrial sheds defacing the downs as Greek temples. She wouldn't be caged by the builders; there were still vast open spaces where she could walk, communing with herself and planning new creative works. What would she write next, she asked herself—another book? "Merciful to be free, entirely to think this out; needn't write a line I dont want to, or squander a moment on repetition."

Back in London the gloom of "mausoleum talks," as Leonard called them, pervaded the atmosphere, and Virginia looked forward to getting out of England altogether. The Woolfs usually spent two or three weeks touring on the Continent in the spring; this year they were going to Greece—a fairly long and complicated journey, which would take them away for a whole month. They were both in the mood for an adventure after the morbid concerns of the past few weeks. Their old friends, Roger Fry and his sister, Margery, had agreed to come with them. The plan to travel sociably in company with the Frys was in part a reaction to Lytton's death, reflecting Virginia's desire for greater intimacy with the friends who remained. The trip had a complex meaning for her, echoing some of the decisive events of her earlier life. She had made the pilgrimage to Greece many years ago, in 1906; then it was a difficult journey to remote places— "not so much a holiday as an expedition," which the Stephen brothers and sisters approached as high adventure. Thoby and Adrian rode on horseback from Trieste to Olympia, where they met their sisters, together with a friend, Violet Dickinson. Virginia filled her notebook with polished descriptions of the Greek landscape, literary exercises that ignored more mundane and crucial details. Toward the end of the trip Vanessa was prostrated by a mysterious nervous illness, and after their return to England Thoby came down with typhoid fever and died. In the aftermath of his death, Vanessa agreed to marry Thoby's close friend Clive Bell, whom she had previously turned down. Now in 1932, with Lytton gone, Virginia chose to revisit the places associated with that painful time, as if seeking reconciliation with her past self.

In her volatile state she held on to the ideal of lightness and anonymity, anchored herself in an impersonal vision, continuing to resist the seductions of fame and publicity. On March 20 she wrote to her friend William Plomer that a French critic, Floris Delattre, had published a study of *Le roman psychologique de Virginia Woolf*. She dipped into the book with some repugnance—it was not what she would call "lively reading, but then its difficult to see one self as a mummy in a museum: even a highly respectable museum." The tome repelled her, she told Ethel the following day; she couldn't read it, "because I hate my own face in the looking glass." Her dislike of most literary analysis extended to her own essays, which she was still revising for the second *Common Reader*. Surveying them, she said, induced "a kind of dancing agony at the futility of all criticism, and mine more than all—such childs play. Such caper cutting about folly they are."

The mindlessness of the literary industry was apparent to her on March 28, when she had tea with Ethel's novelist friend, Maurice Baring, who lived in a seaside house a few miles from Rodmell. Among the guests was a certain Captain Grant, a partner in the publishing firm of Peter Davies, who epitomized the attitudes she had escaped by founding her own press. The chinless captain struck Virginia as "the very spit and image of a soldier in Punch . . . so suave, masculine, foolish; exactly a round peg in his hole. All the slang right & the snobbery & the culture & the self-possession. Has killed animals in every part of the East. Talk, of course, wildly detailed & emphatic and useless about Greece." Having dispatched Greece, the obtuse captain invited Virginia to write a hack biography for his firm, suggesting that she pay an assistant to get up the facts for her. He blithely boasted that his mission was to make his company less highbrow, adding that he especially enjoyed "making suggestions to authors." Virginia received his compliments with silent contempt and exclaimed in her diary: "That chinless man to suggest to me. Pah!" In self-defense against the insidious captain and his allies in the literary establishment, she had developed her doctrine of anonymity, which meant shunning publicity and liberating one's creative work as far as possible from material concerns.

The vacuous tea party was relieved by farce at one point—an incident that Virginia gleefully tucked into a letter to Vanessa. Two men came round with trays of sandwiches. She didn't like the looks of the footmen or the sandwiches, but she took one of the latter—anchovies, which she loathed—and dropped it into her handbag. Later her host asked her for a match. She reached absently for her lighter and handed him the sandwich.

❧

Roger and Margery Fry, with whom the Woolfs departed for Greece on April 15, belonged to a leading upper-middle-class Quaker family. Roger was one of the most influential art critics of his day, as well as a painter and former curator of paintings at New York's Metropolitan Museum of Art. As the organizer of the famous Post-Impressionist exhibition of 1910, he almost single-handedly introduced the masterpieces of contemporary French painting to a reluctant English public. His books ranged through the whole field of art history. His sympathies were broad, and he vigorously promoted new movements in the arts; his literary tastes were reflected by his translations from the advanced symbolist poems of Mallarmé.

Roger's connection with Virginia and her circle went back to 1911, when he and Vanessa Bell had had a brief love affair. Their sexual relationship had soon ended—she had found his vitality and moral earnestness exhausting—but Vanessa kept a strong emotional hold on him and they remained lifelong friends. In the early thirties Vanessa's daughter, Angelica, detected a courtly flavor in the tone of their conversation, as if they could not quite admit that the affair was over.

Virginia admired the clarity and enthusiasm with which Roger made paintings come alive for his readers and lecture audiences, qualities she traced back to his Quaker upbringing. Still rarer, she said, was the blend of thought and feeling in his writing, the determination to check and verify his impressions rationally, though he "always allowed his sensibility to correct his brain." His honesty and sense of social responsibility were admirable. His weakness, if it can be called one, was an openness to new ideas, which sometimes deteriorated into gullibility. Leonard Woolf remarked that though Roger had been trained as a scientist, he was "capable of believing anything," from the latest cure for all ailments to a theory that the earth would be inherited by the birds. There was something fantastic about Roger—he

Figure 6. Julian Bell kneeling, Quentin Bell behind him, and Roger Fry, with Quentin's papier-mâché sculptures, at Charleston, 1931.

was a magpie, his pockets crammed with useful implements, his conversation brimful of curious facts. His friends had affectionately nicknamed him the White Knight, after the elderly horseman in *Through the Looking-Glass* who fell out of his saddle and fitted steel anklets on his horse "to guard against the bites of sharks." Two years earlier, in 1930, when Bloomsbury celebrated Angelica's eleventh birthday with an Alice in Wonderland costume party, Roger came wearing white Jaeger tights, chain armor, and green whiskers. A Woolworth collection of "candles, mousetraps, tweezers, frying pans, scales" dangled from brass chains wrapped around his body. He took the party by storm, completely eclipsing Virginia's long ears and woolly paws—she came as the March Hare.

Roger was a favorite with Angelica, who found him pleasantly alarming. "His fine white hair, parted in the middle, gave him a feminine appearance," she wrote. "His eyebrows were tufted, while beneath them his eyes lived in vital intensity behind gold-rimmed spectacles." He showed magic lantern slides of paintings, holding a long white wand with which he revealed the secrets of spatial form. During those public lectures, Virginia said, his face wore an unforgettably animated expression.

Margery Fry, the fourth traveler to Greece, shared her brother's intellectual and moral earnestness but lacked his engaging sociability. Sensitive about being an outsider in Bloomsbury, she was wary of Virginia—and with cause. On board ship, sailing from Venice to Athens, Virginia tried to conciliate the reluctant Margery while Leonard and Roger played chess. At the same time she wrote to Vanessa that the stout Quaker lady, wrapped in a white pelt, conjured up an image of an "elderly yak." She conceded also that Margery had performed very deftly during their whirlwind art tour of Venice—she had debated with Roger about the shape of a pillar and the design of bald heads in a painting, keeping him so busy that he never probed "the poor ignorant Wolves," whose naïveté about art would otherwise have been exposed. In a letter that crossed Virginia's in the mail, Vanessa described Margery as the quintessential English spinster: in her youth she had loved a man but refused to go to bed with him; then he was killed in the war and she never formed another attachment. The conventlike discipline under which they were all brought up—she was one of six unmarried Fry sisters—stifled romance. Vanessa speculated that perhaps Margery, who ran Roger's household for a time after his first wife's nervous breakdown, was too much in love with her brother to accept anyone else. In her middle years she devoted herself to penal reform and pursued an academic career. Eventually she became principal of Oxford's Somerville College, where she promoted higher education for women. The many academic honors she had received, she told Virginia, could not compensate for her childless life.

✢

The friends arrived in Athens on April 20, and from there they sallied forth on a series of day-trips to neighboring landmarks. They went on two longer motor tours as well—through the Peleponnesus (April 25– 28) and then to Delphi (April 30–May 2). One of Virginia's first acts after arriving was to revisit the Parthenon, which had remained vivid in her imagination through the years, surfacing in *The Waves* as an image of marble columns at the world's end. The ancient temple seemed taut and shiplike, more solid and robust than she remembered it. The sight of those stark yellow pillars radiating against a blue sky startled her; she recorded the moment tersely, observing only that "my own ghost met me, the girl of 23, with all her life to come." (Virginia was twenty-four years old in 1906, but she didn't notice her mistake and repeated it later on.) She was intensely aware of past and present, noticing that in the intervening years she had shed most of the youthful sentimentality that had colored her earlier visit. Fifty and gray-haired now, she had lived to an age when one especially values lightness and energy. Her desire to execute a vital "flourish in the face of death" underlies the gaiety of her accounts of Greece. Her letters home are filled with mythical landscapes and fantastic anecdotes in the spirit of Lewis Carroll. Their bright, reflective surfaces hide the darker thoughts within, while drawing some of their richness from those shadows. In her letters, as in her fiction, she uses fantasy to defend herself against disturbing memories of her youth.

On May 1 she wrote a typically fanciful letter to her nephew Quentin Bell, revealing that Roger, who suffered from piles, was nevertheless determined to go everywhere and see everything. "Some part of Roger's inside is coming through, so that he cant sit or stand— but this makes little difference. Its merely a question of going behind a hedge now and then with a buttonhook." Arriving at Delphi, they had found that it was the Greek Easter; whole sheep were roasting over open fires, golden eagles soared overhead, and the villagers, carrying candles and corpses on biers, marched about "singing wild incantations." The Frys, with their manic reasonableness, could be as entertaining as any of the sights. "Roger is a fair shower bath of erudition—Not a flower escapes him. And if it did, Margery would catch it. Between them every bird beast and stone is accounted for. We talk almost incessantly, and yesterday had the great joy of smelling a dead horse in a field. No sooner smelt than 12—no—15 vultures descended from the azure and proceeded to pick it. They have long blue bald necks like snakes. Sometimes a tortoise crosses the road—sometimes a lizard." Virginia's fable introduces corruptible bodies in order to humorously disinfect them—Roger has his inside coming through, but the problem is mended with a buttonhook. The evil-smelling field and the carrion-eating vultures are offset by the homely, reassuring tortoise and lizard. Virginia used a similar Aesopian tone in telling Vanessa her impressions of Margery. She had been ingratiating herself with "the Yak," who considered her a snob of snobs. Virginia was brimming with goodwill, as she wryly explained: "I do my best to climb off my perch and roll on the floor; and sometimes she likes me; and then she's fearfully humble." When she praised Margery for her political astuteness, Margery protested that she was not well informed, merely good at bluffing. The exchange didn't erase Margery's suspicion, though, that Virginia was one of those lofty aesthetes "who exist by virtue of their white petals." Meanwhile, Leonard beat Roger in game after game of chess, which caused hard feelings between them, because Roger would get into trouble and take his moves back, and then complain that Leonard was playing too slowly.

During their day-trips in the country around Athens, Virginia had the sensation that they were driving through a landscape "so ancient that it is like wandering in the fields of the moon"—stony mountain vistas, ageless olive trees and fertile valleys winding down to deserted bays—a landscape closer to 300 B.C. than to the tea shops and kennels of the English countryside. Returning from Delphi on May 2, they made a side trip through wild terrain in order to visit Hosias Loukas, a remote Byzantine monastery. The trip provided Virginia with "a fine sample of Fry tenacity." It began with an argument between Roger and their driver. Roger insisted they must take the most direct route toward the mountain—it was clearly marked on the map as a main road—and though the driver objected that it was dangerous, almost impassable, Roger was adamant. In the morning, as they were about to start, the driver announced that they had just recovered the bodies of two tourists killed when their car plunged off that road into the precipice. Though still unconvinced, Roger finally agreed to drive around and approach the monastery from another direction. Virginia summed up the excursion in her usual fabulating style. After a long bumpy detour, followed by a climb to the summit in the midday sun (Roger rode up on a mule), they reached the monastery, which was a complete anticlimax. They found that the celebrated "mosaics were very inferior and the Monks were very annoying, and we didnt get back to Athens till 8.30 at night, having broken a spring, punctured a tire and run over a serpent." Nevertheless, Roger came away in the best of spirits and with undiminished energy, remarking that they had gained invaluable insights into the Greek mind.

All in all, their mood, Virginia said, was "as sweet as nuts and soft as silk." The luxuriant shower baths of erudition, the tireless search for masterpieces and out-of-the-way sights, the cranky chess games, as well as Virginia's Aesopian friendliness and Margery's humility, persisted throughout the trip. Furthermore, the Frys, who were keen painters, hardly stirred out-of-doors without canvas, paint boxes, and easels loaded on their backs and strung around their necks. Whenever they passed a visually interesting spot, Roger would say, "I must make a note of that." Brother and sister would get out their kits and sketch or paint, which gave Virginia and Leonard some relief from the hectic pace of their sight-seeing. On May 2, after ten days of touring, Virginia noted that Roger had done about twenty pictures. Painting did not stop the Frys from talking. They were able to do both at once, and kept up a steady stream of questions and observations so that there was rarely a quiet moment. Virginia thought their volubility comic and endearing—they were so sensible and well informed. At some other time or place she might have hated it, but their pursuit of information, like voices in a crowded room, freed her to commune with herself. She was exhilarated by the outer sights and people she met, and at the same time her inner eye glimpsed visions of the Greece she had visited in 1906. The Frys were too busy with flora and fauna, architecture and iconography, to pay much attention to her moods. Roger did notice that she was unusually silent, and satisfied to stay that way. "Virginia in particular doesn't seem to want to talk [he wrote to Helen Anrep]. I think she gets immense pleasure from just having experiences."

She liked him and Margery; her appreciation deepened as they traveled together, but their preoccupation with knowing and classifying everything occasionally made them seem like relations of the Mad Hatter and the Mock Turtle. "They hum and buzz like two boiling pots," she wrote Vanessa. "I've never heard people, after the age of 6, talk so incessantly." What's more, their appetite for facts was insatiable and "at the most trying moments when Roger's inside is falling down, and Margery must make water instantly or perish, one has only to mention Themistocles and the battle of Platea for them both to become like youth at its spring." Because they shared an intellectual tradition and Victorian upbringing with her, they caused Virginia to define her own position. In spite of their interest in art, the Frys lacked the artist's vision. Their obsession with pure facts was almost inspired—like one of Lewis Carroll's fantastic creations—but it was also limiting. The point was clarified when Margery caught Virginia smiling at her own thoughts and said that "no Fry had ever done that," whereupon Roger added, no, they had "no power of dissociation." He meant, as Virginia understood him, that they lacked the imaginative power to break things down and reassemble them into new compounds. And that explained why, in spite of their attention to visual details, they were such bad painters—because, she concluded, "they never simmer for a second."

Still, her respect for Roger kept growing—he was so humane and indomitable—"far and away the best admirer of life and art I've ever travelled with." She enjoyed his enthusiasm for obscure masterpieces and his recurring shout, "Oh come and look at this! My word thats swell—very swell"—pointing to some mosaic high up on a church ceiling, some white, "vindictive" Christ that he said was better than he'd ever imagined. As for Greek architecture, the ruined temple at Aegina demonstrated what genius can do in a small space, achieving perfect proportions, and it was therefore much finer than the one at Sunium built on exactly the same plan. Six inches of difference between their proportions were as crucial as the difference between a cart horse and a thoroughbred stallion. It all depended on the precise intervals between columns and the curves of the capitals. One afternoon in the Byzantine church at Daphnis, Virginia watched him surveying the interior, visually feeling his way along pillars and mosaics, as if his mind were a sensory organ deployed by some "prodigiously fertile spider." Then she turned to the open door and looked out at the rows of olives and pines, their lights and shadows forming "waves on the grey hillside." Exercising her power of dissociation, she could reconcile the two different dimensions—Roger and the olive trees, the church interior and the rhythmic groves around it.

※

[Virginia to Vita Sackville-West, May 8, 1932]

Sea was round us at Nauplia—the waves lapped my balcony and I looked down into the hearts of fish. And then we crossed an appalling pass, winding round and round, every sweep higher, and one wheel or the other perpetually balancing over a precipice 3,000 feet of sheer rock beneath. How I trembled! Then suddenly swooping round a corner to come upon a flock of goats or another car, and to have to back, with the hind wheels brushing the tops of pine trees. But we got through safely and so to Delphi, where an Englishmans skeleton, the son of my oldest friend, had been found, dangling from a tree in a gorge, with a gold watch between the ribs. There I bathed my feet in the Castalian spring; and all the rocks were covered with pale purple campanula. . . .

Yes it was so strange coming back here again I hardly knew where I was; or when it was. There was my own ghost coming down from the Acropolis, aged 23: and how I pitied her!

Reviving the past was painful as well as exhilarating; the day before writing this letter Virginia had visited the Parthenon again and now, using almost the same words as upon her arrival, she said that the ghost of her past self came to meet her. But the words are framed in a new way, revealing how much the encounter unsettled her. "I hardly knew where I was; or when it was . . . and how I pitied her." The 1906 trip to Greece, which began as a naive literary pilgrimage, ended with disaster. Three of her traveling companions returned to England seriously ill, and while Virginia took care of her sick brother, whose typhoid fever the doctors fatally misdiagnosed, her great friend Violet also lay ill with typhoid across London. Vanessa was still an invalid. Virginia's world, already shattered by several deaths, was crumbling completely, and she could not attend to herself. Fearing that news of Thoby's death would be a dangerous shock to Violet, the doctors advised Virginia to conceal it from her at all costs. For almost a month, till Violet accidentally read the truth in the newspaper, Virginia wrote her letter after letter, giving details of Thoby's recovery, including accounts of his state of mind, current reading, and fond thoughts about Violet. The thoroughness with which Virginia entered into the deception suggests that she was deceiving not only her friend but herself, muddling fantasy and fact together, so that she truly no longer knew where she was or when it was. This was the dissociated girl whom Virginia pitied intensely.

The obsessions of her youth, those ghostly presences, still inspired her to shape and rearrange events, turning fact into fiction, though she did so now as a disciplined artist. But her letter, with its manic account of a three-thousand-foot drop onto sheer rock and a lost climber, reflects her fascination with falling. The remains that have just been discovered near Delphi suggest a mythical landscape where Virginia bathes her feet in the Castalian spring. The skeleton with the gold watch between its ribs broods over the scene as her car's back wheels hang over the precipice, brushing the tops of pine trees. One of Roger's letters also describes driving through the mountains. "The excitement [he wrote] comes from the fact that the road is so full of holes that the car has to go along the very edge up terrific heights but we have a marvellous driver. . . . Sometimes there's a ravine cut by rain right across the road and one has to stop dead and just creep down and up with tremendous jars." Virginia's version, as a comparison with Roger's shows, was based on facts, but she had so rearranged and saturated them with her own attitude as to make them sound like an Elizabethan chronicle. Every word was fiction and every word was true.

ॐ

Summing up her impressions on her last day in Athens, Virginia concluded that this was the best holiday they had had in many years. She had come to Greece with a vague idea of reviving memories of her youth, and the country itself, which she found altogether wilder and more civilized than she expected, made her aware of her own English tightness and respectability. Youthful images of gentle peasants and a landscape "perfectly free of vulgarity" charmed her, and she imagined escaping to a mountain retreat where "every inch has its wild flower." She indulged a vision of coming to Crete every year with a tent, living simply on bread, yogurt, and eggs, a sensual existence without reading and writing, but incorporating her artistic values into daily life. She would slough off "the respectable skin; & all the tightness & formality of London; & fame, & wealth; & go back & become irresponsible," that is, recapture a mythical innocence. Crete, where she had never been, though she had heard its beauty praised, was the appropriate place for this fantasy; she explicitly linked it to youthful memories of Cornwall, concluding that she "could love Greece, as an old woman . . . as I once loved Cornwall as a child."

Her utopian musings were intertwined with friendly, slightly baffled observations of Margery, whose kindness to hotelkeepers and bootblacks, and whose genuine concern for the peasants, made her humanity shine. Yet Margery lacked some essential quality. Of course, Virginia said, she had missed having children and therefore was condemned "to paint and botanise and watch birds and philanthropise for ever instead." She was another victim of the Victorian Angel in the House. During her youth her mother, Lady Fry, forbade her to laugh at men's stories lest they think her fast. Curbed and muzzled in this way, she had suffered intense boredom, the marks of which she carried ever afterward, for having learned not to laugh as a young woman, she could not do it now that she was old. In spite of her good-hearted nature, she lacked charm or spontaneity. Virginia told Vanessa an anecdote about the Fry character. Margery had recently got round to discussing her blighted youth with her mother, who was now ninety-seven. Looking back at the way she had raised her daughters, keeping them shut up "in so many band boxes pouring out tea and watering flowers," Lady Fry had a change of heart and admitted to Margery that she had made a mistake. Unfortunately, this effort of imagination came forty years too late. None of her daughters had married, and as for Margery, all her thwarted maternal instincts had fixed on her gifted brother. "I daresay it would be better if she married Roger," Virginia wrote.

Such specimens of Victorian family history coincided with Virginia's ideas for her book about women and the patriarchal order, which she had been working out in her mind "subterraneously" among the ravines and ruined temples. Thoughts about inequality between the sexes blended subversively with the quaking aspens and the smell of orange blossoms. At times she was so immersed in her ideas—about women's condition and the power of anonymity—that she hardly knew where she was, whether in Greece or England. Moreover, while the Frys were busy painting she had read Middleton Murry's biography of D. H. Lawrence and concluded that Lawrence's excessive maleness impaired his writing, because "the male virtues are never for themselves, but to be paid for"; the question of practical consequences, "what will pay," was always present in his work as an impurity. Later in the decade she would incorporate these ideas, together with the utopian vision inspired by Greece, into her arguments against the established order.

7   *Anonymity and Rhythm*

After her vision of freedom and "incandescent pillars," Virginia had difficulty adjusting to the London routine of dinners and parties; thoughts about Carrington and Lytton troubled her again. In the fluctuating rhythm of her life, the spring of 1932 formed the trough of a wave, a physical and emotional nadir. She went out a great deal and often felt numbed by the insincerity of the people she met. The increasing demands upon her time and attention made her wary of all publicity. As a writer she believed that art should be egoless and impersonal, and she was amplifying her "philosophy of anonymity" in response to growing violence and social disorder. Anonymity, as she used the term, referred not only to self-effacement but to an unknowable core or center of the being, which flourishes in obscurity. But at the same time her desire for fame was strong and often pulled her in the opposite direction or in both directions at once.

On May 25, ten days after returning from Greece, she was on the verge of severe depression, nearer to one of her "climaxes of despair," she told Ethel, than she had been in years, and for no very good reason that she could see. She had had an unpleasant encounter with Vita's cousin, Edward Sackville-West, a novelist and heir to the Sackville title. He had quarreled with Vanessa's companion, Duncan Grant, and meeting them both at a party, she had tried to arrange a truce, making the blunder of humorously inviting Eddy "to behave like a British nobleman." Thoroughly nettled, ignoring the ironic tone of her appeal, he went home and fired off a peevish note protesting her "cheap" remarks—to which she replied angrily that her reference to his social standing was "intentionally half-humorous. . . .

To urge either you or Duncan to behave like a gentleman is too silly even for me." Virginia could be formidable when aroused, and her caustic words made Eddy back down, but she hated squabbling and for a while, till the quarrel was patched up, she dreaded meeting him at parties. Behind the trivial wrangle lay a more far-reaching disturbance, a sense of the pointlessness of her own existence, intensified by a visit to the Chelsea flower show, where the hard middle-class faces seemed to taunt her. This mood colored an incident on May 22, when, driving home from Richmond, she and Leonard chanced upon an accident. A crowd had gathered near Mortlake Bridge; people were looking at a boat overturned in the river. The Woolfs stopped their car and got out. There were several fully dressed people in the water and a disheveled woman floating on her back while someone pushed and pulled her through the water. They reached the shore and climbed out. Virginia was struck by the sight of a dripping elderly man scrambling up the bank, trousers plastered to his legs, while the spectators looked on impassively. She found it "a sordid, silent spectacle—this heroic rescue. Middle class people in full Sunday dress immersed in cold water." The immersion suggested a break in surface reality, a "miracle," but the scene brought no vision of "terror or sublimity"; it seemed merely grotesque, a symptom of her own and the general dissociation.

Virginia was also disturbed by problems at the Hogarth Press. The ups and downs of publishing—they were issuing about two dozen books a year—cut right across her literary interests. She did the equivalent of a full-time editor's job, reading manuscripts as they came in and promoting books and authors. Moreover, she helped in other phases of the business—from writing advertising copy to wrapping parcels for the post when a large order was due. Sometimes she set type for one of the limited editions that the Woolfs still printed by hand. She accompanied Leonard on business trips, traveling their books to provincial booksellers. She was constantly drawn into Hogarth Press affairs because she and Leonard lived above the shop. The press occupied the basement of their house at 52 Tavistock Square— musty, stone-floored rooms that had once been a kitchen and servants' quarters. Behind the house, across a small open courtyard, stood a windowless, skylighted studio, where Virginia did her writing. In cold weather she sat in front of a gas fire with a notebook on her knees and a typewriter beside her, smoking hand-rolled shag cigarettes. Her studio doubled as a storeroom. Employees coming in to replenish their stock found her there, surrounded by bales of books, like a soldier among sandbags. In the run of her daily life the press was only a few steps away down a corridor. When Leonard was printing in the back room she heard machinery clanking across the courtyard, accompanied by distant noises from the street. She returned manuscripts to the front office, where, like an interrupted symphony, the clatter of three clerks typing, gossiping, and filling orders resumed each time she opened the door.

During that spring Virginia was disconcerted by the constant tension between Leonard and John Lehmann, whom the Woolfs employed as manager of the Hogarth Press. The twenty-five-year-old Lehmann, a poet with entrepreneurial ambitions, was a Cambridge friend of Virginia's nephew Julian Bell. He had joined them with the hope that eventually, if they got along, he would buy into the business and become a full partner. John provided a useful link with the younger generation, helping the press attract new writers like Christopher Isherwood, Stephen Spender, and C. Day-Lewis. As a prospective partner, the sharp, persistent young poet ran up against the Woolfs' reluctance to give up real control over their brainchild. Leonard had the self-made man's strong and often inflexible ideas about how the business should be run. At first, while John was learning the ropes, Leonard was an admirable mentor; his caustic analysis of the way the book trade worked enabled Lehmann to learn "the essentials of publishing in the most agreeable way possible." Leonard regarded the press, which was still small enough to be managed by one person, more as a labor of love than as a source of income. "If Leonard had a fault," Lehmann wrote, "it was in allowing detail to loom too large at times. A small item that could not be accounted for in the books, a misunderstanding about a point of production would, without apparent reason, irritate him suddenly to the extreme, he would worry it like a dog worrying a rat until indeed he seemed the rat and the detail the dog." This irritability, Lehmann believed, grew out of Leonard's long anxiety about Virginia's health.

In spite of Lehmann's youthful, almost cherubic, appearance, he had a stubborn streak of his own and resented being bossed by Leonard, especially about procedural details that he felt quite capable of settling himself. The two men quarreled fiercely. Vanessa, who was fond of her son's friend, tried to mediate, arguing that John worked hard for meager wages. But Leonard saw no excuse for what he dismissed as slipshod practices, and the conflict, though smoothed over, stayed unresolved.

Figure 7. John Lehmann and Virginia, photographed by Leonard in the garden at Monk's House, c. 1931.

Virginia wrote in her diary on May 25 that she felt almost over-whelmed—the problem of what to do about John merged with a host of other anxieties. She named them in disjointed phrases, observing what a torment it was to feel things as intensely as she did, to be so often "screwed up into a ball," to be so appalled by the rapacious-ness of people that she could hardly imagine enduring it for another year, let alone twenty, although there was at least one mitigating fac-tor: Leonard's "goodness, & firmness; & the immense responsibility that rests on him." The pettiness of her own grievances merely proved that she had been infected by the general sterility. She compared her childlessness to Vanessa's rich maternal state; she regretted her self-consciousness about clothes, which turned shopping into pure tor-ture. The sorrows spilled out, her thoughts leaping from Bond Street fashions to cosmic disorder and back again. There was no sanctuary where she could rest and say, "Time stand still here." She remembered "the hard raddled faces in the flower show yesterday; the inane point-lessness of all this existence. . . . Shall I write another novel; contempt for my lack of intellectual power; reading Wells without under-standing; Nessa's children; society; buying clothes; Rodmell spoilt; all England spoilt; terror at night of things generally wrong in the uni-verse." She used the diary here therapeutically, not only to record her depression but to defuse her anxieties by writing them down. The im-age of violence expanding in concentric waves round Rodmell to en-gulf England and ultimately the world reveals a charged visionary state, rising above her narrow personal concerns. Its energy breaks through the pall of depression. From that point her thoughts circled back somberly to Carrington's suicide and the shadow it cast on the future. She remembered the dark night when she saw "all the violence & unreason crossing in the air: ourselves small; a tumult outside: something terrifying: unreason." She had asked herself then: "Shall I make a book out of this? It would be a way of bringing order & speed again into my world." The warning about unreason, almost biblical in effect, prophesied an advancing shock wave that would soon be felt by everyone. Though she began with a judgment of sterility, she went beyond it, regaining confidence at the end by contrasting the two ex-tremes of social anarchy and creative power, resisting unreason by in-voking her art as a writer.

The next day, after discussing her depression with Leonard, she commented that she was suffering from a conflict between the critical and creative sides of her mind. She had been doing the analytical work of revising her essays, while at the same time her awareness of social disorder increased, impelling her to use her critical faculties more fully. The times required one to oppose "unreason" with clear and forceful arguments, but how could she satisfy those demands and still practice her art? Having understood the conflict, she could try to satisfy both claims, and the cloud that had prevented her from concentrating lifted. Her struggle against depression on May 25 led to her experiment a few months later with a hybrid form of "novel-essay," an attempt to combine fiction and social criticism, and it raised questions that absorbed her for years to come.

Her fear that things were "generally wrong in the universe" coincided with a heightening of tensions in Europe. It was increasingly obvious that war was inevitable, as many of her friends believed. Surveying the public mood in 1933, Leonard Woolf wrote that a change of attitude took place around the middle of the previous year. Up to that time the League of Nations enjoyed solid popular support, but the league's disarmament conference, which began in February 1932 and deadlocked with twenty-seven incompatible plans on the table at once, had extinguished any hope that reason would prevail. Europe was dominated by resurgent national movements and the rise of Hitlerism. Leonard reported that intelligent Europeans of all nationalities shared a common pessimism about the future. The remark he heard most frequently was, "We are back again in 1914." Describing Britain's muddled position on disarmament, the historian A. J. P. Taylor cites London's vulnerability to air attack, which should have led the British delegates "to jump at the idea of abolishing all aerial warfare. They made a mess of their case. Negotiations over disarmament, by getting down to details, usually reveal dangers which have not been noticed before and send the participants away eager for greater armaments. This conference was no exception."

Virginia heard Maynard Keynes's view of the European situation at a lunch given by him on June 1. The conversation was dominated by another guest, George Bernard Shaw, who at seventy-four had the vivacity of a man in his twenties. His compulsive talk veered from the mysteries of letter writing and the Irish character to Shaw's own method of writing history—he made up what he expected people would say and then found facts to support him. The force of his wit was somewhat diminished by his self-absorption. "His face is bright red [Virginia remarked]; his nose lumpy: his eyes sea green like a sailors or a cockatoos. He doesnt much notice who's there." From the other side of the table she overheard Keynes assuring Mrs. Shaw that the political outlook was about as bleak as it could be; all in all things had "never been so bad. We may go over the edge—but as its never been like this, nobody knows. One would say we must." She commented ironically that Keynes made these dire pronouncements while they were all digging in to a very substantial lunch. She remembered his words the following day, driving through Hyde Park, where she observed a steady stream of Rolls-Royces and well-fed people and nurses wheeling perambulators—all unconscious of walking "on the verge of a precipice." Struck by this imposing display of wealth and luxury, she sensed that they were all perilously sleepwalking, like innocents in a slapstick movie. Behind her satirical tone lurked that premonition of violence and unreason that returned in the small hours of the night.

On June 5 Virginia declined an invitation from Kingsley Martin, the editor of the *New Statesman* and one of Leonard's close political associates, to contribute a weekly Books column to that paper, saying it took her three or four mornings to complete an article that most journalists did in one. Behind her refusal loomed continuing conflicts with John Lehmann at the press. All their nerves were frayed, and Leonard was showing the effects of the difficult spring. John suspected that he was "suffering from a severe nervous crisis, cause unknown." John's diary gives a vivid sketch of the situation as he saw it, a picture of a haggard, almost hysterical Leonard persecuting him with "repeated invasions of the office, anxious examinations of work being done, nagging tirades and unnecessary alarms and impatience about what is progressing steadily and in advance of the time-table." An intolerable situation—which they tried to resolve by making a new agreement. John would remain as an editorial adviser, coming in to the office for two hours a day; they would hire someone else to do the managing—an arrangement that would give him more time for his own writing. Leonard, in spite of his irascible temper, conducted the negotiations in a fair and even forgiving spirit. Virginia, for her part, urged John to be "more malleable, & less pernickety," promising to come out of her studio more often and help them get along till the agreement went into effect in September.

At the end of June she was struck again by the volatility of political fortunes when the Russian émigré Prince Dmitri Mirsky, came to dinner on June 27, bringing a "dubious" Russian lady. Virginia confided uncharitably to Ottoline Morrell: "On Monday have Mirsky and his prostitute." He was a literary historian and convert to Communism whom Leonard had met at the Paris flat of Jane Harrison, the great classical scholar. Mirsky was writing a Marxist study, *The Intelli-*

gentsia of Great Britain, which was published in England in 1935. The book described Virginia Woolf as the central figure in the artistic circle identified with Bloomsbury and "unquestionably a great artist," but added that her bourgeois emphasis on individual suffering diverted readers away from material reality "to a world of esthetics." At dinner with the Woolfs, Mirsky announced that he was fed up with living in boardinghouses; he was leaving his post as a lecturer at the University of London and returning to Russia. He had the taut look of a man who has suffered, biting off words as he spoke with trap-mouthed ferocity. To Leonard he seemed totally imbued with Russian fatalism. The Woolfs objected that by returning to Russia Mirsky would be putting his head in a noose. He merely shrugged off their warnings, looking unhappy as he did so—a man going to meet his fate with eyes wide open. Virginia imagined that abstract future in starkly concrete terms: "I thought as I watched his eye brighten & fade—soon there'll be a bullet through your head. Thats one of the results of war: this trapped cabin'd man: but that didnt lubricate our tea." If she had confided this thought to socialists like Shaw or Beatrice Webb, both of whom toured and admired Soviet Russia soon afterward, they probably would have dismissed her as a fantasist. But she was right. As she foresaw, Mirsky died a few years later of unknown causes in one of Stalin's labor camps.

❧

During the summer Virginia had another explosive quarrel with Ethel, whose violent and demanding temper severely strained their friendship. It started with a letter she wrote to Ethel on July 1 stating her exasperation with the constant visitors—a plague of people asking to see and be seen by her, which barely left her time to write or to read. She fixed somewhat grimly on the passive voice of the verb "to see": "Every day it's the same—somebody insists on being seen; has a claim; will be hurt if I dont." Such "seeing" was a sterile ritual, an offense against life's natural rhythms. And ironically "the people I do want to see. . . . I see only in a crush: and some I never see at all." All of which neatly evaded the question of when she could see Ethel.

A week later, while dining with friends in a hot and noisy room at the Ivy, a London restaurant, Virginia suddenly felt everything waver and fade out. She revived to find Clive supporting her and a woman standing by with smelling salts, a scene that was followed by a jolting ride home in a cab and "the absolute delight of dark & bed."

The aftereffects of the episode were relatively mild—it kept her in bed for a day and forced her to cancel a lunch date with Florence Hardy, Thomas's widow. But considering how much her health depended on maintaining a delicate balance, she was impelled to ask herself, "Why do a single thing one doesn't want to do?" She liked the downright advice that Joseph Wright, a philologist whose biography she was reading, got from his mother and passed on to his future wife: "Always please yourself—then one person's happy at any rate." Ethel heard about her fainting spell from Vita and couldn't resist offering some advice; she observed that Virginia for various reasons—her desire to please, love of fame, the "magpie element" in her character—lacked the strength of character needed to "refuse aspirants to interviews." She must harden herself, Ethel said, and devise a system for screening out these casual "aspirants"—advice to which Virginia replied indignantly that she never, never saw strangers—the visitors who came had personal claims on her. She could not send a polite form letter to some old friend of her parents or companion of her childhood. The problem had nothing to do with casual "aspirants to interviews"—how she detested the phrase—and how aggravating that Ethel imagined her spending her time "in a rose coloured tea gown, signing autographs"—as if she were a vain prestige-seeker who welcomed all comers. Should she remind her adviser how their own friendship began? Irritated though she was, Virginia ended on a more conciliatory note, admitting this much: that she got "one of the most intense pleasures in life from 'seeing people'. . . . And hence my difficulty; hence my fainting."

It might have ended there, but Ethel insisted on justifying herself in person. She came on July 21 and staged a terrific scene, whipping herself up into such a frenzy that it could have passed for a lovers' quarrel, though a completely one-sided one. Virginia complained afterward that Ethel had pulled a degrading "stunt"—alternating between abusive and adoring postures, "being august; despairing; melodramatic, & wobbly & weak all at the same time" and finally threatening to exit on this tragic note. Virginia was tempted to let her go, but thinking about the telegrams and explanations that would follow, called her back, scolding and teasing her until she appeared to have calmed down. Subsequently Virginia tried to dismiss the whole boring scene—there was no malice in it, just that Ethel couldn't restrain her flamboyant nature—and she speculated that the old woman's "lust for emotion" was generated by a devouring ego, which drove her to bully and do "the powerful stunt . . . seeing herself, dramatising herself instead of being anything." Ethel was unable to see others or to find her own essential way of "being" because her grasping self got in the way.

Still, Ethel's violence had a fascination, if only of a negative kind, rousing such disturbing echoes that Virginia felt horrified by her own response to it. The scene lingered in her imagination and suddenly attacked her when she was least able to defend herself. She had relived it all in a dream, she wrote Ethel a week later, and woke feeling such horror, "so degraded—so humiliated—as I used to feel, after a scene with Nelly," that it would haunt their friendship from now on. Nevertheless, her tone for the most part was sober and dispassionate; Virginia admitted that their very different styles and temperaments had caused a misunderstanding, for which no one was to blame. But a few lines later she recoiled from the memory of that loathesome scene—it was poison—she still feared the infection, which had unnerved her, and felt sickened, "not only by you—by myself also." Virginia added the reasonable conclusion that Ethel had a right to air her opinions, even to indulge in violent outbursts if she wished. But given her own, no doubt exaggerated, sensitivity, their future seemed to her "full of difficulty."

Virginia's stern, pontifical tone, laced with cries of self-disgust, had an immediate effect on Ethel, who replied contritely that she, too, found the quarrel excruciatingly painful—the thought of being a mere *thing* that Virginia tripped over was so unbearable that she would do anything to avoid its happening again—even give her up, though in that case the sun would go out for her. Moved by her appeal, Virginia agreed, somewhat doubtfully, to continue as before, though she became more cautious about seeing Ethel alone.

"Seeing" remained a charged word for Virginia, expressing the conflict between her public career and her need for privacy. Ironically, she received more than her share of attention from strangers who didn't know who she was—even in London she never simply blended into the crowd. Leonard reported that she could not go anywhere without being stared at. People found something "strange and disquieting" in her appearance—not merely that her clothes were slightly eccentric, but that she radiated some special aura that made Cockneys in the street nudge each other and laugh. This unwanted attention converged with the social duties imposed by her career. She reflected at a moment of extreme fatigue that people didn't know "what they do to me when they ask me to 'see' them: how they hold me in the scorching light: how I dry & shrivel: how I lie awake at night longing for rest." In her reverse idiom, "seeing" people meant being seen by them, held to the light and exposed to their indifferent eyes. And the pressure on her was increasing. *The Waves* had recently sold its ten-thousandth copy—more than any of her previous books; like her father, she was progressing from visibility to eminence. When she spoke of a "scorching light," she meant that she expected nine visitors in four days, not including her brother, sister, and niece. She valued anonymity, therefore, for practical, as well as moral, reasons.

❧

Goldsworthy Lowes Dickinson, who had written movingly to Virginia after reading *The Waves*, died on August 3. Virginia heard the news at Monk's House, where she had gone for the summer. Her memories of that "fine charming spirit," whom she regretted not knowing better, blended with thoughts about some vague immensity surrounding us, some "splendour" inherent in being "capable of dying," though the design, if it existed, lay beyond human comprehension. In spite of these thoughts, life at Rodmell seemed reassuringly sane and stable, anchored after the day's work by domestic pastimes, which she outlined at the end of a letter to Vita, sketching her simple country life for her former lover: "I must go and put my pie in the oven; then we have ice cream to follow—you know we have a frigidaire—with fresh raspberries. Then we turn on the loud speaker—Bach tonight—then I watch my baby owls learning to fly on the church tower—then I read Lord Kilbracken—what a good book—then I think what about bed." An apparently seamless blending of old and new pleasures—Bach and the Frigidaire, Victorian memoirs and baby owls.

A week later, in the midst of a severe heat wave, Virginia had another fainting spell, falling down among her roses—a more serious attack than the one in the restaurant, echoing the heatstroke she had suffered two summers earlier. The episode, which had important consequences later that year, was acutely unpleasant and painful. She also found it intensely interesting—like having a veil lifted for a moment, enabling her to "break through the usual suddenly and so violently." She used an image from the racetrack to describe the fit that shook her whole body. She was sitting on the terrace with Leonard and suddenly "the galloping horses got wild in my head." The "horses" were set off by the strain of entertaining her mother-in-law, who had come to lunch, along with Leonard's brother, earlier that day. The old lady had been "ravishing"; she had brought a gift of her own pearl earrings, almost bringing tears to Virginia's eyes. But these polite, distracted encounters with her in-laws, especially with opinionated old Mrs. Woolf, were always an ordeal. After the visitors left, she and Leonard sat in the garden, enjoying the evening breezes; the freshening air still carried a ghost of the day's heat. Before them lay the receding downs and the silhouette of Mount Caburn, drawing back into darkness after having "burnt like solid emerald all day." Through the stillness the predatory "white owl was crossing to fetch mice from the marsh." Virginia was thinking of "cool and quiet" when suddenly her heart "leapt; stopped; ran away, like a four in hand. I cant stop it, I said. Lord, now its in my head. This pounding must must must break something." She fell among the flowers. Leonard rushed to the house and brought back ice cubes to put under her neck. She lay there for half an hour, countless fragmentary thoughts racing through her mind, while Leonard hovered anxiously nearby. Finally she felt well enough to drag herself to her room. To Ethel, who demanded to know precise details, she confided that she used the chamber pot, but was shaking too badly to hold the thermometer between her teeth. The effort of getting into bed caused another spasm of "pain, as of childbirth; & then that too slowly faded; & I lay presiding, like a flickering light, like a most solicitous mother, over the shattered splintered fragments of my body."

Her account describes an invading force storming through her body and finally centering on her womb. Having touched all the bases of emotions, mind, and sexual being, it subsides and leaves her bending like a "solicitous mother" over that devastated body—an image of fragility and power, the artist swaddled in pain and observing it from the outside, as if giving birth to herself. Moreover, by dwelling on the metaphorical horses—"this struggling team in my head: galloping, pounding"—she further absorbs the attack into her own personal mythology, her self-image as a creature who is impelled by uncontrollable natural forces. The sexually charged horses are aligned with the sensibility that makes her a writer, and that periodically runs away with her. Natural rhythm, she said in "A Letter to a Young Poet," is "the most profound and primitive of instincts."

She had used an equestrian metaphor not long before, in *The Waves*, to describe the writer's sense of rhythm. Neville, who is based on Lytton Strachey, struggles to write a poem, but the unruly words baffle and leave him behind: "How they gallop," he says, "how they lash their long manes and tails." And at the end of the novel Bernard, the author's surrogate, who insists that "the rhythm is the main thing in writing," pictures himself as an allegorical horseman riding forth to defy Death. For Virginia in August 1932 these poetic images blended with her impressions of an actual visit to the Lewes racetrack, where, among the families guzzling their picnics and bookies barking the odds, she had a vivid glimpse of the horses galloping past, lashed by red-faced jockeys. Admiring their lean, muscular beauty, she immediately noticed that the windy downs beyond the track looked so wild she could "rethink them into uncultivated land again." The straining horses provided an image of the course of life between real and ideal states, the motley crowd and the remote fields on the horizon.

Later, in September, she used a variation of the racetrack metaphor when the editor of the *Times* invited her to write a memoir for her father's centenary, which would be on November 28. She thought of refusing, but eventually wrote a brief, graceful essay. In the interval, while she hesitated, her mind was filled with memories, some of which she jotted down for Ethel, praising Leslie Stephen's complete sincerity, unworldliness, and vitality as a mountain climber; she also remembered, though her views were doubtlessly biased, that "he was beautiful in the distinguished way a race horse, even an ugly race horse, is beautiful." In the completed essay she recalled that he would often burst into "a strange rhythmical chant" as he climbed the stairs to his study or strode along in the country. Racing and climbing and writing all demanded careful attention to inner rhythms—a balance between instinctive and trained impulses.

The doctors whom Leonard and Virginia consulted about her heatstroke or "nerve exhaustion," offered very little help, beyond the superfluous advice to stay out of the sun. When she returned to her routine a few days later, Leonard would not let her carry anything and followed her around devotedly, like a dog. Though she made light of her fainting spell, it was serious enough to limit the number of people she could see and to free her from unwanted duties. During September she worked on the last chapters of the satirical *Flush*, which she had set aside for months—it was the slightest of her books—indulging herself in "easy indolent writing."

In the midst of this expansive time John Lehmann suddenly announced that he could not work for them anymore and was leaving the press. His letter arrived on September 1, the day on which their new agreement was to go into effect, just as Virginia was giving tea to T. S. Eliot and his wife, Vivienne. Leonard saw this decision to renege at the last moment as a childish outrage and declined to send any answer. Virginia also thought that John had behaved crassly, but at bottom she was not displeased. She was happy to be free of the egotistical young man's presence next door to her studio. No need to tolerate his vanities and jealousies anymore: "What a mercy. Now I can roam about the basement unperturbed." John disappeared completely from their lives for a time, moving to Vienna, where he witnessed the political upheavals that were shaking Europe and edited a periodical, *New Writing*. He eventually made his peace with the Woolfs and returned to the Hogarth Press in the late thirties. But at this point his departure simplified Virginia's life, happily coinciding with her feeling that her illness had cleared the air. Looking back now, she declared it a particularly "happy lively summer."

In this mood, feeling more kindly toward herself, she was able to extract some humor from her thin-skinned hatred of publicity. On September 16 she flew into a sudden panic on learning that an unflattering photograph of her was going to appear in a book about her life and work by Winifred Holtby. The discovery spoiled her day's writing, but her account of the event involved a delicate transaction between her fear of exposure and ironic self-knowledge. Too agitated to concentrate, she scribbled in her diary, "making myself form my letters, because—oh ridiculous crumpled petal—Wishart is publishing L's snap shot of me . . . my legs show; & I am revealed to the world (1,000 at most) as a plain dowdy old woman." The parentheses about her wilted vanity, though written with a trembling hand, set the whole incident in perspective. She admitted to having a "complex" about privacy and legs, which was aggravated by recent news that the fields around one of her favorite "ivy-blooming" walks were to be auctioned off and new monstrosities would no doubt be built there. This was another item in the "complex": her private moments walking beside the river and her modesty about her long legs both were linked to a fear of violation. Earlier that same day the meadows and downs had entranced her, and now, mixing reverence with self-mockery, she added that their atmosphere seemed "almost entirely satisfactory (oh my legs in the snapshot). I mean, I can fasten on a beautiful day, as a bee fixes itself on a sunflower." The countryside epitomized "the old habitual beauty of England: the silver sheep clustering; & the downs soaring," a vision that made her mind glow with sensations like those inspired by her sister's children, but perhaps they were even deeper because almost religious. "This has a holiness. This will go on after I'm dead."

She pondered a different kind of survival. Yesterday she and Leonard had brought plums from their garden to an ailing Rodmell neighbor, ninety-two-year-old Mrs. Gray, who sat facing an open door framing a seven-foot-by-four-foot section of the downs, but her weak eyes focused on nothing. Her legs were swollen, and she was confined to her chair. Having outlived her children and friends, she prayed for death every night, but the parish doctors wouldn't let her die. Their insistence on prolonging life at any cost, Virginia said, displayed a remarkable "human ingenuity in torture." The old woman, bearing the cross of her worn-out body, presented one of life's casual atrocities, "a rook on a barn door, but a rook that still lives, even with a nail through it."

The danger of being disabled and imprisoned was one of Virginia's chief horrors. As for her anxiety about the frontispiece of Holtby's book, it was premature, since the publisher ultimately cropped the offending legs out of the picture.

Legs, walks, downs formed a chain whose links also involved her writing, her father's ghost, and her own deep rhythms, including the galloping "horses." The effects of her fainting spell were offset by her vivid awareness of the downs and the power of the natural world. A liberating summer, she concluded, and hoped to indulge for a little while longer in ordinary pleasures, such as gossip with friends. The artistic furor would return soon enough. She had inherited her father's nerves, and recognized his legacy in her own temperamental "shying and jibbing," but she intended to spur her imagination on and put those wilder impulses to work in her writing: "Yes, my thighs now begin to run smooth."

✌

Virginia's sense of power persisted after she returned to London at the beginning of October. She was optimistic about her ability to go on changing and developing; now, at fifty, growing old held no terrors for her. The two months at Rodmell had enhanced her sense of freedom—she felt she was "backed" by the downs. Her plans to write a new book were crystallizing, and before beginning she explored some underlying assumptions in her diary. Her remarks were inspired by D. H. Lawrence, whose legend had flourished since his death in 1930. Reading his collected letters, she took stock of her own values in the light of Lawrence's prophetic claims. Woolf and Lawrence never met—she had seen him once in the distance on a station platform, that was all—and yet they were connected through common friends, especially Katherine Mansfield and Ottoline Morrell, both of whom had played important parts in Virginia's life. Rumors of Lawrence had reached her long before she read any of his books. Belatedly taking up *Sons and Lovers* in 1931, she admired his evocations of working-class life. The scenes had a special vividness, as if played against an invisible "green curtain" that accentuated every object and event, but she concluded that his rootlessness and insecurity had prevented him from finding an artistic form to connect them. Still, she deplored the persecution he suffered and sympathized with his campaign against the conventional pieties. She considered herself an outsider, feeling that the oppression she suffered as a woman far outweighed her privileges as a lady. They were potential allies, but their rebelliousness took them in politically opposite directions: Lawrence preached an authoritarian form of pagan vitalism, while Virginia aligned herself with pacifist resistance to authority.

On October 2 she summed up her reaction to Lawrence in a few disconnected phrases. "Not that he & I have too much in common—the same pressure to be ourselves; so that I dont escape when I read him." The elliptical sentence points in both directions at once; he and she don't have very much in common, she says, and then reverses herself by admitting that they both display "the same pressure to be ourselves"—that is, a tenacious egotism. The difference, she added, is that he gives in to it, so that reading his work she feels confined rather than liberated. The writers she admired most, like Proust, enable one to forget oneself and discover other worlds.

The harshness of Lawrence's struggle had made him doctrinaire, and she hated his bullying. Since her youth, when she had been tormented by some religious cousins who tried to convert her, Virginia had violently resented any attempt to get a finger into her mind. Furthermore, having been sexually abused by her half brothers, she was particularly sensitive to any encroachment on her personal space. Intending to fly past all doctrinal nets, she deplored Lawrence's need to fit everything into his "system," which smacked of self-aggrandizement. He used an ideological yardstick to measure people and beliefs, whereas art demanded objectivity, the power to grasp "things in themselves."

This dislike of systematizing shaped Virginia's plans for her new novel, provisionally called "The Pargiters" [ultimately *The Years*], which would follow a typical English family from Victorian times to the present, exploring sexual repression and patriarchal rule. She sought an alternative to Lawrence's kind of reductive analysis, which in practice came down to the "repetition of one idea." Certainly her chronicle needed some framework of social thought, some unifying pattern, but her "system," if she must have one, should be inclusive and nonlinear. "Why all this criticism of other people? Why not some system that includes the good? What a discovery that would be— a system that did not shut out."

✣

When Virginia began writing "The Pargiters: A Novel-Essay based upon a paper read to the London/National Society for Women's Service," as she titled the first draft, she was again concerned with the insidious Angel whose influence she had warned against in her 1931 speech. Her book had the Stracheyan aim of exposing Victorian lies and self-censorship that still exerted a "crippling and distorting effect" on English society. The "novel" portion consisted of five excerpts from an imaginary family chronicle, and each episode was followed by an explanatory essay. The fictional scenes would convey the lived reality, she said, enabling her readers to forget themselves and momentarily become their own great-grandmothers. The essays provided social commentary and background information. Virginia eventually found this composite form too unwieldy and split her novel-essay into two separate books, but from October to December she wrote 60,000 words, equivalent to a small volume in its own right, most of which she absorbed into later drafts.

"The Pargiters" was a liberating exercise in which Virginia went beyond the aesthetic and social boundaries she had observed in the past. Why not say everything in one expansive chronicle? Attempting this, she discovered that much of what she knew about the lives of her grandmothers had simply been invisible, outside the range and beyond the resolving power of her earlier fiction. Both her anger and her idealism had been obscured by those constraints. She welcomed the prospect of opening her mind, no matter how grim the facts might be, and pledged "to take in everything, sex, education, life &c; & come, with the most powerful & agile leaps, like a chamois across precipices from 1880 to here & now." Her subject, she announced exuberantly on December 19, was "the whole of human life." This first draft was devoted to excavating bits of Victorian history, bleak cameos of sexual repression—the little girl who is traumatized by a man exposing himself to her in the street and doubly traumatized by her inability to tell anyone about it; the sex-starved young women peering through the blinds at a gentleman caller next door, while their sister warns them: "Don't be caught looking"; the repressed undergraduate writing false, sentimental love poems to his cousin Kitty, whom he hardly knows. Virginia balanced these disquieting scenes with an account of an enlightened relationship between the sexes. In the fifth episode Kitty, the daughter of an eminent professor, encounters a new attitude to women in the home of an Oxford scholar who rose from the working classes. Mr. Brooks in "The Pargiters" was modeled on Joseph Wright, the author of a monumental dialect dictionary, whose biography Virginia had read earlier that year. Born in poverty in 1855, Wright taught himself to read at the age of fourteen, and with the support of his mother, became an eminent philologist. Teaching a course for the AEW, the Association for the Higher Education of Women, he fell in love with Lizzie Lea, a clergyman's daughter, who shared his philological interests; he married her with the promise that there would never be a lord and master in their home. They should be one and equal. Virginia quoted his love letters to his future wife: "I should lead a most unhappy, and I will say, a most miserable life—depend upon it—if you could, under any possible circumstances, ever become a mere *Hausfrau*. . . . It is my greatest ambition that you shall *live*, not merely exist; and live too in a way that not many women have lived before, if unlimited devotion and self-sacrifice on my part can do anything towards attaining that end." Woolf's fictional Brooks family practices sexual equality, and Kitty feels she can be herself in their modest house as she can never quite be in her own much grander home. She has the revelation of a new world where women need not try to emulate the "Perfect Woman" of Wordsworth's poem, who shines with an "angelic light," but can develop their real talents. The episode is lightly written, with a hint of Wonderland in the picture of the big-boned Kitty feeling much too large and well dressed among the knickknack-laden tables and afraid of bumping her head on the ceiling. The spirited echo of Lewis Carroll suggests that Virginia, like Kitty, found the vicarious crossing of class boundaries liberating.

The freedom to concentrate uninterruptedly on her work was the central discovery of the winter of 1932, which she described as "a great season of liberation." Armed with the excuse that the doctors had ordered her to rest, Virginia began to shed unwanted social obligations. The delicate state of her health gave her "permission" to turn down invitations and to see only the people she wanted to see. She exaggerated her fragility at times, telling Nelly to make her illness sound worse than it really was. By keeping to this more restricted regime, she hoped within a year's time to escape the compulsions of fame and be "free & entire & absolute & mistress of my life. . . . Nobody shall come here on their terms; or hale me off to them on theirs." Thanks to her tired heart, she wrote uninterruptedly every morning, spent most evenings reading vast amounts, as she loved to do—not only piles of manuscripts but real books—and saw her friends in between, at teatime.

Her reclusiveness was only relative—she went out often in October—but on November 2 she had another fainting spell, caused by excitement about her writing. She woke at night in a state of "incandescence," which again brought on the galloping horses in her heart. She lay there struggling to rein them in, reasoning with herself—her writing would be stalled if they ran away with her, she must resist—murmuring, "Death I defy you &c." Finally she woke Leonard, who supplied an ice pack and an infusion of sensible talk to calm her nerves. The event justified stricter limits on her social life and gave her still more time for writing. She had never felt happier, she said, citing the intimacy of her life with Leonard and her writing; she wished it would all go on just this way for another fifty years. Her novel-essay poured out at breakneck speed—all the "facts" branded on her memory long ago by silence and domestic tyranny.

Virginia's reaction against social lies and insincere talk caused friction with some old acquaintances, like Logan Pearsall Smith, the editor and essayist. He belonged to an upper-class set that Virginia knew well from her youth and found increasingly repugnant. Their differences were symbolized by the contrast between fashionable Chelsea, where Logan lived, and her own unprepossessing Bloomsbury address. She disliked Chelsea's bland snobbishness and chauvinism; Logan, an American who had lived in England for many years, didn't even have the excuse of being born to it. He had been spreading malicious rumors about her and her friends but wrote her an arch letter asking why she didn't ask him to come and see her—after all, he gossiped about everyone. Virginia replied that she was never quite sure what Logan really meant, since his words were so often ironic and easily misunderstood. But she conceded that an afternoon of mutual mockery might be quite enjoyable. Logan was welcome, she wrote caustically, to "come and laugh at me and my work and my friends to my face, and I'll do the same by you." The tête-à-tête actually took place on December 15; over his teacup, Logan fished for compliments and made slyly disparaging remarks about the female sex, leaving Virginia bored and offended. She wrote a Boxing Day letter to Ottoline Morrell (a hostess who had suffered similar abuse and would sympathize) declaring that Logan was "coarse and rank and would, if he were a fish, stink, to put it plainly."

Open hostility was far preferable to the polite lies that made her doubt the point of her existence. She would rather risk the galloping horses—they at least were her own and in some way related to the rhythms of her writing. The same runaway impulse inspired "The Pargiters," which, as she said at the start, would move through time "with the most powerful & agile leaps, like a chamois across precipices." On December 19, having written herself out for the moment, she noted that she had recently walked along noisy Southampton Row, obliviously declaiming bits of fictional scenes, and warned herself not to take any risks crossing the road till the book was done. All in all, the preceding weeks had flown by in "such a race, such a dream, such a violent impulsion & compulsion" that she hardly knew where she was. Her praise of anonymity, to which she later gave a political accent, began as a defense of that private inner rhythm against dissonant crowds and traffic. Rhythm was all.

❧

Virginia set her novel aside for the Christmas holidays at Monk's House. The Woolfs stayed in the country from December 20 to January 14, 1933, during most of which time she was intensely busy making final revisions of *Flush* at the rate of ten pages a day. She considered it an unsatisfactory piece of writing and looked forward to getting back to serious work in "The Pargiters." The opening Victorian episodes again reminded her of Lytton's influence—how they had conspired together in their youth against stifling elders. Sometimes in a queer lapse, she seemed to hear him talking in the next room, the effortless talk, which "I always want to go on with." Her real tribute to Lytton would not be the insignificant *Flush*, but her new social chronicle, which would continue the dialogue they had begun a quarter of a century ago. Summing up in her diary on the last day of the year, she spoke to Lytton directly, as if answering her old ally in the next room. "You will understand," she said.

[Virginia's diary, December 31, 1932]
Yes, of course this autumn has been a tremendous revelation. You will understand that all impediments suddenly dropped off. It was a great season of liberation. . . . I said I will no longer be fettered by any artificial tie. I therefore spoke out in my own voice to Eddy & tried to circumscribe Logan. Well—it is always doubtful how far one human being can be free. The ties are not purely artificial. One cannot cut a way absolutely straight. How-

ever, I secured a season of intoxicating exhilaration. Nor do I intend to let myself pay for it with the usual black despair. I intend to circumvent that supervening ghost—that which always trails its damp wings behind my glories. I shall be very wary, very adept—as now—writing languidly to avoid a headache. To suppress one self & run freely out in joy, or laughter with impersonal joys & laughters—such is the perfectly infallible & simple prescription. . . .

If one does not lie back & sum up & say to the moment, this very moment, stay you are so fair, what will be one's gain, dying? No: stay, this moment. No one ever says that enough.

Back in May she had felt there was no refuge anywhere—even the downs were being spoiled—no fields she could explore and "expand in & say Time stand still here." Now, quoting a key passage from Goethe's *Faust*, she came to a happier conclusion. Her appeal to the moment, "Stay you are so fair," repeats Faust's words but reverses their meaning. In Goethe's drama, staying the moment means losing one's soul. Faust's speech proposing his famous wager with Mephistopheles reads roughly as follows:

> If ever I grow fat and lazy,
> That instant let me be undone,
> If ever you can lie and flatter
> To turn my head in self-conceit
> Or tempt me with mere pleasure,
> Let that be my last day—
> That's my wager.
>   Done.
>   And so be it.
> If ever I say to the fleeting moment,
> Stay, you are so beautiful,
> Then take your manacles, lock me up,
> I'll gladly go to the devil then—
> Ring my death knell on that day.
> Then you can boast you've won the wager,
> Then let the clock hands crumble
> And time come to an end for me.

Faust, who has mastered every field of knowledge and found them all hollow, consorts with the Devil in order to escape despair. He tests human limits, ignoring moral and social restraints, in hopes of justifying his existence. Virginia subverts Goethe's dichotomy between the mind and senses by implying that the self expands and grows whole in moments of arrested time. During this age of crises she feared being overwhelmed by political events. Her enumeration of social "facts" in "The Pargiters" and her appeal to stay the moment were equal and opposite responses to this pressure. Her diary reflects her own Faustian wrestling with nihilism. She invokes an adversary, a ghost of depression that trails behind her "glories." Naming that shadow in the midst of her celebratory mood, as one might admit lean years in times of abundance, she incorporates it too into the privileged moment.

She reminded herself to remain "very wary." Her defense against overexcitement, which could cause a dangerous crash, was to take refuge in simple objects and a regulated domestic life. Anonymity implied a privileged space, a sphere of domestic privacy and artistic vision, both of them hidden from intruding eyes. It meant cultivating her own inner rhythm amid "impersonal joys and laughters." In her fiction she discovered meaning in a worn pair of boots or a frayed lamp wick, exploring those wells of emotional truth. She had a grasp of the raspberries in the Frigidaire and the owls on the steeple. Speaking out in her own voice to Eddy and Logan, though such gestures were always only partial, sharpened all her faculties and powers of truth-telling. Unchaining her memory in "The Pargiters," she recovered hordes of facts she didn't know she knew.

Virginia struck her own bargain with the negating spirit, proposing to test human limits and perhaps expand them. Often in the course of her writing she reached "the verge of total extinction"—the phrase is not an exaggeration. She drove herself toward her limits, risking nervous exhaustion, but at the same time she was adept at stopping just short of it, so she could go on working. Her well-being depended on maintaining that rarefied creative state. Recovering the past in "The Pargiters," she predicted that it would be painfully difficult to turn that breathlessly plotted matter into fair copy. She looked ahead to another trial of strength, a test she would have to pass in the future.

Having broken artificial ties in this "season of liberation," Virginia also needed to propitiate the ghost "which always trails its damp wings behind my glories." It was her antagonist and double. She could not have gone so far without that shadow, spurring her on.

8 *The Firing of Nelly Boxall*

During Virginia's youth the typical upper-middle-class family had several servants living in the house—a cook, two or more maids, and a nurse for the children. The Stephen household had seven servants. After World War I smaller families and new labor-saving devices simplified the formal arrangements that had once helped all these people to coexist under one roof. When Virginia boasted about serving ice cream with her raspberries, she was certifying the arrival of a silent revolution at Rodmell. The luxury of owning a Frigidaire ended the need to shop every day. Fewer trips to the store meant less dependence on servants. Modern conveniences—a telephone, a hot-water heater, wireless radio, gramophone—changed the shape of daily life.

The Woolfs had owned a motorcar since 1927—another convenience that simplified their domestic routine, especially at Monk's House, which was several miles from trains and shops. It also made commuting to the country easier and more pleasant. Being able to explore Sussex, driving across the downs in any direction they wanted, gave expansiveness to their weekends and holidays. "What a free life that is," Virginia said in 1932, still a little awestruck by the power they had bought with their literary earnings. They owned a relatively modest Singer car, but in January 1933 they were waiting for the dealer to deliver a bigger and more luxurious vehicle—a Lanchester. After many delays the car finally drew up in front of Monk's House on January 14, a day of billowing clouds when the sky seemed hung with "silver shields." Leonard was pruning in the garden; Angelica and Julian, over from Charleston for the afternoon, were about to go to the shop for sweets.

It was an expensive machine with a green enameled body and a silver convertible top, "beautifully compact modelled firm," Virginia boasted, adding that it was "not too rich—not a money car." She said this to reassure herself about the Lanchester's image—the larger Lanchester rivaled the Rolls-Royce Silver Ghost, and though the Woolfs' car was a scaled-down 18-horsepower model, its thoroughbred credentials were a source of pride and embarrassment to Virginia. The Woolfs, who lived very modestly, disliked any form of conspicuous consumption, but they needed a good working car not only for commuting to Rodmell but for their trips around England to place Hogarth Press books with booksellers. Riding in that elegant carriage, Virginia felt protected and sealed in, as in a Pullman. She wrote to Vita, who was away on a lecture tour of America, archly piling on the metaphors: it had the speed of a swift, the power of a tigress gliding along Bond Street and Piccadilly. Virginia relished chic new technical terms that made the car sound like a yacht: she loved the futuristic fluid flywheel; the capacity to "cruise" at fifty miles an hour. Compensating for this enthusiasm, she gave the car a satirical nickname, "The Deluge," conjuring up the Rolls-Royces lined up in Hyde Park, their owners riding in smug comfort toward oblivion. The Deluge— a jibe aimed at upper-class complacency and an ironic tribute to the coming class war. Like the Frigidaire and the wireless, the sleek Lanchester parked in the village street embodied the restless modern age. For the Woolfs it was a tangible sign of privilege and hard work.

They planned to give the car a test run that spring by driving over the Alps to Italy. Touring would be easy and carefree—the Continent seemed to lie open before them. It was at this precise time that the Nazis became rulers of Germany. Hitler's appointment as chancellor on January 30 didn't cause undue alarm in the outside world. Considering its revolutionary character, the Third Reich came into being with deceptive smoothness—the pieces fell into place easily, guided by swift, well-planned actions that left no opportunity for resistance: the Reichstag fire on February 27, used by the Nazis as a pretext to undermine parliamentary government; the general election of March 4, in which Hitler consolidated his power; and the Enabling Act of March 23, which authorized him to rule by decree. Within less than two months he had subverted the feeble Weimar Republic and seized absolute dictatorial powers, hiding the coup d'état behind a facade of legality. During these events England's rulers, driving with their eyes fixed on the rearview mirror, held on to their obsolete notions of what was politically expedient and acceptable—a position that Hitler skillfully exploited. His enemies thought of him as a bumbler who would get lost in bureaucratic mazes, he said. They were waiting for him to ruin himself by mismanagement, but he would cut the Gordian knot: "We shall not wait for them to act. Our great opportunity lies in acting before they do. We have no scruples, no bourgeois hesitations. . . . They regard me as an uneducated barbarian. Yes, we are barbarians. We want to be barbarians. It is an honourable title."

Dictatorship, which as Woolf saw it was rooted in domestic tyranny, formed an implicit background to "The Pargiters," an invisible ambience that subtly colored her novel. She described her difficulties with the book as a collision between social commentary and fiction: the question was how to incorporate both commentary and "ordinary waking Arnold Bennett life in the form of art"? "The form of art" can transform everything, ideas, facts, images, enclosed within its sphere, but her wish to address topical issues, to offer an epitome of the "present day," as well as a Victorian retrospect, made that magic difficult to achieve. When she returned to the book at the end of January (the week Hitler met his first cabinet) she decided to omit the interchapters and compact her message into the story itself, fearing that the essay portions would make the book too didactic. This change only displaced her problem to a different level. The original "novel-essay" reflected a dichotomy between art and politics, poetry and fact, which deepened as she continued. Her novel of facts demanded close attention to the present state of the world, which kept changing and changing again as she adjusted to the prevailing mood. The anarchic present impinging on her writing made it increasingly hard to achieve the proper tone.

᪥

Virginia was working out her political ideas, which gradually evolved toward a more militant position. On March 26 she wrote to the vice chancellor of the University of Manchester, who had offered her an honorary doctor of letters degree, regretting that she could not accept it, since she opposed writers' accepting public honors of any kind. She smoothed over the refusal with a polite formula: "I am sure that you will understand my point of view." Most likely the vice chancellor did not understand; he would not have been gratified to know how thoroughly she disapproved of the system of professorial ranks, lectures, and examinations. She particularly disliked the reduction of English literature to an academic field—a system that shut out ordinary educated readers. To Dame Ethel, who had herself been "corrupted" by honors, she sardonically denounced such rituals and decorations—what use are they, she said, "when the only honour is blue blank air, no more and no less—whats the point of this honour worship? Mumbo Jumbo!" The Manchester offer came just as she was in the midst of writing a scene in "The Pargiters," in which Elvira, voicing Virginia's own anger, charges that English society is utterly corrupt and resolves not to collaborate with the system or accept its bribes. How odd, she thought, that the defiant Elvira's fictional situation so precisely coincided with her own—"I hardly know which I am, or where: Virginia or Elvira; in the Pargiters or outside." Afterward, at a dinner given by Susan Lawrence, the Labour MP, one of the other guests, the wife of a Manchester professor, said how much she looked forward to seeing Mrs. Woolf receive her degree—a compliment that caught her by surprise. The professor's wife ran on effusively till Virginia interjected awkwardly: "But I wont take it"—whereupon there was a general argument about the meaning and usefulness of such gestures. Virginia felt exposed and priggish, but only superficially. Inwardly she knew she was justified and felt not the least tempted by "all that humbug." She was pleased that Vanessa, who was present at the dinner, strongly agreed and put forth some of the same arguments she would have used; it was reassuring that she and her sister shared the same instinctive distrust of such publicity. Virginia's disgust with "mumbo jumbo" merged with her account of stunted lives in "The Pargiters" and her anger against the patriarchal elite.

She worked intensively on "The Pargiters" and, having brought the narrative up to the 1907 episode, she took time off during mid-April to plan an essay about Oliver Goldsmith, deferring her novel till after their Italian holiday. The essay's rough outlines emerged during her ten-day Easter stay at Rodmell. Its theme was that Goldsmith lived in a time of transition between two strikingly different cultural stages. In the mid-eighteenth century writers who had formerly relied on aristocratic patrons now addressed ordinary men and women, who bought their work from a bookseller for a few pennies. The new public's tastes were crude, but the writer gained the "dignity of independence"; though Goldsmith no longer enjoyed the prestige of riding in an earl's carriage, he dressed as he liked and made friends and enemies without worrying about offending a noble magnate. Goldsmith was free to travel and broaden his outlook, tramping Europe's roads and exploring its major cities. He preferred to be called a "citizen of the World rather than an Englishman." He marveled that the French and English were at war in Canada over bits of fur for edging their muffs and must therefore kill one another and steal the land from the aboriginal people to whom it had belonged for thousands of years.

Virginia heard more news of the disturbing changes going on in Europe shortly before leaving for Italy; on April 28 she met Ethel's old friend, the great conductor Bruno Walter. A slightly disheveled man with an unself-conscious intensity that suggested genius, Walter spoke obsessively about the "poison" of Hitler, which he couldn't get out of his system. He had led the 150-year-old Gewandhaus Orchestra of Leipzig but was now shunned by former friends and unable to work in Germany because he was a Jew. He said that even the persecution of the Jews paled in comparison to the general collapse of civilized values. The change had come with astonishing speed. He had sailed home right after Hitler's rise to power, and the atmosphere among the ship's passengers was dense with political innuendos and veiled threats. In Leipzig he had the sensation of being spied on; the streets echoed with marching soldiers and the wireless blared military music—the memory tormented him and he seemed "very nearly mad" with revulsion. How was it possible that Germany, with its music, its culture, had succumbed to "this awful reign of intolerance"? Virginia respected the intensity with which he lived his feelings—his views impressed her and reinforced her own pacifist position. A few years later, writing her antiwar manifesto, *Three Guineas*, she echoed Walter's plea to resist the oppressors by nonviolent means. "We must refuse to meet any German," he insisted. "We will not trade with them or play with them—we must make them feel themselves outcasts—not by fighting them; by ignoring them."

The Woolfs left for their holiday on May 5, driving along the French Riviera and on into Italy as far as Siena. The Lanchester's smooth-riding suspension, the freedom to design their own timetable, the impromptu picnics beside mountain streams, delighted Virginia, in spite of some tense moments when the fluid flywheel stuck. Still, she longed for the "intoxicant" of writing and couldn't stop making up scenes of "The Pargiters" during the trip. On May 12 they visited the house where Shelley was living at the time when he drowned. The local people and surroundings at Lerici looked much as they looked a hundred years earlier. The atmosphere of the windy bay and the breaking waves pervaded the house, and Virginia imagined Mary Shelley pacing the balcony, waiting for Shelley's small schooner, which had already capsized in a squall at sea. So Shelley had been instantly transported into a mythical realm, becoming a myth himself—the drowned poet "rolled round with pearls." Virginia also noted that the waterlogged body had been washed up a few miles away and burned on the beach with Shelley's friends looking on. All in all, the house at Lerici, so full of the sea, was for her "the best death bed place I've ever seen."

Her impressions of Tuscan hills and friendly peasants were darkened by reminders, especially in the towns, that a Fascist dictatorship, mercifully an inefficient one, usurped that ancient heritage; she joked about the blackshirt listening under her window, feeling divided between love of Italy and hatred of Fascism.

On their way home they spent a very hot night in Vienne, where Virginia picked up her letters and learned that the Book Society had chosen *Flush* as a monthly selection, which would earn her between £1,000 and £2,000—probably more than they paid for their Lanchester. Along with this came word that Cynthia Mosley, the wife of the British Fascist leader, whom Virginia knew casually, had died of acute appendicitis at the age of thirty-four. The moment was sharply etched. Virginia was sitting at a cafe, eavesdropping on the nearby tables: a typist and some young clerks gossiped about hotels at Lyons, and she mused about their lives, and how poverty blinded them to anything outside their circle. Children played in the street, soldiers from Morocco passed in military cloaks, men kept going into the public urinal—she saw their legs at odd angles below the partition. The moment became charged with significance: "highly pictorial, composed, legs in particular," its mundane uniqueness registering on her mind with great clarity.

☙

She struggled to pick up the thread of her novel after her return from the Continent, and in that transitional stage she glimpsed something she often took for granted, the creative "synthesis" of her being, "how only writing composes it: how nothing makes a whole unless I am writing." That was a first approximation; there was a more essential truth having to do with the two levels on which her mind worked. On the surface, writing for her was often a grim struggle, all effort and despair, but on a deeper, less conscious level, she was simultaneously shaping and ordering her ideas. Even while she seemed to flounder on the surface she felt a deep sense of rightness as the inner picture shifted and resolved, coming "into focus: yes: the proportion is right." Writing, with all its surface strain, ensured "proportion," while the inability to write implied disorder, loss of control, which referred not only to her art but also to her daily life. A day with her mother-in-law, she said, "burst 'the proportion.'" Being immersed in her novel conferred stability and brought "the whole universe to order. I can see the day whole, proportioned."

In speaking of "proportion" Virginia was echoing Mary Wright, the dictionary-maker's wife, whose biography of Joseph Wright had inspired the first draft of "The Pargiters." In her diary Virginia dashed off her own highly condensed version of Mary Wright's dialogue with her future husband: "She said 'make details part of a whole—get proportions right'—contemplating marriage with Joe. Odd how rare it is to meet people who say things that we ourselves could have said. Their attitude to life much our own." The aphoristic summary, "make details part of a whole—get proportions right," is as much Virginia's invention as Mary Wright's, stating her own "synthesis." The original passages, which Virginia found so congenial, clarify her point of view in "The Pargiters." Mary Wright focused on the question of how to balance her duties as a housekeeper with a life of intellectual inquiry. It is up to a woman, she said, not to allow the petty details of every day's work to absorb her mind. Rather she should make them "take their fit place, and form part of a whole. A great many 'details' are not 'isolated forms,' because they touch on general principles, and if you keep your eyes on principles, the details will dovetail in." Furthermore, she said, it is essential to spend "a goodly proportion of one's days in simplicity and truthseeking. . . . I want to get hold of the relative proportions of things, and not lay too much stress on what does not matter." In noting and telescoping these ideas about "getting proportions right," Virginia generalized them, avoiding any specific reference to the details of housekeeping and marriage. While remembering their original context, she applied her aphoristic phrases mainly to the craft of writing, compounding the puns on "right" and "Wright." Virginia's idea of rightness was concretely based on a whole and proportioned "day," a wholesome amalgam of writing and domestic activities—the equivalent of Mary Wright's "simplicity and truthseeking."

Her inner sense of right proportions could carry her through a noisy public meeting, though speeches and ceremonies, even in a good cause, seemed increasingly futile. On June 20 she attended the Congress of the Women's Cooperative Guild, a society that sponsored stores and educational programs for working-class women. Virginia had supported the guild since World War I when she acted as secretary of her local branch. In spite of her sympathy for its aims and her respect for the working-class women in the hall, who were a hardy, down-to-earth lot, she hated the event. The speeches by the Labour Party bigwigs, Margaret Bondfield and Susan Lawrence, were loaded with fake optimism and ringing phrases about the coming "triumph of cooperation," and the new world they would all live to inherit. A galling denial of the real dangers ahead—not an iota of truth in it, Virginia lamented, "not a word that fits—all wind blown, gaseous, with elementary emotions." It made her feel merely vacant, hollow, though she restored herself by remembering her work. Such quasi politics were worse than useless; the day had far less reality, she reflected, than if she had spent it writing in her usual concentrated state.

Summer 1933 provided a rare calm interlude when she was able to enjoy the pleasures of village life and concentrate on "The Pargiters" without much distraction. Her retreat at Monk's House offered many whole, creative days spent writing in the morning followed by the usual walk and later typing and revision of what she had written in the fresh early hours. Dispensing with a conventional plot, her novel progressed in minutely observed domestic scenes, like the homely, evocative moments captured in Dutch genre paintings. Virginia needed such quiet intervals, often devoted to simple household chores, in her own day, and since taking greater control of her social life, she had more time for "the dear old repetitions." She wanted her long walks and a "perfectly spontaneous childish life" with Leonard, she said, punctuated by "dinner; tea; papers; music; I have a dread of 'seeing' people."

They had a steady stream of visitors at the end of August, sometimes unwelcome ones, like Leonard's colleague Kingsley Martin, the liberal editor of the *New Statesman*, whose solemn opinions and sloppy table manners irritated Virginia. In spite of her grumbling, she was highly sociable, but she keenly enjoyed the quiet intervals between visitors, remarking that those days were "rightly balanced. . . . How happy, when people go, to get our dinner, & sit alone, & go to bed in my airy room where the rising sun on the apples & asparagus wakes me, if I leave the curtain open." A few days later, on September 2, she recorded a brief neighborly exchange with Percy Bartholomew, the gardener, who brought in the slop pail while she was boiling the kettle. He said, "You've never had such a summer." "No," she replied, "its been fine since Christmas"—which was true not only of the weather but of her mood. Leonard was overseeing improvements in the garden, to be paid for by her earnings from *Flush*—they were having the old pond in back regrouted and digging a new one. That day she thought of a new, still provisional title for "The Pargiters"—

"Here & Now" and later she remembered that Goldie Dickinson had used the phrase "here and now" in his tribute to *The Waves*; he praised the book as both timeless and contemporary—belonging to "here and now" while presenting universal themes. "Here and now" suggested the novel's dual aims: to combine an overview of the years leading up to the modern age with close-ups of present-day rooms and their inhabitants or, as she put it, "the press of daily normal life continuing."

A happy summer, she noted on September 26, adding that she had even forgotten an idea she meant to write in her diary, she was so beguiled by the pleasures of "feeding the gold fish, of looking at the new pond, of playing bowls." Absorbed in writing her domestic chronicle, exposing past lies and their toll on the present, she was content for the moment in that self-contained world. The story often seemed grim, but it was of her own making and she was sustained every day by "the dear old repetitions." For a brief moment the world beyond the downs and across the English Channel faded into the distance. The summer's day harbored no reflections to cloud her happiness.

❧

On September 9 T. S. Eliot, with whom the Woolfs had had friendly, though formal, relations dating back to 1919, when the Hogarth Press published a collection of his poems, came for an overnight stay at Monk's House. Tom, as Virginia called him, had just separated from his wife after seventeen years. Vivienne Eliot came from a distinguished artistic and intellectual family—she was a talented dancer and writer whom Eliot had married during World War I. Then she was a vivacious young woman with a satirical eye and the gift of finding comically low motives for her friends' innocent acts. During the twenties, as Eliot's career and reputation flourished, she progressively disintegrated, eventually displaying "full-blown paranoia with delusions," according to one psychiatric opinion. In the process she grew addicted to the drugs her doctors prescribed for her illness. Eliot was devoted to his wife, taking care of her with longsuffering patience, though the action of his puritanical nature on her high-strung and impulsive one probably made things worse. By the early thirties Vivienne was a semi-invalid; on one occasion in 1932 she visited the Woolfs wearing a tattered white satin dress and carrying an ether-soaked handkerchief whose odor wafted through the room. In a photo taken by Leonard she seems to shrink into herself, a gaunt woman with her eyes cast down and hands stiffly hidden behind her. During that visit

Figure 8. T. S. Eliot, Virginia, and Vivienne Eliot at Monk's House, 1932.

she was alternately hostile and amorous, exuding such an aura of disorder that Virginia dreaded seeing her again.

At the end of 1932 Eliot, who had accepted an invitation to lecture on poetry, left for a six-month residence at Harvard, and upon his return in June 1933, he refused to see Vivienne, informing her by letter that their marriage was over. She tried frantically to find out where he was. Virginia wrote to Quentin Bell that Vivienne had accused her and Ottoline of being Tom's mistresses and threatened to come after them with a carving knife—a joke with just a tinge of genuine alarm in it. The grieving Vivienne was also rumored to have created a shrine of flowers and photos of Tom in her flat. After years of forbearance, Eliot was adamant about parting from her, and on September 9 he assured Virginia that Vivienne was merely trying to manipulate him. It was all an act, though the actress almost believed it herself. "He wont admit the excuse of insanity for her," Virginia reported, "thinks she puts it on; tries to take herself in."

Virginia was amused and disconcerted by Eliot's transformation into an important personage. She regretted the disappearance of the shyer, more tentative poet. His behavior in the marital crisis reinforced an impression of prim self-importance. Writing to him while he was lecturing at Harvard, she had satirically lamented that most of the manuscripts submitted to the Hogarth Press were now "about a man called Eliot; or in the manner of a man called Eliot—how I detest that man called Eliot! Eliot for breakfast Eliot for dinner—thank God Eliot is at Harvard. But why? Come back soon." An inverted compliment behind which lurked her dislike of the public role writers were encouraged to play. Seeing Tom, fresh from America, with his ego buoyed by international renown, started her debating with herself again about the seductions of fame and the blight of publicity.

[Virginia's diary, September 10, 1933]
He is 10 years younger: hard, spry, a glorified boy scout in shorts & yellow shirt. He is enjoying himself very much. He is tight & shiny as a wood louse (I am not writing for publication). But there is well water in him, cold & pure. Yes I like talking to Tom. But his wing sweeps curved & scimitar like round to the centre himself. He's settling in with some severity to being a great man. Keats wasn't that. . . . [He] said that people exaggerate the intellectuality & erudition of his poetry. "For example Ross Williamson in his book on me. . . ." He says that very seriously. I couldnt quote Holtby with the same candour. . . .

His father was a brick merchant in St Louis . . . & died alas, in 1919 before Tom had become—well, happily his mother lived to see him what she called (& I daresay Tom too) a great man. What a queer naïve vanity all this is! But of course, when you are thrown like an assegai into the hide of the world—this may be a definition of genius—there you stick; & Tom sticks. To shut out, to concentrate—that is perhaps—perhaps—one of the necessary conditions.

Virginia's skepticism applies both to Tom's self-importance and to the "great man" idea itself. She sees him as a hybrid, the private and hidden poet merging precariously with the absurd figure of the "glorified boy scout," still immature and plagued by his narrow puritanism. The well water deep within him is rarely accessible; the poetic gift that should free him perversely hardens into the instrument of self-love, the sweeping wing becomes the cruel scimitar. She admits his power of concentration and ability to shut out, which is "perhaps—perhaps" a sign of poetic greatness. She says this reluctantly, as if against her better judgment; the "perhapses" reflect her desire for a different image of the artist, one more like Keats, who never lived to play the great man. Eliot's penetrating force "may be a definition of genius." She thought his poetry succeeded at times through sheer violence, but she also felt a narrowing—the sharply pointed lines did not permit much scope, only attacking "a minute province of his imagination." And after all there are finer ways to impress the world than by sticking in its hide.

Her mixed feelings have another source. Behind magisterial Tom lurks the father who dominated her youth and from whom she first got her idea of greatness. She portrayed Leslie Stephen in *To the Lighthouse* as the tyrannical Mr. Ramsay, who exhausts his wife with demands for sympathy. To the children, jealously vying with him for their mother's attention, he seems reduced to an inhuman thrusting engine, a cruel "beak of brass, the arid scimitar of the male, which smote mercilessly, again and again, demanding sympathy." Mr. Ramsay plays the notes of the intellectual keyboard in serial order, having trained himself to concentrate and shut out, suffering agonies because of his inability to sound the furthest notes of the scale, where greatness lies. Virginia's ironic portrait of her father carried with it the knowledge that she could never satisfy such standards—in spite of her gifts she could never be what he would have admired most—a "great man."

Tom Eliot's disturbing vanity impelled her to examine her own position more closely. His influence oddly complemented that of Ethel Smyth, another great egotist, to whom she had given some practical advice about writing earlier that year. In June Ethel asked her to read the manuscript of her new collection of essays about women's musical careers, *Female Pipings in Eden*. Virginia thought the facts Ethel stated about discrimination in the male-dominated musical world were compelling. She made a powerful case, but she weakened it by including a list of her own accomplishments and grievances, which invited critics to dismiss her as a childish, self-absorbed woman. The personal asides in the midst of the factual record made Virginia blush. She herself had discussed women writers in *A Room of One's Own*, and she had fictionalized her own character, turning herself into an emblematic figure, so as to avoid the indecency of egotism and special pleading. "The mention of 'I' is so potent," she argued, it leaves "such a deep violet stain—that one in a page is enough to colour a chapter." Reading the revised book in November, she was pleased that Ethel had omitted most of the preaching, thereby greatly strengthening her case. The absence of 'I' freed her to find her natural athletic rhythm, galloping "over turf as springy as a race horse."

In October a flurry of requests from various strangers for interviews and photographs provoked Virginia to write to the editor of the *New Statesman*, urging readers to resist the publicity mania. Her letter asks well-known artists and intellectuals not to allow accounts of their home life and private personalities to be published in the papers, but rather to resist the subtle coercion of publicists, admirers, and purveyors of official culture—a modest proposal with radical implications. She admitted that by publishing her plea for privacy she drew attention to herself—a contradiction that reflected her complex attitude to public action, at once engaged and seeking detachment. At the same time she tried to persuade herself that it didn't matter what the magazines and papers said about her, that reviews and notices were no more than minor distractions, mere "rain drops." But her sensitivity made them much more important than that metaphor suggests.

She was implicitly addressing the odd pair of egotists, Tom and Ethel. She had at last got hold of her "philosophy of anonymity," she wrote in her diary on October 29, the day after the *New Statesman* letter appeared. That letter, she said, was a crude, partial statement of her views, an outgrowth of the previous winter's liberating decision to cut meaningless social ties. Her response to male writers, like Eliot, who could tempt her to pursue that deceptive phantom of "greatness," was to refuse to play by their rules: "I will not be 'famous' 'great.' I will go on adventuring, changing, opening my mind & my eyes, refusing to be stamped & stereotyped. The thing is to free ones self; to let it find its dimensions, not be impeded." Her mind was supple and diverse, shunning formulas and doctrines, devising ways to include rather than shut out. Honoring that principle, she resolved to read the New Testament, having been a nonbeliever since her childhood.

On the same day she invoked another, more special sense of the term "anonymity" in a letter to Ethel. She was going to a dinner that night in honor of her mother-in-law's eighty-fourth birthday, a large gathering of Jewish in-laws, which made her highly self-conscious. Her deepest need as a creative artist was "not to be aware of [herself]. And all these people insist that one must be aware of oneself." Unconsciousness and anonymity, she told Ethel, were the only conditions in which she could write. Not being aware of oneself meant having access to the deeper unconscious self that shunned daylight and fed all her creative life. In a similar vein, she struggled to overcome her extreme sensitivity to criticism and her concern about her public image. On November 22 she noted that she had resisted the temptation to read an article on her work in *The Criterion*, T. S. Eliot's magazine. For the moment she rose above the battle, looking on from the distance at a mere effigy of the eminent Virginia. "One sees people lunging & striking at a thing like a straw horse & its not me at all." The thought of giving up all concern for her reputation and being entirely private exhilarated her—she woke at night feeling "astonishingly happy." Was this how her sister, who enjoyed the balance and perspective she lacked, felt all the time—this serene detachment? It would leave Virginia a great deal of energy to spend on Leonard and the things she really cared about. But as she enjoyed this "great liberation" an inner voice reminded her that her own natural state was different from other people's. She achieved her calmness by dissociating herself from ordinary concerns and vicissitudes rather than by engaging with them. That tendency, and the dangers it brought, were implicit in her abrupt question about the euphoric state: "I wonder whether this is related to any of the famous human feelings"—a statement that recognized that her vision was often outside or beyond the common wavelength.

She hated the idea of hardening into a figure, a public statue of an eminent writer. Rather than further polishing the style she had perfected in the twenties, she was changing it, partly following the ex-

ample of Henry James, whom she had been reading during her trip to
Italy. Unlike his tame imitators, he had the "power to break his mould
callously," to smash the finespun type of sentence he had invented and
start anew. Similarly, in "Here and Now" [the new working title, later
The Years] she exercised a hard discipline, forcing herself, she said,
"to break every mould" and create new forms of expression to contain new ways of feeling. "But this needs constant effort, anxiety &
risk. Here in ["Here and Now"] I am breaking the mould made by
The Waves." Breaking molds, tearing down the stereotyped patterns
in which her work was stamped—those disruptions would help her
in the long run to get the proportions right.

Her "philosophy" interwove two separate strands, an artistic/vi-
sionary strand and a political/iconoclastic one. Fusing the two, she
evolved her own prophetic voice, though she did not, like D. H. Lawrence, impose a dogmatic system. Politically, "anonymity" armed her
against the danger of being co-opted by the establishment, flattered
or bribed into standing in for the "great man." Artistically it produced a more accessible style, combining fact and vision and addressed to a wider audience. Though she valued her privacy highly,
she ultimately wrote her manifesto and submitted her militant views
to public scrutiny, only insisting on defining the issues in her own
terms. Her aim was to break patriarchal molds and launch her own
nonviolent insurgency.

∽∮∾

Virginia once said to Ethel: "Everyone I most honour is silent." A
silence resonates in Virginia's diaries and letters, where the people
she cared about most are always present but are drawn less vividly
than her lesser friends. Leonard and Vanessa were too close, her un-
derstandings with them were shared silently or gained in small daily
increments too elusive to record. Virginia and her sister wrote to
each other often; their letters are practical, down-to-earth dispatches,
only rarely revealing the deeper connection between them. A similar,
less profound, silence surrounded Virginia's feelings for Vanessa's
children.

Her twenty-three-year-old nephew, Quentin Bell—"the dreamy
charming slow one," she called him—had been ill on and off for
months. In the summer he came home from a trip to Spain with a case
of whooping cough. Then in August he contracted pleurisy, requiring
a long recuperation at Charleston. They feared that he might need an
operation, but the doctors concluded that both illnesses were tuber-

cular and ordered him to spend three months in a Swiss sanatorium for his lungs. Vanessa arranged to fly with him to Geneva, and on November 3 the Woolfs drove them across London to Croydon airport. Virginia and Leonard stood on the roof, watching the plane take off, a sight that impressed her with its ominous dissociative power. The machine seemed to grow rarefied before her eyes; the propellers turned over, spun faster, and "simply evaporated: then the aeroplane takes a slow run, circles & rises." Watching it diminish and slowly melt into distant space, carrying Vanessa and Quentin remorselessly away, confirmed her own sense of remoteness. "This is death I said, feeling how the human contact was completely severed. Up they went with a sublime air & disappeared like a person dying, the soul going." The intense sensation later inspired an impressionistic sketch, "Flying Over London," about an imaginary flight in which the pilot, after circling the countryside, turns the plane's nose upward, climbing toward a serene altitude where the world recedes and "extinction" becomes desirable. Death impends. She feels herself being carried further, she welcomes the thrust that takes her where every glimmer of light and knowledge is dulled, but the pilot, like Charon ferrying the dead across the River Lethe, is sheathed in flames. Having reached that extreme limit, the plane turns back, slowly descending to the world of gasometers and football fields. The passenger detects far below millions of anonymous insectlike figures, which resolve themselves, as the plane descends, into the familiar social orders—business magnates in Rolls-Royces, women kneeling with scrubbing brushes on front steps. The world as it is, the common day—returning to which the plane makes its quick, bumpy landing; everything stands still for a moment; the scene revolves, the fantasy dissolves, and she hears the pilot announce that, because of engine trouble, the flight just due to begin has been called off.

Virginia's diary entry about the actual scene at Croydon ended cryptically: "I saw the plane become a little mark on the sky. A good funeral could be arranged"—perhaps evoking an ancient funeral ship carrying the dead on their last journey.

These thoughts anticipated her anguish three days later, when Vanessa was due to return and Virginia sat waiting for the phone to ring announcing the plane had landed, but no word came. She was entertaining Lady Simon, the social reformer, and making polite conversation, while inwardly sure they had crashed. The plane, delayed by dense fog over Paris, circled for a long time above the airport before landing. The calm and self-possessed Vanessa had arrived home after the flight and dissolved into tears. Later, hearing her account of the Alps as seen from the air, Virginia conceded that they were probably the most beautiful of earthscapes—their father had climbed them all in his youth—and she prayed that Vanessa would never, never fly again. "Oh my God," she exclaimed to Vita—"how I hate caring for people!"

During the following months, she wrote regularly to Quentin at his mountain retreat, a series of indiscreet and entertaining letters, full of shrewd insights and fantastic guesses about the people she met—a gallery of characters. Like her mother, who had a vocation for nursing, she believed that a dose of satire was fortifying and helped to cure most ailments. Half the joy of seeing people, moreover, was in entering other worlds, where she gathered clues from which to spin her fictional yarns. With Quentin she enjoyed playing the indecorous aunt who would say anything. The news about Mary Hutchinson's daughter, Barbara, for example—friends about whom she really must be discreet, but . . . Barbara was engaged to one of the Rothschilds, a Jew, which was all in his favor, Virginia said, but she wondered. . . . He had brought Barbara a little present in a cardboard box, which she opened after he left, and out tumbled the family jewels, masses of them, studded with diamonds and red rubies. The richest young man in England, so smug and self-satisfied—Virginia predicted the marriage would not last. And she reported with relish that Vanessa was of the same opinion, "didn't like the flavour of the Jew. Like raw pork, she said. Surely rather an unkind saying?" Unkind and archly anti-Semitic too, but Vanessa had said it, not she.

One of her visitors was Stephen Spender, who came and talked nonstop about his own writing and the careers of the great poets. "A nice poetic youth . . . bright eyed, like a giant thrush," but egotistical and, being very young, painfully obsessed with a need to assert his genius in the eyes of a doubting world. Spender lived for the moment in Maida Vale, a London neighborhood of homosexual writers, including E. M. Forster, W. H. Auden, and William Plomer, all of whom were romantically attached to working men rather than to members of their own class. Virginia wondered, "Why this passion for the porter, the policeman and the bootmaker?" Referring to their Maida Vale address, she unkindly christened them "the Lilies of the Valley" —a kind of sarcasm she rarely indulged in now, evoking the homophobic and xenophobic attitudes of her youth.

Increasingly disenchanted with the English ruling class, Virginia still had close connections with influential members of the establishment, like her first cousin H. A. L. Fisher, warden of New College, Oxford. On November 30 she stayed overnight at the impressive Warden's Lodgings, which had been an official residence since 1370. Cousin Herbert, a historian, had served in Lloyd George's government during World War I, and his talk was brimful of anecdotes about "when I was in the Cabinet." That taste of power, hobnobbing with Arthur Balfour and Winston Churchill, was for him "what a Christmas tree is to a child." The visit, she told Quentin, helped her to get a more rounded view of contemporary life. Herbert and his wife, Lettice, were completely absorbed in their official functions, and while Virginia was with them she could see it all made perfect sense. They had tradition behind them—dignified, tasteful, and bloodless. She caught a glimpse of England's rulers, who seemed to loom over Herbert's shoulder. They were flat, conventional figures, lacking in imagination and human warmth: "small; but not evil." Telling his stories about the great days of 1916, Herbert became one of them, playing his own approved version of the great man—suave and tight-lipped, "like a butler used to the best families."

She attended a reception at which her bald, priestly cousin led shy undergraduates to meet her, like victims approaching an altar. There she stood, making meager small talk—"Are you first year or third year?"—asking about a familiar surname or place, till she ran out of subjects and fell back on the sales at Selfridge's. She could see that some of these awkward, fresh-faced boys would have been amusing companions if the gathering had not been so artificial—"if only I could have lain on cushions and shied roses at them." But no, the air echoed with polite phrases and institutional bells, each hour bringing round new duties. Lettice Fisher, who managed her husband's demanding social schedule on a very modest income, had been transformed by the effort into a hard, cheese-paring "henwife." She was very kind by nature, but forced into a mold that excluded imagination and humor, she confirmed Virginia's dislike of the institutional life that had destroyed her spontaneity. "Why," Virginia asked, "are officials so noble but so chilly?" Looking at the Fishers, she glimpsed a procession of stately Wardens and harried wives—she had portrayed one such couple in "Here and Now"—receding into the past.

⁂

Having brought the narrative of "Here and Now" to the eve of World War I, Virginia paused over the Christmas holidays and prepared for the next chapter by rereading old diaries from the war years, when her marriage was in its early stages. Looking back at their beginnings, she concluded that what Leonard and she had made of their lives was good. They were creative and hardworking; they were still developing, establishing friendships with younger writers, like Stephen Spender, Kathleen Raine, and William Plomer, living fully and adventurously, their days embedded "in a rich porous earth." She had reordered her social life and followed a simple, well-balanced routine. On Wednesday, December 20, 1933, for example, she worked during the morning and evening hours—wrote her Goldsmith essay from the sketch she had made in April, and after dinner read and approved a fiction manuscript for the Hogarth Press. In between, she and Leonard walked Pinka, whose sight was failing, round the square; Virginia walked to Oxford Street, looking for a dinner service, and saw china cups she liked at Waring's. Back home around teatime, she dropped in on Vanessa, whose house was two blocks away in Gordon Square— "Angelica cutting out silver paper beasts." Before bed the Woolfs listened to a Haydn symphony on the wireless. A "fairly specimen day."

Ironically, the chief constraint on her freedom now was the old system of keeping a live-in servant, which they continued mainly out of inertia. Her relationship with Nelly Boxall was as charged as ever. Virginia oscillated between easy familiarity and extreme irritation with her cook. When Nelly was in a friendly mood, Virginia felt that their long history enriched all the common domestic chores, adding a luster, "like lichen on roofs." More often, though, she felt exasperated by this baffling stranger, who served and washed up, whose daily life was entwined with her own in a disturbing compound of distrust and intimacy. Tension between her and Nelly reached a new peak early in 1934 when Virginia was ill with flu and a headache.

The house at 52 Tavistock Square was full of workmen. First came electricians to redo the wiring and install an electric boiler for hot water. They were followed during February and March by a parade of painters and plasterers, the landlord having decreed that they must redecorate every room in the house. Furthermore, a surveyor had determined that the floors were in danger of collapsing under the weight of their books, and must be propped up with steel posts, an expensive job that the Woolfs had to pay for. Through all this activity, Virginia struggled to get back to writing "Here and Now" after weeks of illness. Her relations with Nelly were already strained by a quarrel about an oven. The Woolfs wanted to install an electric oven, but Nelly stubbornly refused to try the new contraption. The tension finally erupted into another fierce row about her day off. Nelly stormed out in a rage and her employers ate eggs for lunch; that evening they were reduced to having an expensive, badly cooked dinner at a local pub—it was the last straw. Virginia silently vowed to fire Nelly once and for all by Easter.

She had made the same vow a number of times before and been persuaded to relent. Nelly had lived with them for eighteen years, and Virginia had periodically felt oppressed by her intrusive presence in the house for more than a decade. "Everyone I most honour is silent," she had said, and garrulous Nelly was always with her. Long ago Virginia had observed that her servants regarded talking as a social ritual, irrespective of what they said. Resting on the drawing room sofa one day during an illness, she heard Nelly and Lottie gossiping, as on countless other days, with a neighbor outside on the doorstep. It went on and on, and she jotted down her impressions of their chatter in telegraphic phrases: "Wonder expressed—loud laughter—agreement . . . more & more emphatic . . . talk with them a kind of muscular activity I think, for they never say much: repeat one thing over & over." The melody of their talk, now flowing, now staccato, was imprinted in her mind by countless repetitions. In 1929, looking through her diary, she had thought the story of her relations with Nelly offered a revealing focus on her own life, the sort of clue she often looked for in diaries.

Now, in February 1934, the tension in the house was almost unbearable. At the same time she was watching the steady deterioration of the political climate. The talk between her and her friends focused on the worrisome recent events in Europe. Austria's right-wing Chancellor Dollfuss had brought in troops to suppress the workers who controlled the municipal government in Vienna. On February 18 Virginia noted in her diary that Socialists and Fascists had been fighting pitched battles in the streets, civilians were being shot down; the news came closer to home than usual since John Lehmann, who had coolly dropped in to offer the Hogarth Press his latest book of poems, had just returned from there. People considered Dollfuss's successful coup the beginning of the end, Virginia wrote to Quentin—an omen that Mosley's British Fascists would be in a position to seize power within the next five years. "I suppose you and Julian will be in for it. What Angelica will live to see boggles me."

These prophetic fears merged with the daily discomfort of having workmen in the house. The Woolfs lived amid hammering and the reek of paint; they camped beside stacked furniture, eating on their laps, tripping over piles of books and rolled-up carpets, contending with a dust of plaster that sifted into their teacups. Virginia struggled to get back into her writing, in spite of the painters and puttiers—in spite of Nelly, who was "gay & garrulous as a lark." She refused to be provoked into the usual violent scene, which took so much out of her. Often in the past she had discharged her anger and afterward weakly agreed to a reconciliation, but not this time. Her restraint made Nelly suspicious, so that their encounters became rounds in a silent duel, the servant probing while her mistress evaded her. One day Nelly said indignantly: "You show no confidence in me; you dont treat me like a maid." To which Virginia longed to reply, "Then go!" but she bit her tongue and was silent. When the hammering and painting was at its worst, the Woolfs moved for three days into a borrowed room at the Strachey house in Gordon Square, where two of Lytton's sisters still lived. These domestic disruptions were overshadowed, however, by the Nelly problem. Virginia's visceral dread of the final scene interrupted the flow of her writing and spoiled her pleasure in everything. Nelly grew more insistent as Virginia retreated, following her around with ingratiating offers—"Do let me make you a cup of tea—you look so tired"—the sort of motherly care Virginia found hard to resist. Nelly could be "angelic" when she wished and she cooked admirably.

Virginia was determined not to discuss her plans with Leonard, suspecting he would try to dissuade her.

Her emotions were turbulent. For ten days she had spent the afternoons dusting books, returning them to their shelves, row after row, the clouds of dust echoing her unsettled feelings. Years of habit and familiarity were flickering and dispersing like motes in the air. New prospects opened—she hardly recognized her studio, it seemed larger, with clean white walls that had formerly been smoky. Firing Nelly would free her from the demands of an outmoded social system, she told herself, though uneasily, because in some part of her mind the system still spelled comfort and security. Servants, like family members, were domestic fixtures, human furnishings that one accepted in spite of their warts and blemishes. She renounced all that—it had been a suffocating way of life. She would cultivate anonymity from now on, using daily servants, who had fewer claims on their employers, or perhaps hiring a more self-sufficient live-in maid—it would be a great gain of freedom, though perhaps a loss of something as well.

The dust swirled round her—a vortex of anxiety now that the showdown was close—all in all, she said, some of the most disagreeable days she had ever known. She bit her tongue and controlled her dread "until I almost died of it." She meant to give Nelly notice the day before their departure for Rodmell, leaving as little time as possible for the inevitable recriminations. And she spent the last twenty-four hours feeling like the "executioner & the executed in one." It would pass, she told herself—"the immitigable day" of waiting, which was worse than the event itself. She had decided and there was no other way. "This has to be lived I say to myself." She had to keep in mind all their former quarrels and suppress any subversive thoughts about the difficulties of working for two such high-strung people as the Woolfs.

On March 27, six weeks after their quarrel about the oven, Virginia called Nelly into the drawing room, that pleasant room with the high windows framing plane trees in the square, the light falling full on the table stacked with books and periodicals. Nelly stood at the door, exposed and defensive in the full light "with her funny rather foolish mulish face puckered up." Virginia made the speech she had prepared, keeping to her script, saying they must part, the strain had become too great, addressing Nelly "correctly . . . persuasively," distancing herself with polite phrases: "And I expect you want to get another place too." So reasonable, and when Nelly started to protest, Virginia cut her off. This was something new—Nelly reduced to silence, standing there baffled while Virginia handed her a check for £25 and a £1 note for her mending; Nelly just managed to say, "But you dont owe me anything" before Virginia was gone down the stairs and out to her studio in back, leaving her cook in possession of the house.

Afterward, when the first shock wore off, Nelly unleashed the expected "storm of abuse and apology, and hysterics and appeals and maniacal threats." She said they couldn't make her go; she refused to accept Virginia's notice, stuffing the check, a generous gift for the time, back into her pocket and appealing to Leonard, who stayed out of it. Appealing to their class consciousness, she complained about the damage to her social standing among the servants in the neighborhood—they would blame her for being let go. She pressed so hard that Virginia, who had been chased out of her studio again by workmen, fled and walked up and down Oxford Street in a cold wind to get away from her. She and Leonard left for Rodmell the next day amid abuse and tears. Nelly stood at the sink with a wet cloth in her hands, glaring; Leonard put out his hand, but Nelly drew back, reproachfully: "No I really couldn't Sir." They walked out the door and she called after them, "No, no, no, I will not leave you." To which

Virginia replied firmly: "Ah but you must." They slammed the door behind them.

Virginia wrote the whole story to Ethel, whose appetite for mundane facts was as great as ever. When it came to it, Virginia said, she didn't feel guilty or have any regrets. Rather, she was left with an overwhelming sense of Nelly's egotism and how that had undermined her in the past. "Indeed I saw so deep into her poor muddled terrified but completely self seeking mind that I felt a thousand times reassured." At Rodmell, as the knowledge that she was no longer mired in that semifeudal relationship sank in, a luxurious calm descended on her. Nelly wrote and sent messages, anything she could think of to make her change her mind, but Virginia didn't answer.

Nevertheless, she soon found a replacement for Nelly—the "steady silent unselfish Mabel [Haskins]"—whom Leonard found irritating but tolerated for Virginia's sake. Though she still relied on servants, she had renounced the Victorian model of family life, as she had moved away from the heavy furniture and high, curtained rooms of her childhood.

As for Nelly, she appeared publicly fifteen years after Virginia's death in a brief BBC radio interview. On her best behavior, she revealed nothing about her own feelings and very little about Virginia—mainly her tastes in food—confiding that "she liked veal schnitzels with mushrooms and the trimmings and was very fond of good soups and her favorite pudding was crème brûlée or ice cream with hot chocolate sauce." When Virginia baked bread or prepared her dinner she "used every dish in the place and left all the washing up." Nelly also recalled that Virginia always praised her cooking and was very kind when she had to go to the hospital. "She came to see me in the ward carrying a huge pineapple and came straight up to the bed and cuddled me up."

The only hint of any differences between them was Nelly's final remark that after leaving the Woolfs, which she was sorry to do, she went to work for Charles Laughton. The movie star and his actress wife, Elsa Lanchester, rented a flat in nearby Gordon Square, which enabled Nelly to keep up her friendships with the other servants in the neighborhood. She found Laughton and Lanchester, who kept irregular hours, so that the house often seemed like a well-run madhouse, exasperating at times, but they respected her sense and forbearance. According to Lanchester, she was an admirable cook.

9   *Acts in a Play*

During the spring and summer of 1934 Virginia wrote the final "Present Day" episodes of "Here and Now." Recapitulating the novel's themes in the long finale, she could perceive the whole pattern spread out before her. All the dramatized scenes and period details she had recorded so swiftly as they rose up from her subconscious contributed their various notes to a complex musical development. Planning the last scenes, she concluded that the party at the end, in which three generations of Pargiters celebrate an all-night family reunion, would convey "the submerged side," that is, the psychological underpinnings, of the preceding chronicle of "facts." The bulky 200,000-word manuscript she had worked on for two years in such a trance of enthusiasm and defiance now formed a coherent, though unfinished, artwork with a life of its own.

And it was new—almost the opposite of anything she had ever written before, a fact that exhilarated her. On July 25, at the beginning of her long summer break at Rodmell, Virginia looked ahead with a sense of her good fortune and privilege. The previous day she had discharged all her current social obligations—she had tea with Leonard's old mother, who was settled in seaside lodgings an hour's drive away at Worthing; then she had listened to Mr. Fears, the village postman, assess the outlook for the local Labor Party—and now she counted on two full months of immersion in her writing, time enough to finish the first draft, a prospect that restored order and proportion to her world. It was "a wild windy hot day—a tearing wind in the garden; all the July apples on the grass." That was the scene outside her garden lodge: a vision of cultivated wildness that confirmed her sense of freedom. She would not be forced into a predetermined mold as a writer; she would not repeat herself or be enslaved by other people's expectations, but she would carry her latest experiment all the way to its unpredictable conclusion. Such freedom, she told herself, could be achieved only by accepting "constant effort, anxiety & risk." Approaching the limits of her own experience, struggling to give some shape to its randomness and disorder, she felt fully energized, awake, and reassured that she was still capable of finding "a fresh form of being, that is, of expression, for everything I feel & think." The new form, which renounced poetic obscurity and moved toward a more accessible language, reflected her heightened political awareness. In "Here and Now," she concluded, "I am breaking the mould made by The Waves."

That is to say, she had moved on from the lyrical visions of her earlier work to an interest in transcribing daily life, though surface details became increasingly charged with symbolic meaning as the novel proceeded. With its emphasis on dialogue, "Here and Now" raised questions about the relationship between novels and plays, a theme that coalesced with some of Virginia's ideas about Shakespeare. She had seen Macbeth in April and observed that the stage production created a special kind of reality that novels might approach in their own way. Using the dramatic medium, which demanded "coming to the top," Shakespeare had captured the full range of human experience. Virginia reflected that a novel might combine "the different levels of writing," going directly from objective facts to the underlying psychological plane without the narrator's intervention. She was trying to do that in "Here and Now" by means of musical rhythm and design. Further on, she speculated that fiction could present the "upper under," that is, embrace above and below in a single imaginative act. This fusion of "the different strata of being," she believed, would recreate the synthesizing mode the mind naturally adopted in thinking.

✣

Earlier that spring, before settling in to finish the first draft of "Here and Now," Virginia had taken two weeks off to tour Ireland with Leonard. The romantic mythology of that country, which she had never visited before, inspired one of her fantasies of disaster, blending satire and premonition: she would be "windswept into the sea," she wrote to Vita, overtaken on some wild island "where the seals bark and the old women croon over corpses of drowned men." She and Leonard drove from Rodmell through a rural England that seemed al-

most untouched by the twentieth century, and on across Wales, where
storm clouds alternately darkened and threw shafts of sunlight onto
sheep-dotted hillsides. They reached the landing at Fishguard on
April 27. That evening Virginia sat in the hotel lounge, waiting for the
ferry, which sailed at midnight. Spying on the other patrons, she pondered the obtuseness of the English middle classes. Outside, a gale
was raising choppy waves on the Irish channel; it would be a rough
crossing, they said. But Virginia watched a married couple across the
room—country gentry, by the look of them—engrossed in the daily
sports page, reading choice bits of cricket news out loud and discussing the fine points. Impossible to keep her attention focused on the
novel in her hand, Proust's *Sodome et Gomorrhe*, with that solid
down-to-earth couple opposite her—just the sort of people Ethel admired, who never gave a thought to artistic squabbles or dictators
or any of the matters that worried her Bloomsbury friends. She laid
Proust aside and wrote to Ethel instead, drawing a satirical sketch of
these admirable English whose faces wore a look of "perfect suitabil-
ity. . . . How calm, how right, how deeply rooted they are." In a voice
that carried across the room the lady told her husband that she had
strained her innards and must see a doctor. No sign of a chink in her
complacency. Virginia's comment was barbed with irony: "Lord, how
I wish I could be them." She observed the careless ease with which the
husband called the waiter and ordered a drink, using exactly the right
tone of voice. "Yes, thats the way to say it. . . . Heres the small
whiskey and soda—now how well they drink it!" Virginia lived in an
altogether less stable world than theirs, always in flux and tumbled by
the waves. Their respectable figures were a perfect foil for her own insecurity and defiance. Yes, a fierce wind was churning up the sea, she
wrote to the churchgoing Ethel; the ferry would sink, and with any
luck she would see God about two o'clock that morning. She elaborated the same theme in a second letter, addressed to Quentin, assuring him that these would be the last lines he received from her. It was
"pouring and howling" outside, she said, with some poetic license,
and by dawn her body would be tossing on the ocean floor, like one
of Tom Eliot's drowned sailors. But unlike Tom, she had no religious
faith to soften these forebodings. "What shall I say to the conger eels?
when they nose me at dawn."

Next day, after an uneventful crossing, Virginia observed the desolate beauty of the Irish countryside, an impression that persisted during their visit to the novelist Elizabeth Bowen, at whose family estate
they spent the night. Bowen's Court was a gray stone mansion, a
"great barrack," like a half-empty town house set in a deserted land-

scape, though it overlooked a fine meadow with trees in a ring. They visited an ancient wishing well where Leonard wished that their dog, Pinka, wouldn't smell; in spite of some character and charm, the Bowens' big house suggested "desolation & pretension cracked grand pianos, faked old portraits, stained walls." It confirmed her first impression of Irish life as "ramshackle & half squalid."

The Woolfs toured the southern coast of Ireland, driving to Waterville, where on May 1 Virginia learned from a two-day-old copy of the *Times* that her older half brother, George Duckworth, had died. The news baffled her—she hardly knew whether because it meant so much or so little. He had been an important figure in her childhood, and his incestuous embraces had traumatized her after her mother died. But he had played an insignificant part in her adult life; she had seen him only a handful of times in the past twenty years. Here in the wilds of Kerry, his death seemed very far away, and at the same time it produced a dizzying "sense of time shifting & life becoming unreal," individual selves obliterated, while the world went on indifferently without them. She had felt a "genuine glow" during a rare visit to George's home the previous year, and for the moment the memory renewed a certain attachment, though anger followed it closely. Her feelings were hopelessly jumbled together, "one from this year, one from that"—he had pervaded her childhood and now all that was gone. She recalled some of the kindnesses he had done her and the other Stephen children: taken them out for teas and bus rides, taught them to hold their cricket bats straight, spent countless hours entertaining them. Virginia wrote to Vanessa that she felt more affection for him now than ten years ago. His "half insane quality," the eccentricity of his opinions about family and food, seemed almost endearing, but then she remembered reading a memoir by Vanessa, and the thought of George's influence on their young lives flooded her with horror.

Years earlier, in 1921, she had demolished his character in an essay written for an association of Bloomsbury friends, the Memoir Club. The George Duckworth she knew as a girl was a well-bred young bachelor with a decent income. Tall, handsome, and a firm believer in "moral rectitude," he was eagerly sought after by London's fashionable hostesses. He was, of course, "abnormally stupid," but this did not prevent him from shining in society. He had the virtue of being a true English gentleman, who "would run miles to fetch cushions . . . and remembered the birthdays of aunts and sent turtle soup to the invalids." The catalogue of George's philanthropies went on and on. A certain Miss Willett of Brighton wrote an ode on his heroism—for on a trip abroad he had saved an Italian peasant from drowning. The ode, which compared him to the Hermes of Praxitiles, had been one of their mother's treasured possessions. All very well, Virginia added, but "if you looked at him closely you noticed that one of his ears was pointed; and the other round; you also noticed that though he had the curls of a God and the ears of a faun he had unmistakably the eyes of a pig. So strange a compound can seldom have existed." Greatly favored by their mother, whom he adored, George had indulged in outlandish displays of feeling. "When he had a tooth out he flung himself into the cook's arms in a paroxysm of weeping. When Judith Blunt refused him he sat at the head of the table sobbing loudly, but continuing to eat." After Julia Stephen's death, dutiful, oppressive George insisted on taking Virginia out to dinners and dances where she would meet other eligible bachelors like himself. These social gatherings, with their superficial glamour, bored and overexcited her. George's affectionate displays grew increasingly erotic, and he began invading Virginia's bedroom, still under cover of brotherly devotion. She described one such incident after their return from an evening in high society; she was in bed, almost asleep, when the door opened noiselessly. "'Don't be frightened,' George whispered. 'And don't turn on the light, oh beloved. Beloved—' and he flung himself on my bed and took me into his arms." How far these intimacies went is unknown; the adolescent Virginia was too disturbed and embarrassed to protest. Eventually Vanessa, who also suffered George's illicit embraces, complained to their family doctor, and his abuses stopped.

Virginia's extreme self-consciousness about her appearance in public, her clothes complex, was a permanent consequence of George's habit of inspecting her before their outings into upper-class society. She remembered being looked up and down like a show horse and feeling terribly exposed in an odd green dress she had improvised with her small allowance. The memory of George's moral disapproval—for he found the dress shamefully eccentric—still made her wince, as did the contempt in his sadistic verdict: "Go and tear it up."

She was moved enough by his death to sob sympathetically when she met his widow afterward, but on the whole she felt a very qualified distress. "No, I'm not seriously sorry," she confided to Vita, "only selfishly, that my past is now further away and the grave I suppose nearer."

❧

At a westernmost point of their Irish tour, near Galway, the Woolfs stopped on a cliff overlooking the sea, where they saw the Aran Islands outlined in the distance. A hectic, blustery day. The massive clouds drew apart, spilling a shaft of light; Virginia and Leonard picked bright-blue gentians in a fierce wind that almost blew them off the cliff—so she wrote to Elizabeth Bowen, again struck by the notion of being windswept into the sea. In her diary she noted the intensely blue-black shimmer of the water with its high, crested waves. "People gathering sea weed & heaping carts. Extreme poverty."

Touring on from Galway to Dublin, where they spent two final days before returning home, Virginia visited landmarks associated with Jonathan Swift, whose biography her father had written, and whose legendary love for two young women had affected her own family history. At Saint Patrick's Cathedral she read the "tremendous words" of Swift's epitaph, and standing in front of his tomb, heard an indignant verger protest that the bishop had removed a brass plate marking the spot where, according to tradition, Swift's beloved Stella lay buried beside him. Silly prudery, Virginia declared, to separate these unmarried lovers; besides, "if Swift was buried in [Stella's] grave, that seems to amount to marriage." The Woolfs had also driven into the countryside near Dublin to visit Marlay Abbey on the Liffey, the home of Swift's other love, Esther Vanhomrigh, known as Vanessa. They saw the deserted sham Gothic house from the distance, but the grounds were closed and Virginia imagined Vanessa seated there in a green bower of trees down by the river. Looking at the heavy foliage and bricked-over cathedral windows, she considered the climactic moment when Vanessa wrote to Stella, demanding to know whether the rumors that Stella had secretly married Swift, who was her guardian, were true. The impulsive letter of a passionate young woman. There followed "the famous interview with the blue eyes," as Virginia called it. Swift, who could not bear to be interfered with, came to Vanessa in a rage, flung down her letter, and left without saying a word. She feared his diatribes and had spoken of his "killing killing words," but this silence was truly deadly. Virginia recorded the scene in her essay on Swift. "When the full force of those bright blue eyes blazed upon her, when he flung her letter on the table and glared at her and said nothing and rode off, her life was ended." Within a few weeks Vanessa, who had been in poor health, was dead.

These events had special associations for Virginia. The naming of a child can be a prophetic act and Leslie Stephen had a stepchild named Stella, who came to him with his second wife, Julia Duckworth. When another daughter happened to be born on Stella's birthday, he named her Vanessa, invoking Swift, whose biography he was writing at the time. He published it three years later, in 1882, the year Virginia was born. The story of Swift's ambiguous attachment to two young women, one of whom was his ward, resonated with Leslie Stephen's own dependence on his daughters and his special relationship with Virginia, who would become his literary surrogate and inheritor. Stephen, who suffered from nervous irritability, had written sympathetically of Swift's "egotistic attachments." Virginia's account of Swift's role as guardian of Hester Johnson (Stella) applies precisely to Leslie Stephen and herself. "His influence was everywhere—upon her mind, upon her affections, upon the books she read and hand she wrote, upon the friends she made and suitors she rejected. Indeed, he was half responsible for her being."

༈

All in all, Virginia thought Ireland a melancholy place, in spite of the charming people, who lived up to their reputation as great talkers. Dublin struck her as a parody of a capital that fed on "the dregs of London." There was a pervasive second-rateness, enforced by poverty and the aftereffects of the civil war; behind that lurked bitter anti-English feelings, which puzzled her, since she had received a cordial welcome from the working people and shopkeepers, most of whom shared the attitude of the porter at the ferry: "We dont want this hate—it does nobody any good." The ordinary people were sensible, she concluded, and hatreds were deliberately fomented by the politicians. The Irish malaise was reflected by the eloquent inn-keeping lady at Adare, who addressed the Woolfs in melodious, well-formed sentences—an accomplished performance, though Virginia detected "something heartless" behind her loquacious mask. The landlady's eloquence was too studied, too much of a performance, her phrases acting as an intoxicant to soften the depressing atmosphere. "They spend their lives in talk," Virginia noted elsewhere, "dont mind poverty so much." She felt relieved to get back to the tidy English countryside, where in every roadside inn the prosperous gentry met to gossip and drink their pints "under pictures of famous race horses . . . these dwellers in the very heart of the land." She was so fascinated by the other patrons in one inn that Leonard had to warn her to stop staring.

On their way home the Woolfs stopped off to see Stratford-on-Avon, which lay on their route. The "fine unself conscious town" invigorated Virginia; after the staginess of Ireland, Shakespeare's memorials seemed refreshingly modest. His garden was in bloom; the spacious house where he lived had been pulled down, but she imagined he had sat at a window overlooking similar flower beds, writing *The Tempest*, and heard the chapel clock strike, just as it did then. The whole town, where handsome Elizabethan cottages and solid eighteenth-century houses lined the riverbank, radiated "sunny impersonality." Shakespeare's spirit pervaded the place without imposing itself—she could feel him as a disembodied presence that seemed to murmur, I am here, "but you wont find me not exactly in the flesh." He was down-to-earth and elusive; escaping the tyranny of egotism, he had no wish to impose himself on others, and his spirit conferred a sense of freedom. Virginia's diary placed him as the central figure in a utopian idyll. "He is serenely absent-present; both at once; radiating round one; yes; in the flowers, in the old hall, in the garden; but never to be pinned down." Entering the church, she saw the comically florid Shakespeare bust by an unknown sculptor, and the plain slab over his grave, both standing in contrast to the loftiness of Swift's memorials. Shakespeare's epitaph, admonishing the visitor not to stir his dust or move his bones, confirmed her feeling that he was "all air & sun smiling serenely & yet down there one foot from me lay the little bones that had spread over the world this vast illumination." That radiance and freedom epitomized the state she called "anonymity"—impersonal, absent-present, here and not here, impossible to pin down. Her Shakespeare had embraced ordinary daily life and shrewdly escaped its deceptive entanglements.

"Sunny impersonality" was precisely the quality she sought in her own writing—she was thinking of the finale of "Here and Now"—and her vision of Shakespeare coincided with her conception of that episode. Stratford's luminous atmosphere celebrated the creative life. Its sturdy, unpretentious buildings, surrounded by flowering gardens and embedded in "the very heart of the land," provided an admirable haven, a modest and stable community where, she imagined, Shakespeare found serenity amidst "the rage & storm of thought." Also an escape from the egotism of the "great man." She observed approvingly that he had left nothing that could reveal his personal tastes or habits—hardly even his signature, of which only one genuine copy existed, as the caretaker told her, and all his other belongings, books, furniture, pictures, had been obliterated by time. So at the end of "Here and Now" old Eleanor Pargiter glows with happiness, thinking that the furnishings of her Victorian youth have disappeared and her vision survives. To leave nothing behind but a luminous body of works, to be completely absent-present and beyond the desire for fame, to pour all of oneself into creation, was Virginia's idea of the artist's heaven. "Now I think [Shakespeare] was very happy in this, that there was no impediment of fame, but his genius flowed out of him, & is still there, in Stratford."

♧

Back home and writing again, Virginia reminded herself that the end of "Here and Now" demanded cunning and patience—she must allow time to let "the soft subconscious world become populous." After finishing the manuscript she would have the job of cutting and revising; it would be fully a year, she thought, before the book appeared in print. She immersed herself in the work, but the static of political events occasionally distracted her and filtered into her writing. On July 1 the papers reported that Hitler had ordered the killing of hundreds of his Brownshirt followers, including their commander, Ernst Roehm, the closest thing he had to a friend. These were summary executions justified only by Hitler's unsubstantiated claim that the victims had plotted a coup against him. The army high command, which despised the million-man Brownshirt militia, greeted the decapitation of this rival army with approval. By condoning murder, including the murder of a leading member of their own caste, the generals undermined their moral authority and independence, opening the way for Hitler's absolute rule. Soon afterward his decrees became Germany's sole law.

The Woolfs recognized that the bloody purge reflected an accelerating descent into barbarism. Two years earlier, after Carrington's death, Virginia had seen an apparition of "violence and unreason crossing in the air," and subsequently the conductor Bruno Walter had confirmed that vision with his account of Germany's Nazification. Now the reports of Hitler's bloodthirstiness revived Virginia's desire to write a political tract, "On Being Despised," about the connections between fascism and the oppression of women, though it would have to wait till after she finished her novel. The Roehm purge moved Leonard also to begin writing his book *Quack, Quack*, which presented an analysis of the totalitarian movements and their apologists. Europe was in crisis, he argued, because the elites had joined forces with the "barbarians" to prevent democratic reforms and keep the majority out. Following the examples of Carlyle, Nietzsche, and Spengler, many intellectuals had joined in this quackery, appealing to the primitive instincts that lurked beneath the surface of civilized life. "The psychology of civilization," Leonard wrote, "is of comparatively recent growth, a thin crust of reason, culture, and humanity which covers and conceals the hot passions and instincts of an animal and the crude delusions of a savage." Consequently, every society harbors respectable citizens who conceal "the heart of a gorilla or savage under a uniform, evening dress or golf-jacket." Such rhetorical figures as the gorilla are embedded in long passages of dry political analysis, but Leonard underlined his point again in the photographic illustrations, which show the contorted faces of Hitler and Mussolini haranguing their followers. Both portraits are paired with images of Polynesian war gods, whose ferocious masks echo the dictators' snarling faces, and as the text explains, reflect the same barbaric intention to cow their enemies. So much for fascist claims of racial superiority. Virginia's comments about the Roehm purge were equally charged, although her emphasis was different. On July 2 she noted that Osbert Sitwell had phoned her to discuss literary matters, and then brought up "this monstrous affair in Germany," to which she responded vehemently.

[Virginia's diary, July 2, 1934]
"One of the few public acts" I said "that makes one miserable." Then trying, how ineffectively, to express the sensation of sitting here & reading, like an act in a play, how Hitler flew to Munich & killed this that & the other man & woman in Germany yesterday. A fine hot summers day here & we took Philip [Woolf] Babs & 3 children to the Zoo. Meanwhile these brutal bullies go about in hoods & masks, like little boys dressed up, acting this idiotic, meaningless, brutal, bloody, pandemonium. In they come while Herr so & so is at lunch: iron boots, they say, grating on the parquet, kill him; & his wife who rushes to the door to prevent them. It is like watching the baboon at the Zoo; only he sucks a paper in which ice has been wrapped, & they fire with revolvers. And here we sit, Osbert I &c, remarking this is inconceivable. A queer state of society. If there were any idea, any vision behind it: but look at the masks these men wear—the brutal faces of baboons, licking sweet paper. And for the first time I read articles with rage, to find him called a real leader. Worse far than Napoleon.

While Leonard associated the killers with demonic nature (the gorilla or savage), making them seem larger than life, Virginia invokes

Figure 9. Virginia, reluctantly wearing dark lipstick; photo by Man Ray, 1934.

the baboon or the juvenile and cuts them down to size. Her sardonic tone deflates conventional invective. Monstrous though their crimes are, the perpetrators are ordinary and absurd—playground bullies or clownish apes. Her piled-up adjectives suggest inarticulate rage— "meaningless, brutal, bloody"—which she sharpens by recording some concrete details of the murder of General Kurt von Schleicher, Hitler's predecessor as chancellor of Germany. The mental snapshots flash by so rapidly that she can just fix them: the general at home having lunch, the invaders' boots scraping across the parquet floor as they drag him away from the table and shoot him in front of his wife, whom they shoot too when she tries to intervene. Bloody reports impinge on the innocents at the zoo. Following her usual method of blending fantasy and naturalistic facts—the sucking baboon and the iron boots—Virginia brings the murderous event into focus, and highlights her own impotence as a spectator of these events. Concluding the entry, she observes that the summer heat and the just-delivered letters, which included two invitations and a check from her American publishers, had already begun to dull her awareness. Before it faded further, she aimed an angry blast at Ethel, who had received her musical education in Germany and defended German nationalism: "How can you or anyone explain last week end!" she wrote. "Hitler! Think of that hung before us as the ideal of human life!" The reproach was linked to her general disgust with the respectable middle classes who talked about cricket and horses and went to church on Sunday. She was equally appalled by their literary surrogates, like Ethel's friend Maurice Baring, who wrote genteel novels. The English, she knew, would dither and pronounce the old truisms while totalitarian vandals continued their conquest of Europe.

The political dangers came up frequently during her conversations with her friends at Rodmell, where the Woolfs saw a good deal of Maynard Keynes, whose views about German economic activity provided a warning of the greater turbulence ahead. On August 7 he came to tea and reported that the German manufacturers were unable to pay a relatively small bill for cotton cloth in Lancashire. Why?—were the Jews withdrawing their money? But the German government was still buying up supplies of copper, an essential mineral for the weapons industry, which suggested that they were secretly rearming, starving their domestic economy in order to supply the army. "They're doing something foolish—no Treasury control of the soldiers." Later in the summer she recorded a tea party conversation about the threat to civilization. The barbarians were winning all over Europe, Leonard argued, citing the disturbing number of present and would-be dictators: Hitler, Mussolini, Pilsudski, Schuschnigg, and Mosley. The conversation deeply depressed Leonard's colleague, Kingsley Martin, who said he saw no point in continuing his work editing the left-wing *New Statesman* "if there's no future for our civilization." That morning, Virginia noted, she had been writing a fictional scene in which Peggy, a young doctor, thinking of the constant news reports about brutality and torture, protests angrily against people who think only of their personal ambitions, literary intellectuals who go on writing "one little book, and then another little book," instead of "living differently." But her outburst offends her listeners, and the episode, which Virginia wrote with burning cheeks and trembling hands, ends in baffled silence. Though Virginia had changed the form of her fiction in "Here and Now," apparently moving toward greater realism, the narrator's oblique view of events excluded any detailed treatment of ideological battles or the gritty facts of political life. There was a large disparity at this point between her reaction to events like the Roehm purge and the impersonal tone of her "Present Day" episodes. Nothing in "Here and Now" matched, or came close to, the violence of her tirade against the Nazi "baboons." Her views about artistic detachment and her hedges against propaganda kept her writing within a relatively narrow emotional range.

Virginia's political distress emerged in a running quarrel with Ethel, whose Christian optimism struck her as another form of insularity. On July 26, soon after arriving at Rodmell, she had heard the church bells tolling across her garden and written teasingly to Ethel: "Why is Christianity so insistent and so sad?" She had noticed that religious moralists often took pleasure in other people's misery. She was reading a life of her own great-great-grandfather, Henry Venn, an influential eighteenth-century evangelical parson, who felt great joy when a worldly lady swallowed a pin, a mishap that inspired thoughts of death, and so led the lady to stop "burning her wings" at public dances and card parties. Thereafter she became "a shining light"—one of those Angels whom our forefathers put on pedestals. The parson's smugness represented everything that Virginia loathed about religion, and she dared Ethel to justify it. "Mercifully she swallowed a pin! How can you belong to such a canting creed?"

Ethel defended herself vigorously, declaring that her faith helped her resist the tyranny of her own excessive egotism. Then she made a bold flanking maneuver, asking whether Virginia, who seemed innately religious, would have lost that faculty if she had not married an atheist like Leonard. She also reminded Virginia of Roger Fry's comment about the classic proportions of certain architectural columns, that such perfection cannot be explained by reason alone. Art shows that there are unprovable truths, and Virginia, whose writing displayed such profound spirituality, must admit that the same might apply to religion.

Ethel's implied criticism of Leonard touched a particularly sensitive nerve, and Virginia opened her next letter with a merciless attack on Maurice Baring's latest novel, which Ethel admired. Ethel had compared Baring's *The Lonely Lady of Dulwich* to Prosper Mérimée's *Carmen*, a suggestion that Virginia received with wry amazement. Baring's work, she wrote, was as "thin as a blade of green that a butterfly makes wobble. *There* [in *Carmen*] the shade is ink black; here thin as weak tea. *There* the sun is blue; here a watered wisp. Its a conjuring trick of a hack. 'Behold my hat! Look well—now there's a rabbit. . . . Thats all it is—a book without roots; veracity, shade or sun. A parasol of a book—an empty white waistcoat." Baring's book epitomized the prim English leisured classes with their hopelessly antiquated ideas. And how, how, she asked, could Ethel praise this "brash?"—which, Virginia explained, meant "babies diarrhoea." She then turned her attention to Ethel's Christian humility, which was a sham and served only to advertise Ethel's own superiority. That brought her to the real sore point: the hypocrisy of certain "religious caterpillars," who assumed that they had a corner on virtue and had the right to convert others. But "my Jew has more religion in one toe nail—more human love, in one hair." Her tone had lost its satirical edge and become simply indignant. "My Jew has more religion. . . ." Here she meant exactly what she said.

Ethel replied at once, declaring that of course Leonard had "more love in his toe nail than most people of any creed whatsoever," though she still deplored his hostility to religious faith. When this didn't mollify Virginia Ethel backtracked further, explaining that she had no wish to offend Leonard, whose passionate atheism was really an inverse spirituality, an overreaction that was part of belonging to "the most profoundly religious race in the world—the race that wrote the Bible." The quarrel, with its implicit background of Ethel's pro-German sympathies, might have grown nasty, but Ethel did not condone Hitler's atrocities, and besides, she cherished her friendship with Virginia. When Ethel came to tea and "did her owl" a week later, Virginia discovered that she was still fond of the voracious old bird, whose ruffled feathers had "added considerably to the entertainment of the weekend. We sat and bawled, about God and Dulwich."

The shouting visit helped Virginia dissipate some of her irritation, and it cleared the air between her and Ethel. Virginia's spirits were lifted too by one of her long rambles on the downs, where on August 29 she discovered an entirely new walk past a lonely farm that lay hidden in a fold between two hillsides. The novelty delighted her. She walked back home beside the gray river, which was overflowing its banks. The sky was covered by clouds and shed pearl gray light over the earth, giving her the sensation of passing through a fine eighteenth-century landscape. Looking at the river, she saw the waters break and a "porpoise came up & gulped. It rained. All ugliness was dissolved." This sense of communion with the land was heightened, after she got back to Monk's House, by a sudden hailstorm—a black cloud overhead sent down torrent after torrent of white ice pellets that lashed the earth wildly while the Woolfs played Brahms on the gramophone.

10 *On Being Despised*

"One's life is not confined to one's body and what one says and does," Virginia wrote in "A Sketch of the Past," but is related to a larger design, a pattern hidden behind the "cotton wool" of daily life. We glimpse minute corners of the pattern, bits of repeated figures, and these glimpses supply the "background rods or conceptions" by which we measure our existence. Varied repetition rules our lives; everything comes round again, each time a little differently, bringing us moments of foreknowledge and déjà vu. Our acts are governed by that figured background, as a poem receives its motifs from the natural world. The pattern engrosses and weds us to something greater than ourselves. "The whole world is a work of art," and our individual lives provide its poetic or melodic phrases—"we are the words, we are the music." The biographer's task, Woolf said, is to reveal her subject's unique motifs, the measuring rods or conceptions that she lives by.

Virginia's diary in the summer of 1934 exhibits one of those recurring motifs of her inner life. She was working on the last chapter of "Here and Now," having spent two years on the bulky manuscript, which extended to nine hundred pages. On September 12 her concentration was broken by the news that her old friend Roger Fry, who had slipped on a rug and fractured his hip, had died suddenly in the hospital. Virginia's friendship with Fry went back to 1910, the year when he organized the first English exhibition of Post-Impressionist paintings. His views had influenced her portrait of the artist in *To the Lighthouse*, which she at one point considered dedicating to him. She wrote the news in her diary, recording the fact in language as plain and direct as a child's. "Roger died on Sunday. I was walking with Clive on the terrace when Nessa came out. We sat on the seat there for a time." She felt dazed and unable to work. The death had cast "a thin blackish veil over everything." Virginia felt the shock most keenly on her sister's account. Though Vanessa's love affair with Roger had ended in 1913, their intimate friendship had continued without interruption; he had been a constant visitor, playing with the children like a favorite uncle. Now she was devastated; the peal of her voice as she came across the terrace crying, "He's dead!" stayed with Virginia. Silent sympathy was the only comfort she could offer Vanessa: "We sat on the seat there for a time."

Observing her own state of mind, Virginia remarked that she hardly knew what she felt or how to mourn Roger's death; her tears flowed, but "the famous human feelings," as she called them, baffled her like an exotic garment she had never learned to wear. "Women cry, [Leonard] says: but I dont know why I cry—mostly with Nessa." She examined herself, asking whether this numb detachment was the writer's occupational hazard. De Maupassant, whose journals she had been reading, remarked that writers are doomed to sift and analyze everything that happens to them, and can never simply feel. They observe their own reactions even in the midst of crises, recording their state, "after every joy and after every sob." Virginia reflected about her own shocked detachment when her mother died, a memory that seemed to confirm de Maupassant's judgment.

"I remember," she wrote, "turning aside at mother's bed, when she had died, & Stella took us in, to laugh, secretly, at the nurse crying. She's pretending, I said: aged 13. & was afraid I was not feeling enough. So now."

Roger's death echoed that first shock, reviving her old fear of disconnection. Later, in "A Sketch of the Past," Virginia returned once again to the trauma of her mother's death, which had profoundly changed the course of her life. She remembered two deathbed visits, though she had conflated them in her diary. A few minutes after Julia Stephen's death the children were fetched to their parents' bedroom by their half brother, George Duckworth. As Virginia approached the bedroom door her father staggered out into the hall. She reached out her arms, trying to stop him, but he brushed past, seeming not to see her. Entering the sunny room, she noticed the long looking glass and washstand, candles burning in the sunlight, one of the nurses sobbing in the background—a sight that made her shudder with suppressed laughter. Her mother lay in the big matrimonial bed. Unnerved by her father's snub, Virginia examined her own feelings and concluded, half defiantly, half guiltily, that she felt "nothing whatever." Since that time she had often made the same test at moments of crisis and come to the same conclusion. Her mother's face, when she bent to kiss it, was still warm. The next day her half sister Stella led her to say good-bye a second time, and her lips brushed a hard surface, "iron cold and granulated." It was "like kissing cold iron."

Virginia adapted this experience in the opening scenes of "Here and Now," which are set in 1880. The Pargiter children assemble at their dying mother's bedside, but Delia falls back behind the rest of the family and stands looking out the hall window while raindrops roll down the glass. Her father breaks away from the circle of mourn-ers and stumbles past her, blindly reaching out with clenched fists and crying his wife's name. Delia, who is very like her father, silently ac-cuses him of insincerity: his abortive gesture is merely histrionic. "You did that very well, Delia told him [without speaking] as he passed her. It was like a scene in a play." She watches the raindrops sliding down the windowpane, shining and indifferent, and observes that they re-flect an immensity, a deluge that can engulf her and the other mourn-ers. "A wall of water seemed to gape apart; the two walls held them-selves apart," evoking the stillness between two waves. Then the vision dissolves into gray twilight as Delia watches the drops slide to-gether and roll down the pane.

This episode departs from its original in one significant way—it de-picts the father stretching out his arms, whereas in real life it was Vir-ginia who reached out to her oblivious father, who came out of her mother's bedroom and brushed past her, "crying out something I could not catch; distraught." By transferring the gesture to Colonel Pargiter, Virginia reversed or neutralized its effect. She described the same gesture of outstretched arms, similarly displaced, in *To the Lighthouse*, where a central section, titled "Time Passes," frames the mother's death. Unlike the novel's long opening section, which gives a minutely detailed picture of the Ramsays' domestic life during a few hours at their summerhouse, "Time Passes" shifts the focus to the house itself, which stands empty for ten years while sun and rain, vines and creepers, threaten to undermine it entirely. The main actors in "Time Passes" are impersonal forces, like the insidious little "airs, detached from the body of the wind," which nose around the house, probing for weaknesses in its structure, persisting tirelessly as night falls, returning night after night as the seasons change. "What after all is one night?" asks the narrator. "The winter holds a pack of them

in store and deals them equally, evenly, with indefatigable fingers."
Against this background of decay the narrator inserts a brief paren-
thesis, disposing of the novel's main character in a single sentence that
has become a modern touchstone.

"[Mr. Ramsay, stumbling along a passage one dark morning,
stretched his arms out, but Mrs. Ramsay having died rather suddenly
the night before, his arms, though stretched out, remained empty.]"

Focusing on the father's gesture, this convoluted statement again
revises the original disturbing incident. As these fictional variations
suggest, Virginia was doubly traumatized, both by her mother's death
and by her father's failure to comfort her, or even acknowledge her
presence, when she needed him most. Her treatment of Mrs. Ramsay's
death, in spite of its apparent objectivity, reflects deep resentment
against her father; the mood is vindictive. *Mr. Ramsay, stumbling
along a passage one dark morning* . . . So too the overbearing Colonel
Pargiter came out "stumbling," and in her memoir Virginia wrote
that her father "staggered" past her. *But Mrs. Ramsay having died
rather suddenly the night before* . . . By placing the death not only
within brackets but as a casual aside in a modifying phrase, the narrator implies her contempt for Mr. Ramsay and his self-dramatizing
gestures, while underlining his present impotence: *his arms, though
stretched out, remained empty*. The last redundant clause rubs in the
uselessness of such gestures; the arms that are empty now will remain
so forever.

Centering on that bracketed statement, the whole "Time Passes"
section, with its description of blind natural forces, reflects a chilling
dissociation from human concerns. The section is sandwiched between two detailed accounts of ordinary domestic life, but the novel
treats the "sane" and the dissociated states with impartial detachment, giving no indication that one is more legitimate than the other.

❧

Virginia's life in the days following her mother's death took on a hal-
lucinatory quality. Friends came, voices murmured behind the drawing room door where her widowed father sat; after a while a visitor
emerged with a tearstained face. The family lived in artificial light
behind drawn curtains, a hushed atmosphere that intensified the
sense of unreality. "We were made to act parts that we did not feel; to
fumble for words that we did not know." Her mother's memory became entangled with "the conventions of sorrow," and all the particulars of that vivid personality were blurred by the general fog.

At one point Virginia went to meet her brother Thoby, who was coming home for the funeral, and found the glass arcade of Paddington Station lit by the setting sun, a sight that flooded her with emotion. She stood on the platform, bathed in the brilliant red and yellow light as the train steamed into the station, "gazing with rapture at this magnificent blaze of colour." The scene shimmered as if a burning glass had been laid over everything. Another illumination came while she was reading a book of poems in Kensington Gardens: the words grew transparent; she seemed to look through them into a radiant sphere where "poetry was becoming true." Years later, evoking such visionary moments in *To the Lighthouse*, she conjured up a beacon on a rock. But at thirteen her euphoria decayed very quickly, and the gloom seemed deeper afterward. Returning home, where she heard her father crying as he paced back and forth in the next room, Virginia felt that nothing she said or did was true any longer.

A similar chill touched her now after Roger Fry's death. The simplicity of his funeral, at which friends gathered without ritual or speeches, steadied her but did not dispel the sense of futility. The body lay nested among flowers in a bright room whose doors opened onto a garden—silence blending with music. The sight of the coffin slowly receding through the crematorium gate, while they played anonymous old music, inspired a "tremendous feeling" of tragic loss and defiance. She returned then to writing the last chapter of her novel in a state of excitement, convinced that Roger would have approved and, as long as the writing lasted, she enjoyed a sense of being "above time," beyond the reach of the invisible enemy who had silenced him. The excitement of writing the end of "Here and Now," she later said, tinged Roger's death with "all the colours of the setting sun." She finished the first draft of "Here and Now" on September 30, and laid down her pen without euphoria, but with a sense of "peace & breadth, I hope." That tentative "I hope" reflected her misgivings about the manuscript, which was more than twice as long as *The Waves* and would require endless rewriting. Now that she had reached a lull in her work, the delayed impact of Roger's death struck her— a "terrible blankness" that she warded off by concentrating on her sister's suffering, simultaneously affirming and denying her own feelings. His absence exposed "such a blank wall," she said. "Such a silence. Such a poverty. How he reverberated! And I feel it through Nessa."

✣

With the ordeal of the next publication in mind, she steeled herself against public exposure. On October 11 the *Times Literary Supple-*

ment carried an ad for Wyndham Lewis's *Men Without Art*, which contained a chapter on Virginia Woolf's work. Knowing Lewis's hostility to Bloomsbury and his destructive zeal as a critic, Virginia expected a vicious attack, but she couldn't resist the temptation to read his comments, feeling attracted, she said, by "the queer disreputable pleasure in being abused," which was inseparable from other illicit pleasures, such as martyrdom and publicity. Lewis's commentary, she reported, charged that she was "a peeper, not a looker, a fundamental prude." Given Virginia's shyness about being seen in public, the inverse of peeping, these remarks stung, and she resolved to face them squarely but never to adjust her vision in order to conciliate her critics. Her writing flourished, she said, when she retreated from the light into a mysterious zone of "populous obscurity." Lewis's abuse had some value, it even gave her an "odd pleasure," insofar as it propelled her toward her own shadowy realm. And after all, "being dismissed into obscurity is also pleasant & salutary." So she reasoned with herself, trying to draw the sting but at the same time aware that her desire for obscurity could go too far. Her dislike of public exposure was balanced by a fear of being forgotten. She expected that her literary reputation would decline within the next few years, it was inevitable; her work might prove ephemeral, and she foresaw abrupt "shoots into nothingness" opening to engulf her. Facing the abyss of nonentity at about two in the morning, she remembered that Yeats, whom she had met at Ottoline's, had described *The Waves*, along with *Ulysses* and Pound's *Cantos*, as a representative work of the age. At the thought, energy surged through her and she felt "a driving eyeless strength"—her primal self, unseen and indifferent to fame, advancing with the blind concentration of a mole.

She noted on November 15 that she had survived the "awful moment" when she was forced to settle down to reread and rewrite "Here and Now" and in fact had found it a great relief. She foresaw a "damnably disagreeable" struggle to reduce that heap of pages to coherence, but her complaints were merely precautionary—routine formulas to appease the jealous gods.

At the end of the year the Woolfs and Bells collaborated in the presentation of an amateur theatrical for family and friends—one of Bloomsbury's regular private entertainments. Virginia took time over the Christmas holidays to polish off "Freshwater," an occasional piece in celebration of Angelica Bell's sixteenth birthday. The farcical play, based on a sketch written in 1923, provided comic relief from the seriousness of "Here and Now." The entertainment presented on January 18 in Vanessa's studio to an audience of about eighty guests was a ribald tribute to Bloomsbury's Victorian antecedents, with Angelica playing the precocious actress Ellen Terry, who had in her time represented a new artistic generation.

In "Freshwater" Ellen appears as a spirited girl wilting in an artistic hothouse ruled by three eminent Victorians: her husband, G. F. Watts, called "the modern Titian," his friend, Alfred Tennyson, who declaims poetry, and Virginia's great-aunt, Julia Margaret Cameron, a pioneer of portrait photography. Ellen is sixteen, like Angelica, and spent years on the stage as a child actress before marrying Watts, an elderly Pre-Raphaelite painter. His estate on the Isle of Wight provides a cloistered realm of blossoming apple trees and perpetual nightingales. "The moon's shining. And the bees on the thorn. And the dews on the lawn," sighs Nell Terry, feeling misplaced with her aging and high-minded companions. She is modeling for her husband, whose painting *Modesty at the Feet of Mammon* is full of sexual symbolism, though he shows no carnal interest at all in his young wife. Later, wandering along the seashore, Nell encounters a handsome naval officer who offers to take her away from this artificial island to a down-to-earth place where she will feed on sausages and kippers, an irresistible delight. Nell has been dreaming of nothing but omnibuses and pavements. So she feeds her wedding ring to a porpoise and runs away with the sailor, who owns a big house in Gordon Square, Bloomsbury, leaving the sylvan airs and faded garlands behind forever. And that is how the present artistic generation, of which both audience and players are members, got started.

⁂

The work of revising "Here and Now" to reveal the inner light that infuses mundane objects sometimes caused Virginia such difficulty that her head seemed about to split. The strain intensified with news that another old acquaintance, Francis Birrell, had died of a brain tumor on January 2. A few days later, still shaken, she gratefully acknowledged the happiness of her domestic life with Leonard. They had spent Christmas and New Year's at Monk's House, and the nearness of the downs calmed her by reflecting something stark and elemental, a landscape in harmony with her mood. "Oh what miles I've walked," she wrote to Ethel, "right into remote valleys; with a thorn tree, and a shell. I always think the ice has only melted off the downs a year or two ago—the primeval ice—green ice, smooth ice." On January 11, after another morning of struggling with her intractable novel, she felt unable to concentrate—she had intended to read Dante but felt too numb to continue, and her thoughts reverted to death, a dangerous turn, for which the antidote was to fix her attention on something practical: the act of pulling on her galoshes and walking the fifty feet from her lodge across the rain-soaked garden, a gale blowing the trees, to the house, where lunch was waiting—scrambled eggs and sausages for Virginia, liver for Leonard and Louie Everest, the new daily help. The concreteness of these facts reassured her, and she was fortified by learning from Louie "that lamb's liver is more tender than calf's . . . thus filling up a blank in my knowledge of the world." Perhaps she could fool death by concentrating on eggs and sausages and the succulence of lamb's liver.

T. S. Eliot came to tea with the Woolfs on February 4. He and Leonard engaged in a philosophical argument about war and pacifism, but at one point Eliot began talking with deep feeling about his religious beliefs and the meaning of immortality, giving Virginia a rare glimpse of the unhappy soul behind his urbane mask. She was struck by the fact that in spite of his influence and celebrity he "got so little joy or satisfaction out of being Tom"—quite the reverse, success seemed to have alienated him still more. She was fond of this "lonely very sensitive man, all wrapt up in fibres of self torture, doubt, conceit, desire for . . . intimacy." Her attitude to him had been evolving. Two months earlier, at a dinner party, she had admired the ease with which Tom played his role as a great man, noting how solid and authoritative he had become. She added that this "divine authority" no longer made her feel frozen out—she could ignore it and still engage the shy, self-deprecating poet whom she had once described as "a dear old ass." Tom's struggle had inscribed new lines in his face. His head, she noted, was "very remarkable; such a conflict; so many forces have smashed against him: the wild eye still; but all rocky, yellow, riven & constricted." Fixing on the wild eye, Virginia concluded that she and Tom were alike in their reliance on evasion and disguise. The sincerity of his religious faith impressed her, and at the same time she felt unsettled, aware of "a vast sorrow at the back of life this winter."

The shadow of totalitarianism. Virginia's mood responded to the darkening atmosphere. Her daily labor of rewriting "Here and Now" on the typewriter, whose clatter she disliked, produced not just the ordinary wrestling with words but deeper irritability, hints of a vast sorrow, which sometimes made her lose all patience with "that blasted Chapter . . . that d——d chapter." She was painfully philosophical about the likelihood that her writing would be "hated & despised & ridiculed." By late March she and Leonard were proposing to spend a lazy fortnight wandering among tulips in Holland, and from there they would fly to Rome, where Vanessa would be settled during the spring. Virginia mentioned this in a letter to Quentin Bell on April 3, but a week later the plan underwent a major change. It was to be a motor tour, beginning in Holland, and then taking the direct route south to Italy, which, as Virginia remarked, meant driving across the length of Germany, "concealing Leonard's nose," that is, his Jewishness. Not the simple relaxing holiday they had originally planned, but a "heroic" tour. In her letter to Quentin before the change of plan she ironically summed up the Nazi menace, using dark satire, as she often did, to defuse or contain her anxieties. Leonard predicted the Germans would shortly drop poison gas on London, she wrote, killing not only expendable young men like Quentin, but even upstanding people like herself. She imagined a "yellow fume" descending as she walked along Oxford Street and herself sinking into the gutter. The Teutons would roll in, and Bloomsbury would be transformed into "a Platz with a statue of The Leader." What was needed was an alternative to that martial figure, which Quentin could supply by carving a sculpture of "a great flaming Goddess"—an anti-fascist declaration and tribute to Bloomsbury all in one. This grim flight of fancy tapped into the collective psyche, its bold images cutting through the abstractions of politicians and editorial writers. Virginia had been steadily thinking about fascism from her own angle—that is, asking how and why the petty aggressions of daily life sometimes escalated into full-blown atrocities. Lately she had felt a great urge to write a straightforward anti-fascist pamphlet as a prelude to her proposed book on women and the professions. She discussed the idea with Leonard on February 26, just as he was on the verge of finishing his tract *Quack, Quack*, and concluded that her plan would have to be deferred until she had developed her own approach, to which Leonard's specialized knowledge could add very little, since in writing "its the person's own edge that counts." In the meantime she continued gathering material for future use, recording the experiences of her cousin Janet Vaughan, a doctor, who had lost her fellowship because the male medical establishment considered women incapable of advanced research. Subsequently she noted similar facts about the legal profession, which was suffocating under hidebound traditions, and the lord mayor of London's ceremonials, which were scandalously wasteful.

Virginia's dislike of militarism and the patriarchal state dominated her impressions of the Tower of London, that massive barrack and "dungeon place," which she and Leonard toured on March 26. She described it as "the reformatory at the back of history; where we shot & tortured & imprisoned." The display of crown jewels seemed merely tawdry, and the parade of drilling soldiers in the courtyard, stamping and wheeling in unison like machines while a sergeant major barked hoarse orders, was a degrading spectacle.

Political anxiety colored Virginia's fierce reaction to a conversation with E. M. Forster at the London Library. Forster remarked that the Library Committee, to which he belonged, had discussed whether they should select a woman member. The remark carried personal associations for Virginia, since her father had been president of the library during the 1890s, having succeeded Tennyson in the job. She thought Forster was about to invite her to join the committee, and prepared to refuse, but he confided that the other members had opposed the selection of a woman. Back in Leslie Stephen's time they had selected a Mrs. Green, the widow and collaborator of a well-known historian, and she had proved extremely troublesome; now the committee would not even consider Forster's mild endorsement of the opposite sex, insisting that "No no no, ladies are quite impossible." Virginia heard the story in silence and went on her way without telling her old friend that she was deeply offended. He had not said that her name had been mentioned, but she assumed it was. To be disqualified from the body that her father had headed, to imagine being put forward and dismissed, made her burn and shrivel. Leslie Stephen, she remembered, had willingly spent his evenings in the objectionable Widow Green's company. Virginia's hand trembled as she wrote about the incident. She rarely used her diary as a vehicle for fiction, but this event provoked such a rush of feelings that she began at once inventing a little fictional scene for her book on the oppression of women. In the sketch a woman who has politely refused a public honor confides her contempt for the whole rigmarole to a friend.

[Virginia's diary, April 9, 1935]
    And they actually thought I would take it. They were, on my honour, surprised, even at my very modified & humble rejection. You didnt tell them what you thought of them for daring to suggest that you should rub your nose in that pail of offal? I remarked. Not for a hundred years, she observed. . . . Yes, these flares up are very good for my book: for they simmer & become

transparent: & I see how I can transmute them into beautiful clear reasonable ironical prose. God damn Morgan for thinking I'd have taken that. . . .

The veil of the temple . . . was to be raised, & as an exception she was to be allowed to enter in. But what about my civilization? For 2000 years we have done things without being paid for doing them. You cant bribe me now.

Pail of offal? No; I said while very deeply appreciating the hon. . . . In short one must tell lies, & apply every emollient in our power to the swollen skin of our brothers so terribly inflamed vanity. Truth is only to be spoken by those women whose fathers were pork butchers & left them a share in the pig factory.

Virginia's rage hung in an uneasy balance with her artistic impulses: on the one hand, a need to hurl the insult back at those who had inflicted it and on the other, a desire to harness that energy for her creative work. It was a variation on the conflict between art and propaganda; while she burned and vowed to refuse all bribes, the professional writer in her plotted to turn her anger into clear, effective prose. She had misgivings, though, about the widening gap between her feelings and the reasonable public voice of her essays. She imagined distilling her anger till it grew beautifully "transparent," and almost in the same breath damned Forster for cooperating with the pork butchers. Reason demanded concealment and dictated polite phrases that made her want to gag: "While very deeply appreciating the hon. . . ." But her anger would remain unspoken "for a hundred years"; it would simmer and mature, she supposed, while the pork butchers went on filling pails with offal—an image that echoed other grievances—against abusers like George Duckworth with his pig's eyes, and against the Nazi butchers with faces like baboons.

Looking back at her account of the library incident three days later, Virginia concluded that the entry would provide some useful phrases for her book, in spite of its ranting tone. At the same time she noted that she and Leonard were settling their travel plans and had decided to drive to Rome via Germany. They expected, according to Leonard, that a leisurely drive would give them a better understanding of both "international politics and human nature." The motives behind this plan were complicated, since it was a time of "emphatic scares," when Leonard brought home new reports of imminent war after every committee meeting. Virginia treated the trip as an occasion for black humor, predicting that they would be interned or flayed alive, because

"Leonard's nose is so long and hooked." In his biography of Virginia, Quentin Bell noted how their route had astonished him at the time, since any minor mishap on the road could have provoked "a frighteningly unpleasant incident" with dangerous consequences for Virginia's health. The British Foreign Office had privately advised Jews not to travel in Germany, which the Woolfs knew, and their decision to go ahead seemed inexplicable; this was the only time, as far as Bell knew, when "Leonard took an unjustifiable risk with Virginia's nerves." In retrospect, Leonard explained that the decision grew out of a state of denial and (in spite of his general skepticism) a surprising faith in the immunity conferred by a British passport. "It seemed to me absurd that any Englishman, whether Jew or Gentile, should hesitate to enter a European country." Both he and Virginia wished to get a feel for the country, and to check their forebodings against the reality.

They were concerned enough about the dangers to consult a diplomat who lived in a village near Rodmell. Ralph Wigram, a younger member of the Foreign Office, had just returned from Berlin, where he had assisted Foreign Secretary John Simon in his talks with Hitler. He seemed uneasy about the question of Jews in Germany, declining to discuss it on the telephone, but he and his wife came to tea at Monk's House on April 22. The Wigrams made a disturbing impression. Ralph wore iron braces on one of his legs, hobbling about with a crutch. His wife, a pale blond woman, growing fat, resembled "an old daisy or other simple garden flower; if a flower could look very unhappy." Virginia thought her gloom reflected faint disgust with her husband's deformity, which was aggravated by the burden of caring for a retarded child. In manner and temperament Wigram seemed a typical representative of his breed: "a nice rigid honest public school Englishman." He began talking at once, describing the herdlike docility of ordinary Germans and the mesmerizing effectiveness of their leader. Nothing to support the theory that the Nazis were primitive barbarians who would fail through their own incompetence—on the contrary, Hitler had impressed Wigram as an extremely capable politician. He had delivered a forceful and detailed analysis, speaking for twenty minutes at a stretch without notes and displaying complete command of the issues. This performance coincided with hints of frightening volatility. An impenetrable figure who had neither ideals nor principles, only calculations about power, who openly boasted that he would restore Germany's military strength and erase her defeat in the last war. Hitler's impressive speech and threatening attitude had shaken the English delegation. Virginia formed a general picture of a "completely equipped & powerful machine" dominating a population of willing slaves, stamping his image on them like "a great mould coming down on the brown jelly." The situation seemed all the more frightening when one asked how England's rulers would fare in a real showdown with such an opponent. Virginia concluded they would not be much better equipped than Wigram, in which case the future looked even bleaker than she had thought. "Here in England we havent even bought our gas masks. Nobody takes it seriously. But having seen this mad dog, the thin rigid Englishmen are really afraid. And if we have only nice public schoolboys like [Wigram] to guide us, there is some reason I suppose to expect that Oxford Street will be flooded with poison gas one of these days. And what then? Germany will get her colonies."

As for the Woolfs' trip, Wigram dismissed the Foreign Office warning as nonsense, offering his private opinion that there was no reason for them not to go, though they should be careful to stay away from any Nazi parades or public ceremonies. As insurance, he gave Leonard an introduction to Prince Bismarck, a counsellor at the German Embassy, who was affable and reassuring. No grounds for apprehension, the prince insisted—of course they must go to Germany! He presented Leonard with a letter advising all German officials to render the distinguished English travelers all possible assistance. The document might be useful, Virginia wrote Ethel, "since our Jewishness is said to be a danger—(not seriously)."

At dinner on April 28, three days before her departure, Virginia discussed the task of finding substitutes for war with her activist nephew, Julian Bell. Julian argued that his generation craved danger and adventure—bullfighting, mountain climbing; "the danger emotion" was driving young people to join the Communist Party, which offered the excitement of fighting for a cause and the solace of a coherent worldview. Virginia pointed out that the romance of war palled very quickly—there were more durable excitements. Nothing, Julian replied, could match the twin stimuli of "lust and danger." One might hope to divert people toward less destructive fantasies, but that could only be done very gradually. Throughout the conversation Virginia was struck by both her nephew's vibrant energy and his blindness to his own motives. She did not name those motives—one can infer that she was thinking of his attachment to Vanessa, which Julian considered "about the most satisfactory human relationship I have," and from which he had distanced himself by rejecting Bloomsbury's pacifist ideals. Virginia had her own reasons for feeling on shaky ground about pacifism after having diagnosed the menace of "this mad dog" Hitler. The conversation moved her to begin sketching her "Professions book" again, but she was aware of swimming against an irresistible tide. She understood what Julian meant by "the danger emotion," and the image of Wigram, "hoisting himself about on a stick," cast a shadow, suggesting the futility of appeals to reason. "What is the use of trying to preach," she protested, "when human nature is so crippled?"

⁓

London's streets were festooned with streamers and its public buildings covered with flowers. Blue paper crowns and red roses appeared on lampposts, flags flew from windows; at night the streamers shone purple and pink against the black sky. All England was preparing to celebrate the twenty-fifth anniversary of King George V's ascension to the throne, a festival intended to mark the return of prosperity and evoke past imperial glories. Virginia, who saw little reason to celebrate, was content to be going abroad. On May 6, Jubilee Day, she and Leonard were touring the Dutch countryside, where the cows wore coats and cyclists skimmed along "in flocks like starlings." Everywhere they observed the complete domestication of nature— earth and sea tamed, farms and towns dividing the land between them in a harmonious pattern. The streets were crowded with prosperous burgers strolling past endless shops and immaculate sixteenth- and seventeenth-century houses. "Old ladies combing their cats in the window," Virginia wrote. "Not a beggar, not a slum—even solid wealth"—which suggested a degree of complacency remarkable even by English standards. She felt as if she had been transported back to a time before 1914, when war seemed a thing of the past, like the bubonic plague. The Dutch represented middle-class civilization in its purest form, Leonard concluded, and considering conditions in the rest of Europe, this haven of beauty and bad taste had much to recommend it.

Leonard had brought along a tiny passenger, Mitzi, a pet marmoset, which perched on his shoulder as he drove or curled up amid the luggage in the backseat. He had rescued the sickly animal from her indifferent owners the previous year and nursed her back to health, and she had grown passionately devoted to him. Leonard was proud of his success with her, noting that marmosets rarely lived long in captivity and that his methods of nurturing and training worked better than those of the zookeepers. Since the weather in Holland had turned very hot, they drove with the convertible top of the Lanchester rolled down, and Mitzi drew small crowds wherever they stopped. People were entranced by the squirrellike ball of fur peering round her master's head, while her tail hung down his jacket front. They oohed and aahed about "the dear little creature," brimming with goodwill and banal questions. Mitzi eased the formalities of travel, endearing herself and the Woolfs to strangers, inspiring them with a warm sense of common humanity. Virginia gave no sign of sharing these sentiments about animals or people.

The border crossing into Germany was guarded by grim-looking soldiers who made Virginia nervous. While Leonard went through customs, she sat in the car, trying to concentrate on her book, Lawrence's *Aaron's Rod*. After a while she realized that ten minutes had gone by since Leonard had disappeared into the office with the barred windows, and she wondered whether she should go after him. Dutch customs had taken less than a minute. To her relief he emerged just then and the guards passed them through. She noticed how much her sense of freedom had already eroded. When the officers smiled at Mitzi, she and Leonard responded with exaggerated delight: "We become obsequious," she remarked—"the first stoop in our back." Leonard reported that the delay in customs had been caused by an incident involving the driver ahead of them, a peasant with a farm cart. The customs officer sat in front of a wall decorated with Hitler's portrait. When the peasant driver approached his desk the official burst into a violent tirade against the "insolent swine" for not taking his cap off in front of the Führer's image. "This office is like a church!" he shouted. Witnessing this scene, Leonard had the uneasy feeling that he might need Prince Bismarck's letter after all. The intimidating display, which he half suspected was staged for his benefit as a foreigner, suggested that "savagery" had already penetrated deeply into German daily life.

Leonard's uneasiness mounted as they drove on the autobahn between Cologne and Bonn; they seemed to be the only car on the road, which was guarded at twenty-yard intervals by soldiers with rifles. In Bonn they found the road closed ahead, and the policeman redirecting traffic informed them that the "Herr Präsident" was coming. Looking for an alternate route through the city, Leonard blundered into the very situation Wigram had warned him to avoid. It seemed that the whole population had turned out in the streets to await Göring, who was expected to arrive shortly. The sidewalks were crowded

Figure 10. Reich Party Day parade in Germany, 1935.

with flag-waving children and townspeople standing behind a line of storm troopers. The Woolfs had no choice but to drive down the single narrow lane between the spectators, who formed a seemingly "unending procession of enthusiastic Nazis." To make matters worse, the banners across the road bore slogans such as, "The Jew is our enemy," and "There is no place for Jews in——." An unnerving scene, though they need not have worried. The festive crowds, like the Dutch, instantly fell in love with the darling marmoset on Leonard's shoulder, which they greeted with shrieks of delight, Heil Hitlering to the little animal and its masters. Ranks of cheering schoolchildren swam past, and Virginia gravely waved back. They drove on for mile after mile, hemmed in by the "docile hysterical crowd," whose programmed cheers and laughter grew increasingly oppressive. Finally, unable to stand it any longer, Leonard pulled off on a side road and they found a large, empty hotel overlooking the Rhine. They were the only guests in the dining room, whose windows offered a view of coal barges passing on the river. After dinner they tried to sound out the manager on the subject of the new regime. He was very wary and would say nothing, but when Leonard mentioned that they lived in Tavistock Square, he suddenly decided he could trust them and poured out his story. He had worked as a waiter in a restaurant on the Thames and had returned to Germany a few years ago in order to marry; before leaving England he had actually been offered a job managing a hotel in Tavistock Square, which he turned down because his new wife spoke no English. They were trapped here. Business had fallen off sharply after the Nazis came to power; formerly, university students had come up the river from Bonn to drink and carouse, but now they were kept busy doing military exercises and had no time for pleasure outings. "If one says a word of criticism," he confided, "one is in danger of being beaten up. It is all processions and marching and drilling." Germany had become a prison and they would never get out.

The grim atmosphere relaxed somewhat as the Woolfs traveled further south, though all the towns displayed enormous placards announcing that Jews were not welcome, and they had to imagine how the people crowding round Mitzi would have reacted had they known Leonard was a Jew. Mitzi gained them friendly attentions wherever they went, all tinged with unreality. At Augsburg, in heavy traffic, a smiling policeman made the other cars wait and waved the marmoset and her owners to the head of the line. Leonard grimly observed that he never needed to show Prince Bismarck's safe-conduct letter, for "it was obvious to the most anti-semitic stormtrooper that no one who had on his shoulder such a 'dear little thing' could be a Jew."

Before this trip Virginia had indulged in ironic warnings of disaster, reminding her friends that Leonard's long nose marked them out for persecution, and casually including herself among the potential victims. "Our being Jews is said to be a danger," she had written to Ethel. In the event, they had received accolades and favors. Virginia carried away a vision of expectant crowds hailing a tiny ape as they waited to catch sight of the apostle of racial purification. Though her nerves were frayed, she preserved a very English coolness in public. Her travel diary adopted the same cool, objective tone, though she had appraised the crowds and described the hollowness of their laughter: a "stupid mass feeling masked by good temper." The German tour left her feeling drained and dispirited. She reported the existence of the anti-Jewish placards and said no more, as if her shudder at their hatred dissolved in thin air. Nothing had happened—only that Virginia, who planned to write a tract "On Being Despised," had sensed the presence of violence and unreason that she could not defuse with her gallows humor or transform, like Wyndham Lewis's insults, into a source of disreputable pleasure.

❦

The drive through Germany left obscure tracks, like an interference pattern or a charged silence. After crossing the Austrian border Leonard advised Virginia that she could now tell the truth again. She said no—some parts of reality, or of her power to register it, had been obliterated. "I have forgotten 2 days of truth." The journey to Rome, where they met Vanessa and her children, provided relief from this numbed state. In his autobiography Leonard observed that ordinary people in Italy had been acquiring civilization for more than two thousand years, and even the Fascists had not been able to pervert their humane spirit. It was obvious that he and Virginia would not "require either a marmoset or a Prince Bismarck to protect [them] from the native savages." Still, political disintegration had reached an advanced stage here too. Mussolini had recently made territorial claims on Abyssinia, threatening to use force if they were not met, and that unresolved crisis hung in the air.

During her stay in Rome, Virginia received a letter from the prime minister offering to recommend her for the Companions of Honour, an award to be included in the King's Birthday Honours. She took the offer as an opportunity to refuse still another bribe and to tease Ethel, who had been made a Dame of the British Empire, about the custom of wearing a little red ribbon to advertise one's social or artistic standing.

The return trip via France was an anticlimax: rain fell in a gray, featureless landscape that made Virginia long to be home rewriting "Here and Now" again. After hours of seeing the world through a dripping car window, she was relieved to stop at Chartres, where they visited the cathedral just as night was falling. Standing in the nave, Virginia saw stained-glass windows between dark arches and pillars, like "the skeleton & eyes of the cathedral glowing there. Mere bones, & the blue red eyes." A high stone gallery accented by bursts of intense color: "so bare, so architectural, a statement of proportions, save for the fiery & deep blue glass, for the glass varied from gloomy to transcendent."

They arrived home at Monk's House on May 31 to find that their pet spaniel, Pinka, had suffered three mysterious fits and died suddenly the day before. A depressing loss that made Virginia feel they had buried part of their private play life in the orchard.

The holiday interlude, with its passage through Nazi Germany, had upset her, and she spent several days relaxing, doing small chores, waiting to settle again into her fertile "unconscious" state. Reviewing the unrevised portion of "Here and Now," she felt intense aversion to "this cursed dry hard empty chapter." Its hard-edged style, composed in implicit defiance of her earlier poetic mode, seemed a misguided attempt to get out of her own skin. At the same time, she began plotting the novel's finale again, remarking that it depended heavily on dialogue and grew increasingly playlike. The dramatized scenes should combine architectural solidity and airiness, creating a new narrative form. "The arches and domes will spring into the air," she had written before the trip, "as firm as steel & light as cloud." Now, as the book came back into focus again, her anxieties subsided. On June 6, walking across Regents Park at twilight, she saw the flower beds glowing in the mist, vivid as stained glass. An ecstasy of light emanated from "the blue and red mounds of flowers burning a wet radiance through the green grey haze." The sight activated her imagination so that phrases of unwritten stories flooded her mind. Shortly thereafter she engrossed herself in carving out the last chapter of "Here and Now," reshaping the long original draft into highly condensed episodes, a task that proved difficult. Her brain felt congested and words came slowly, as they had done when she wrote *The Waves*; she wondered whether that meant the book was good, and kept on with her labor, noting that the main problem was to clarify its structure: "I feel I have a round of great pillars to set up."

Figure 11. A page from Virginia and Leonard's Monk's House album.

Figure 12. Virginia among red-hot pokers in the Monk's House garden, 1931.

Figure 13. Angelica and Vanessa Bell at Charleston, c. 1932.

Figure 14. Angelica, Vanessa partly hidden, Clive Bell, Virginia, and Maynard Keynes in front of Virginia's writing lodge, 1935.

Figure 15. Leonard with the spaniel Sally, after June 1935.

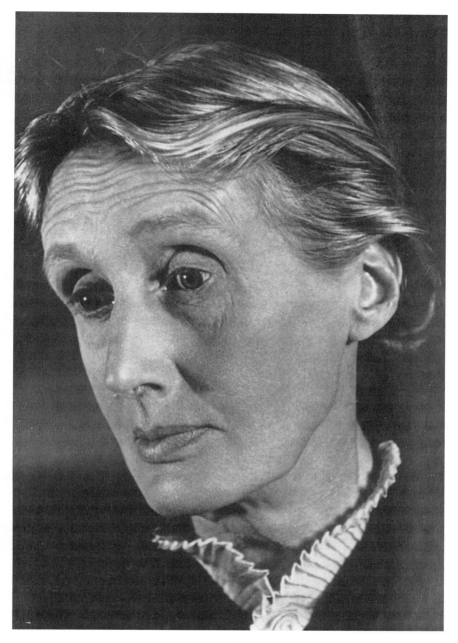

Figure 16. Portrait of Virginia, London, 1939. Photographed by Gisèle Freund.

Figure 17. Vanessa Bell clasping her hands, David Garnett, Virginia, Angelica petting Sally, Quentin, and Leonard at Monk's House, c. 1940.

Figure 18. Two large elms at Monk's House, named by the Woolfs "Leonard and Virginia"; her ashes were buried in the earth beneath "Virginia," which was later blown down in a storm.

11 *Slow Motion:* The Years

After reading Stephen Spender's long poem *Vienna*, about the massacre of Austrian workers by right-wing troops, Virginia wrote to him on June 25, 1935, noting the difficulty of reconciling politics and poetry. Spender's desire to teach made him focus too narrowly on surface events, and so neglect their inner meanings. Poetry should tap into the depths of one's being, she said. "Here again my hatred of preaching pops out and barks. I dont think you can get your words to come till youre almost unconscious; and unconsciousness only comes when youve been beaten and broken and gone through every sort of grinding mill." Her comments continued the argument she was having with herself, coming directly out of her struggle to revise "Here and Now," which seemed increasingly problematical. While she advised Spender not to mix poetry and political action, she was longing to write a polemic herself, and had just told the Argentinian editor Victoria Ocampo that she planned to issue a sequel to *A Room of One's Own* denouncing fascism, but had to finish her novel first. Her decision to exclude all except the most general political ideas from "Here and Now" meant censoring some powerful arguments that went all the way back to the original novel-essay form of the book. She felt a need to issue her own political manifesto, and the more carefully she avoided the polemical tone in her fiction, the more those arguments obsessed her. Occasionally, as she followed events during the summer and fall of 1935, the urge to write her anti-fascist book, which she now referred to as "The Next War," grew overwhelming, and she quickly sketched passages of the book before returning to her novel. Though it mainly existed in her imagination, the twin or phantom book had followed the track of "Here and Now" at every stage, absorbing excess anger and unwritten protests. Writing her novel demanded strict restraint, whereas planning the polemic was a release, a breakthrough to unfamiliar ground where, Virginia said, her feelings ran "absolutely wild, like being harnessed to a shark." The intensity of this reaction was a sign of how much anxiety she was holding in check. There was an undercurrent of disappointment, too, because in separating fiction from social commentary she had given up the attempt to get her whole meaning into one book.

It took great self-discipline to continue working on "Here and Now," since she had been tied to her desk for months now, typing and retyping the corrected manuscript. The sheer mechanical drudgery, combined with the difficulty of reshaping plotless episodes, exhausted her; she longed to pick up her pen and feel the sentences rounding themselves sensuously under her hand again, remarking that these typed phrases drawn from an already existing draft did not satisfy her like handwritten ones that sprang "fresh from the mind." But no, she had to keep on banging at the keyboard. and the end of the "impossible eternal book" kept receding toward the horizon.

✤

Rapid social changes also disturbed Virginia. Her democratic principles were sometimes subverted by inherited class attitudes that had endowed her with a weakness for aristocratic hostesses and a fascination with royalty. When Leonard reduced Mabel, whom he found annoyingly slow, to tears one day by complaining about the coffee, Virginia, instinctively applying the standards of her youth, remarked that he could never be genial and easy in his dealings with servants due to "not being a gentleman."

Her own attitude toward Peggy Belsher, their attractive young secretary at the Hogarth Press, who had recently married a clerk in the customs office, was sympathetic and condescending. On July 18, shortly before their summer move to Rodmell, the Woolfs went to have tea with the newlyweds and were given a tour of their house. The obligatory visit reminded Virginia how much the old class distinctions had faded—a change that was confirmed for her by the array of glossy new goods in the shops along Tottenham Court Road. She accepted socialist arguments for a fair distribution of wealth, but disliked the materialism that seemed to come with greater equality. In "Here and Now" Eleanor Pargiter and her friend Nicholas dreamed of a utopian new world; in actual practice the advent of the new world was signaled by a deluge of cheap bedroom suites and cases of cutlery. Looking around Miss Belsher's house, Virginia noted that the young people lived more comfortably than her own parents had lived at Hyde Park Gate fifty years earlier. The newlyweds enjoyed their possessions and showed them off eagerly, feeling so pleased with themselves, so certain that happiness lay in "having what everyone has." Miss Belsher, who had her husband under her thumb, intended to keep her drab maiden name at work rather than use her husband's, Standgroom. Virginia read the signs of the times ruefully, welcoming the freedom they reflected and deploring the couple's apparent indifference to anything beyond their own material interests. "They have the world they want. Bedroom suites are made for them; all Tot. Court Road is theirs; the world is to their liking." The scientific progress that had provided furnishings for their house had also produced powerful weapons—and perhaps in view of the political dangers, Miss Belsher did not intend to have children—but she and her husband were content to take the world as they found it. Virginia commented crisply that her secretary was "quite on top of the situation. Patted my shoulder. No snobbishness. No sense of class differences. And science has helped them to electric toasters."

All the political talk that summer was about Mussolini's threats against Abyssinia, which shared a boundary with the Italian colony of Somalia. He had been preparing to absorb this weaker neighbor into Italy's African empire, and since 1928 the border between the two countries had disappeared from Italian maps. Attempts to end the crisis through the League of Nations had failed. Now, with troops massing on the border, the league made a last attempt to arrange a compromise. Virginia's days were dominated by "Here and Now," which she was retyping yet again—she had finished a "first wild retyping" on July 17 and was now hoping to produce one hundred pages per week—but the background was filled with talk about the latest war threat. On August 21 she noted that the blackberries were ripe at Rodmell; there were no mushrooms to be found; Stanley Baldwin, the Conservative leader who had succeeded Ramsay MacDonald as prime minister, had returned from his vacation retreat at Aix-les-Bains to conduct an emergency meeting of the cabinet; and Mitzi had got loose, their maid having forgotten to close the door, and had spent last night in the open.

On September 4, with the league about to convene a last-ditch session on Abyssinia, she observed that the papers called this the most critical day since King George V declared war in 1914. She added in the margin of her diary that she had decided to call her novel "The Years," a title that evoked her preoccupation with time's passage in *To the Lighthouse* and *The Waves*. The day before she had been in London and had seen pro-fascist slogans chalked up on the walls: "'Dont fight for foreigners. Briton should mind her own business.' Then a circle with a symbol in it"—the flash-in-circle insignia of Mosley's British Union of Fascists. She had bought an expensive tasseled umbrella for twenty-five shillings, her first new one in years, feeling self-conscious when a man on the bus eyed it and her. In the morning it was pouring and she used the umbrella in the garden. She and Leonard stumbled on an agony in the grass: a snake eating a toad, which it had half swallowed and was sucking down very slowly. Leonard poked its tail with a stick. It seemed to her that the prey was choking its devourer—a burst of violence in slow motion that rooted in her mind. "The snake was sick of the crushed toad," she wrote, "& I dreamt of men committing suicide & cd. see the body shooting through the water." These images—Italy poised to swallow its helpless neighbor, fascist slogans, snake and toad, and a suicidal body in the water—converged. That night, listening to a shrill radio broadcast about Mussolini's refusal to negotiate, Virginia felt a tremor of fear for her country—an unexpected reaction, since she did not believe in patriotism. Next morning the papers were less melodramatic, predicting that the crisis would drag on for some time and that hostilities were not imminent. Virginia remarked on the blustery weather and the murky political climate: "Violent wind & rain; violent sun & light, & they go on talking, threatening, advancing & retreating at Geneva."

She thought of the snake and toad after attending the annual Labour Party Conference in the domed pavilion at Brighton on October 1. The climax of the conference came in a clash about whether England should be ready to back up economic sanctions by force if Mussolini invaded Abyssinia. The party leader, George Lansbury, who spoke for the old school of international socialists, nominally supported the League of Nations and its collective security system, while opposing sanctions against Italy, which he thought increased the chances of war. Leonard Woolf described him as "one of those sentimental, muddle-headed, slightly Pecksniffian good men who mean so well in theory and do so much harm in practice. He was a convinced believer in the desirability of having the best of two contradictory worlds, of undertaking the obligation under the League to resist aggression without providing the arms which would be required for the resistance." Speaking after Lansbury, his rival, Ernest Bevin, responded with a personal attack whose ruthlessness still troubled Leonard's conscience many years later. In his autobiography he wrote that Bevin had "battered the poor man to political death—Lansbury afterwards resigned the leadership—and, although I was politically entirely on the side of Bevin in this controversy, I could not help shrinking from the almost indecent cruelty with which he destroyed the slightly lachrymose, self-righteous Lansbury."

Virginia's reaction was tougher and more skeptical than Leonard's. While he focused on the issues, she looked at the event, observing not only the speakers but the dynamics of the meeting and the ways in which the atmosphere encouraged showmanship rather than reasoned argument. Lansbury's performance, which was based on the role of "the battered Christian man," moved the audience, and Virginia herself, to tears. She found it fascinating to watch, "as good as any play," but it was worse than useless in relation to the political debate, only obscuring the issues. Bevin's truculent speech was just as calculated as Lansbury's; sinking "his head in his vast shoulders till he looked like a tortoise," he denounced the squirming party leader as one of those people who "like to go hawking their consciences about," claiming some dubious moral superiority, while he, Bevin, merely recited the facts, unpleasant though they were. Virginia suspected both of these showmen of having ulterior motives. "Too much rhetoric, & what a partial view: altering the structure of society: yes, but when its altered? Do I trust Bevin to produce a good world, when he has his equal rights? Had he been born a duke—" The speakers' views, designed to manipulate others and shaped by the audience's prejudices, were necessarily partial. The right hand did not know what the left was doing, and Bevin, in spite of his rhetoric, would be a natural autocrat if he came to power. His crushing attack against Lansbury, like "a snake who's swallowed a toad," was the most dubious part of the whole spectacle, but it did not make her like the victim any better. Neither side, she observed, neither the idealists nor the pragmatists, had any thought of extending equal rights to women. At one point a woman spoke for her sex, protesting that it was time they quit doing the washing up—a frail genuine voice, refreshingly clear, like "a little reed piping, but what chance against all this weight of roast beef & beer—which she must cook?" Virginia also listened sympathetically to the dissenting voice of a radical pacifist who wanted to meet aggression with nonresistance, urging that England should set an example by handing over her own tropical colonies to an international body. She shared the pacifist's views, but being a political outsider, "uneducated and voteless," she took bitter comfort in the thought that she was not responsible for the current mess.

The noise and excitement of the meeting reverberated in her head the next day, distracting her from her work, but the interruption was worth it, she concluded, since it had provided her with new ideas about the structure of society and ways to change it. One might begin by observing mundane domestic matters, like their own relationship with Louie Everest, the cook-housekeeper at Rodmell, who had just said that she enjoyed doing for them and was sorry to see them return to London—"thats a piece of work too in its way." How could she reconcile her political instincts with her responsibilities as an artist? Leonard, with whom she discussed this while walking across the marsh, said that "politics ought to be separate from art." Of course she agreed, but that formula did not resolve her anger or change her desire to join in the fight against fascism. The Labour Party Conference had moved her to articulate her position. She had been so aroused by the lone woman's voice demanding freedom, so repelled by the aura of masculine authority, that she spent the next three days in a state of "wild excitement," dashing off a chapter of "The Next War" [ultimately *Three Guineas*]. The timeliness of her theme was apparent when, on October 3, while she was in the midst of her pacifist argument, Mussolini did in fact send his troops into Abyssinia. The League of Nations swiftly voted economic sanctions, which had no noticeable effect.

Writing to Ottoline Morrell on the eve of returning to London, Virginia described the flooded Sussex countryside, with "the marsh overflowing and gigantic storms coming over the hills" and the wet tree trunks flecked with deep brown, a turbulent beauty that contrasted with the ugly disorder in world affairs. Leonard flicked on the news and instantly she felt herself jolted out of her own imaginative world into the other, discordant one. "When even I cant sleep at night for thinking of politics, things must be in a fine mess. All our friends and neighbours talk politics, politics."

⁂

In addition to dashing off sections of the shadow anti-fascist tract, Virginia had begun planning another book, a biography of Roger Fry, which she had agreed to write after prolonged discussions with his sister, Margery. Virginia had hesitated because the sensitivities of

Fry's relations and friends would make it hard to give a fair picture of his private life, but her love of the genre—she was constantly reading lives and letters and urging her friends to write their memoirs—prevailed. She began reading and taking notes in September, having collected a great mass of letters and other documents. The biographical research, which she did mainly in the evenings, helped to ease the strain of revising *The Years*, since it allowed her to use "quite the other side of the brain," but it also increased the pressure on her to finish the novel quickly.

Virginia's sense of belonging to two incompatible worlds, in one of which she was a detached artist and in the other an angry outsider, was accompanied by abrupt swings in her judgment of *The Years*. The work compelled her at times, but she also felt increasingly restless and dissatisfied with it, sometimes experiencing both elation and gloom in a single hour or blending them in a single paragraph of her diary, as she did on October 27. She began the entry in an expansive mood, vowing not to hurry her writing, which she had reread and judged rather good. She would allow the book to mature, even if it took another year. The insistence on a leisurely pace was unusual for Virginia, who made timetables and measured her life by the pages she had written. The next sentence suggested that her mood was anything but leisurely and her imagination furiously active. "In spite of the terrific curb on my impatience—never have I held myself back so drastically—I'm enjoying this writing more fully & with less strain . . . I mean its giving me more natural pleasure than the others. But I have such a pressure of other books kicking their heels in the hall its difficult to go on, very slowly." The work stimulated her so much that she had to exert terrific self-control not to pursue every new idea; her slow progress in that mesh of pleasure grew almost painful. A few days later she remarked that her attempt to mix "fact and fiction," that is, to plan her tract before finishing *The Years*, had stalled her writing, and she regretted being unable to control the "terrible fluctuation between the 2 worlds."

This divided state was reinforced by a series of "specimen days," which is the term Virginia used for days dominated by social and professional chores, or, as Quentin Bell has said, specimens of "the distraction, worries, absurdities, that make up one's life." She generally spent her mornings writing, but her afternoons and evenings were crowded with mundane business and overshadowed by the ominous political situation. The realm of "nonbeing" continually encroached on her creative hours. Describing a "specimen of the year 1935" in her diary on November 5, she provided a frame of public events, beginning with the forthcoming wedding of the king's third son, the Duke of Gloucester. England was on the eve of a general election, she reported; there had been warnings of a fascist revolution in France, and Haile Selassie's troops were fighting the Italian invaders in Abyssinia. London basked in pleasantly mild November weather. In the afternoon of that day she visited the BBC, where she heard a man talk some twaddle about literature, and from there she went on to represent the Hogarth Press at the *Sunday Times* Book Exhibition. Then two further engagements, each with a political slant. At five-fifteen she received a visit from the Baroness Nostitz, Field Marshal Hindenburg's niece, whom Virginia had agreed to see because Ethel Sands, an old acquaintance, asked her to. An embarrassment. The baroness, who was trying to recruit young English poets to lecture in Germany, casually let drop that things were better under Hitler. Virginia recorded the remark without comment, declaring the lady a hard, impassive aristocrat, "marmoreal and monolithic and precisely like a statue in a street." The baroness was followed by an Indian who told of being brutally kicked out of a first-class railway carriage by British colonials in Bengal. After he left, a phone call came from E. M. Forster asking her to meet the French man of letters Jules Romains. A specimen of typical activities that fed her novelist's hunger for insights and inundated her with more facts and impressions than she could absorb.

She saw *Murder in the Cathedral*, T. S. Eliot's play about the martyrdom of Thomas à Becket, on November 12. The play's poetic speeches, which she had liked when she first read them, sounded thin and lifeless on the stage. Eliot presented a rarefied religious drama, and Virginia reacted with anticlerical vehemence, writing to Ethel, the usual butt of such complaints, that the world needed "sanity and substance and not the puling of green sick American eunuchs." His high-minded sentiments made her feel she had been "rolling in the ash bin; and somehow filled my mouth with the bones of a decaying cat thrown there by a workhouse drab." Nevertheless, she still loved Tom in her "spasmodic fashion." Three days later she told Ethel not to take her outburst seriously, it was just a "violent flare," though such gut reactions had their value, and the play still struck her as a series of disembodied soliloquies. She summed up her irritation in a letter of Bloomsbury gossip to her nephew Julian Bell, who had been in China since September, teaching English literature at Wuhan University. She was repelled by Eliot's tone, she wrote, "the tightness, chillness, deadness and general worship of the decay and skeleton." The reasonings about spiritual pride and sacrifice at this time of real atrocities had annoyed Leonard so much, she had almost had to carry him out of the theater, shrieking.

As the year ended Virginia was close to finishing her revision of *The Years*, but not at all certain that it was really final. Ironically, this chronicle in which time itself figured so largely had upset all her working timetables. She told herself again that there was no hurry, she was not "time's fool"; she could enjoy this final stage at her own pace. On November 27, after a series of specimen days that kept her from writing, she commented in the ironic voice of someone who is keeping her spirits up and knows it: "I cant write, yet, Heaven help me, have a feeling that I've reached the no man's land that I'm after; & can pass from outer to inner & inhabit eternity." This mirage of "eternity" would vanish when she got back to the real grind of revision. Even the present mood was subverted by the drab image of no-man's-land, suggesting not transcendence but battlefields, as if she had unconsciously drawn her vocabulary from "The Next War."

During the Christmas holidays, which the Woolfs spent at Rodmell, Virginia did and did not finish *The Years*. On December 28, revising the final pages, she asked herself whether she would ever write a long novel again, considering how hard it had been to hold the whole work in her mind for almost three years. It seemed doubtful that she would. "Nor do I even attempt to ask if its worth while." The following day, having just written the last words, she drew up a list of all she still needed to do, to condense, sharpen, and cut out repetitions, before preparing the manuscript for the printer. Still, the work had left her with an impression of "vitality, fruitfulness, energy. Never did I enjoy writing a book more, I think." The dubious sound of that last "I think" reflected her uncertainty about whether the effort was worthwhile after all. The book had less intensity than *The Waves*, she added, but it was more complete, presenting the whole of life, and it had exercised every part of her mind.

The intense effort of the last few days had given Virginia a severe headache, and outside a heavy rain had turned the meadows into mud. She ended her 1935 diary by sketching the present moment, a coda of phrases set to the beat of her inner life. "A wild wet night—floods out: rain as I go to bed: dogs barking: wind battering. Now I shall slink indoors, I think, & read some remote book."

❦

Virginia's misgivings about *The Years* intensified as she rushed to get the manuscript ready for Leonard to read before they sent it to the printer. She had spent more than a year, since November 1934, at the typewriter, a process of "perpetual compressing & re-writing always at that one book" and longed for the physical relief of writing fresh sentences again. On January 16 she lamented that she had seldom been more completely miserable than after rereading the ending. She turned for comfort to Leonard, who reminded her that she always complained when she was finishing a book, but she said no, it had never been as bad as this—it was "such feeble twaddle—such twilight gossip" and it went on at such length. She relented the next day, finding some pages that created a rich, ample fictional world, but the hopeful mood didn't last. She told her friends that the book was dull, empty, an awful bore, and in her grimmer moods cursed herself for attempting "to do all the things nature never meant me to do," but one had to take the risk, she said, or be left "to moulder in ones own dung." On March 16 she noted for her own future guidance the constant shifts in judgment that had made the last few months excruciating. She had never, since her first novel, *The Voyage Out*, suffered "such acute despair on re-reading, as this time." In her numb misery she thought of simply throwing it away, but she kept on typing and "after an hour, the line began to taughten." Later, rereading again, she thought it might be her best book. The repeated cycles of despair followed by renewed hope severely frayed her nerves; they suggested the presence of an unresolved conflict in her conception of the work, but she kept on typing.

Politics created tensions she could rarely escape because Leonard's constant Labour Party activities pervaded the background of her life. On March 7 Hitler, who had been emboldened by the failure of the League of Nations to stop Mussolini in Abyssinia, marched his troops into the demilitarized Rhineland, thus violating the Versailles peace treaty, while France and England did nothing, again revealing the impotence of the European democracies. "As you can imagine," Virginia wrote to Julian, "we are all under the shadow of Hitler at the moment." She felt that the guns had come very near their private lives; she dreamed about war constantly and seemed to hear the roar of guns behind the facade of ordinary Mondays and Tuesdays. Even Vanessa and Duncan, who were usually indifferent to matters not related to painting and the arts, began conversations by asking, "What is your opinion, Leonard, of whats-his-name?" Virginia's friends debated the use of sanctions, Leonard arguing that the danger was so great—they were on the verge of the worst catastrophe in six hundred years—that they must forget private differences and support forceful action by the League of Nations. Virginia was not persuaded, agreeing with Aldous Huxley's pacifist argument that sanctions merely intensified patriotic fervor—they had brought the Italians rallying round Mussolini—and made matters worse. She believed in seeking root causes at the local and domestic level, starting with the many social groups that existed in order to exclude people and so make it harder to resolve conflicts. It was the wrong way to live, she told Julian Bell, "to draw chalk marks round ones feet" and say to outsiders, "You can't come in."

A real outsider called on her a few days later. On the evening of March 19 a fainting girl tapped on the basement window at the Hogarth Press to ask for a drink of water. She had been walking all day, looking for work, and had eaten nothing since her morning cup of tea. The Woolfs took her into their kitchen, fed her hot soup, and sent her home to her room at Bethnal Green with a slab of tongue, two eggs, and five shillings. Poverty and unhappiness were fostered by the class system, Virginia thought, and in view of her private income and connections, she felt personally responsible. It was all the worse because the girl, who spoke educated English and was a Jew like Leonard, accepted what was offered her so humbly, asking if they could afford it. Virginia felt ashamed as well as guilty, but there was nothing she could do. (A few days later, though, she reported that Leonard was interviewing a Miss Bernice Marks, otherwise unidentified, who may well have been this young woman.) In her diary Virginia observed that such episodes, which tended to grow stylized and lose their vividness as she recorded them, called into question the very act of writing. The girl's real presence had spoken a powerful language of its own. "Some horror become visible: but in human form. And she may live 20 years. . . . What a system."

Virginia's pent-up nervous energy poured out in one of her letters to Ethel, who as usual inspired personal confessions. The grind of revision, which still filled Virginia's freshest hours, demanded an ascetic devotion that drove out other more worldly activities—she had pared down her social life by refusing visitors and invitations. Work on the manuscript had become a sacrifice, an end in itself, gobbling up everything, even her vision of the book, which had dwindled almost to nothing as she concentrated on knitting sentences together and inserting commas.

[Virginia to Ethel, March 10, 1936]
I dont really get quit of my script till dinner: work from 10 to one: then 5 to 7. if work it can be said to be: anything more

dreary cant be conceived. And the book disappears; I suspect its
bad; but what do I care, once I can write End: and never look at
it again. Forgive this egotism. Still more, forgive this dulness. I've
been seeing no one. My friends die or fall ill. Sybil Colefax is now
a widow—poor woman—still wants to come and dine. I read
only solid history or Dickens to ease my mind of commas. Love
seems a thing I've never felt or hope or faith either. Why, I ask
does one do this sort of task? and who sets it? Whats the point?
A 3 month sitting in a cellar. When the sun sinks I go owling
round to Nessa. There we tell old tales by the light of a candle.
Harold asks me to meet Lindbergh—no I cant. [Lady] Oxford
asks me to meet [Mrs. Wallis] Simpson—the new Royal harlot—
cant again. . . . Oh and politics go on all day, every day. L. is entirely submerged. I might be the charwoman of a Prime Minister.
But we will come out of the tunnel one of these days, in the sun,
on the grass—can I believe it?
      Yes inky and bitter and old
      Ink you know dries bitter like gall.

Virginia's artistic vision had disappeared, along with the book and
the sense of why she was writing it, leaving only the despotic task itself. Art and politics came together for once in the gritty image of the
tunnel, representing all the anxieties that drove her to turn sacramen-
tal ink into gall.
  On March 11 Virginia reported they had decided to have the novel
set in galleys as soon as she finished the current draft, without waiting for Leonard to read it in typescript, as he usually did. Instead, he
would read the galley proofs when they came from the printer. Quentin Bell speculates that she was afraid to hear his verdict and therefore
delayed that moment as long as possible. Leonard explained that she
wanted galley proofs, rather than the more restrictive page proofs, so
that she would feel free to make extensive further changes. But they
were also speeding up the publication process, condensing two steps
into one by setting the book in type without Leonard's preliminary
comments. They still planned to publish it in the fall, partly motivated
by the fact that Virginia's earnings during the last year had fallen below her expenses and she was eager to make up the difference. She
risked losing the two to three hundred pounds they had paid for the
typesetting if the book turned out to be worthless, but it was a relief
to have committed herself.
  She approached the end of her revisions in such a high-strung state
that Leonard insisted they spend some days at Rodmell, where she

could do the last pages in relative quiet. But in her present obsessive mood, the move made very little difference, especially since it rained much of the time and a bitter north wind rattled her windows. She stumbled to her garden lodge every morning, hardly noticing what was around her, and was often in despair about the book. Her work had become a numbing routine that left her feeling as if she lacked eyes, ears, and nose and was shut off from the ordinary world, but she was determined to persevere. On April 9, having finally sent off the last batch of manuscript to the printer, she reported that galleys of the opening chapters had already arrived and were sitting on her desk; she must now begin correcting "six hundred pages of cold proofs"— a horror. The feeling she had described to Ethel, of being trapped in a tunnel, had progressed to an awareness that she was headed for a breakdown. She would descend further into the tunnel, pay for doing things nature never intended her to do; the signs told her that a "season of depression" was just ahead, a necessary collapse: "after congestion suffocation."

It happened a day later; her nerves rebelled, bringing on a vicious headache that prevented her from writing at all. On April 14 she wrote to Ethel, who was eager to hear about her health, that she had spent days lying totally befogged on two chairs, and had risen from the chairs in order to go to bed. As for her novel, she had stuffed the proofs into a cupboard and would not look at them for at least a month. She later added that she had not yet read *The Years* through even once from beginning to end, and had forgotten what it was about. At times she was so reduced she could not read the newspaper or form letters. Perhaps that would change in the fall; for the moment she did nothing but "look at a starling in the rain."

⚜

"After congestion suffocation." Virginia had predicted the consequences of her long drudgery before the first of the headaches began. They came in succession, one following another so closely that days and weeks blurred into a continual illness. She did no original writing, not even in her diary, and struggled to correct some pages of her proofs for as long as her nerves could stand it—generally an hour or less a day. In early May, when her health seemed to be improving, the Woolfs set off on a motor tour of Devon and Cornwall, hoping that a visit to the west country, which she had loved as a child, would restore her completely. On May 11 they stopped near Dartmoor, and she wrote to Vanessa from the hotel's sitting room, where the armchairs were all inhabited by kindly old couples; a sleeping dog began to snore, which inspired a conversation between Leonard and a maiden lady about dogs in general and whether spaniels snore in particular— an eminently respectable scene, Virginia concluded, that simply demolished all one's fears about the end of civilization.

She had just read Ethel's latest autobiographical volume, *As Time Went On*, and recommended it to Vanessa, seasoning her enthusiasm with malice. The portraits of Ethel's friends were amazingly vivid, she said, "considering she writes like an old turkey cock scattering the gravel with its hind legs. . . . Showers of gravel fly, but there they are." Virginia added demurely that she would try to use the same technique when she wrote her own memoirs. She immediately refurbished these opinions in a second letter addressed to Ethel herself, converting them into elaborate praise of Ethel's spontaneity and artlessness, with only a bare hint about the old turkey cock's lack of style. Reveling in her freedom after the constraints of the preceding weeks, she used Ethel's memoir as an occasion for her own verbal acrobatics.

[Virginia to Ethel, May 11, 1936]

How you do it, God knows—I mean I can't see how its done— how face after face emerges, when there is apparently so little preparation, no humming and hawing, all so inconsecutive and unpremeditated,—all roads winding this way and that—streams running, winds intersecting,—how then do all these people stand and live in their own element with the life of their own time rushing past, as might be fish caught in a net of water: living, breathing and about to shoot on—the whole torrent pouring past, nothing frozen and final as happens with the usual skilled hack? . . . And you yourself preside—if it weren't truer to say that you encircle, like some rush of air and sun—(for you're very genial, as well as searching). . . . I'm obsessed with a desire that you should paint me: not a thing I often feel; but what a revelation it would be, painful no doubt: but like seeing the true soul, picked out from its defacing shell, its confining and twisting convolutions, by the silver sharp pin, or sword, of Ethel's genius.

Virginia respected Ethel's homely virtues as a writer, but her fanciful rhetoric carried her a step further than she would otherwise have gone. The suggestion that she wanted Ethel to draw her literary portrait was unusual, considering how intensely Virginia hated having her private life discussed in public. Having recently described Ethel's character as "Shakespearean," she embroidered on that fancy with the image of a sunny encircling presence wielding a silver pick and exuding an air of impersonality, like the spirit that pervaded Stratford. She skipped impulsively from there into the vision of her own self freed from its convoluted shell by the magic probe of "Ethel's genius"—a manic note that gave a hint of the illness still hanging over her.

The climax of the Woolfs' trip was a visit to Talland House in St. Ives, where Virginia had spent many childhood summers and which provided the setting for *To the Lighthouse*. She crept into the garden at dusk, peering into the windows and perhaps feeling haunted by the thought of seeing her own doppelgänger looking back at her.

The illness flared up again after Virginia returned to London; on May 27 a friendly lunch with Vita, who was still a romantic figure, left her in such a nervous state, so excited by her racing thoughts, that she could not sleep. The sedative she took jangled her nerves still more, and she spent the following night lying awake, looking at the bottle of chloral hydrate and fighting the temptation to swallow another dose. The episode terrified her, she told Ethel, because sleeplessness had preceded the onset of her worst mental breakdown years ago, initiating that awful, violent time "when I couldn't control myself."

The struggle to regain her balance and go on working in spite of severe headaches dominated the summer of 1936. The silence of her diary during this period—she had kept it without a break since 1917—signaled the intensity of the struggle. She broke her silence for a moment in June with three short entries, the first of which reported that she had been fighting off catastrophic illness for two months. "Never been so near the precipice to my own feeling since 1913," that is, close to a suicidal state. She reported feeling better at the moment, but the reprieve was followed by another relapse. On June 21 she wrote that she had spent "a week of intense suffering—indeed mornings of torture—& I'm not exaggerating—pain in my head—a feeling of complete despair & failure—a head inside like the nostrils after hay fever," which again was followed by some relief, but she could not depend on it—any slight shock set off the headache and depression. "My brain is like a scale: one grain pulls it down. Yesterday it balanced. Today dips." She went on correcting her proofs whenever possible, though she moved at a glacial pace. The effort of repressing her creative enthusiasm and avoiding all excitement demanded heroic self-control, she said, "like the iron clasp of a statue on a horse's reins."

Figure 19. Virginia in the upstairs sitting room at Monk's House; fireplace tiles designed by Vanessa.

Virginia's mock-heroic image of herself as a public statue suggests the ambivalence of her struggle. She was both horse and rider: the arrested thoroughbred and the commander reining herself in with an "iron clasp"—a bronze parody of fire and spirit. She began her summer holiday at Rodmell early in order to avoid the clamor of London, vowing to keep some remnant of her identity by spending an hour a day on her proofs, even if she corrected only two pages out of the six hundred. On July 20 she hinted to Ethel that she was battling something worse than illness. "If I were to tell you the history of the past 3 months—if I were ever proud of myself, it would be that I did not—well, well. I dont want to go into it." In spite of their danger, her bouts of illness had a certain fascination. While under way, they roused her with compelling terrors. "You cant think what a legacy insanity leaves behind it," she wrote—"how the spectres come out on a sleepless night." Sometimes, when the worst was past, the terrors seemed almost seductive, and she remarked that the inner voyage brought its own compensations, because "one visits such remote strange places, lying in bed."

She needed all her cunning to control the midnight specters; her writing, which was her chief defense against suicidal depression, also could bring the illness on, and this left her very little room to maneuver in. If she worked a few minutes too long, her system rebelled, and if she refrained from writing, the void opened before her. As for the pain, she had no word for it—"headache" was too tame to convey the fierceness of the attack, which was like "enraged rats gnawing the nape of my neck." All summer she fought a tense, immobile battle, inwardly racing, and outwardly inching along, almost frozen into a statue. She cursed the book and her woolly head, but kept on correcting, subdividing her time, writing for half an hour if she couldn't manage an hour; sometimes she was reduced to limiting her work periods to ten-minute intervals. The world turned very slowly; a page was longer than a chapter had once been; a bare trickle of inspiration sustained her. She was nearly extinct and yet monumental in her perseverance. Looking back later, she commented: "I wonder if anyone has ever suffered so much from a book, as I have from The Years. . . . Its like a long childbirth. . . . Every morning a headache, & forcing myself into that room in my nightgown; & lying down after a page: & always with the certainty of failure." The galleys struck her as appallingly dull and repetitive, and her work seemed like childbirth in reverse, a kind of suffocation, the snake choked by the toad it was swallowing.

She had greatly simplified her life, and when the illness subsided she enjoyed the tranquil daily routine at Monk's House. Leonard worked at his desk and tended the garden; at night he carried a lantern out among the zinnias, plucking snails, whose shells she heard him cracking. Virginia corrected a few pages of her galleys in the mornings. Afterward she took short walks, drowsed over a book, played a game of bowls, and cooked their dinner. She rarely saw any visitors. The outer world, with its conflicts, was far away, she wrote Vanessa, and "all vanities are less than the slug on the Zinnia."

In this peaceful atmosphere her anxieties subsided and her health slowly improved. At the end of August she concluded without much regret that she could not finish correcting *The Years* in time for fall publication and it would have to wait till 1937. She heard very little political news. Early in the summer, at the height of her "coma," she had resigned from the Committee of Vigilance, a group of anti-fascist intellectuals, and received so much abuse as a result that she vowed never again to sign a petition or attend a conference, adding that Leonard, with his passionate commitment to political causes, did more than enough for them both. Of course she intended to write her anti-fascist tract—the need was greater than ever. The visit of the starving young woman had reminded her that one cannot withdraw, that social disorder will track one down in one's own neighborhood. The situation in Europe had deteriorated further with the outbreak of civil war in Spain, where Franco's armies had been fighting the loyalist forces since July 16.

✣

Virginia's breakdown, measured by the period when she was too ill to write in her diary, had lasted more than six months. She began the diary again on October 30, remarking that she would not try to analyze the previous summer—it had been extraordinary, but it was safer to keep her mind on the present. Three days earlier she had visited Sybil Colefax, the fashionable hostess and collector of literary lions, with whom she had been on guardedly friendly terms for years. Lady Colefax was a society woman who valued her own social position and prestige above all else. When her devoted husband died, she went right on dining out and appearing at parties without a break, a fact that intrigued Virginia, who couldn't decide whether her behavior reflected extreme callousness or remarkable courage. Now Sybil was selling the house in Chelsea where she had entertained so lavishly and auctioning off most of its contents. Virginia arrived for her visit to find strangers wandering in the rooms and price tags on the furniture. Sybil, whose face usually reminded her of "glossy red cherries on a hard straw hat," looked pale and had chiseled grooves on either side of her nose. She was nervous and distracted, but still engrossed in social maneuvering, having been "too long exposed to artificial light to do without it." She couldn't help posing, Virginia thought, amused by Sybil's attempts to appear poetic and unworldly for her benefit, but still one had to admire her pluck in adversity. She tried to say something consoling about the gifts Sybil had given her friends, and when Sybil returned the compliment, Virginia would not hear it, insisting on the importance of Sybil's social offerings to "living people." Virginia had met Arnold Bennett, George Moore, Noel Coward, and many others in Sybil's brown dining room. The memory inspired her with affection for her hostess, even though she had often found the gatherings themselves tedious. She wanted a closer contact with Sybil, who seemed to share the impulse, but her bustling mask forbade any genuine intimacy. "My bare hand rested for a moment on her bare hand. This is sympathy, I felt: but it must not be emphasized or prolonged." The warning reflected the power of Sybil's social role, her retreat from personal contact, which Virginia emphasized by repeating the words "bare hand" twice, as if she had reached through a barrier and touched a member of some exotic species. In any case, the maid interrupted them, calling Sybil away to see someone at the door, and then Sybil's car was ready; she had errands to run before a concert and supper party and offered to drop Virginia off.

On November 1 Virginia finally sat down to read the corrected galleys of *The Years* from beginning to end. She found the book bad through and through, as she feared—every other sentence needed rewriting, and the episodic form made it seem like mere twilight gossip. She forced herself to read on in a state of "stony but convinced despair," and finally, too depressed to finish, she dropped the pile of proofs on Leonard's desk, "like a dead cat," muttering there was nothing to do now but throw it on the fire. Her mood created a dilemma for Leonard from the start. He had read all of Virginia's novels as soon as she finished them, and had always given his honest opinion, but this time he feared that anything less than complete approval would bring on a major breakdown. Virginia herself did not doubt the outcome and was resigned in advance. She took a long walk, feeling that a weight had been removed from her shoulders, which should have been a relief, except that it was accompanied by a sense of loss and dislocation. "Now I was no longer Virginia, the genius, but only a perfectly insignificant yet content—shall I call it spirit? a body? And very tired. Very old." The day passed in this strained detachment; in the afternoon several nondescript visitors came, and afterwards she went to the Sunday *Times* book show, where she chatted with old acquaintances, feeling dead the whole time. Back home she became seriously depressed as Leonard read on and on without saying anything, and she dozed off in a stupor, as if the blood had stopped flowing to her brain. Suddenly Leonard put down the proofs, having read about a third of the book, and declared it "extraordinarily good—as good as any of them," a response so different from what she expected that Virginia was reluctant to believe him. "Miracles will never cease," she wrote ironically next day as Leonard read on. Without quite doubting his sincerity, she felt perplexed and uneasy; perhaps she detected some hint of reserve in his voice.

He did not tell her the whole truth about his reaction. In his memoirs Leonard recalled reading with a growing sense of relief—*The Years* was a book most writers would have been proud to publish, but he added that it was well below the standard she had set in *The Waves* and *To the Lighthouse*. Worrying about her health, he praised the book more enthusiastically than he would have done if she had been well, though he also said that it was too long in the middle, and needed cutting. Virginia heard him, he added, with feelings of relief and exhilaration. Her diary presented this episode in a different light, indicating the charged quality of Leonard's comments and her own vacillation between pleasure and disbelief. She announced his final verdict on November 5: "The miracle is accomplished. L. put down the last sheet about 12 last night; & could not speak. He was in tears. He says it is 'a most remarkable book—he *likes* it better than The Waves.' & has not a spark of doubt that it must be published." She added that she accepted Leonard's sincerity, having seen how moved he was, but was uncertain about her own judgment. Being a born skeptic, she was suspicious of miracles, and this one was no more plausible than most. "I hardly know yet if I'm on my heels or head— so amazing is the reversal since Tuesday morning. I have never had such an experience before." Underneath it all her opinion had not changed. A few days later she wrote Julian that she thought the book was bad and not worth publishing but she would go ahead with it on Leonard's advice. "I'm so sick of it I can't judge."

She had just finished an article on "The Artist and Politics" for the Communist paper, the *Daily Worker*, declaring that artists, who usually tried to stay clear of political debates, must renounce their detachment in times of crisis such as the present. The artist's general interest in human passions and awareness of mass feelings would necessarily draw him or her into the struggle, for "the practice of art, far from making the artist out of touch with his kind, rather increases his sensibility." Artists could not ignore the voices calling them to emerge from their studios and workshops, and must become politically active to ensure their own survival and that of their art. Virginia coupled this article with telegraphic jottings in her diary about the fighting in Spain. "I am tired this morning: too much strain & racing yesterday. The Daily Worker article. Madrid not fallen. Chaos. Slaughter. War surrounding our island. Mauron over, & G. Brennan. Dine with Adrian tonight." Gerald Brenan, who had been Carrington's lover and lived in Spain for many years, had returned to England because of the civil war. Virginia also noted that she no longer cared about anyone's opinion of *The Years* so long as she was rid of it, juxtaposing the thorny book, the workers' defense of Madrid against fascist troops, and the common pattern of teas and dinners.

12 *An Inch of the Pattern:* The Years

The Memoir Club had been formed by a group of Virginia's old friends who met to hear each other's autobiographical essays and indulge in serious gossip. On November 8, 1936, Virginia wrote to Molly MacCarthy, promising to read some brief notes at the next meeting, though she protested that it was not her turn, and besides, nothing interesting had happened to her lately. Writing the memoir gave her some relief from the job of making final cuts and revisions in *The Years,* to which she reluctantly returned every morning. Her tongue-in-cheek essay on the theme "Am I a Snob?" described her attitudes toward the aristocracy and ended with a detailed account of her recent visit to Sybil Colefax. As a young woman, Virginia wrote, she had known a titled lady who picked up bloody bones from her dinner plate and fed them to the dog with such complete indifference to the guests at the table that forever after she symbolized "human nature in its uncropped, unpruned, natural state." Aristocratic drawing rooms were enlivened by the whims and eccentricities of their owners, generating an excitement that one never felt in bourgeois company. Virginia found the fabled creatures irresistible, like racehorses or rare species from the savannas, she told the Memoir Club, and if she had to choose between meeting Einstein and the Prince of Wales she would "plump for the Prince without hesitation." When she spoke these words on December 1, she had just heard the latest rumors about the former Prince of Wales, now King Edward VIII, whose willfulness and indifference to public opinion were becoming notorious.

The news that the king intended to marry the unsuitable Mrs. Simpson was making headlines everywhere except in England, where the papers had loyally imposed a blackout. Virginia heard about the crisis from Kingsley Martin, who had been asked to prepare and hold an article stating the king's side of the case. His informant spoke in strict secrecy about the "sexual difficulty" behind the king's attachment to the lady, who was just going through her second divorce. The day after the Memoir Club meeting, the bishop of Bradford publicly deplored the king's irregular churchgoing, and on December 3 the papers, following his lead, made their first discreet references to the dilemma posed by Mrs. Simpson. The story was out, and everyone was suddenly discussing the scandalous romance, which provided a diversion from depressing international bulletins. Virginia observed that "all London was gay & garrulous—not exactly gay, but excited," and she reported a variety of opinions, ranging from the grocer's young woman, who said, "She's no more royal than you or me," to more democratic observers arguing, "Hang it all—the age of Victoria is over. Let him marry whom he likes." Meanwhile, the nobs at Clive Bell's exclusive club looked glum as undertakers. For Virginia the scandal was a fascinating reflection on the English character—a family affair playing out on a national scale and crystallizing collective attitudes toward class, sex, and power. Considering the public impact of his actions, the king's motives were shockingly petty, and the political culture had reached new heights of triviality: "We are all talking 19 to the dozen," she wrote on December 7, "& it looks as if this one little insignificant man had moved a pebble wh. dislodges an avalanche. Things—empires, hierarchies—moralities—will never be the same again." By this time people were beginning to tire of the crisis, grumbling that the king kept the nation hanging in suspense "while he sits, like a naughty boy in the nursery, trying to make up his mind." The absurd spectacle crowded every other bit of news out of the papers, Virginia added—nothing about Spain, Germany, Russia—they all yielded to limelight photos of Mrs. Simpson getting out of her car and revelations about her luggage. As Keith Feiling, Neville Chamberlain's biographer, observed, "for two precious months, while the Duce's son-in-law Ciano was at Berchtesgaden, while Germany signed the anti-comintern pact with Japan and while Fascist soldiers entered Spain," the British government was solely preoccupied with this one insignificant man's desire to marry an American divorcée.

On December 10, with the abdication apparently inevitable, Virginia reported that the remaining public sympathy for the king had evaporated, yielding "to a kind of sneering contempt. 'Ought to be ashamed of himself,' the tobacconists young woman said," a comment that typified the general disillusionment. Although royalty lived in beautiful cages, as everyone knew, people still expected them to represent wild, uncropped nature. The king had punctured that myth, being merely spoiled and self-indulgent. Mary Hutchinson had heard from high-placed friends at court, she told Virginia, that he was terrified of losing Mrs. Simpson, whose ardor seemed to be cooling, and therefore his "bourgeois (her word) obsession with marriage. . . . She says all his friends think him insane. He could have gone on with Mrs. S. as mistress till they both cooled: no one objected." Far from representing feral instincts, the king was domesticated and dependent on a skirt. People felt subtly humiliated by the thought that such a snare had made him throw away his kingdom, Virginia remarked, and to her surprise, she minded it too. She quoted some of the gossip suggesting that the king's desire for a respectable union came down to the quest for a more perfect orgasm: "Apparently the King's little bourgeois demented mind sticks fast to the marriage service. Mrs. S. gives him, unlike all the other mistresses, physical relief; her time synchronizes with him." What a kingdom, Virginia concluded.

A public announcement was scheduled for that afternoon and she took the bus to Westminster, where she joined the crowd in front of the House of Commons. Scanning the faces around her, she detected crosscurrents of sadness, shame, and excitement, impressions that were heightened by the shining rows of lamps and the clear yellow-brown light round the silhouetted Houses of Parliament. Out of the crowd loomed Ottoline Morrell, looking distressed. They met another old acquaintance, Bob Trevelyan, talked a while, and strolled on, still talking, till they came to the carved facade of a public building with great lighted windows framed by white stone. From one of those windows, Ottoline said, Charles the First had stepped out to have his head cut off. For a moment they seemed to have stepped out of the present age, traveling back to an earlier time—the buildings, the lights, the red-and-silver-uniformed guards standing at attention, all belonged to an aristocratic England of the past. Virginia imagined "walking in the 17th century with one of the courtiers; & she was lamenting not the abdication of Edward . . . but the execution of Charles. Its dreadful, dreadful, she kept saying." Ottoline's thoughts reverted, indignantly, pityingly, to the present king's dilemma—certainly he was the victim of his own undeveloped character, acting as he had always done, like a "poor silly little boy—He always lost his temper. No one could ever tell him a thing he disliked."

Later, listening to the king's abdication speech, Virginia detected a note of vulnerability and along with it the marks of "a set pigheaded steely mind." The occasion itself was impressive—that "very ordinary young man" speaking from his tower at Windsor Castle, while the country came to a standstill, the streets deserted, everyone listening to him say all the correct things about the prime minister and the constitution, and then those ritualistic phrases about being unable to rule without "the help and support of the woman I love"; about having been denied the blessing enjoyed by his brother, the new king, of "a happy home with his wife and children," which was a bit cloying, but Virginia's imagination was stirred by the scale of the event—one man addressing the world.

❧

The aftereffects of Virginia's long ordeal with *The Years* had mostly worn off, and on December 30, on the verge of returning the final proofs to the printer, she felt completely free of that burden for the first time since February, her spirits springing up "like a tree shaking off a load." She would enjoy going about again and seeing people, but she reflected that work was an absolute necessity for her; she needed to plan her writing in advance and always to have two or three projects under way. At the moment she looked forward to dashing off her anti-fascist polemic, now titled *Three Guineas*, and the biography of Roger Fry, which would carry her a long way past the publication date of *The Years*. Her creative energy had revived and she could write without constant fear of falling apart. "No emptiness."

In *The Years* she had kept her attention fixed on external facts, and gradually, through hints and indirections, evoked the inner lives of her characters. By refining her objective narrative till objects themselves became charged with meaning, she had discovered how to combine "the external and the internal. I am using both, freely," she had written. "And my eye has gathered in a good many externals in its time." Each episode opens on scenes of domestic life, depicting eleven points on the calendar from 1880 to an unspecified time in the mid-1930s, slices of life with long stretches of darkness between them and no transitions, so that episodes glide past like scenes observed from a moving train as figures appear in lighted windows and then are gone. The episodes present the inconclusive saga of the Pargiter family, whose members reappear at various, seemingly random, stages of their lives, and the whole work is tied together by the strong presence of Eleanor Pargiter, whose visionary humanism forms a major theme. Her story contains parallels to Sophocles' *Antigone*, a tragedy referred to throughout the novel, in which a young woman is buried alive by a tryannical king. Eleanor's history suggests a parable of living burial and renewal, a long underground passage, and final emergence into the light.

The book is divided into three unequal parts, though without corresponding headings in the text—the prewar years 1880–1914 (episodes 1–8), the World War I period (episodes 9–10), and the "present day" (episode 11)—tracing stages in Eleanor's spiritual development. As the oldest of Colonel Pargiter's daughters, she was expected to run her father's household and take care of him when he grew old, sacrificng her life to his—a duty she performed uncomplainingly. After her father's death in 1911, when she was fifty-five, she set off across Europe, traveling to Greece, Italy, and Spain. Back in England, she continued to work for social reform, having rejected the conservative dogmas of her Victorian upbringing. Her progress toward a tolerant vision cuts across the reactionary interlude of World War I, growing stronger as the destruction increases. Reaching the present day, lucid as an old prophetess, she knows that civilization is threatened again by the spread of fascism, but nevertheless concludes that things are better now than when she was young. Considering the impoverishment of those good old days, she refuses to indulge in nostalgia and insists that she never had anything one could call a life. She has nothing now but the present moment in which she warmly reaches out to her family and friends. Her final vision of a young couple coming home at dawn to begin a new life is serenely confident, though the daily news of preparations for war seems to belie her faith in human renewal.

The novel's tone subtly adjusts as the characters come to know themselves better over the years. In the episodes set before World War I, the narrator remains relentlessly objective, reporting domestic scenes without comment, and with very limited attention to people's inner lives. This deceptively neutral style, with its parade of domestic "facts," imitates the stifling atmosphere of the patriarchal household, where strong feelings are kept under control by rigid social restraints. The Pargiters' quiet desperation is reflected by their inability to speak about their feelings or even to finish their sentences. The book avoids dramatic climaxes, observing the ordinary routines of daily life in meticulous detail, and each episode ends with a literal or metaphorical darkening, as each restored fragment of the past fades back into obscurity, submerged in the onrushing stream of time. The ending of the pivotal eighth episode, "1914," describing cousin Kitty's vision on a hilltop in northern England, seems to be an exception. She has just returned to her estate from London, and the countryside strikes her as pristine, uninhabited, a refuge from the pressures of the city, which she left the night before after presiding at an arid dinner party. As she looks at the patchwork of light and shadow before her, the hazy distant fields shimmer with a dancing wavelike motion. "Light and shadow went travelling over the hills and over the valleys. A deep murmur sang in her ears—the land itself, singing to itself, a chorus, alone. She lay there listening. She was happy, completely. Time had ceased." The scene happens on the very eve of World War I and against that background Kitty's formulaic statement that "time had ceased," which is reported in the same matter-of-fact tone as the weather, becomes darkly ironic.

This mock resolution prepares us for a deepening of the irony in the following "1917" episode where a family dinner party is interrupted by a German air raid. The dinner, given by Eleanor's cousin Maggie, is an ordinary event, but the war makes it extraordinary by breaking down old barriers and inhibitions that prevented people from speaking openly to each other. Eleanor has just met the Polish idealist Nicholas, who says we can't create a just social order, our laws and religions are flawed, "because we do not know ourselves"—a thought she has often had herself, though she never said it. The air raid siren interrupts them, and danger creates a sense of communion, though they know how absurd it is to talk about freedom while crouching in a cellar. After the danger has passed, Eleanor notices that it has had a liberating effect. "A feeling of great calm possessed her. It was as if another space of time had been issued to her, but, robbed by the presence of death of something personal, she felt—she hesitated for a word—'immune?' Was that what she meant?" The irony is pointed, for Eleanor feels released from the pettiness of merely personal motives, and at the same time she feels more in tune with herself, as if the exploding bombs in the distance had given her new vitality. Why must they go on living like "cripples in a cave," she asks, aware that the voluble Nicholas understands her and she can forget her English reserve.

The episode reveals a severe split between personal and public moralities, a conflict that oppresses Maggie's French-born husband, Renny, who is infuriated to be sitting in a cellar while outside, in the air above him, men try to kill each other; Renny remarks with intense self-disgust that he helps them to make shells. He is a passionate man, Eleanor thinks, a man who feels many things at the same time—love of country, hatred of war—and is tormented by contradictions. The whole experience of the evening—the air raid, and Nicholas's idealism and Renny's suffering—breaks open Eleanor's own protective shell and brings her a moment of fuller self-knowledge. For the first time in her life she has met a man she could have married, she thinks, coming out into the dark street—he is married to her cousin, and it is twenty years too late. She has never felt that way about anyone, never allowed herself to think such thoughts. She walks down the street reflecting that Renny and Maggie have a happy marriage, a fact that adds piquancy to her turbulent feelings. Meanwhile, the fan of a searchlight probes the night sky for German zeppelins, seeming "to take what she was feeling and to express it broadly and simply, as if another voice were speaking in another language." For a moment the moving band of light seems to merge with her inner illumination; then the light stops to probe a patch of sky and she remembers the air raid, which had temporarily slipped her mind. Her ability to forget the war so easily in spite of the air raid suggests the persistence of her own inner light.

❧

The juxtaposition of spiritual growth and political disintegration carries over into the "present day" episode. Throughout the long party at the end of *The Years* Eleanor, who is now in her seventies, ponders the apparent split between private and public spheres, while the interweaving voices of her family and friends present variations on the theme. Trying to talk about social reform, the search for liberty and justice, a new world in which people will live differently, they often lose the thread and peter out into silence. The earnestness with which they sift through the old outworn phrases, hoping for some new insight, suggests the depth of their insecurity. They refer to the fascists only indirectly, as if naming them would magically increase their power. Eleanor's nephew, North, who has recently returned home after long years as a solitary sheep farmer in Africa, is shocked by the changes in England since the war and finds the atmosphere stifling. He complains that the dominant note is materialism, people talk endlessly about money and politics, and those who share his own interests in poetry and the life of the mind have been reduced to silence. North resists the various political orthodoxies and goes on trying to think for himself. He wants to conjure up a more spontaneous way of life that flows like the pure jets of "the hard leaping fountain. . . . Not halls and reverberating megaphones; not marching in step after leaders, in herds. . . . No; to begin inwardly, and let the devil take the outer form." He is drinking a bubbly punch, and the sight of the bubbles rising in his glass suggests that freedom does not mean separation from the mass. It is possible to join the collective stream and still preserve one's unique individuality, learning to unite "the bubble and the stream . . . myself and the world together." But such an ideal is illusory, he admits, looking at the people around him, since he has lost his faith in the traditional forms of patriotism and religion, and no longer fits in anywhere.

North's sister, Peggy, a hardworking doctor who can't erase the fascist brutalities from her mind, insists that it is immoral to go on merely cultivating one's private garden. The news placards on every street corner, with their reports of killings and torture, summon decent people to act. She bristles when Eleanor remarks that Maggie and Renny have a happy marriage, which shows that people are happier and freer now than in the past. Eleanor is referring only to domestic life, but Peggy silently protests that talk about personal happiness is meaningless. The world is on the verge of disaster; they are all "only sheltering under a leaf, which will be destroyed. And then Eleanor says the world is better, because two people out of all those millions are 'happy.'" A short while later Peggy suddenly denounces her brother, North, for his petty ambitions and lack of social consciousness. She had not meant to lash out in this way. The people around her were playing the game of drawing a composite picture of a monster with a woman's head, bird's neck, tiger's body, and elephant's legs, a grotesque image that made Peggy laugh helplessly. Relaxing for a moment, she imagined a state of wholeness and freedom beyond the limits of "this fractured world." She wants to tell North about that comforting moment, but instead she finds herself scolding him, predicting that he will marry, have children and "write little books to make money." When she tries to explain her meaning, she can only repeat herself, but in a more vicious tone, insisting that he will "write one little book, and then another little book" instead of "living differently." Looming behind this are all the current arguments about art and political commitment. Peggy hears silent voices insisting that writers cannot afford the luxury of detachment; their works must have a message and be socially useful. She is drawn to such certainties, but is unable to support them in practice. The abruptness of her outburst reflects not only her dissatisfaction with North but her ambivalence about the doctrinaire mood of the time. Although she is outraged by the growing savagery, she shares her brother's distrust of political slogans and party discipline. Her angry conscience urges her to speak, but some inner resistance muffles her voice, and she ends up, like most of the Pargiters, uttering broken phrases and unfinished sentences. North is surprised and hurt by her outburst, and at the same time he senses how much they have in common. Though they are temperamental opposites, sister and brother are both trying to recover the idea of a shattered unity—North's reconciliation of self and world, Peggy's glimpse of wholeness—and for that they need the guidance of Eleanor, who instinctively ignores the battling ideologies and finds a practical middle ground.

Of all the Pargiters, Eleanor comes closest to conveying the author's point of view and the central premise of *The Years*. At one point while revising the book Virginia commented that she had pared down a thicket of details in order to keep them from obscuring the overall design. "I want to keep the individual," she wrote, "& the sense of things coming over & over again & yet changing. Thats whats so difficult: to combine the two." To combine the two, repeating the motifs while observing their constant changes, meant somehow reconciling the extremes of order and contingency. Life, Eleanor concludes, resists all our attempts to summarize or explain it, being composed of an endless series of chance events and sensations. As Virginia wrote in "Modern Fiction," impressions come from all sides in "an incessant shower of innumerable atoms." Eleanor can remember "millions of things" that mass themselves and move apart like dancing atoms but convey no coherent plan, seeming to move in random paths. Everything is in motion and passes away. And yet she perceives an idea of order, though she suspects it is merely a comforting fiction. She once owned a brush shaped like a spotted walrus, an ink-corroded object that used to lie on her desk and has now disappeared, but the self that remembers the brush and feels the keen sensation of being here "in this room, with living people," has survived. It pleases her to meditate on that persistent kernel of being or identity; she has sometimes drawn it in symbolic form as a dot with spokes radiating from it, a child's image of light. That luminous point, moving along with the world and still unmoving, enables us to interpret the pattern of our experiences. Just then she notices her old friend Nicholas, who is watching a hesitant girl at the door. Eleanor hears him say certain words in her head, and a moment later he says them out loud. He has said them before at similar moments, and that pattern of his being corresponds, she imagines, to some regularity in the outer world. "Does everything then come over again a little differently? she thought. If so, is there a pattern; a theme, recurring, like music; half remembered, half foreseen?" This sense of recurrence and change coming together, of past and future linked on some other plane, pervades the final scenes of the novel. The thought of a unifying order entices and baffles Eleanor. It "gave her extreme pleasure: that there was a pattern. But who makes it? Who thinks it? Her mind slipped. She could not finish her thought." She can't ask Nicholas to help her; her idea is too fragmentary to explain, even to a close friend, and besides, he is engaged in conversation with Sara, the poetic Pargiter cousin whom he loves but does not marry because he is a homosexual. The music strikes up for a dance, and Eleanor watches couples wheeling "slowly, intently, with serious faces, as if they were taking part in some mystic rite which gave them immunity from other feelings." They seem to be making a wordless statement in another language. The dancers' immersion in the present moment, their "immunity" from random distractions, satisfies her. A moment later Nicholas asks Sara to dance, and Eleanor reflects, as they circle away, that their laughter and love for each other reveals "another inch of the pattern."

Eleanor moves naturally from contemplating unity to solving practical problems, intuitively finding a midpoint between North's poetry and Peggy's politics. She unties the knot in her handkerchief—that is, she performs a small, disinterested act of kindness. The knot is a reminder to ask her brother, Edward, to help a gifted working-class boy, her porter's son, get into Oxford—a gesture across class lines that involves untying several knots: of egotism and social discord. Eleanor's quiet goodwill cuts across and dispels North's dark vision of crowds chanting mindless slogans. He feels that he has been "in the middle of a jungle, cutting his way towards the light; but provided only with broken sentences, single words." But Eleanor, simply appealing to Edward, who offers to see the porter's boy, exemplifies the virtue of local efforts that work without the help of loudspeakers and organized marches. The concreteness of Eleanor's act helps to relieve North's confusion, and he imagines ways to loosen the constriction within himself. "For he had had enough of thinking alone. Thinking alone tied knots in the middle of the forehead."

North's impulse to end his isolation is a small, inconclusive gain. The Pargiters' voices continue weaving their verbal tapestry, which is still absurdly misaligned, like the composite figure they drew together on folded paper. But the interplay of ideas and opinions is amplified on another plane by images that culminate in a cascade of lights and petals as the novel ends. Though all their voices are choked and tentative, the imagery steadily celebrates the inner light. The progression of images, which begins with a luminous sunset, includes Eleanor's memory of a wartime searchlight and the restoration of a flower from beneath the grime of a Victorian painting. Eleanor, whose name is a variant of the Greek word for light, explicitly connects the light with the core of her being. "Perhaps there's 'I' at the middle of it, she thought; a knot; a centre; and again she saw herself sitting at her table drawing on the blotting-paper, digging little holes from which spokes radiated." The light is blocked by her sister Milly, who has grown so fat that flesh has almost overgrown the diamond rings on her hands, but it revives in Eleanor's dream of lolling candles whose golden glow fills her with happiness. It flashes from a gleaming sixpence and is reflected by Kitty's silver evening shoes; it blossoms in the flowers heaped up on the basement tables where the Pargiters have their dinner at dawn. The atmosphere darkens again at the end when Eleanor fails to gain her brother Edward's attention—an alienating moment that chills her with a premonition of death. "For her too there would be the endless night; the endless dark. She looked ahead of her as though she saw opening in front of her a very long dark tunnel. But, thinking of the dark, something baffled her; in fact it was growing light. The blinds were white." In that light the old brothers and sisters, grouped together for a moment, look statuesque and eternal, as if carved in stone. Maggie holds out a bunch of beautifully arranged flowers and Eleanor, stepping to the window, looks down at a taxi in the brightening square.

⁂

Like Woolf's earlier novels, *The Years* subtly evokes the passing of time and the growth of the inner light, but it is less successful in its attempt to create a social panorama. Endorsing Eleanor's inner vision and her emphasis on improving one's own neighborhood, *The Years* implicitly rejects mass political action, which often involves violence. As loudspeakers distort the human voice, so party loyalties dislocate personal relations. In her own way Virginia had tried to write a political novel, but one that was free of polemical content, which was probably a contradiction in terms. Focusing mainly on the politics of family life, she nevertheless aimed to evoke the ideological struggles of the day. Proper aesthetic distance, she believed, would protect her against her own suffocating anger, and to a certain extent it did, but she could only make it work by minimizing the ferocity of political hatreds. In one of the novel's few explicitly political statements Eleanor angrily tears up a picture of a fat, gesticulating dictator—clearly meant to be Mussolini—and flings the paper on the floor, denouncing him as a "damned . . . bully." Strong language, coming from this very private woman. The "damn" startles her niece, Peggy, but it is merely a whisper in comparison to Virginia's actual rage against the Nazi baboons who murdered von Schleicher or the pig-factory magnates of the London Library. The narrator's refusal to name the dictator is a typical gesture of avoidance. The same tamping down happens with Peggy's outburst against North and his "little books," which Virginia felt so keenly while she was writing it that her cheeks burned and her hands trembled. But there is no voice to project those turbulent feelings in the published scene. Peggy is unable to say what she means, and can only fall back on her lame phrases about living differently.

Guarding against preaching of any kind, Virginia set limits in *The Years* that not only filtered out the darker realities but also prevented her from elaborating her own humanist position. Her charcters find it painful to express any faith or put their convictions into words, as if lies have defiled language itself and shamed them into silence. On their way to the final party, Eleanor and Peggy pass a monument to Edith Cavell, a World War I nurse, who was executed by the Germans for helping Allied prisoners of war escape, an excessively harsh sentence that made her a cause célèbre in England. Peggy, whose brother died in the trenches, bitterly says the statue reminds her of "an advertisement for sanitary towels." But Eleanor reads out the sentence cut in the stone pedestal, remarking that to her it has always seemed "the only fine thing that was said in the war." Cavell's last words, which never actually appear in Woolf's text, are an appeal for Christian forbearance: "Patriotism is not enough. I must have no hatred or bitterness for anyone." The sentence sums up one of the novel's central pacifist themes, but the narrator leaves it to her readers to supply the words from memory if they wish. All persuasion, no matter how enlightened, seems futile now, for it only adds to the din of political argument, and the only reasonable course is to keep silent.

The novel's references to the persecution of Jews are oblique in a different way. Eleanor's eccentric niece, Sara, lives in a poor neighborhood in a run-down house, where she shares her bath with another tenant, a Jew who leaves rings of grease and black hairs round the tub. London, Sara warns North, is a wasteland, a polluted "city of dead fish," its streets filled with crowds of wage slaves who spend their lives running the soulless machine. The Jew in her bath, she says, would drive her to become a member of that conspiracy, if she did not have a shining talisman in the form of a letter to a newspaper editor who knew her father at Oxford and will presumably hire her to write for him. Although her little parable seems anti-Semitic, Sara's whimsical, mocking tone makes it something else: an abridged satire. (The Jew is a workingman "in the tallow trade" and hardly fits the racist stereotypes.) Sara's flights of fancy reflect her refusal to take bigotry seriously; she neutralizes the poison by treating it with her own odd humor. Once again, though, the episode understates the power of racial hatred, whose virulence Virginia had seen for herself during her trip through Germany.

Her toning down of *The Years* in order to exclude polemical notes is illustrated by her final cuts in the book's middle section, which Leonard thought too long. A deleted "1921" episode, set in a rather ugly postwar England, reveals a side of Eleanor's character that is darker and more misanthropic than anything in the published version. The end of the episode derives from Virginia's vision of destruction the night after Carrington's suicide, when she walked with Leonard along a blue street lined with demolition scaffolds and "saw all the violence & unreason crossing in the air: ourselves small; a tumult outside." As Grace Radin has pointed out, the jagged demolition site against the urban sky was one of the "seminal images" that inspired Woolf to write this novel. In the deleted "1921" episode Eleanor walks through central London after dining alone in a restaurant where the dullness and rapacity of the other diners made her recoil in disgust: "What apes and cats we are." Looking into brightly lit shop windows she feels threatened by the nihilistic pulse of the street and sees the city as a jungle; young men with "the faces of beasts" swagger past, singing a crude song and force her off the pavement. Walking on, she passes a block where a big shop is being pulled down and sees "a line of scaffolding zigzagg[ing] across the sky"—a jagged image prefiguring the lightning-bolt emblem of Mosley's British Union of Fascists. In the "Present Day" episode North will see the (unnamed) flash-in-circle chalked on a building. Eleanor in "1921" regards the irregular scaffolding as a sign of "something violent and crazy in the whole world tonight. It was tumbling and falling, pitching forward to disaster. The crazy lines of the scaffolding, the jagged outline of the broken wall, the bestial shouts of the young men, made her feel that there was no order, no purpose in the world, but all was tumbling to ruin." This is not the sane, reflective Eleanor we meet elsewhere but a depressed woman who suffers black moods and angers, who is revolted by the strangers around her, and sometimes feels, as Virginia did, an intense loathing for the whole human race. By deleting the "1921" episode, Virginia avoided undercutting the later account of Eleanor's enlightened old age, but she did so by reducing the complexity of the portrait, and therefore the resonance of the final episode.

Ironically, the silence that blankets *The Years*—all these refusals to name the totalitarians, all these attempts to defuse the evil by laughing at it or ignoring it, all these diversions of anger—constitutes a violence that Virginia inflicted on herself. Cutting out the "1921" episode distorted the book's outlines and was an act of imaginative self-mutilation, which she later regretted. Like the other omissions, it reflects her attempt to split herself into separate artistic and political halves, the same painfully artificial division that nearly prevented her from finishing the novel.

✢

Her anxieties had subsided, but she knew that the publication of *The Years* on March 15, 1937, would revive all her doubts about the book; she expected bad reviews, which would be immensely depressing. The best defense was to immerse herself in her work, and on January 28 she began writing her anti-war book, *Three Guineas*, noting that at least for the moment the labor of creation eclipsed all other interests. Perhaps the excitement of being involved again in that "happy tumultuous dream" would carry her over the period of hostile criticism when her novel appeared. In the meantime she was extremely busy, since Margaret West, the Hogarth Press's manager for four years, had died suddenly of influenza and pneumonia. Leonard had taken over the job of running the office, conferring with authors and correcting proofs, while they looked for a new manager. Virginia helped with all these duties while the press was in upheaval.

Passing Miss West's empty office, she reproached herself for not having gone in more often when she had the chance, not having taken a personal interest in the lively Miss West, who had worked with cheerful efficiency "in the basement room where she sat surrounded with neat papers; a spotted horse; a carved wooden flower, & a piece of green linoleum." Virginia's regret about her own aloofness merged with a more general distress, for Miss West's death had brought to the surface "a viper's nest of malodorous feelings." For many years she had lived with her elderly lover, a Miss Howlett. But Miss West's assistant at the press was also in love with her. The two rivals tried to share the responsibilities of caring for their sick friend, but they were so jealous that they could not cooperate, and they bungled the job— a fascinating display of sordid attitudes. Virginia thought they had in fact "killed her with their wild idiocy." She detected the shadow of that deadly triangle in the bad feelings at the funeral, which was a grim charade in rain and fog, with a small group of Miss West's friends standing in dispirited silence during the hymn—about "saints receiving their due; alleluia," Virginia commented—while the only person singing was the undertaker's man. The coffin slid away then, and Miss Howlett, an old crone with knotted hands, stiffly accepted condolences from the other mourners. The submerged bitterness of the gathering seemed to obliterate the genial image of Miss West. Virginia, who hated funerals, complained that the last rites made no more impression than if "she had been a kitten or a puppy." A few days later the bereaved assistant came crying to Virginia that Miss Howlett had accused her of killing her friend, and shortly afterwards she quit her job at the press.

These events were entwined with the news that Julian Bell, who had become involved in a messy love affair in China and longed for straightforward political action, had decided to resign his teaching job and go to fight for the loyalist cause in Spain. Most disturbingly, he planned to sail directly from Marseilles to Spain without returning to England. Knowing his fascination with danger, Vanessa wrote imploring him to come home and consult his friends first, and the impulsive, good-natured Julian agreed to do so. Vanessa was plunged into gloom and gripped by dire forebodings. Virginia felt the shadow hanging over her sister and had her own misgivings. "Nessa was in one of her entirely submerged moods," she wrote. "Always that extraordinary depth of despair. But I must fight, thats my instinct." She discussed the question of political responsibility with the self-absorbed young Stephen Spender, who had just accepted an invitation to broadcast in Spain. Spender thought that Julian was right— they must stop fascism before it spread to France and England. He added that the Communist Party, which he had joined that very day, "wanted him to be killed, in order that there might be another Byron"—a remark that interested Virginia, since she had just been speculating about the "psychology of vanity."

Throughout February, as the publication of *The Years* drew nearer and her fear of a public drubbing increased, she felt "like the man who had to keep dancing on hot bricks." She worked on *Three Guineas*, struggling to keep up her morale, boasting wishfully that the critics could not touch her, her hide was as thick as a rhinoceros's. On February 20, when she stood in front of a pile of review copies ready for mailing, the truth shaped up very differently. She could just hear the critics whooping with joy as they attacked her work; they would call it "the long drawn twaddle of a prim prudish bourgeois mind." She imagined, even more bitterly, that her friends would greet the book with awkward silence. She expected the worst, and writing it down in her diary made the prospect seem a little more bearable, but her relative calm was over. She hoped to conquer her anxiety by falling back on her "philosophic revelation" of 1932, when she had vowed to resist the seductions of fame and cultivate anonymity. She would shrug off the critics' "whistlings & catcalls," refusing even to defend herself, remembering "how little they matter in the sum! how little they count with other people—how little the goodness or badness of my books affects the world." So she tried to practice humility; she told herself she was immune to sneers, but her nerves refused to obey her. On March 1 she wrote Ethel complaining that her new book was so bad that if Leonard had not prevented her, she would have tossed it in the wastebasket where it belonged. Besides, she loathed publishing and being "hooked and hauled to the surface when my natural dwelling is in the dark at the depths." She launched into a rhapsodic vision of Ethel, whose indomitable spirit reminded her of a majestic oceangoing ship attended by dolphins. The hyperbole was a safety valve, providing some relief as Virginia screwed up her courage to cope with the imminent public exposure.

In her diary that day she examined her nervous state, probably aggravated by the onset of menopause, with almost clinical precision. She felt chilled and isolated. Her sensations were vivid and extremely unpleasant: "A physical feeling as if I were drumming slightly in the veins: very cold: impotent: & terrified. As if I were exposed on a high ledge in full light. Very lonely. . . . No atmosphere round me. No words. Very apprehensive. As if something cold & horrible—a roar of laughter at my expense were about to happen. And I am powerless to ward it off. . . . It affects the thighs chiefly." Once, looking into her own eyes in the mirror, she recognized what she saw there as the terror of a rabbit in the road dazzled by headlights. She probed further, observing that her being was divided. On the surface she was aquiver with anxiety, as if dancing on hot bricks. But there was a detached observer inside her, an uncanny self lurking in some deep pool. "For I can burrow under & look at myself displayed in this ridiculous way & feel complete submarine calm: a kind of calm moreover which is strong eno' to lift the entire load." It was a calm she could not command at will, however, and would not invoke lightly if she could.

At night, when the funk was on her, she fell into the grip of a "cold madness," which alternated with periods of merely ordinary furor. "I'm going to be beaten, I'm going to be laughed at, I'm going to be held up to scorn & ridicule," she predicted with a hint of self-parody. She could see it was going to be bad, but not really as bad as all that. At the same time she noticed the strange fluctuations of her health, and on March 7 she drew a fever chart, reporting that her temperature had hovered around 103 and 104 for the past few days, though it was now back to normal. This was the "fatal week" of publication, which would test her severely, but she had several lines of defense: she could think about her next book, her economic independence, and her very full private life, which was "unthrowable." As for *The Years*, she had her own standard—that would neutralize the world's criticism. "It's going to be pretty bad, I'm certain . . . but the point is that I myself know why its a failure & that its failure is deliberate." Later she explained to Stephen Spender that she had wished to give a broad social panorama, turning her characters' "faces toward society," and had therefore neglected to flesh out the individual portraits sufficiently. She wanted it all to coalesce at the end into "one vast many-sided group," a collective figure that transcended any single life, suggesting the possible "recurrence of some pattern; of which of course we actors are ignorant." In doing this she was creating a more comprehensive version of the six-sided figure formed by her characters in *The Waves*. The effort failed, of course, but she had expressed her own point of view; she had exposed social evils while refusing to repeat the predictable calls to battle. As a woman, fighting was alien to her, she told Spender, and "[violent] action generally is unreal. Its the thing we do in the dark that is more real." Which clarifies what she meant by calling *The Years* a "deliberate" failure. Novel-writing, she acknowledged, is not an isolated act that can be cordoned off from the give-and-take of public events. She chose not to say anything that would add to the general divisiveness, not to use political mayhem as an artistic subject. These scruples required her to tone down conflicts and eliminate the darker vision of the "1921" episode, setting aside for the present her aim to unite "the different strata of being."

⚘

There is no end to the tricks publicity and public opinion can play on one. The first reviews were quite good and the ones that followed were enthusiastic, praising her lyricism, her domestic scenes, her evocation of time, her strangeness. They seemed to vie with each other in admiring the beauty of her writing—which was delightful, of course, but it was disconcerting too to find herself appearing in such a different light than she expected. On March 19 she wrote in her diary that the papers "say almost universally that *The Years* is a masterpiece. . . . Now this is one of the strangest of my experiences. . . . If somebody had told me I shd. write this, even a week ago, let alone 6 months ago, I shd. have given a jump like a shot hare."

A review by Basil de Selincourt pleased her particularly. Unlike the anonymous reviewer in the *Times Literary Supplement*, who had described *The Years* as a mere "series of exquisite impressions," de Selincourt had seen that it was a "constructive" book, addressing serious social issues. He had picked out two key passages near the end, one about Nicholas's ideal of social progress (he never manages to communicate it) and the other about the caretaker's children who sing raucously for the party guests (their accents make the words of the song incomprehensible)—complementary visions, as de Selincourt suggested, of an unimaginable future. So the book would be taken seriously, Virginia concluded, and its meaning debated. Her strategy of keeping the artistic and polemical voices completely separate would work, with *The Years* stimulating public interest so that *Three Guineas*, coming closely after it, might find a receptive audience.

The favorable reviews did not inspire Virginia with confidence, however. "No one has yet seen the point," she remarked. She was sure Ethel would not like the book and advised her not to bother reading it; she could get the gist if she wished from the "Present Day" episode and even that was of dubious value: "Its all very bad, but well meant—morally." The assumed indifference did not protect her from the shock of an unfavorable review by the poet Edwin Muir, who found *The Years* disappointing after the imaginative richness of *The Waves*. Muir wrote that the narrative does not draw a line connecting the various stages of the characters' lives; they don't develop, and so they "do not become real, they only become old. One has the feeling that Mrs. Woolf has almost left them out." There are some brilliant scenes, he added, but since the characters are flat, the book is dominated by the pattern Woolf has stretched over them, and the pattern seems "cold and artificial and mainly external."

This was the kind of attack she had expected, and it instantly drowned the approving voices and put out the lights. "EM says The Years is dead & disappointing. . . . So I'm found out & that odious rice pudding of a book is what I thought it—a dank failure. No life in it. Much inferior to the bitter truth & intense originality of Miss Compton Burnett." Muir had conceded that the book displayed occasional brilliance, but Virginia knew it was a pudding through and through. The poisonous thought woke her at four in the morning and clouded the following day. Her spirits revived in the evening with the help of another favorable review, and she decided it was healthy to meet some resistance after all the lulling praise. In fact, she now felt invigorated and more carefree *because* she had been abused by Muir, whose criticism made her brim with new ideas. She declared that "the delight of being exploded is quite real. One feels braced for some reason; amused; roused; combative; more than by praise. . . . I feel once more immune, set on my own feet, a fighter." At the same time Maynard Keynes, whose opinion she respected, said he thought *The Years* was her best book, more moving and tender than its predecessors. She was intrigued by the incongruity of these two opinions—apparently *The Years* was both her most human book and her most inhuman one. Her ideas had been turned on their heads, and the reversal could be reversed, and then reversed again—an absurd discovery that illustrated the ironic pleasures of "being exploded." In a more sober mood, as if that part of her mind was independent of her unruly ego, she examined her novel with calm impartiality, explaining to Stephen Spender that she had tried to present too broad a panorama, "muted down the characters too much in order to . . . keep their faces towards society; and altogether muffed the proportions."

Still, the completion of her work, together with the unexpected applause, put her into an optimistic frame of mind. She woke in the small hours of the morning on April 9 with the thought that she felt completely content, and her happiness was not just a passing fancy but rather her reward for putting up such a fierce fight to finish *The Years*. The awareness of having won the fight inspired her. "I lay awake so calm, so content, as if I'd stepped off the whirling world into a deep blue quiet space, & there open eyed existed beyond harm; armed against all that can happen." She had had such serene moments, which she had never known before in her life, several times since the previous summer, when she would write three sentences and crawl back into bed. The feeling had surprised her in the midst of her "worst depression, as if I stepped out, throwing aside a cloak, lying in bed, looking at the stars, those nights at Monks House." She focused on the singularity of the experience, describing it as "the worst summer of my life, but at the same time the most illuminating."

The final irony was that *The Years* earned her a lot of money. It sold well in England from the start, and on June 1 she noted that it was doing even better in New York, and was now the number one bestseller in America, having already sold far more copies than any of her previous books. Perhaps readers were longing for a humane voice. *The Years* remained at or near the top of the list throughout the summer and continued there into the fall, rivaling the year's leader, *Gone with the Wind*, and outselling Steinbeck's *Of Mice and Men*.

13 Antigone's Daughters

Virginia's pleasure in the success of *The Years* was only slightly damped by the thought that her present happiness was probably as illusory as her past despair. She was still breathless after the long struggle, and wanted the quiet of Rodmell, where she and Leonard went for ten days at Easter. On the morning of March 27, 1937, she received a phone call from a *New York Times* reporter, asking for an interview—just the sort of attention she most wanted to avoid, though she said he could look at the outside of their house in Tavistock Square. She returned to her log fire—it was a cold, blustery day—picturing the downs with their patches of snow lit by shafts of sunlight and shrouded by sudden "octopus pouring" storms that turned the day inky black. She could see the distant rounded slopes of the downs from her terrace, and enjoyed them in every kind of weather; the vista framed by her garden and the old churchyard and steeple next door enclosed more beauty, she said, than could be absorbed by one pair of eyes—"enough to float a whole population in happiness, if only they wd. look." That afternoon a black Daimler drew up in front of the house, and shortly afterward a dapper man in tweeds appeared in her garden, looking around and jotting in a green notebook. She found herself ducking her head so as not to be seen through the window, while Leonard, having ignored the stranger for a while, finally told him "no Mrs. W [doesn't] want that kind of publicity," and escorted him back to his car. A trivial incident, but she recoiled in disgust, feeling that a bug had walked over her skin and wanting to crush it, angry that she was not safe from prurient eyes even in her own house. She scrawled some rough lines about the trespassing reporter, alias "John Bug," describing him as an unwanted guest sitting in her garden, taking up space and air, asking "to be seen," a squirming, thick-lipped egotist with a doughy face and "a hole for a mouth." She devoted forty-one lines to this blubber-lipped specimen, this "John Bug; James Bug Bug Bug Bug," who reminded her of a glistening semi-transparent insect, "as if while he talked he sipped blood," his pale body growing engorged with a blue-black fluid, one of those noxious creeping things one finds crushed on some lodging house wall.

The stranger had asked "to be seen," but of course he came to spy her out with his insect eyes, for being "seen" was only an excuse for seeing, and the thought of those prying eyes severely jangled Virginia's nerves, arousing an anger out of all proportion to the actual offense but corresponding to some violence of her own, a shadow of the previous year's chaotic state.

The incident brought on a severe headache, which gradually wore off the next day; her optimism returned, but she felt wary, and recalled some lines from Wordsworth's "Elegiac Stanzas," written after a friend's death, in which the poet considered former pleasures and found them illusory: "Such happiness wherever it is known is to be pitied for tis surely blind." But the warning did not apply to her, she protested—she had earned her happiness the previous summer, when she had looked into the void and kept her hold on reality. She permitted herself to savor that achievement, ignoring her own warnings in *Three Guineas*, which she was immersed in writing at the moment, her angry and ironic indictments against dictators and patriarchs who were preparing for war. The writing itself gave her intense pleasure, allowing her to observe the growing power of the infantile bullies, without being paralyzed by it.

She had another source of anxiety. Julian had come home, ostensibly to sort out his future plans, but in fact, Virginia soon realized, merely to act on them; his mind was made up—one way or another he intended to go to Spain. The only question was how he could get Vanessa to agree to his plans, for she grew distraught at the very idea, and he had promised not to do anything without her consent.

He was a disheveled young Apollo, with holes in his clothes, unruly hair, and a disarming smile. Tall, and physically imposing, he still seemed at times to be an overgrown child, a child playing at poetry and politics, enjoying the excitement of a good argument and always eager to sharpen his wits on any new problem. Very careless about danger—which showed in his slapdash way of driving a car and his eagerness to fight the toughs who tried to break up left-wing demonstrations. David Garnett, who had been part of the Bell household during World War I, remarked that Julian had grown up without fear or self-consciousness—"was not punished as a child, but reasoned with," and even at the age of twenty-nine his face often wore "the lovely sulky look of a half tame creature." He was attractive to women and had had a series of love affairs, none longer than a year or two. His departure from China had been speeded by the fact that he was caught making love to his department head's wife. Back home, Julian felt oppressed by the insularity of England and of his own ingrown family circle; he needed to go where the fighting was, to test the reality of danger. Virginia observed that he had matured during his eighteen months in China; the taut lines around his eyes and mouth reflected self-control and determination; also a shade of bitterness, "as if he had been thinking in solitude. . . . Something to me tragic in the sadness now." Of course there were constant reminders of the charming, impulsive Julian she had always known.

Hoping that her friends could persuade him that he would be most useful taking a political job in England, Virginia invited Julian to meet Stephen Spender and Kingsley Martin. Spender's lover had enlisted in the International Brigade in Spain and been thoroughly disillusioned; Martin was an expert on military affairs. Both of them would introduce some realism about the war, she thought, and puncture some of Julian's illusions about loyalist heroism on the battlefield. The political discussion at dinner on April 14 began with a general agreement among the men that pacifism was no longer an option for any responsible person. Surprised that the talk had taken this turn, Virginia silently reaffirmed her own vow never in any way to aid or abet the warmakers, but she said nothing. Having dismissed pacifism, her guests went on to invoke Kingsley Martin's military expertise with talk about hand grenades, bombs, and tanks, deploying military jargon with the zest of amateur tacticians. Julian's pugnacious attitude impressed her; she found his hard-line arguments, peppered with hooting laughter, rather uncouth, "yet honest, yet undisciplined, yet keeping something up his sleeve." He had thought through his political position while in China and had written two long essays arguing that the history of his own generation was essentially tragic since they were forced to abandon humane values "and follow what is evil: violence, compulsion, cruelty. We must do this because this is the rational choice of the lesser evil, because only by doing so can we hope to avoid complete extinguishing disaster." The values represented by the dubious father figures, Clive Bell and Duncan Grant, who had been conscientious objectors in World War I, were impractical and probably obsolete. "At this moment to be anti-war means to submit to fascism," a fact that made most political discussions seem silly and self-indulgent. Seen in the light of hindsight, Julian's essay on "War and Peace: A Letter to E. M. Forster," shows a grasp of basic realities that eluded most of his contemporaries. He argued that it was pointless trying to placate the Nazis, since Hitler's signature on a treaty had no more value than Al Capone's; concessions only stimulated the dictator's rapacious appetite. Furthermore, the anti-fascist coalition was extremely shaky; the Marxist members were zealots and true believers who longed to abase themselves "before the proletarian saviour." Indispensable as wartime allies, they were "mainly evil" in practice, in spite of being "mainly right" in their interpretation of history. In order to resist the insidious appeal of fanaticism, it was necessary, he said, to rely on the integrity of the fighting soldier or military leader, "whose courage may deliver us from fear, and good sense from hate and enthusiasm." Paradoxically, the military outlook, with its realism and distrust of ideological purity, offered the best defense of the endangered humanist values and artistic life. Unlike the professional politicians, real fighting men knew too much about war to be blinded by hate and enthusiasm.

Having convinced himself that his only choice was between fighting and "being tortured in a concentration camp," Julian concluded that he would much rather "finish off with a decent fight." The meeting with Spender and Martin had merely confirmed him in his determination to go to Spain. Action and excitement were as essential to his peace of mind, he said, as the freedom to paint was to Vanessa. She reluctantly agreed to a compromise: he would go as a noncombatant ambulance driver, which was quite safe; the relief organization, Spanish Medical Aid, had already sent out several groups of volunteers and there had been no casualties, he assured her—only one man lightly wounded. The information did little to alleviate her fears. She had always believed in personal freedom and had to accept Julian's choice, but she was certain that he would be killed. Consenting and grieving, she clung to him that spring while he studied Spanish and first aid, and learned to drive heavy vehicles. The coming separation brought them closer than they had ever been.

On June 5 the Woolfs dined with Clive and Vanessa to see Julian off. Virginia, who was feeling guilty for having casually rejected one of his essays, asked him to write something for the Hogarth Press while in Spain. He said he would, talking very fast as usual and with sudden stops and starts. Later he sat in the car, which wouldn't start, frowning and radiating vitality, in his shirtsleeves; suddenly the car jerked into motion and he called out, "Goodbye until this time next year." The unspoken feeling behind this good-bye, Virginia noted, was that it might be the last. She shared Vanessa's premonition that he would be killed, but unlike her sister, she was "determined not to think about the risks. . . . I had a couchant unexpressed certainty, from Thoby's death, I think; a legacy of pessimism, which I have decided never to analyze."

✿

Writing *Three Guineas*, Virginia remarked, was like being suspended in a "magic bubble" that protected her from external shocks. She was particularly aware of this when she saw Vanessa alone in her studio and observed the awkward contrast between her own hopeful mood and her sister's depressed spirits. The two of them tiptoed round the subject of Spain, which hung in the air and made speech and silence equally distressing. Finally Vanessa began to talk politics, and Virginia was disturbed again by the swamp of "immeasurable despair just on tother side of the grass plot on wh we walk—on wh I'm walking with such energy & delight at the moment. The reaction from last years 9 months gloom & despair I suppose."

Her happiness was blind, no doubt. Sometimes, when she was tired or distracted, she would become violently aware of "the pale disillusioned world" outside her magic bubble and think of Julian near Madrid. Thoughts of Spain and Vanessa's fatalism threatened to unhinge her work, but she could still ignore them. Her instinct, she had said, was not to give in, but to fight. As usual she had a hectic social schedule—so many visitors that on July 7 she reached her limit and so missed a cocktail party for Matisse, whose reputation as a prime bore almost equaled his fame as a painter. She enjoyed some pleasant interludes at Rodmell, including a rare long weekend without any intrusions from the outer world, just the homely routines of village life. "Not a voice, not a telephone," she marveled. "Only the owl calling; perhaps a clap of thunder, the horses going down to the Brooks, & Mr. Botten calling with the milk in the morning." The heat shimmered in a white cloud above the hills, and hay in the meadows stood high enough to cover her as she lay beside the river.

Julian wrote Vanessa from Spain, sounding a little breathless but in excellent spirits and eager to witness real battles. He had spent his first few days waiting to be assigned to a hospital, and in the meantime had driven for long hours on bad roads, picking up supplies and wounded men. In comparison to the other drivers, most of whom were "wreckers," he was a model of responsibility, he said, careful to keep his vehicle oiled and in good running order, though he had once braked too fiercely and broken a passenger's nose against the windshield. Madrid gave a surreal impression of normality in spite of the closeness of the fighting—one could take the subway to the front. "It's utterly impossible to give the full fantastic effect of it all. But I find it perpetually entertaining and very satisfactory."

Virginia wrote in her diary on July 19 about the death of Janet Case, who had taught her Greek when she was an adolescent girl. She had been in love with this austere woman who made her work so hard at Greek grammar and exhibited such a passion for Aeschylus and Euripides. Virginia remembered going hot and cold before her lessons, and later, when she was recovering from a mental breakdown, having Janet come to stay with her while Leonard was away. They had lost touch in recent years, but in April Virginia had learned that her old teacher was dying of cancer, and visited her in the New Forest, where she shared a sunny thatched cottage with her sister, Euphemia, known as Emphie. In contrast to Janet's dignity and reserve, Emphie's manner was a little scatterbrained and cheerfully voluble. Entertaining Virginia while Janet dozed in the next room, she let fall a few tears and unself-consciously confided her sorrow. It was such a bore, she said—they had planned to enjoy old age together, and this illness came just when they were ready to begin a new phase. "So many things we wanted to do . . . to go to Holland & look at birds." Even so, she did not radiate any gloom, Virginia noted, still retaining some of her "natural gaiety." Leaning an elbow on the table, her eyes fixed on something beyond the immediate scene, Emphie talked about her faith that death was not the end. "Whats 70 years? So short—so short—Whats it all for I ask if it ends now? Oh no, we go on—I'm convinced of that. It cdn't be possible otherwise." Her sister, though, did not believe as she did, and never went to church. Janet was too weak to talk for long, but she told Virginia that she had read one of Gerald Heard's books and shared his belief in "some sort of life in common, not as individuals. Some mystic survival. The young wanting it." She was firm about rejecting conventional religion and the hope of personal immortality.

Shortly before Janet's death Virginia agreed to write her obituary because it would please Emphie, although she felt it was a meaningless gesture. Janet had composed her own funeral service, writing a few words about gentleness and faith on a page, with a blank where the day could be filled in; she wanted nothing said aloud, but asked that an adagio from Beethoven be played for the mourners. There was "something fitting & complete about the memory of her, thus consummated," Virginia said, which made any other memorial seem redundant. She thought again about the two sisters and how the harumscarum Emphie had provided some emotional ground and foil for the classicist Janet, who was the "steadfast contemplative [sister], anchored in some private faith wh. didn't correspond with the worlds." And Janet was always shy about saying what she felt; her letters were cool and matter-of-fact, except that the last one began, "My beloved Virginia." But none of this did her justice, or gave an adequate idea of "how great a visionary part she has played in my life." The vision had been transformed by long absence, though, becoming "a part of the fictitious, not of the real life."

Virginia's reflections on Janet's death merged easily with other subjects in her diary—the latest reactions from readers of *The Years*, a visit to her mother-in-law—and she ended with an account of a Rodmell Labour Party meeting at her house, where the members were harangued by a guest from the village, a "shell-shock Major . . . who talks to mice & holds toads in his hand." The major surprised the company with a distracted tirade about "force & religion, which is heredity . . . its all a question of thinking isnt it, & you cant talk to a Spaniard, but you can to a Mahommedan, & thats what I feel, religion's at the back of it"—such a rigmarole that Virginia had to fix her eyes on a lighted cigarette end in order to keep from howling.

This vision of inanity was the last relatively lighthearted note in her diary for some time to come. On the next day, July 20, she got a message that Julian had been wounded in an air raid at Brunete and died in a Madrid hospital a few hours later.

※

Vanessa lay in bed, red-eyed and dough-faced, contorted with grief. Virginia came that first night and sat with her and came the next day and the day after, wrote notes canceling her appointments, explaining to her friends that Nessa liked to have her, so she was with her as much as possible; she haunted the studio at Fitzroy Street. She was the only person, aside from Duncan and the children, who could comfort Vanessa by her silent presence and could speak comforting words about their shared past, their intimacy. She invoked Julian without piety or self-consciousness, talking on simply to connect Vanessa to something outside her, not hindering or denying her grief, leaving her free. Later Vanessa remembered "lying in an unreal state and hearing [Virginia's] voice going on and on keeping life together as it seemed when otherwise it would have stopped."

The violence of Vanessa's grief blotted out everything else, renewing Virginia's oldest feelings of solidarity with her sister. She had privately criticized Vanessa's overprotective attitude toward her children, and heartily envied her for having them, but now she could only remember her suffering. When Vanessa recovered enough to travel, they drove her to Charleston and Virginia moved to Monk's House, from which she continued her attendance, coming over almost daily, and sending ardent letters when she could not come. She was doing what she had never done, nursing the formidable sister who had provided her with emotional ballast since childhood and protected her after their mother died—a role reversal that distressed and excited Virginia. She took some comfort from being with Vanessa's family, feeling very close to Duncan, Quentin, and Angelica, and "losing completely the isolation, the spectator's attitude in being wanted." In spite of the "expression mania" that made her write about everything, she could hardly get herself to say anything about Vanessa's breakdown in her diary. Finally she jotted down some fragmented notes about the last traumatic days in London.

[Virginia's diary, August 6, 1937]
But one must get back into the current again. That was a complete break; almost a blank; like a blow on the head: a shrivelling up. Going round to [Vanessa's studio] that night; & then all the other times, & sitting there. When Roger died I noticed: & blamed myself: yet it was a great relief I think. Here there was no relief. An incredible suffering—to watch it—an accident, & someone bleeding. Then I thought the death of a child is childbirth again; sitting there listening. . . . Then we came down here last Thursday; & the pressure being removed, one lived; but without much future. Thats one of the specific qualities of this death—how it brings close the immense vacancy, & our short little run into inanity. Now this is what I intend to combat. . . . I have to go over though every other day to Charleston. We sit in the studio door. It is very hot, happily. A hot bank holiday—a child killed at the top; aeroplanes droning. The thought of Julian changing so queerly, no so usually: now distant, now close; now

of him there, in the flesh; now some physical encounter—kissing him surreptitiously: & so on. . . . A curiously physical sense; as if one had been living in another body, which is removed, & all that living is ended. . . .

Nessa is alone today. A very hot day—I add, to escape from the thought of her.

"I shall be cheerful, but I shall never be happy again"

"I thought when Roger died that I was unhappy—"

Virginia's diary emphasizes the sheer physical impact of Julian's death, returning to that theme again and again—from the opening "blow on the head," to the pain of "someone bleeding," to the echo of childbirth and the curious feeling that her connection with another body, which was like part of herself, had been severed. Haunted by Vanessa's inarticulate cries, she sensed that the sounds her sister uttered in mourning echoed and reversed the cries that accompanied Julian's birth. As for herself, she cultivated the art of "sitting there listening." Her listening, her ability to hear those echoes of childbirth, informed the words she spoke to Vanessa—speech itself becoming part of the art of listening—which is why Vanessa later said that Virginia's arrival was the only point in the day she had looked forward to.

Like Vanessa, she linked Julian's death to that of Roger Fry, recalling her numb detachment at Fry's funeral. At that time, she says, she "noticed"—that is, she remained cool and analytical, watching herself and others with Maupassantian objectivity, and then felt guilty for doing so, but nevertheless found that detachment was a great relief.

Not now—now she was at the mercy of her physical sensations. The daily visits were very hard work; often, when Vanessa was in a "submerged mood," Virginia found herself flopping on the surface of those deep waters, "like a dilapidated fish." Julian was a shimmering, changing presence, a mirage coming close and growing distant in the summer heat. These strained hours contrasted with the quiet of Monk's House, where she found Leonard working at his desk or in the garden, doing his chores, as he had done for the past nineteen summers. She felt a little guilty about leaving him to fend for himself so much. He had filled the house with oak logs bought from an old man with a wagon, and their scent, mingling with masses of lilies, pervaded the rooms. Vines had grown densely over the low windows, changing the dining room into such "a green cave" that they had to eat in the kitchen. In the distance across the meadows the downs had turned "the colour of lions" in the heat. Their beauty was tinged with sadness. Vanessa was still shaky, and some days, tottering round the garden on Quentin's arm, she looked like an old woman. The frail figure reminded Virginia of her father's last days. She was aware that Vanessa had depended on Julian for companionship after Roger Fry's death and her state made Virginia wonder whether she would ever fully recover. She reflected that Julian had a "queer power over her—the lover as well as the son. He told her he could never love another woman as he loved her." Angelica Garnett gave a similar account of their amorous attachment in her memoir, *Deceived with Kindness*; their closeness was obvious, she said, to anyone who had watched him "leaning over the back of her chair, and the quality of the smile on her face." Angelica went further, exploring motives that Virginia had preferred not to analyze. Julian's departures for China and Spain, she believed, were driven by the need to escape from the rarefied atmosphere of Bloomsbury, and especially his mother. He had written a friend before going to China that the exile might be regarded as "a genteel form of suicide." From abroad he had assured Vanessa that it would be hard for him ever to marry, since he was so much more devoted to her than to any of his mistresses. Having learned that even China with its intrigues was not distracting or remote enough, Julian tried to escape Bloomsbury's seductive grip by going to war. Angelica concluded that "it was a supreme effort to gain his freedom, without if possible hurting his mother." Impossible, of course. Virginia, for her part, was unwilling to probe deeply into the link between Julian's desire for violent action and his attachment to his mother. He had told Vanessa that "feelings about war and excitement [are the] only really serious thing we are different about," a statement that reflects both their intense intimacy and his search for a stimulant or antidote to counter her influence.

Virginia skirted round the subject of incest in a memoir dated July 30, remarking that she and Julian were united by a "passion" for Vanessa—"not too strong a word for either of us." She wooed the grieving mother with declarations of sisterly love, and humorously hinted at more illicit feelings. On August 17 she confessed to being "more nearly attached to you than sisters should be," and having recently acquired a telescope, she warned Vanessa that she would point it in her direction and pry into her bedroom. "If you notice a dancing light on the water, that's me. The light kisses your nose, then your eyes, and you cant rub it off; my darling honey how I adore you, and

Lord knows I cant say what it means to me to come into the room and find you sitting there. Roger felt the same." Her comment about the spot of light that won't rub off referred to her own frequent demands for kisses and Vanessa's instinctive shrinking from any demonstrative act.

Eddy Playfair, who was Julian's great friend, came to Monk's House to focus Virginia's new telescope; at this time in mid-August he gave Vanessa two letters that Julian had asked him to deliver in case of his death—an uncanny message, written two years earlier, when Julian was on his way to China, to assure her that whatever happened, he felt no bitterness or regret. He loved her more than anyone else, he said, and had done so "ever since I can remember." He had enjoyed "an extraordinarily happy and complete life," having been born into a highly civilized society, and having done almost everything he wanted to do; he could die "with considerable equanimity. . . . I'd much rather a violent finish in hot blood, you know: indeed, I wouldn't mind losing a few years for one." He had repeated this point elsewhere, declaring that he preferred "finishing off with a decent fight [rather] than just going phut in a lethal chamber." The farewell letters insist that he is not at all depressed or feeling washed up, but they also display a strikingly indifferent attitude to his own survival. Although he promises that he will not take unnecessary risks, he clearly expects to die a violent death, a thought that does not daunt him. His consoling assurances that he has well and fully lived convey a sense of closure, a surface optimism disguising much darker moods. This fatalism irked Virginia, who complained that he had taken an easy way out and would have shown more character if he had "stayed in England & faced drudgery." She conceded though that the self-sacrificial gesture had a certain grandeur: "it was fine, as all very strong feelings are fine; yet they are also wrong somehow; one must control feeling with reason."

✤

Toward the end of September Virginia was again writing *Three Guineas* from ten to one every morning and plotting the book in her head after lunch, while she tramped the three miles or so to the village of Piddinghoe or Tarring Neville, the race of ideas driving her all afternoon "like a motor in the head over the downs." As usual, her walking rhythm enlivened the pace of her prose. Back home, she played bowls in the garden with Leonard from five to six, and spent an hour reading before cooking dinner. Afterward they listened to the news on the radio. Then she returned to her reading, and drank a cup of hot chocolate before going to bed. In practice, she rarely finished a "specimen day" without interruptions from visitors. She was deeply immersed in her tract, which had now become an implicit dialogue with Julian, detailing the reasons for not fighting, and impelled by the memory of his teasing laugh, which sometimes reminded her of Clive Bell's. It haunted her that Julian, who had been Bloomsbury's first child, absorbing all their liberal ideals and growing into such an open, uninhibited youngster, had nevertheless rebelled against his elders' pacifism. Why did he, in spite of his rational and humane upbringing, have such a need to fight? "He had to be killed in Spain," she wrote— "an odd comment on his education & our teaching." There were other disturbing questions—about her own relationship to her sister: so much unsaid on both sides, such closeness and constraint between them. Irony, too, in the fact that her writing was flourishing and she would have been very happy that summer, if Julian's death—"that extraordinary extinction"—had not nullified it all. "I do not let myself think. That is the fact," she wrote on September 26. "I cannot face much of the meaning. Shut my mind to anything but work & bowls."

She and her sister were alike in their reluctance to confront certain personal subjects. While Vanessa dominated others with her monumental reserve and stillnesses, Virginia distracted and beguiled them with artful words and fantasies. Both were intensely private. The rule of reticence was so strong that Vanessa could not thank Virginia directly for her loving care. Looking for a way to speak while still remaining silent, like Midas's queen whispering her secrets to the reeds, she told her feelings in a letter to Vita, who relayed the message to Virginia on September 21. "I cannot ever say how Virginia has helped me," Vanessa wrote. "Perhaps, some day, not now, you will be able to tell her it's true." Some day, not now—defensive phrases that suggest her anxious withdrawal from her sister's embrace. Virginia found the message profoundly touching—as if it revealed more about Vanessa's inner life than any direct confession could have done. Invoking silence, as she did when her deepest feelings were involved, Virginia wrote Vita that the message "meant something I cant speak of." It was a reticence beyond the reach of conscious choice, a condition that mirrored the unnaturalness of the young dying before the old and "the sight of Nessa bleeding." She could not fall back on her usual posture as a cool, detached observer, an artist whose main responsibility is to carefully "notice" and record the event. She had been severely shaken by Vanessa's grief and forbidden to say anything about it. "I can do nothing with the experience yet. . . . Whats odd is I cant notice or describe."

⁂

On October 13, a day after finishing the first draft of *Three Guineas*, Virginia saw Philip Hart, the surgeon who had operated on Julian in Madrid, and heard a more detailed account of his death. He had taken cover under his ambulance during an air raid and been hit in the side by a shell fragment, which penetrated one of his lungs; he was conscious when they brought him in to the hospital and asked what his chances were—they were negligible, but Hart lied that they were 80 percent. Julian seemed in good spirits, looking ahead to the operation, completely focused on the moment, and he died quietly that night after it was over. Hart added guiltily that they should not have sent him out to the battlefield, he was far too inexperienced, but they had not yet realized how dangerous it was—half the drivers in Julian's unit were killed.

Deeply upset, not knowing how to fit his death into the scheme of things, Virginia returned to work, revising the draft of *Three Guineas* for the printer. The last stages of the writing had been colored by a special urgency, she said, since thoughts of Julian had blended with ideas that had been taking shape ever since her visit to Greece in 1932. She felt his presence more and more, challenging her, testing her arguments, and wrote under intense pressure, galloping through her mornings, the ideas spurting out of her "like a physical volcano."

That imaginary presence made her hold on to her loved ones more tenaciously than ever. On October 22 she woke from a nap with an impulse to take a flying trip to Paris, where Vita was vacationing with her sister-in-law and lover, Gwen St. Aubyn. She consulted a timetable and began making plans—but when Leonard said he would rather not go, her enthusiasm waned and she canceled the trip. After twenty-five years of marriage she did not want to be separated from him even for a weekend. The thought of how attached they were flooded her with happiness; she told him so as they walked under the plane trees in the square, "love making"—an idyll whose radiant clarity resembled fiction rather than fact, a world that followed the shape of her desires, from which she received "enormous pleasure, being wanted: a wife. And our marriage so complete."

Three days later she had an ecstatic moment driving in a gale with Leonard along the sea front while storm winds blew spouts of white water high up against the shore; the turbulent sea absorbed and filled her with delight: a "great spray fountain bursting to my joy over the parade & the lighthouse. Right over the car." They parked at Cuckmere and staggered down to the shore against the wind, which almost blew them off their feet, and stood gasping behind a shed, watching the surf, birds shooting past through the spray. The great curling waves exhilarated Virginia, who wrote teasingly to Ethel, asking why the smash of water satisfied all one's "religious aspirations. And its all I can do not to throw myself in—a queer animal rhapsody, restrained by L." An exaggeration for Ethel's benefit—but the melodramatic note reflected a desire to lose herself in pure sensation. Wild "rhapsodies" naturally conjured up the leap into oblivion, and there were very few steps from the one to the other. She indulged such fantasies, knowing that she could rely on Leonard to restrain them—a combination of freedom and discipline that defined the limits of their happy marriage. They conspired, as she had suggested in her memoir of Julian, to "control feeling with reason."

✕

The Hogarth Press had become a serious burden, making greater and greater demands on the Woolfs' time and energy. They considered letting it lapse, or reducing it solely to an outlet for their own books, but they had spent twenty years turning it into a viable publishing house and were unwilling to let it go now that it was thriving. Then in December Leonard felt ill, perhaps he had caught a chill—but there was blood in his urine, which suggested prostate or kidney disease. Virginia remarked with horror that "this cursed year 1937" still had them in its grip and would not pass without inflicting new torments. Leonard's symptoms grew worse during their Christmas holiday at Rodmell, preventing him from gardening, and the doctor ordered him to rest. Reduced to living on rice pudding and spending most of the day in bed, he still got through a great deal of work, but the importance of lightening his work load was obvious. He could not go on functioning as a full-time publisher, writer, political editor, and adviser to the Labour Party, all at the same time. On January 2, 1938 he wrote to John Lehmann (the letter was in Virginia's hand, but signed by the bedridden Leonard), inviting him to buy out Virginia's half share of the press. Lehmann, who had been seeking a home for his literary magazine, *New Writing*, would have a chance to publish the work of young writers and would oversee the actual day-to-day operations of the press, receiving a salary as managing director. He and

Leonard would make all policy and editorial decisions together as equal partners, thus ensuring that the press kept the special character that the Woolfs had defined for it.

Meanwhile Leonard stayed in bed while the doctors tried unsuccessfully to diagnose his illness. Their tests were inconclusive, and the possibility that he would need an operation loomed over them. Virginia tried to immerse herself in the final revisions of *Three Guineas*, and occasionally succeeded. When she was in the grip of anxiety, time seemed to slow to a crawl, she said, and only the work on her tract restored some semblance of normality: "then the time passes." After two weeks Leonard's symptoms disappeared, and on January 13 the doctor reported that he appeared to be normal, though they would have to wait a month to be sure he was really in the clear, but Virginia was sure that nothing serious was wrong and that the doctors knew nothing. In her letters to Vanessa, who had gone away for a month to her winter retreat in the south of France, she had understated her anxieties while the outcome was uncertain, but now she wrote at once, announcing her "amazing relief." She guessed that his symptoms had been caused by a blow to his back from a car door handle—but no matter, so long as the threat of an operation was averted.

The agreement with Lehmann was practically settled, she noted on February 3; he had met with the current office manager, Dorothy Lange, and was preparing to assume his new duties. It was the day before Julian's birthday, and she wrote a few lines to Vanessa, saying that she remembered seeing him in his cradle, and adding how much she wished she could help her sister. Vanessa replied that she wouldn't have survived without Virginia's help, and felt very grateful, though she couldn't show it.

Leonard had been reading the completed manuscript of *Three Guineas* and announced his approval, praising her "extremely clear analysis." She was disappointed by his very moderate appreciation; she had written the book in a fury, loading it with bold satirical strokes meant to provoke and rally dissenting women, but Leonard found the satire mild. He admired her reasonableness when she had meant to speak with tongues of fire. She reminded herself that one must always expect an "extreme diminution of force," that is, a gap between the intensity of the writer's feelings and the pale sentiments that trickled through to a reader. She could not expect her social analysis to have the same kind of emotional force as her novels. No—though she had hoped for a more full-blooded response from Leonard, it was enough to know her tract had some practical value, and that she had done "a good piece of donkeywork."

⁂

Three Guineas takes the form of a letter to the chairman of an anti-war society, outlining the writer's views about fascism, the causes of war, and the oppression of women. She argues that the patriarchal system, as reflected in the universities and professions, promotes competitive and authoritarian impulses that lead to war. Her analysis, which presents documented accounts of discrimination against women, branches and subdivides, generating enough pages, including over sixty pages of notes and references, to fill a volume. The extended "letter" has some elements of a serious political treatise, but its tone subtly subverts conventional discourse, since the ironic narrator parodies the social scientist's style and embroiders on her findings in humorous and poetic language. Her voice is so personal and distinctive that the book often sounds like fiction, and where social reporting is paired with metaphorical flights, as when she discovers fascist eggs deposited in the newspapers by reactionary male correspondents, the fact and the fiction blend into a new compound. Like most of her books, *Three Guineas* is an experiment, a hybrid form, combining social commentary and poetic satire.

Pointing her satire, the narrator poses as an innocent collector of facts and figures, a neutral observer, who is naively astonished by the hypocrisy she finds in English society—astonished that women are paid so much less than men; that they have so little power to improve their daughters' educations; that venerable institutions like the universities, the church, the bar, and the medical schools conspire to exclude them. Digesting these facts, she reflects that women have gained some advantages from their status as second-class citizens, since they are thus saved from the corrupting influences of power and privilege. They do not have to accept conventional ideas of success, but can define it in their own terms, embracing spiritual values that the patriarchy ignores. Her remarks apply mainly to a small minority of women who come from upper-middle-class families but do not share their brothers' wealth or outlook. She calls these invisible women "outsiders," to suggest their existence as a separate, unrecognized class. Her account of their liberation after centuries of domestic servitude forms the major subplot of *Three Guineas*, and her satirical voice, when she describes these women, acquires prophetic intensity. For having known obscurity and deprivation in the private house the outsider can give new meaning to the traditional monastic vows of poverty and chastity (though not obedience), to which the narrator adds the additional articles of "derision and freedom from unreal loyalties." She defines these terms for her own class. "Poverty" means making enough to live on but no more. "Chastity" means practicing one's profession for its own sake and not for money or fame. "Derision" means refusing honors and continuing to dissent in spite of ridicule. "Freedom from unreal loyalties" means rejecting class pride and claims of national or racial superiority.

Politically, the outsider must obey her own inner law, and since the desire to fight "is a sex characteristic which she cannot share," she should refuse to support the war-makers in any way, cultivating an attitude of complete "indifference," which means eloquent silence and noncooperation. In order to stiffen her resolve she should remember that England enslaved her in the past and still oppresses her in the present. "As a woman," she will say, "I have no country. As a woman I want no country. As a woman my country is the whole world." Active indifference, the narrator argues, is not a colorless negation but a moral choice that can have strong psychological effects, forming part of a larger effort to change the social order—a vision of renewal through detachment.

Virginia had mulled over these ideas for a long time, but Julian's death gave them greater immediacy, and she remarked that she was always thinking of him as she wrote. Rather than censoring her anger, as she had done when she cut large chunks out of *The Years*, she intended in *Three Guineas* to use it creatively. Sophocles' *Antigone* again provided a blueprint of the struggle against tyranny. There is a continuous line of descent, the narrator says, from the ancient tyrant, Creon, who buried the dissident Antigone alive in a rocky tomb, to the Victorian paterfamilias and the totalitarian dictator, with ranks of professional men, politicians, generals, and bureaucrats behind them. Her indictment here is harsher than it was in *The Years*, though not as bitterly outspoken as in her diary. She describes the petty Creons who infest England at present as caterpillar worms, voracious creatures that lay their misogynist eggs and go on circling head to tail round "the sacred tree, of property," the mulberry, whose leaves they devour. Shifting the metaphor, she adds that the pursuit of wealth and professional advancement is, in the words of a prominent churchman, "mind-and-soul-destroying," blinding the pursuers so that they are unable to enjoy nature or art and lose their sense of proportion. "So competitive do they become that they will not share their work with others though they have more than they can do themselves. What then remains of a human being who has lost sight, and sound, and sense of proportion? Only a cripple in a cave." An ironic echo of the destruction Creon brought on himself and his kingdom by burying Antigone.

His most active descendants at present are the fascist dictators whose zeal is displayed in some photographs she has received in the mail with appeals for aid to Spain—pictures of ruined houses and "bodies of dead children killed by bombs." No need to go to Spain in order to fight the fascist plague, she says; the dictator's followers are active in England, the infestation is spreading, and one should first help to "crush him in our own country." One might begin with the college where young women are trained to enter the professions and imitate their male patrons. She imagines lighting a fire that will consume that building and along with it burn the old hypocrisies, though the flames in her vision are poetic and Elizabethan. "Let the light of the burning building scare the nightingales and incarnadine the willows. And let the daughters of educated men dance round the fire and heap armful upon armful of dead leaves upon the blaze." Not that she is not tempted to start a real fire, but reason tells her to use her energy to light up another building, the poor house where professional women live on their meager earnings. Help them to make the windows blaze like a lighthouse, and after centuries of indignity and abuse their mothers "will laugh from their graves." Even now, she adds heatedly, she would gladly throw the fighting word "feminist," which has caused such antagonism between men and women, into the ritual flames. "Let us write that word in large black letters on a sheet of foolscap; then solemnly apply a match to the paper. Look, how it burns!"

The narrator's satirical humor is edged with fire. She remembers Spain, but it would be futile and self-defeating to enlarge that conflagration. Sophocles' *Antigone* again suggests another kind of response, for though the ancient poet condemns Creon, he also draws a psychologically complex portrait of the tyrant, endowing him with a share of our common humanity, so that when the curtain falls the audience can even feel some sympathy for him. Though she detests the dictator and fears him, she seeks to lift the brutal mask and discover the frightened creature behind it—a grotesquely overgrown version of a small boy strutting and stamping around the playground to gain attention, possessed by infantile rages and longings. Unreason. His acts are abhorrent, but his blindness is pitiable. Placing him thus, she concludes that we must declare him, as Prospero did Caliban, a noxious insect, but our own creation, and admit that we "cannot dissociate ourselves from that figure but are ourselves that figure." We cannot withdraw, disclaiming responsibility—that is impossible, since reality is twofold: "the public and private worlds are inseparably connected," and any evil in the one is amplified in the other. We have made the public world and must change it, as we have made the dictator and must remove him.

This imperative brings special dangers, the narrator warns, for one must not use the dictator's methods to defeat him. She particularly emphasizes the vulnerability of her own literary profession. Again Antigone reminds us how important it is to preserve the truth by preserving the separation between art and propaganda. The artist is a thoroughbred, she says, trained to a high state of awareness, and if writers endorse the lies and simplifications of propaganda, their visionary powers will atrophy and literature will grow sterile, suffering "the same mutilation that the mule has suffered; and there will be no more horses."

Finally, hating all forms of regimentation, outsiders will refuse to organize in chapters or cells, but will rely on many personal dissenting acts. An Outsiders' Society, if it existed, would be the very opposite of most such bodies—informal, without leaders, dues, or even an office to meet in—its name would be shorthand for many spontaneous private acts, or a way of reinventing society itself by introducing the values of domestic life into the public domain. Similarly, the narrator imagines a gathering of artists and intellectuals to replace the existing educational institutions, a "poor college; in which learning is sought for itself; where advertisement is abolished; and there are no degrees; and lectures are not given, and sermons are not preached."

She is under no illusions that these are anything more than utopian inventions; she can hear an imaginary reader asking her to stop dreaming "about ideal worlds behind the stars" and to turn her attention to actual facts in the real world. She admits that her campaign of active "indifference" to all war-making activities will have few supporters and that the Outsiders' Society may have no members aside from herself. But if her book encourages even a few women to reject the culture of violence, it will have practical value and change some lives.

Virginia's program for outsiders is limited, dismissing organized political action and appealing to a very small class of women. At the same time, it is radical in its aims. In addition to her militant pacifism, she advocates complete freedom for women to pursue any careers they choose and to receive equal pay for their work, including their domestic work as mothers. She wishes to end class privilege and traditional hierarchies, bringing about the gradual disestablishment of the ruling class. In the meantime, while awaiting the creation of a better world, she sends a guinea to each of three charitable appeals—for a women's college, a group of professional women, and an antiwar campaign. The revolutionary thrust of her proposals is softened by the narrator's ingenuous tone, her fastidiousness in pursuing the truth, and it is further complicated by her use of poetic imagery. "I so slaver & silver my tongue," Virginia remarked, "that its sharpness takes some time to be felt." Antigone's ironic daughter, armed with reason and pronouncing judgment. Sometimes she observes "men and women working together for the same cause," but more often she encounters "a monstrous male . . . decorated like a savage with feathers" and discovers new evidence that her country has always treated her as a slave.

Virginia predicted that these arguments would shock her readers, arousing strong hostility on both the right and the left, and doubted that she would have many friends left after the book appeared.

≫

While she was making her final corrections in *Three Guineas*, events on the Continent took another turn for the worse. Austria's Nazis had put increasing pressure on the government, and when the chancellor ordered a plebiscite to enlist popular support for Austrian independence, Hitler moved to annex the country to his third *Reich*. German troops crossed the border without resistance; they marched into Vienna on March 12 along swastika-draped avenues lined with cheering crowds. Recording this event in her diary, Virginia paired it with the show trials then going on in Moscow, in which Stalin eliminated political rivals by bringing trumped-up charges of treason against them. Insanity—a reversion to the Middle Ages, she called it, noting that Stalin's methods matched Hitler's, "like drops of dirty water mixing." She could do nothing except go on working, but it was hard to concentrate, since Leonard's political activities constantly reminded her of the crisis. The public world intruded into the room next to hers with a hectic round of Labour Party meetings, editorial conferences, urgent phone calls and negotiations. Kingsley Martin, distraught as usual, talked at great length and pointlessly about emigrating "from our doomed Europe." Virginia summed up the grim outlook in her telegraphic style: "England, as they say, humiliated. And the man in uniform exalted. Suicides. Refugees turned back from Newhaven. Aeroplanes droning over the house." The rumors of war made Julian's death "somehow not pointless," but the springlike and indifferent weather, displaying "a bland sunny blue," seemed to dismiss violence, and she could not grasp his defection. It baffled her that Julian was not there "to see the daffodils; the old beggar woman—the swans." Visiting Vanessa at Charleston, she sensed his presence and felt he might materialize at any moment.

After a few days the political storm subsided and the newspapers went back to covering the Torso case, a lurid unsolved murder; Virginia observed that the underlying motives for war were as great as ever—Hitler was insatiable—and "when the tiger . . . has digested his dinner he will pounce again."

She was busy with the usual social engagements—inviting Elizabeth Bowen to tea, planning a party, buying a dress—mundane activities that created an illusion of normality. It was false, but she took some comfort from the fact that she had joined the fight against fascism on her own terms. *Three Guineas* was her bid for legitimacy and independence. She had taken a risk by attacking national shibboleths, and the boldness of the venture exhilarated her. To be sure, the risks for her were mainly emotional—publishing the tract would probably not affect her sales or her literary reputation—but given Virginia's fine-tuned nervous system, public hostility and ridicule could be dangerous in themselves. She sent off the final proofs on April 28 with great satisfaction, declaring that she felt "entirely free. Why? Have committed myself. am afraid of nothing. Can do anything I like." The bravado of her words, like an escaped prisoner's, reflected some anxiety about publicly adopting a militant position. She defended herself in advance, as she had advised outsiders to do, by embracing her unpopularity, listing the negative advantages she would gain from it. "No longer famous; no longer on a pedestal; no longer hawked in by societies: on my own forever." In any case, she was financially secure and could ignore the pressure to deliver the same saleable goods she had delivered in the past; she "need never recur or repeat. I am an outsider. I can take my way: experiment with my own imagination in my own way. The pack may howl but it shall never catch me." More bravado, behind which lurked the specter of Europe going up in flames; it could happen at any moment—"one more shot at a policeman" and they would arrive at August 1914 all over again. She heard growling overhead and saw the sharklike form of an airplane through the wavy glass of her window. She lamented that *Three Guineas*, which she had written with such passionate conviction, would be consumed in the coming debacle "like a moth dancing over a bonfire."

Looking back, she saw *The Years* and *Three Guineas* as "one book," a composite work on which she had labored with elation and despair for the past six years, the tract transposing her fictional themes into a polemical key. By spinning off her social critique into its own separate enclosure, she had avoided the need to dramatize her anger, that is, to enter into it fully with her novelist's imagination. She had preserved her artistic detachment, but limited the scope of her fiction, a failure that still rankled. To Ethel, who read *The Years* in February, she wrote that she loathed the book, and saw "a sweat stain, a tear stain, a gash—200 pages cut—on every existing page." In *Three Guineas* she tried to complete the original design of her essay-novel, venting her anger within a medium she could safely handle. The tract's satirical commentary, in which an excess of reason masks an excess of feeling, mirrors the disorders of its time.

14 *A Purple Background*

Virginia's main fear now was of an anticlimax. What if the book she had written with such passionate conviction fell flat and vanished without making any impression at all? She was equally afraid of attracting the wrong kind of attention, for in spite of its political content, *Three Guineas* was deeply personal and might even be described as "autobiography in public"—a mode she hated. The book had evolved from her realization in 1933 that she need not court public approval or play the role of the famous writer, but could "go on adventuring, changing . . . refusing to be stamped & stereotyped." That revelatory moment, when she had felt a "mysterious hand" reaching out to her and vowed to practice her philosophy of anonymity, had marked a "spiritual conversion." The last phrase was inaccurate, she said, but it conveyed the euphoria she felt about being free to write on her own terms. She had rushed round London on that day, buying a magnifying glass and extravagantly tipping a street musician who told her his life story. The whole episode had liberated her to write her polemic against the patriarchal establishment. Now she felt a trace of the usual dread before publication, but it was outweighed by "the immense relief and peace" she had gained by committing herself.

Furthermore, she was immersed in her writing again; on two successive days, April 1 and 2, 1938, she had composed the opening pages of two books, her biography of Roger Fry and a new satirical novel. This double venture, which was like a "dive into darkness," had partly insulated her against the impact of surface events. She still had some misgivings about the Fry biography, for which she had been reading letters and taking notes since 1935. It was to be full of facts and based on solid research, but she would have to be discreet and selective in her account of Fry's personal life in order to protect the privacy of his family and friends. Authorized biography, which she had never written before, seemed an uncongenial mode, leaving little room for the poetic imagination. On the other hand, Roger's life would give her the chance to explore an important influence from her own artistic past, and the book would be an offering to Vanessa, a memorial to her former lover. Virginia found the painstaking work both tedious and bracing. On April 12, when she had written twenty pages, she remarked that she relied on this "sober drudgery" to distract her and steady her nerves. Although she resented having to stick to the facts, she welcomed the formal discipline and the engagement with Fry's aesthetic doctrines. His rational humanism, dating back to happier years before the war, offered a respite from the rigid ideologies of the 1930s. She spent most of her mornings working on the biography, but sometimes she rebelled against her diet of facts by turning to the new novel. The story was set at a country house, where a group of family and friends were sitting out on a summer's night, chatting about village business—water and sewage and bits of their past lives. The scene was sandwiched between two satirical prayers, the first saluting an old oil lamp and the second invoking a grub-eating bird, homely figures representing spirit and nature.

Virginia's sense of absurdity, always alert, was activated by a sudden declaration of love from Philip Morrell, Ottoline's sixty-eight-year-old husband. He had courted her several times before, first discreetly inviting an affair in 1917, and again, with greater ardor, in 1927. He had treated her with awkward deference, stressing his own inferiority and her beauty and intelligence, not to mention her terrifying wit. These charms had inspired him to overcome his natural shyness. Virginia was unmoved by his mournful posture, knowing that he had had an illegitimate child by his secretary during the war and a string of other affairs. She had managed to evade his clumsy advances while staying on friendly terms with Ottoline.

Early in 1938, when the Morrells were both recovering from serious illnesses (Ottoline had suffered a stroke), Philip read Virginia's second novel, *Night and Day*, and wrote her on January 31 that the entrancing music of her comedy of manners had made him long to be in touch with her again. In his eyes, he said humbly, she was, if possible, cleverer and more beautiful than ever. How vividly he remembered the past—Virginia walking on the downs, riding with him in a car, sitting in a windowseat while his daughter recited "Prufrock" for a group of friends. A series of incidents passed through his mind. Once at a party he had said some foolish thing that hurt her feelings, and had the misery of seeing her face change, without any chance to take back the offending words. Several times, he recalled, she had invited him to spend a weekend with her and Leonard when Ottoline was away, as if she liked him for his own sake, and not just as Ottoline's husband. On one visit she had made up a bed for him in the printing room, with type scattered about among the presses—the most memorable bedroom he ever had. He was still absurdly shy, he said, and longed to see Virginia alone because it was impossible for him to speak freely in front of Leonard or Ottoline. Would she meet him some afternoon at the National Gallery or Westminster? Not that he had anything important to say, he just wanted to see how they got on; he had a longing, he declared, to meet the original Virginia again.

She had written to acknowledge his compliments about *Night and Day*, but avoided any further correspondence. Diverted and repelled by his goatish tenacity, she teasingly described the incident in a letter to Vita. "I have a lover. The husband of a lady in high life. Wishes to meet me clandestinely. I put this in to see if I can rouse jealousy. . . . How odd, this red flower on a grey tree! (He's grey: so am I)."

The one-sided flirtation on Morrell's part ended abruptly on April 21, when he wrote her that Ottoline, seriously weakened by her previous stroke, had died suddenly of heart failure that morning. He was beyond asking for sympathy, which could not help him now, and only asked Virginia to write an obituary for the *Times*, since she had understood Ottoline. He dreaded reading what a stranger might say.

Virginia had known Ottoline for thirty years and often criticized her imperious temper and self-dramatizing attitudes, but in recent years she had come to know another side of her—not the society figure who had attracted artists and courtiers "like a Renaissance princess" but a shy and stoical woman. Grown very deaf, and ailing, Ottoline had retreated from an increasingly ugly world that was "destroying all she cherished." Over tea with Virginia she talked with simple dignity about some obscure but worthy poet or eccentric ancestor, and the intimacy between them seemed stronger than ever before. Now, attending her depressingly bland, conventional funeral, Virginia realized how much she would miss Ottoline and the visits to Gower Street; that light had gone out. Two weeks after the funeral she visited Gower Street in order to choose something of Ottoline's to remember her by, as provided by her will. Morrell pressed several mementos on her—a big green ring, pearl earrings, a shawl and fan. She felt embarrassed about taking so much—"a vulture feeling"—and laughter welled up in her at the incongruous thought of "doing well out of Ottoline." Morrell's behavior was simple and unaffected, but she felt uneasy and was aware of their hands touching as he gave her the ring. Her obituary emphasized the contradictions in Ottoline's character, praising her achievement as a great hostess but acknowledging that her flamboyant personality had often attracted ridicule. Philip declared it the best thing ever written about her, but Virginia disliked the whole genre and complained that "the horrid little pellet screwed my brain."

⁘

It was a relief to turn to the new novel, which she had begun in an adventurous mood and planned to write in a freer, more humorous style than she had allowed herself to use in *The Years*. Remembering how she had suffered with that novel, bidding defiance like Jonah, she begged to be released from grand themes and prophetic visions.

[Virginia's diary, April 26, 1938]
    Dont please impose that huge burden on me again, I implore. Let it be random & tentative; something I can blow of a morning, to relieve myself of Roger: dont, I implore, lay down a scheme; call in all the cosmic immensities; & force my tired & diffident brain to embrace another whole—all parts contributing—not yet awhile. But to amuse myself, let me note: why not Poynzet Hall: a centre: all lit. discussed in connection with real little incongruous living humour; & anything that comes into my head; but "I" rejected: "We" substituted: to whom at the end there shall be an invocation? "We" . . . composed of many different things . . . we all life, all art, all waifs & strays—a rambling capricious but somehow unified whole—the present state of my mind? And English country; & a scenic old house—& a terrace where nursemaids walk? & people passing—& a perpetual variety & change from intensity to prose.

Virginia's mock prayer at the beginning is ironic and paradoxical. She is at the mercy of her artistic demons, but she gains her power from them. She addresses the darkness of her own hidden intentions. Even as she resists that unknown influence, seeking to postpone the moment when she will ardently "embrace another whole—all parts contributing," she is already feeling the seductiveness of the task. Her plea, "not yet awhile," points ahead to the time when she will devote herself to it. Till then she will amuse herself, she says, by sketching the outlines of her new work. She feels free to say anything that comes into her head, and that will form part of her artistic scheme. She describes it in deceptively simple terms, aiming to incorporate "all life, all art, all waifs & strays," that is, linking the collective "all" with the individual and random "waifs." She aims to join their diverse members in "a rambling capricious but somehow unified whole"—and again, helped by that bland "somehow," she bridges the gap between mere caprice and formal unity. Such a result depends on the artist's ability to conquer her egoism, substituting "we" for "I" and obeying the rule of anonymity. By this point her tone has undergone a reversal, changing from the distracted appeal for "something I can blow of a morning" to visions of "perpetual variety & change." The ironies of the opening have been replaced by the artist's earnest involvement in her new formal experiment.

Absorbed in her writing, Virginia awaited the publication of *Three Guineas* on June 3 with relative calm, though her heart beat faster as she sent out the advance copies. Her heart would soon be adopting the same rhythm as the reviews, she predicted, beating "to the time of sneer enthusiasm enthusiasm sneer." The event went by almost painlessly; it was the "mildest childbirth" she had ever had, and the sneers had very little sting. The papers were respectful; most gave the book their blessing, praising the writer's admirable motives and her enchanting style. A review in the *Times Literary Supplement* applauded her fairness and called her "the most brilliant pamphleteer in England," a label that pleased Virginia in spite of herself. *The Listener* took a similar line, noting that she had showed "almost puritanical restraint" so as to ensure that her seductive prose did not subvert "reason and logic." She was "too fair-minded and sincere to want to trip her readers up." The reviewer for the leftist *New Statesman and Nation*, whose views Leonard pronounced foolish but well-meaning, approved "the justice of Mrs. Woolf's demands" and "the beauty of her gospel." In contrast to these conventional voices, the feminist journal *Time and Tide* described *Three Guineas* as a "revolutionary bomb of a book, delicately aimed at the heart of our mad, armament ridden world." This was an isolated voice. Most of the reviewers read only what they wanted to read, the idealistic sentiments of a conventional figure, a Virginia Woolf who existed only in the journalistic imagination. The *Times Literary Supplement* assured readers that this eminent writer had no wish to stir up bad feeling between the sexes—to think she did "would be the grossest misunderstanding," said the reviewer, ignoring the radical content of her proposals. By silvering her tongue, Virginia had made it too easy for readers to minimize the bitterness of her indictment. Furthermore, as Leonard suggested, the shrillness of current political speech made it hard for readers to attend to Virginia's elaborate ironies. She was inconsistent enough to enjoy favorable reviews, even if the papers praised her for the wrong reasons and even if the praise subverted her standing as an outsider. She expected to be vilified, and was pleasantly surprised to escape public abuse. Most important, they had not dismissed her as a charming prattler. "On the whole 3 Gs is taken seriously," she concluded on June 11. "Many high compliments; some snarls . . . but generally kind, rather surprised, & its over."

It was over because the Woolfs had chosen this month for their spring holiday, and by the time they returned the first wave of reviews would have passed. Before leaving London Virginia received some of her friends' first reactions to the book. Ethel had read *Three Guineas* with great enthusiasm, only questioning the harshness of the attack on patriotism. Virginia replied that of course she was patriotic, if that meant loving England, the places and the people, but she could not accept the common linkage between love of country and the fighting instincts. As an outsider she was able to detect the ways in which politicians manipulated people's loyalties better even than Leonard with his Jewish sensitivity. It was important not to succumb to mindless chauvinistic reflexes. "We must enlarge the imaginative, and take stock of the emotion."

Leaving London and these explanations behind them, the Woolfs drove north to tour Scotland and the Isle of Skye, stopping first at a Northumberland hotel, where they visited the wall built by the Roman emperor Hadrian to keep out Scottish marauders. The wall ran like a ruined causeway across the landscape, a frozen wave, Virginia said, with the remains of towers cresting here and there and bogs at its base. Sitting near the wall while Leonard cleaned the spark plugs on their car, she read a translation of ancient Greek poetry and thought about the Roman presence still subtly imprinted on the countryside. The poetry engaged her attention then till her mind whizzed "like an aeroplane propellor invisibly quick and unconscious." The effect derived not only from the words on the page but from the landscape around her—rolling steppes dotted with sheep and cattle, "miles and miles of lavender coloured loneliness," a northern Campagna sprinkled with flowers, wild hawthorn, and the single white thread of a road. The scene shimmered, like the white wildflowers whipped by the wind, as if held in suspension between past and present. Two thousand years ago Roman soldiers, gazing from their lonely forts, had studied the same vistas she saw now. She imagined their encampments of rough barracks, treasure houses, and latrines. The landscape seemed mysteriously charged with meaning. "D'you know how suddenly a country expands an airball in ones mind," she wrote to Ethel—"I mean states a mood completely that was existent but unexpressed, so that at every turn of the road its like half remembering, and thinking it can't be coming, but then it does?—a feeling a dream gives? and also it is oneself—the real Virginia or Ethel?" Deep peace enfolded the ancient battlegrounds.

She remembered with distaste that she had received an unpleasant letter about *Three Guineas* just before leaving London. It was from Vita, who found the book tantalizing, explaining that she was alternately enchanted by Virginia's prose and exasperated by her "misleading arguments." Vita could not publicly challenge these arguments, "for I should always lose on points in fencing, though if it came to fisticuffs I might knock you down. So long as you play the gentleman's game, with the gentleman's technique, you win." The superior tone chilled Virginia like a shadow passing across the earth, though she tried to shrug it off. That evening she wrote an indignant reply, asking whether Vita meant to accuse her of dishonesty—what else could the term "misleading" mean?—and declaring that she had taken "more pains to get up the facts and state them plainly" than with anything she had done in her life. What stung most was the hint that she was merely a dilettante, dabbling at a "gentleman's game."

Her irritation was dispelled by the austere beauty of the highlands; crossing wild passes and "cataractuous" rivers, she discovered country that reminded her of unspoiled parts of Italy or Greece and remote inns where people spoke with such a thick brogue that she had to invent their side of the conversation in addition to her own. She mischievously reviewed the local cooking in a letter to Vanessa: first there was the fish, she said, which some people thought divine but she regarded as a dubious invention. Leonard loved the pastries, but she did not share his enthusiasm, since she disapproved of scones for breakfast and deplored the ginger in the cake. "Still the more frivolous sugar cakes are very good," she admitted. "And the porridge is a dream. Only I loathe porridge." She went on with a litany of "good earthy soup . . . and the splendour of sausage, bacon, ham, eggs, grapefruit, oatcake, grilled ham for breakfast." After all these wholesome edibles it was almost superfluous to add that the people she met, like the baker who was sending her his own shortbread, were "beyond belief nice."

Back in London, she found herself still angry at Vita and wrote again, sharply rejecting the insult to her intelligence. Vita had accused her of writing "specious humbug. . . . And then you sicklied me over with praise of charm and wit." Vita replied in distress that she had sent a letter, which had apparently gone astray, clarifying her clumsy comments. She had never for a moment doubted Virginia's integrity or the accuracy of her facts, but only disputed the inferences she drew from them—a mere difference of opinion. Virginia had argued, for example, that women are natural pacifists, "but is it not true that many women are extremely bellicose and urge their men to fight?" She was horrified that her hasty remarks had caused such a misunderstanding. The minor blowup subsided with apologies on both sides. But Virginia's formidable reaction showed how seriously she took her role as a social interpreter. When it came to historical facts, she was her father's daughter, honoring the twin gods of reason and truth. The suggestion that she had cooked the evidence shocked her as if she had been accused of public indecency.

�֍

The European crisis, which had been simmering since the annexation of Austria, heated up again at the end of the summer when Hitler, seeking new opportunities for expansion in the east, charged that Czechoslovakia had committed atrocities against ethnic Germans in the Sudetenland and massed his troops on the border. France, England, and Russia were bound by treaties to defend Czechoslovakia, and war again seemed imminent. But England's leaders, like the public in general, were reluctant to fight for a small, distant democracy. Hitler exploited their reluctance, steadily escalating his demands while the other great powers temporized, and finally he threatened to invade unless the Czechs ceded major portions of their territory to Germany.

Witnessing these events, and observing military maneuvers in her own quiet village, Virginia felt as if they were "all sitting downstairs while someone slowly dies." On August 6 she watched six tanks with gun carriages clambering "like black beetles" down the hill near Monk's House, and dismissed them derisively as the work of "small boys playing idiotic games for which I pay." A week later she heard that a woman had drowned herself near Rodmell, a widow who lived in a ramshackle farmhouse at a spot on the downs called Mount Misery and had "turned queer" since her son died. Virginia had seen her rambling over the downs with her dog. She had come to the village shop to beg for a small amount of kerosene for her lamp. She was alone in the dark and almost destitute—the farmer wanted to evict her. Finally, having killed her dog, she went down to the river at high tide and jumped in. Her body was washed up near Piddinghoe, on the route of one of Virginia's regular walks.

An obscure death that would soon be followed by a multitude of others if Hitler ordered his million men to start the killing. The idea was so numbing that Virginia could only tell herself to stop thinking about it and go on with ordinary life. "What else can a gnat on a blade of grass do?" They were adding a new room upstairs at Monk's House with glass doors leading onto an open balcony, where they could sit on hot summer nights. Sheets on all the furniture, dust falling, as the workmen hammered. Retreating to her garden lodge, Virginia mulled the problems of Fry's biography. When did his wife go mad, and how on earth was one to "explain madness and love in sober prose, with dates attached?" She and Leonard played at bowls, which was their "mania." They picked dahlias. In spite of politics, they drove to Seaford in order to mate their dog, Sally, and succeeded after considerable coaxing.

This European crisis, Virginia observed, was different from the preceding ones; the danger that England would be drawn into the conflict had finally penetrated the reluctant public consciousness. The papers that had smugly minimized the importance of German rearmament now expressed their alarm. On September 5, a day after the talks between the Czech government and the rebellious Sudeten German minority had stalled, Virginia wrote: "This time everyone's agog. Thats the difference. . . . We are beginning to feel the herd impulse: everyone asks everyone, Any news? What d'you think?"

She had crossed a threshold of her own, approaching a region in which her pacifist convictions provided little guidance. She was only sure that all the political factions were bedeviled and driven by the power madness of a "ridiculous little man. Why ridiculous? Because none of it fits. Encloses no reality. Death & war & darkness representing nothing that any human being from the Pork butcher to the Prime Minister cares one straw about." But to say it was unreal explained nothing. She could make no sense of it. She had refused to let her thoughts dwell on the thugs and henchmen, dismissing them as baboons or pests or nasty little boys. She had cushioned herself against the news of atrocities. Now "indifference," and the derisive attitude that accompanied it, was no longer enough. On September 10 she observed that even if the crisis was unreal—less real, say, than the facts about Roger Fry's life in 1910—the infection had defeated all attempts to control it. She repeated her parable of the destructive little boys, but reversed its direction. "All these grim men," she wrote, "appear to me like grown up's staring incredulously at a child's sand castle which for some inexplicable reason has become a real vast castle, needing gunpowder & dynamite to destroy it. Nobody in their senses can believe in it. Yet nobody must tell the truth. So one forgets." The image of these uncontrollable destructive forces reflected a change of outlook, a deeper insight that went beyond satire. It meant reading the drone of airplanes flying over the downs and the hoot of sirens being tested. Omens. Virginia concluded that they had arrived again at "1914 but without even the illusion of 1914."

While the ordinary villagers at Rodmell were highly skeptical about calls to arms, the local Labour Party candidate for Parliament, an insignificant man who collected matchboxes, was in favor of going to war. During a dinner at Monk's House, the candidate, Mr. Black, talked about his daughters—one bred pet mice and the other painted posters of them. He was mouselike himself, Virginia said, but still keen on deploying all the guns. "And it is thus that the [Labour Party] counters Hitler." His personality seemed to mirror the surreal atmosphere of the present moment. Mr. Black imagined that war would create an opportunity to "build a new state," Virginia added, "& what kind of new state? One in which mice & matchboxes are collected."

On September 13, at the instigation of the Nazis, the Sudeten Germans rioted in Prague and forced the Czech government to impose martial law. While these events were taking place the Woolfs learned that the owner of their house at 52 Tavistock Square planned to demolish the building within the next three years; they would probably have to think about moving much sooner than that. And Vanessa and Duncan were preparing to leave for their house at Cassis in the south of France. In spite of the uncertain political outlook, they set out in their car on September 16, taking Quentin and Angelica with them. Vanessa's absence, Virginia said later, left her feeling she had "no circumference; only my inviolable center: L. to wit."

The crisis came to a head at the end of September. Eager to avoid a war for which England was inadequately prepared, Prime Minister Neville Chamberlain flew to Germany to negotiate with Hitler, and at the same time began pressuring the Czechs to allow the Sudeten Germans to secede if they wished to do so. These maneuvers aroused some opposition, Virginia reported in her diary. By demanding the surrender of a highly fortified border, which would leave the Czechs defenseless, Chamberlain was in effect ordering them to commit suicide. Furthermore, the public's growing awareness that Germany's power would be greatly enhanced caused general dismay. "Everyone calling everyone else a pick pocket. The prospect of another glissade after a minor stop into chaos. All Europe in Hitler's keeping. What'll he gobble next." Nevertheless, Chamberlain flew to Germany again on September 22 to transmit an offer of self-determination for the Sudetenland, but that offer was no longer enough. There would be no gradual transfer of power. Hitler demanded immediate annexation of the disputed areas without an election or other delay, or he would order his troops to invade on October 1. The ultimatum severely rattled Chamberlain and his French allies, who could not quite swallow these demands. The British government hastily initiated a scheme of civil defense and prepared to mobilize for war.

"Never never has there been such a time," Virginia wrote to Vanessa, in the first of several letters describing the week beginning Monday, September 26. It started with a call from Kingsley Martin, that unattractive man whose urgent appeals Leonard could never refuse and whom Virginia had to tolerate for Leonard's sake. It was desperately important, Martin said, for Leonard to come at once to reconcile the Labour and Liberal Parties, to advise someone about something—he was the only one who could do it. The point remained unclear, but Virginia threw her nightgown into a bag, and they set out, planning to stay overnight in London. The streets were crowded—people talking about war, piles of sandbags, trucks delivering planks, workmen digging trenches for air raid shelters, loudspeakers exhorting citizens: "Go and fit your gas masks." Over all an atmosphere of cynicism and unnatural calm—a state in which Virginia went on to buy coffee, while Leonard visited the *New Statesman* office. That evening he brought Kingsley Martin home for dinner. Martin was at his most melodramatic and had dark circles round his eyes. No mention of the urgent problem that had made him summon Leonard. They discussed "the inevitable end of civilization," and Martin explained that Hitler planned to drop bombs on London every twenty minutes for forty-eight hours. He paced feverishly up and down, "hinting that he meant to kill himself." He stopped to call a friend at the BBC for news of Hitler's speech—then in progress—

and reported that the crowds were "howling like wild beasts" in response to the Führer. After some more lugubrious conversation he called again and reported the situation was worse—looking hopeless. "Hitler is more mad than ever. . . . Have some Whiskey Kingsley, said L. Well, it dont much matter either way said K." At last he left, saying he could not sleep and would pace the streets. He clasped Virginia's hand earnestly as if for the last time.

In the morning Virginia retreated to the London Library in order to gather facts about Roger Fry and the Post-Impressionist exhibition of 1910. Later, thinking about Roger, she stopped in at the National Gallery, where an old man was lecturing on Watteau to a group of attentive listeners who seemed to be absorbing a last taste of normal life. Virginia looked at some paintings by Renoir and Cézanne, trying to see them as Roger would have seen them, which helped her, she said, to dispel the prevailing gloom and "get some solidity into my mind." Later she and Leonard met with the seven members of their staff to discuss the future of the Hogarth Press, which was uncertain, since people were not buying books at the moment and shops planned to close. The clerks had fixed up a book-lined stockroom as a bomb shelter, with supplies and mattresses on the floor. They wanted to stay on, and the Woolfs agreed to go on paying wages as long as they could. It was a painful good-bye for Virginia, her dislike of urban chaos conflicting with her guilt about leaving the others behind. She felt like a coward, but reminded herself that the government was urging people to leave the city if they could. It would be a great relief to return to the relative calm of Rodmell. She and Leonard considered what they would need in case they were marooned there, and he took a warm coat while she brought Roger Fry's letters to Vanessa and a pack of stamped envelopes. They left, as they had come, in the rain, on darkening roads. Spectral figures loomed outside their slowly moving windows. "It was pouring terrific torrents," Virginia reported; "the roads packed; men nailing up shutters in shop windows; sandbags being piled; and a general feeling of flight and hurry." Back in Rodmell they learned that the village would have to house fifty children from London and they promised to take two.

The next day, Wednesday, September 28, a cultivated voice on the BBC instructed people who were being evacuated to wear warm clothes and bring no pets. This was followed by an official message to ships at sea, an archbishop saying prayers, and authorities at the zoo explaining their plans to kill all poisonous snakes and other dangerous animals, which gave Virginia visions of "London ravaged by cobras & tigers." The Woolfs received a message that the Hogarth Press manager could not get a key to Tavistock Square, where the air raid trenches were, because the park was for residents only. They tried to tune in foreign broadcasts, but the frequencies were jammed. The multiple uncertainties made everything unreal. At five that afternoon they switched on the radio again, expecting to hear that the war had begun. Instead they heard news of Chamberlain's "sensational announcement." Virginia read Harold Nicolson's account of this dramatic episode the following day. Chamberlain had made a long speech before the House of Commons, outlining the origins of the crisis. He spoke in a tired, mechanical voice, and they all assumed he would end by calling for war. After about an hour someone handed him a note, which he paused to read, adjusting his pince-nez. "His whole face, his whole body, seemed to change," Nicolson wrote. "He raised his face so that the light from the ceiling fell full upon it. All the lines of anxiety and weariness seemed suddenly to have smoothed out; he appeared ten years younger and triumphant." He had received a message from Hitler inviting him, together with Daladier of France and Mussolini, to come to Munich and resolve their differences. Upon hearing this the House went wild; members threw their hats in the air and rushed into the lobbies, shouting. Chamberlain cut short the speech and went to prepare for his departure. The news that mobilization had been postponed for twenty-four hours evoked a general sigh of relief, Virginia said, "like coming out of a dark room."

On Friday morning, September 30, the four powers in Munich signed an agreement accepting all of Germany's demands. Later that day, at the airport, Chamberlain waved a paper that bore his own and Hitler's signatures on it, pledging that their two countries would never "go to war with one another again." He later insisted that he had brought back "peace with honour. I believe it is peace for our time." His words drew frenzied cheers from the largest crowd since the Armistice. At Rodmell, in spite of a hastily organized church service and clanging bells, the villagers were "perfectly sure that it was a dirty business"—that Hitler was preparing to attack when he grew stronger and they were unable to resist.

The crisis had numbed Virginia with an "unreality that clouded all distinct feeling." Now the feelings came seeping back, and she allowed herself to picture the disaster they had escaped—an inferno of bombed-out cities, casualty lists, terrified civilians sheltering behind the bodies of the young. They would have had their "noses rubbed in death" and faced a constant struggle to secure "a thread of liberty"—

their lives boxed in on all sides. She did not know whether she could survive under such conditions. The reversal from yesterday's gloom, when she was sure that bombs would begin exploding at any moment, was so startling that she concluded it was "soberly & truly life after death."

The lull in the political storm coincided with a stretch of actual stormy weather, which Virginia could not help seeing as another omen; in crises like this, she said, one becomes highly susceptible to "weather symbols—roping everything in." The storms persisted for several days. Her feelings of relief, like those of her neighbors, had turned into a peevish awareness that the peace could not last. High winds and pelting rain knocked out electricity in the village, and the Woolfs lit the candles they had bought in preparation for war; they heated their food at the dining room fireplace, or ate cold mutton and windfall apples, which were plentiful. Darkness and silence made the recurring drone in the sky especially ominous. Virginia wrote to Vanessa: "Marshes all a mist, cows sheltering, aeroplanes still booming." Leonard predicted they would have "peace without honour for six months."

❦

Virginia detected increasing disillusionment with Chamberlain's policies when they returned to London on October 16; everyone felt that time was growing short. Vanessa wrote on October 24, praising the beauty and solitude of Cassis. The vines were ripening and the peasants friendly; they had lunch on the terrace every day—a perfect time for Virginia to come. She was tempted by the lure of hot sun and no telephones; the thought of escaping wintry London brought her to the verge of buying a ticket, but at the last moment she realized that she and Leonard were "so unhappy apart that I cant come"—a humiliating fact, she wrote, that revealed the complete failure of her marriage, since attachment reduces one to "damnable servility . . . the worst failure imaginable." In any case, war might break out, and she could not risk going so far away from Leonard. They discussed the sword of Damocles that was hanging over them. He said that he had been obsessed by fear of death for the past two or three years and had to teach himself not to think of it. Virginia replied that she would not wish to live if he died, but as long as they were together she "found life what? exciting? Yes I think so. He agreed. So we dont think of death."

Her social life was busier than ever. She had predicted that her fame would decline and she would fall into obscurity, but just the opposite was true. She had so many visitors and invitations she sometimes could do no more than list them in her diary. On December 1 she recorded eight engagements in four days—in spite of which she had the sensation of merely marking time. It was hard to believe in the importance of what she was doing when Europe was preparing to plunge into chaos. Her books were "intolerably airy and off the point," she told Ethel. The Fry biography involved major drudgery, but she kept on with it, only pausing to dash off an episode of "Pointz Hall" (ultimately *Between the Acts*) when the diet of facts grew too oppressive. Summing up the year's work just before Christmas, she noted that she had brought Roger's life up to 1919 and written 120 pages of the new novel, as well as several essays and stories.

She had a paradoxical sense of hovering at the brink of a fatal accident, when time moves very slowly and speeds up relentlessly. Franco was winning the war in Spain, she noted at the beginning of the new year and she had dreamt of Julian. On January 28, 1939, the Woolfs had tea with Sigmund Freud, whose books the Hogarth Press had published since 1924—a "screwed up shrunk very old man," sitting in a bright Hampstead room surrounded by little statues of Egyptian gods. He was half paralyzed and suffering from cancer of the mouth. It was a strained but impressive interview due to Freud's old-fashioned courtesy and broken English. He presented Virginia with a narcissus. She detected traces of "immense potential . . . an old fire now flickering." He listened intently to Leonard's story about a judge who wanted to punish a book thief by making him read all of Freud's works, and commented: "I was infamous rather than famous." Speaking about the Nazis, Freud said that the poison would take a generation to work its way out. When Virginia remarked that if England had not won the last war there might have been no Hitler he replied that if Germany had won, it "would have been infinitely worse." His final words were: "What are *you* going to do?"— "you" meaning England—and Virginia supplied the only possible answer: war.

The strain of negativity infected her overall mood. She fretted deeply about a loan to her friend, Helen Anrep, who had lived with Roger Fry in his later years. Helen's financial affairs were in disarray, and Virginia lent her £150 to cover her overdraft at the bank. She had worked hard to earn the money and at once regretted her generosity. Helen had often subsidized needy young artists in the past, and Virginia wondered whether her loan was now going "to supply sympathy to sympathy addicts." What a return for her drudgery. The suspicions nagged at her throughout January. She consoled herself with the thought that Roger had given her invaluable criticism of her novels; his comment that her lyrical "inanimate scenes" diverted too much attention to her own personality was worth at least £150. She had done the right thing to honor his memory by helping his beloved companion. Still, when Vanessa remarked that Helen's habits had not changed—"Oh she'll never repay you"—Virginia ground her teeth.

The new truncated Czechoslovakia was disintegrating, and on March 11, while the disorder was coming to a head, Virginia reported that she had finished the first draft of the Fry biography. She felt no elation, focusing rather on the "terrible grind" still to come; given her inadequacies as a biographer, she wondered whether she would be able to finish the work, though she allowed herself "one moments mild gratification" for having at least extracted the facts and outlined the main events of Roger's life. A few days later she noted the end of Czechoslovakia in her diary. The Slovak provinces had declared their independence, and Nazi troops marched into Prague on March 15, making the remainder of the country a German protectorate. Having promised to respect Czechoslovakia's independence, Hitler again proved his contempt for those who had believed him. Virginia quoted Chamberlain's feeble complaint that this action was "not in the spirit of the Munich meeting." The absurdity of the remark made any comment of her own superfluous. All she could say was: "We sit & watch." In the meanwhile she estimated that it would take her three months to revise "Roger Fry" and by then very likely they would be at war. She referred to that disaster with bitter nonchalance: "There's always our dear old war." This "purple background" clouded their Easter holidays at Rodmell in spite of the fine hot weather. The war had caused a deep severance, she said, making everything seem meaningless, and at the same time generating a "community feeling: all England thinking the same thing . . . at the same moment. Never felt it so strong before."

Her reaction to this sinister atmosphere was complicated by Leonard's mother, who had suffered a heart attack in December and was obsessed by her health. Marie Woolf had begun settling her affairs and had offered to leave Virginia either a drawing room chair or a silver sugar caster. But she clung to life with fierce tenacity. On April 27 a particularly dismal tea with the ailing woman left Leonard pondering his own old age. He said he hoped to die before Virginia because, living more in a world of her own, she could cope with solitariness, whereas he depended on their common life and shared pleasures such as the garden. They argued absurdly about who needed the other more. Virginia commented: "I was very happy to think I was so much needed. Its strange how seldom one feels this: yet 'life in common' is an immense reality." As for Leonard, he was upset by his mother's increasing self-absorption and the thought that the spirit can die before the body.

[Virginia's diary, April 28, 1939]

Her lonely old age is so intolerable . . . he said, because she has adopted an unreal attitude. Lived in a sentim[ent]al make believe. Sees herself as the adored matriarch, & forces the children to adopt her attitude. Hence the unreality of all relations. This obsession of hers has also shut her off from all other interests: doesn't care for any impersonal thing—art, music, books. Wont have a companion or reader; must depend on her sons. Constant innuendoes therefore about the goodness of Herbert & Harold; inference that L. neglects her; hints that I have taken him away from his family; absorbed him in mine. So in that crowded pink hot room we sat for 2 hours trying to beat up subjects for conversation. And there were awful silences, & our heads filled with wool. . . . Yet she followed us out on to the stair & made L. swear that she looks better—"Sure Len? Sure I look better?" as if she still clings hard to life & cant be removed. So to walk in the hail in Ken[sington] Gardens; & see the cherry trees livid & lurid in the yellow storm haze. Very cold winter spring.

Virginia was determined to resist the conventional lies that ensure "the unreality of all relations." She applied the same yardstick to her mother-in-law's ordinary human weaknesses as to the dictator's extraordinary lust for power—both represent an "unreal attitude." They impose a frame that does not fit and "encloses no reality," while works of art and intellect provide fitting frames for our experience.

Marie Woolf's emotional blackmailing of her children differed only in degree from other kinds of force. Her resentment against her daughter-in-law for taking Leonard away from his family was a paradigm of tribal prejudice and national pride. There was a continuity between her delusions and the greater delusions of the age. Domestic unreality warps feelings as well as ideas, and Mrs. Woolf's anxious questions added their confusion to the "purple background" that stained the finest of spring days.

15 *To the Altar*

The Woolfs were living next door to a demolition site. Workmen had torn down the two houses next to theirs and erected girders to shore up the outside wall, which had also been the interior of the adjacent house. From the street one saw a patchwork of wallpaper and paint where bedrooms and sitting rooms had once been. At night the traffic on Southampton Row, formerly muffled by the intervening houses, kept Virginia awake. During the day there was constant hammering, and a fine sand sifted in from outside, coating the floor of her studio. Preparing to leave for Rodmell on May 25, 1939, Virginia thought about the time she had spent in that room, sitting in front of the fire with a notebook in her lap and stacks of Hogarth Press publications around her. It had become slightly oppressive, and she reflected that she would write no more books there. Leonard at that moment was negotiating the lease of a new house in nearby Mecklenburgh Square, a quieter neighborhood where their back garden would abut on a park and playground that had once belonged to a foundling hospital. Virginia imagined ending her days sitting in the sun in that "great peaceful garden."

They left Rodmell on June 5 for a two-week tour of Brittany and Normandy, visiting Les Rochers, the château where Madame de Sévigné had written the letters that proved her "one of the great mistresses of the art of speech." Virginia was enchanted, she said, to see a chaise longue and a chamber pot shaped like a tureen that the lady had carried with her on her visits to the court of Louis XIV. The undistinguished château was "made of silver oatcakes," but the old farm buildings, dressed in harmonious grays and whites, suggested natural refinement. On June 18 the Woolfs stopped in Bayeux, where the Feast of Saint John with its midsummer night's celebrations confirmed her sense of a rich tradition—fireworks, people in fancy dress, and a white-robed priest under a palanquin blessing a fishing boat heaped with roses. "Lord, how rapturous and civilized and sensuous the French are compared to us," Virginia wrote Ethel, "and how it liberates the soul to drink a bottle of good wine daily and sit in the sun." How satisfactory too to watch an elderly *bourgeoise* whose neat figure bulged "like a cottage loaf" and an old man in black velvet with silver buttons playing the bagpipe while elaborately costumed youngsters danced and cavorted through the night.

Upon her return to England, she set to work again revising *Roger Fry*. She had now reached the chapter on the Post-Impressionist exhibition in which Fry first introduced the great modernist painters to Philistine England, and she found it appallingly difficult to "get the right proportions." Virginia's friends were all talking about the suicide of Mark Gertler, her old acquaintance and Fry's protégé, who had turned on the gas in his studio after separating from his wife. Virginia had seen him a month earlier, when he came to provide some information about Fry for the biography and vigorously denounced "the vulgarity, the inferiority of what he called 'literature'; compared to the integrity of painting." A difficult, opinionated man and an egotist—too fanatical to take life easily. But he was also a dedicated artist who appeared to be well established, with influential friends and connections. Although she had some doubts about his paintings, she had years before concluded that "his pertinacity would bore holes in granite." Virginia had seen few signs of illness or depression when he dined with them in May, though Gertler talked about an earlier suicide attempt, from which, he said, he had completely recovered, having reached a new stage of development as a painter. Vanessa and Duncan were enthusiastic about his latest show and had pronounced it "a great advance." These were the external facts, but Virginia thought about the inner realities, the private pain that had been too severe to live with—his wife, perhaps—outweighing all the advantages of "his intellect & interest," his absorption in his work. He was poor, of course, and forced to teach, but those were mere incidentals. She knew nothing about why he had done it. His lonely death highlighted the isolation that many artists felt during this appalling time. Moreover, his identity as a Jewish artist made him doubly sensitive to Nazi brutality. After one of Hitler's speeches he had said: "I heard the voice of the brute pouring poison into the hearts of his countrymen—it was awful—like wild beasts."

⅌

Virginia's style in *Roger Fry* was conventional and occasionally flat, as if the crisis atmosphere in which she wrote it discouraged any self-expression. The book presented a sympathetic survey of Fry's life and aesthetic ideas, but made little effort to portray the inner man. Virginia had scrupulously excluded many personal details from the portrait in deference to Fry's family and her own views about privacy. Her account of his artistic career was clear and supple, but unadorned by poetry or humor—an "experiment in self suppression," she called it—her friend's life told as much as possible in his own words, on the assumption that he would "shine by his own light better than through any painted shade of mine." Her self-restraint had a certain point, since it was Roger who had warned her against the temptation to "poetise" and impose her own personality. Like *The Years*, this biography was an attempt to write against her grain and a response to the antipoetic spirit of the times. Leonard later remarked that she had done some violence to her nature by submitting to an "iron pattern" of realistic chronology. She said as much when she was in the midst of revising the manuscript, declaring that she was determined "to plod through & make a good job, not a work of art. Thats the only way. To force myself on. . . . There's no blinking the fact that it is drudgery & must be; & I must go through with it." Her task was to synthesize the facts and create a faithful memorial. She hoped to do a commonplace "good job," relying not on artistic vision but on the self-effacing practice of her craft.

Still, the artistic instincts she denied on one level made their claim on another—the man she was writing about had after all devoted his life to the fine arts—and in retrospect she compared the biography to a musical composition with its statement of themes, development, and recapitulation. She tried to sound all the themes, she said, so they could be "heard together and end by bringing back the first theme in the last chapter." She added that she thought of her books as music before writing them and could only deal with the proliferating factual data by "abstracting it into themes." In "A Sketch of the Past," the experimental memoir she had begun writing in April, she gave another account of this style, with its emphasis on leading motifs, observing that "if life has a base that it stands on, if it is a bowl that one fills and fills and fills," then her own starting point was a childhood memory of lying in bed on a summer morning at St. Ives, listening to the sound of breaking waves and splashing water. Such core experiences were linked to a hidden pattern behind daily life, which in turn set the "background rods or conceptions," that is, the personal yardsticks, one used to measure all events. So Virginia's life was governed by the water's rhythm, the sense of ebbing and flowing that she had acquired during those summers by the sea, and her years filled with variations on that motif. Similarly Virginia presented Roger Fry's core experience in the opening paragraph of the biography. The garden of the house where he lived in early childhood contained a bed of brilliant oriental poppies that first aroused his keen aesthetic sensibilities. She quoted Fry's account of the discovery. He had observed the green buds "with little pieces of crumpled scarlet silk showing through. . . . I conceived that nothing in the world could be more exciting than to see the flower suddenly burst its green case and unfold its immense cup of red." The ecstasy of that moment was the core, the base on which all Fry's later artistic career rested. It provided the design of Virginia's biography, setting aesthetic passion as the dominant theme, the center round which all other interests revolved.

Aesthetic passion, evolving into a mission to bring the new Post-Impressionist art to the Philistines, sustained Fry in spite of his personal unhappiness. In 1917, at the height of World War I, he wrote "Art and Life," an essay arguing that the two realms have distinct and independent rhythms, their histories often taking quite different courses—as Roman pictorial style, for example, remained unchanged while the empire was in the throes of conversion to Christianity. Virginia found a comparable duality in Fry's private life; the hectic rhythms of the freelance critic and painter, "with callers coming, the telephone ringing and fashionable ladies asking advice about their bedspreads," stood in sharp contrast, she said, to the lucidity of the connoisseur retiring to his studio to contemplate Giotto. Fry's life displayed an unusually complex intermingling of both rhythms, the active and the contemplative, each overlaying and modifying the other. The more closely she looked at the details of his life, the harder it was to keep them separate in her mind—was there any clear dividing line at all? she asked. For Fry had found that his aesthetic theories provided indispensable help in facing personal problems. Detachment, he said, was "the supreme necessity for the artist," and he had needed all the detachment he could muster when his young wife suddenly showed signs of serious mental illness shortly after their marriage.

Helen Fry's breakdown formed a rough parallel to Virginia's own history, with Roger playing the same nurturing role as Leonard. To add to the echo effect, Helen's psychiatrists, Savage and Head, had also been Virginia's doctors when she broke down shortly after marrying Leonard. Those ghosts infected her style, coloring the key passage in which she described the onset of Helen's dementia. The crisis began while the young couple were living in Italy, where they had gone because the English climate seemed to affect Helen's lungs. This was a false alarm, but other vague anxieties haunted them. "Certain fears," Virginia wrote, "whether reasonable or fantastic it was impossible to say, kept recurring. They moved from place to place in the attempt to escape from them. Roger Fry, it can only be said, did all that he could to help his wife; his patience and sympathy were indefatigable, his resourcefulness beyond belief. But her obsessions increased. And finally, when they came back to England in the spring the blow fell. Madness declared itself." Simultaneously overblown and wooden, the account reflects the writer's discomfort with her subject, which she describes in stock phrases. "Her obsessions increased. . . . The blow fell. Madness declared itself." Virginia did not allow herself to dramatize or imagine the moment at which Helen for the first time became so agitated that Roger, in spite of his caretaking skills, had to get professional help. Instead of providing details of the illness, she quoted his terse note to a friend: "Last night she was worse. Nothing was omitted to make it horrible. We take her today to an asylum." Virginia's brief authorial comment on Helen's breakdown drew a veil over the event: "The agony that lay behind those words cannot be described," she wrote, "but it cannot be exaggerated."

The tone of the last sentence again suggests Virginia's reluctance to examine Fry's character or motives in any depth. What she left out is revealing. She edited his account of falling in love with Helen Coombe after only a few hours of intense talk, and in improving Fry's prose she obscured the fact that he had anticipated his wife's breakdown from the start; he was fascinated, he wrote, by her wit and by something else, "a strange touch of genius. . . . And there was beauty too and a certain terror on my part at the mysterious ungetatableness of her—I suppose what became her madness later on, but the terror tho' very definite, so that I felt certain of tragedy when I married, added a fearful delight." In transcribing this sentence, Virginia omitted Fry's statement that he "felt certain of tragedy when [he] married," a certainty that gave the romance a somewhat sinister aspect. The omission played down the implication that Roger was attracted to Helen because of her illness, which again had parallels in Virginia's relationship with Leonard.

Virginia was even more reticent about the parts of Roger's personal life that coincided with her own. She mentioned her friendship with him only obliquely and was completely silent about his love affair with Vanessa, which began about a year after Helen, diagnosed as a schizophrenic, was permanently committed to an asylum. Vanessa had advised Virginia to tell the whole truth about her and Roger, sending an important signal to the young. "I hope you won't mind making us all blush," she had written. But Virginia, sticking to her determination not to publish the details of private life, excluded anything that could cause blushes, even among the dead. Everything she knew from personal experience, including Roger's close friendship with Julian, received the same reserved treatment.

She shared Fry's belief that the aesthetic emotion carries a special "quality of 'reality.'" His single-minded concentration on artistic forms was refreshingly objective and remote from practical politics. Though the job of documenting Roger's life was often sheer drudgery, she had vicariously formed a new relationship with him; in some ways she felt closer to him now than when he was alive. The shape of his theories fit the cast of her mind and resonated naturally in her voice. She sensed a crossover between literary and visual forms, Roger's ideas in a different register enriching her understanding. It was illuminating to examine the things he had collected in his studio. Among piles of papers and books, canvases and paints, he had arranged a group of objects for a still life, with a note warning the cleaning lady not to disturb them—a shrine where the artist worshiped indestructible "tokens of spiritual reality . . . the immortal apples, the eternal eggs." Their clarity of form resembled one of Virginia's fictional still moments, her visions of a kitchen table lodged in a pear tree or an old glove that kept the shape of a hand.

Fry maintained that though art depends on material conditions, its essential aim is not to mirror nature but to create its own forms, and therefore its own special reality. This power was exemplified by the work of the great Post-Impressionist painters, who were able to "express by pictorial and plastic form certain spiritual experiences. . . . They do not seek to imitate form, but to create form, not to imitate life, but to find an equivalent for life." Through structural clarity, he said, they tried to achieve a vividness analogous to that of the natural world itself, escaping the limits of mimetic art. "In fact they aim not at illusion but at reality." Their works bewildered visitors to the first Post-Impressionist exhibition, in 1910, antagonizing the London art establishment, as well as the public, by exposing them, Virginia said, to "the shock of reality." The exhibition had brought Fry great notoriety, she added, ultimately making him "the most read and the most admired, if also the most abused, of all living art critics."

While insisting that art and life obey separate and often divergent, rhythms, Fry was highly sensitive to the political climate. In the aftermath of World War I he saw the folly of imposing vindictive peace terms on Germany and predicted that these policies would produce a terrible reaction. The main task now, he said, was to prevent the politicians from destroying the remnants of civilization that had survived the war. Like Virginia, he regarded nationalism, with its appeal to mass emotions, as the most monstrous "of all the religions that have afflicted man." Unscrupulous leaders, manipulating the masses for their own ends, drove Europe closer and closer to anarchy. An epidemic of "emotional unreason" had not only infected Germany and England but also undermined the great tradition of objectivity in France, the country he admired most, making it imperative to promote the civilized detachment provided by the aesthetic emotion.

Fry's critical study of Cézanne, a book that Virginia considered his masterpiece, offered an implicit summation of these values. His argument, she wrote, was that the great painter combined two different and usually incompatible kinds of artistic intelligence—the power of rigorous analysis and of intuitive sensibility; he grasped both the formal design of a work and the minute local gradations of its tone and texture. These powers, Virginia added, had enabled Cézanne to transform ordinary domestic objects, like a few apples, a table, a milk jug, and a ginger jar, into statements of timeless values, so that the objects were "invested with the majesty of mountains and the melody of music."

A similar spirit invigorated Fry's criticism, enabling him all through his life to analyze the most familiar works afresh, as if seeing them for the first time; he refused to repeat himself. In his last years, Virginia said, he often retreated to a small house at St. Remy in Provence, where he could work on his own painting without interruption. In the evenings he would open the door and listen to the nightingales singing and frogs croaking, happily observing that the night creatures "always break the rhythm before it gets quite fixed." His own supple temperament had something in common with those natural rhythms. Though he had never achieved the same mastery as a painter that he displayed as a critic, his practice as an artist sharpened his analytical skills. Adopting the impersonal tone that Fry favored, Virginia commented on the convergence of his critical and creative selves. "As the artist grows older," she wrote, "the critic becomes aware of an increasing richness and boldness in the design. . . . The artist becomes less conscious and so has access to a greater range of emotion. He draws into his theme common things, the milk-pot, the apple and the onion, and invests them with a peculiar reality." But remembering Roger's insistence that analysis was only a crude instrument in comparison to the complexity of the concrete work of art, she went no further.

Roger's puritanical character had been permanently stamped by the twelve early years during which he had wrestled with his wife's mental illness. After Helen's commitment he had turned all his energies to practicing and teaching his aesthetic gospel. His belief in the artist's need for detachment and self-renunciation paralleled Virginia's ideal of anonymity, and her account of his philosophy echoed the prophetic passages of *Three Guineas*. In order to expand and grow, she wrote, the self must learn to resist "the deformation which is possession." Such detachment enabled one to enjoy life fully without succumbing to "the great sin of Accidia which is punished by fog, darkness and mud." The words applied to Roger, but they arose from Virginia's own struggle against depression, her fear of the enveloping "fog, darkness and mud," which one could only defeat, she said, "by asking nothing for oneself."

Roger had welcomed new inspirations to the end, she concluded. "Like the frogs at St. Remy, he broke the rhythm before it got quite fixed."

Leonard's mother at eighty-eight stubbornly insisted on doing everything for herself. Short, fat and impulsive, she had fallen several times, and on June 28 she broke two ribs. She lay in the London Clinic in serious condition, clinging to life and applying such emotional blackmail to her grown-up children that Virginia's sympathies went mainly to the daughter who would have to nurse her. It was cruel to say so, but the old woman had so "contrived to falsify all emotions" that her family could only wish for her to die. A long, drawn-out illness would be even crueler, Virginia thought, because her mother-in-law had "the immortality of the vampire. Poor Flora will be sucked drop by drop for years to come."

Marie Woolf was in a precarious state for three days, during which time Virginia spent hours sitting in a hospital alcove, waiting for word from the sickroom. The doctor had warned them that the patient would probably at some point simply stop breathing. One night Mrs. Woolf felt well enough to joke that Virginia should write a book called "The Fallen Woman." On July 2, after most of the family had left for dinner, they received a phone call at Tavistock Square saying that her condition had turned critical, and she died before they reached the hospital.

Virginia was left with "a regret for that spirited old lady, whom it was such a bore to visit. Still she was somebody." But one could not deny that her character was depressingly banal. She had forced her own rosy version of reality on the unwilling family, who humored her, Leonard said, by pretending to live "in the best of all possible worlds, a fairyland of nine perfect children worshipping a mother to whom they owed everything" and revering the memory of their dead father. Paradoxically, she also had the tough, practical sense of a widow who had raised her nine children alone on a very meager income. But for a long time she had lacked any interest or productive work that could make life worth living. Virginia had discussed that distressing fact with Leonard years ago and concluded that "one should take poison. She has every reason; & yet demands more life, more life." In spite of these thoughts, Virginia had been deeply moved when Mrs. Woolf confessed one of her darkest secrets: that the governess she shared a bed with as a child had given her an unspecified terrible disease. Virginia had received the confidence as a real offering, though she could not respond to the implicit demand for greater intimacy. How would she herself act when she reached that advanced age, she asked—would she "go to the writing table & write that simple & profound paper upon suicide which I see myself leaving for my friends?"

⚘

Crises had come and gone for so long, and with such regularity—the Rhineland, Abyssinia, Spain, Austria, Czechoslovakia—that Virginia in July 1939 heard the latest news of German threats against Poland in a state of numb detachment. Harold Nicolson, from his vantage point in Parliament, predicted there would be war in a month, and the warning sank in, blending with all the previous ones. She felt a dull foreboding and a low vibration in the background, like the audible impression of her frayed nerves. "Over all hangs the war of course," she wrote. "A kind of perceptible but anonymous friction. Dantzig. The Poles vibrating in my room." Walking along the Tottenham Court Road one night on her way to the movies, she was overcome by horror of the crowd—the people seeming so "stunted & vicious & sweating" that she had to order herself to take one step at a time, murmuring, "step out, on, on," in order not to freeze in her tracks. She worried about moving to Mecklenburgh Square. The thought of all those carpets, books, papers, furniture they had to dispose of gave her sleepless nights. She prepared for their usual summer move to Rodmell, knowing that she was leaving Tavistock Square for good and intending to record her feelings about leaving, but in the last-minute rush she had no time to do it.

Arriving at Monk's House on July 25, Virginia found that workmen, on Leonard's orders, had started putting up a new greenhouse; an ugly brick foundation and shed stood in the garden, spoiling the view from her writing lodge. It caused her serious conflict, since she knew how he loved his gardening. While she was taking her bath the following morning, Leonard came in to ask what he should do. The workmen were outside—should he tell them to finish the job or send them away? She felt the fine balance between her own distress and his pleasure. Her account of what followed indicates the shape of their marriage in two spare sentences. "I said, You must decide. So he sent them away." She couldn't stop brooding about Leonard's disappointment, while at the same time she equally resented the intrusion on her working space. Leonard told her to forget the whole thing, but her conscience bothered her. "I'm so unhappy," she wrote, using that "portmanteau word" to signify a mixture of "headache; guilt; remorse . . . The house, L's house . . . oh dear, his hobby—his peach tree—to be pulled down because of me." Altogether it had been a "Greenhouse morning." Since misery kept her from working, she composed herself by reading through her diaries for the past year, which helped because it let her survey a longer stretch of time than the narrow view she got from "grubbing in an inch." She realized then that she had been outfoxed, for hadn't Leonard caused the problem by not consulting her in the first place, and then he had made her feel guilty for being so particular. She was definitely annoyed by his "adroitness in fathering the guilt on me. His highhandedness. I see the temptation. 'Oh you dont want it—so I submit.'" Of course it was a temptation to claim the moral high ground, and he had yielded to it. So they quarreled and then came a reconciliation, climaxed by her shameless demand for reassurance: "Do you ever think me beautiful now?" To which he replied: "The most beautiful of women."

The "great affair" of the greenhouse ended two days later with the decision that Leonard should build an unobtrusive cold frame behind the house. The workmen took down the foundation and shed. "Queer what a relief," Virginia remarked, "to see the shape of the wall & the pink Jackmanna again. How my eye feels rested."

After the dance of self-sacrifice and accommodation, the naive maneuvering for moral advantage, she found their reconciliation sweet. What a specimen of ordinary domesticity—to be squabbling about the garden. Perhaps it was a sign that nothing really disastrous would happen after all. Virginia could still declare that she had "never been so free & happy," though she added the warning from Eliot's "Prufrock" that such idylls only last till "human voices wake us & we drown."

❧

All their belongings were deposited in boxes in vans, Virginia wrote to Vita; they owned two London houses, neither one livable. The Woolfs' move to Mecklenburgh Square coincided with a further escalation of the political crisis. On August 24, the day they had arranged for the movers to deliver their personal belongings, the news came that Germany and Russia had signed a nonaggression pact, thus freeing Hitler to move against Poland—a disagreeable turn of events for the British government, which had pledged to fight if the Germans invaded Poland. Riding up to London by train that morning, Virginia was struck by how subdued and almost indifferent the other passengers seemed to be. The city streets, too, were quiet, in contrast to the stir that had marked the Munich crisis—a sign that people were emotionally exhausted. "Rather like a herd of sheep we are. No enthusiasm. Patient bewilderment. I suspect some desire to 'get on with it.'" All indications were that they would soon have their wish. The government was staging a complete dress rehearsal for war—blackouts, Parliament meeting to pass the Emergency Powers Act, public places closed. Arriving at Mecklenburgh Square the Woolfs learned that the trip was a waste of time, since the man who was supposed to unpack their furniture had been called up for military duty. The foreman took this setback with philosophical calm. No one was to blame, he said. "What can you do against fate?" The new flat was in a state of complete chaos, its passages blocked by crates and boxes. Disorder too at the Hogarth Press, since all the delivery vans had been commandeered

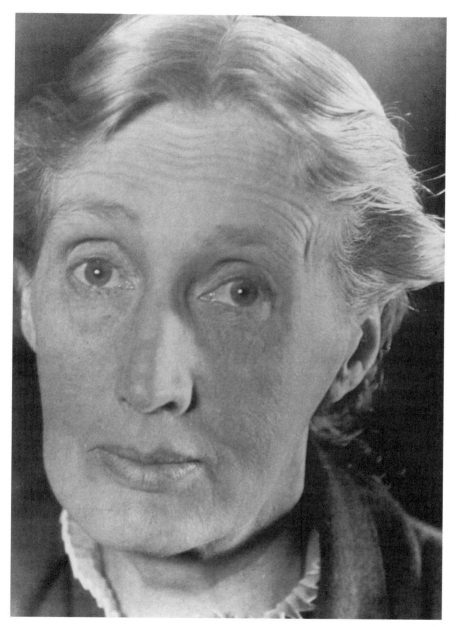

Figure 20. Virginia, photographed by Gisèle Freund, 1939.

and there was no one to transport books to the shops. Although they were comfortably settled in Rodmell for the time being, Virginia was distressed by the general disorder in London. Their private affairs were a mess, she said, and in perfect agreement with the mess the politicians had made.

The modest routines of their life back at Monk's House were hardly affected by the war preparations, but everything had changed. Sometimes, lulled by the country quiet, she allowed herself to imagine that they had escaped to a sunny private island, but afterward the return to reality was all the more painful. Every day they switched on the radio, expecting to hear that the fighting had begun. Hitler's shrill voice came through, denouncing Poland as he had previously denounced Czechoslovakia. Virginia's sense that a way of life was ending and a new dark age was being born gave each summer day a vibrant clarity. On August 28 she walked on the downs, thinking that this might be the last day of peace, and lay down beside a cornstack, registering the emptiness of the land, the indifferent spectacle of pinkish clouds crossing the sky. Later, resisting despondency, she noted how content she felt with her private life and domestic duties; the romance of the commonplace filled her with "bliss day after day. So happy cooking dinner, reading, playing bowls. No feeling of patriotism." Perhaps she could forget the war mania on her private island; but when she thought of the world beyond it, things lost their color, she went numb, a "vast calm cold gloom" enveloped her. The question was how they would survive, "how to go on, through war? . . . Of course I have my old spurs & my old flanks." Work had pulled her through before, and her old flanks had survived several hard races. Besides, she had the fullness of the present moment to sustain her. "Yes, its a lovely still summer evening; not a sound. A swallow came into the sitting room. I talked to the girl who keeps elk hounds on the hill, by the ivy bloom tree. May flies buzz. I am sleeveless in the heat."

There was an ominous note in her language. She kept casually reversing herself, mentioning domestic bliss one moment and numb despair the next, as if the two were unconnected and an impassable gulf separated her sunny island from the stormy outer world. Her memories of the two states came so close together that they seemed about to mingle, but still they remained separate, each untouched by the other, as if applying not only to different phases but to unrelated selves. This split anticipated wartime conditions, with their alternating "normal" intervals and spasms of pure destructiveness—conditions in which dissociation became a strategy for survival.

For now the pleasures of cooking, reading, and talking with her neighbors occupied her, but on another level she struggled against falling into complete apathy. It was important at least to create some order in the new flat at Mecklenburgh Square. They went up to London again on August 31 to see about having their furniture unpacked and clearing the bottleneck at the Hogarth Press—an ironic moment to begin settling in, for on the same day the Germans were preparing to invade Poland. The first bombers crossed the border at dawn on September 1. Back at Monk's House, Virginia observed that the event they had dreaded for so long made no noticeable difference in the village—everything went on with the same deceptive air of normality as before. Leonard was in the garden, putting bags on their fruit trees, and a carpenter was busy installing decorative wooden columns in the dining room.

Though the war had begun, Chamberlain put off a formal declaration for two days, still hoping to negotiate rather than fight. The rank and file of both parties were angry about the delay, and Arthur Greenwood, the Labour Party spokesman, prodded Chamberlain to act, arguing that the time for compromise had ended. His speech in the House of Commons set off an argument between Virginia and Leonard. She objected to Greenwood's call for war. The Labour Party were still outsiders who had no say in policymaking, and she had no faith in the Conservative government. "Its 'they' as usual who do this," she argued. "We as usual remain outside. If we win,—then what?" To which Leonard replied that they had to fight and win in order to stop the spread of barbarism. "The Germans, vanquished, are what they are. . . . All the formulae are now a mere surface for gangsters." A rare political argument—they shared the same goals, but Virginia stood by her pacifism, insisting that force never worked in the long run. Shortly afterward, Chamberlain's ultimatum to the Germans expired without a reply and the argument became moot. Virginia judged that the public mood in Lewes, where she shopped for groceries, paralleled her own. The streets were crowded: cars loaded with bedding; resentful people buying provisions and stuff for blackout curtains, emptying the shelves, but showing no excitement or interest in the war. She concluded defiantly that the uproar was all "bosh & stuffing" compared with the reality of reading one of Tawney's social commentaries or revising a sentence of *Roger Fry*. She reaffirmed her faith in "the reality of the mind." When the material world seemed to recede, growing thin and insubstantial, she fortified herself with the mantra-like reminder that "any idea is more real than any amount of war misery." So she told herself without any great conviction, for at the back of her mind she saw a picture of bombs falling on rooms in Warsaw very like the one where she and Leonard were presently sitting. The image was superimposed on her garden, where the apples shone in the sun.

The air raids had not yet reached England, though Virginia woke to the sound of sirens on the morning of September 6. When she and Leonard emerged onto the terrace, the sky was clear, and there were no enemy planes in sight. Afterward she sewed curtains and helped some expectant mothers who had been evacuated from London settle into a Rodmell cottage. The women quarreled and complained, and Virginia concluded that the day resembled "a long sea voyage, with strangers making conversation, & lots of small bothers & arrangements." The constant stir and disorder made it impossible to concentrate on writing or any other creative work—a first taste of war's tedium. "Force," she declared, "is the dullest of experiences. It means feeling only bodily feelings: one gets cold & torpid. Endless interruptions."

They expected the bombs to rain down at any moment and were not sure when or whether they could return to Mecklenburgh Square, which was still a shambles. They made a flying visit on September 7, unpacked the furniture and laid down some rugs, but left the rooms still cluttered with empty cases and upended tables and chairs. Virginia found London silent, hot, and brooding. At night the unlit streets suggested "a mediaeval city of darkness and brigandage," and she reported a friend's story of hiring a taxi driver who had just been beaten and robbed. The war, she told Ethel, left her feeling as if she had been knocked on the head. She was very relieved to return to Monk's House and feel her nerves unknot themselves as they reached the familiar countryside. They decided it would be best to live at Rodmell for the time being, commuting to London when necessary.

Still no air raids. On September 23 Virginia noted that the Germans had taken three weeks to gobble up Poland with the help of Soviet troops that occupied the eastern half of the country, after which Poland completely disappeared from the map. The Germans paused there to consolidate and plan their next move, while the British government marked time and the French retired into the underground bunkers of their Maginot Line, peering at enemy positions through ingenious optics.

Since she could no longer count on an income from the Hogarth Press, Virginia turned to literary journalism, agreeing to write two articles for the *New Statesman and Nation*, a task that would not only earn her some money but keep her busy until she could concentrate on serious writing. "It's best to have a job," she reflected, "& I dont think I can stand aloof with comfort at the moment. So my reasons are half in half." That is, half economic, and half public-spirited— ironically filling in for other contributors who had joined the war effort. Though being a "journalist" again made her feel that she had regressed thirty years, writing to deadlines gave her a purpose around which to order her days. Her first article, on Gilbert White, the eighteenth-century parson whose *Natural History of Selborne* described the birds and beasts of his native village, absorbed her during mid-September. White's classic introduced the reader to a world where "the gossip is about the habits of vipers and the love interest is supplied chiefly by frogs." Her second subject was equally innocent and remote from the present conflict—a review of a new edition of Lewis Carroll's works, which she finished writing during a visit to London.

They left Rodmell on October 13 to spend a week at Mecklenburgh Square. Virginia was reluctant to go, feeling sure they were driving into a trap; their timing had been so bad lately, she feared they would enter the city at the precise moment when the bombing began, and she spent the first few days with one ear half cocked, listening for the sirens. "You never escape the war in London," she wrote. It was inscribed in the faces of the people hurrying along the sidewalk, in the disorder created by closed Tube stations and irregular buses, in the absence of children and loiterers. A subterranean life—"everyone humped with a gas mask." The shops closed early, and after dark the urban lanes yielded to untamed nature, growing "so verdurous & gloomy that one expects a badger or a fox to prowl along the pavement. A reversion to the middle ages with all the space & the silence of the country set in this forest of black houses. A torch blinks. An old gentleman revealed. He vanishes. That red light may be a taxi or a lamppost. People grope their way to each others lairs." Their flat was still a maze of books and pictures stacked on the floor, chamber pots in the living room and a bed in the dining room. The unfamiliar rooms dwarfed their furniture, the stairs needed fixing and the kitchen was too small. They had a miserable rainy spell during which Virginia stayed indoors, writing and rewriting the Lewis Carroll review, trying to forget how cold her hands and feet were, resisting the mood of "barren horror." One evening she wrote to Angelica Bell, giving glimpses of this claustrophobic city with its blacked-out windows and earth-moving machines digging trenches in the square. She had just pulled down her own blackout blinds, reflecting that "rats in caves live as we do."

By the end of the week life under siege began to seem almost normal, but returning to Rodmell changed the perspective—the surprise and relief were "rather like drawing the curtains and finding it a fine day." The shadow of the city, that medieval forest of houses, still hovered in the background, disturbing the quiet of her country house and garden. She sensed the urban wilderness coming closer, spanning the river, laying its grid over the meadows and downs. She often heard its engines booming in the planes that flew over the village.

⁓

It seemed that people still wanted books in spite of the war, and the Woolfs decided to publish the Fry biography in the summer of 1940, though they expected very modest sales. Virginia was revising the last long chapter, "Transformations."

They waited for an emergency that didn't come and wouldn't go away—the "twilight war," Churchill called it—the great armies lying low and perfecting their plans before committing themselves to full-scale hostilities. One day Leonard remarked that he had "trained himself to cut adrift completely from personal feelings" when necessary, a habit of selective detachment that Virginia found highly desirable. It was only common sense, since the ability to escape the prison of identity "gives one the only happiness thats secure." Such renunciation, which she was far from achieving, offered great advantages. How liberating it would be, she reflected, to be able to hear criticism of one's work while "eliminating oneself." Yes, Leonard's comments were "very subtle & wise," and compatible with her vision of anonymity, which was more easily achieved down here in the country, where one was not constantly being distracted by visiting friends and strangers. She also was finding new approaches to objectivity in Freud's writings, which she had started reading for the first time. She was determined to achieve greater scope and get outside herself; it was vital to defeat "the shrinkage of old age," she told herself. "Always take on new things. Break the rhythm."

They went on with their provisional lives, grimly watching sideshows like the hunt for the German pocket battleship, *Graf Spee*, which was cornered by British ships and took refuge at Montevideo on December 14. The Germans were allowed to stay in the neutral port for two days; then they were required to leave and take their chances against the British fleet waiting just outside territorial waters. Virginia remarked in disgust that journalists and curiosity seekers were chartering airplanes from which to watch the battleship go down, "& several people will lie dead tonight, or in agony. And we shall have it served up for us as we sit over our logs this bitter winter night." The event was spectacular enough, though it ended without a battle. The Germans evacuated the ship, sailed her out into deep water and blew her up; three days later the captain shot himself—a minor break in the deceptive calm of the twilight war. Virginia reported: "Nothing happens in England. Theres no reason anywhere. Brutes merely rampant." She found remnants of sanity among the villagers, who spoke their minds with invigorating bluntness, but most people seemed to be stunned by uncertainty, numbly carrying on while their minds were elsewhere.

Record frosts throughout December and January reinforced the general immobility and isolation. The severe cold froze water pipes and glazed the streets, lining Virginia's favorite walks with icy stubble. When the Woolfs drove their cook and maid, Louie, to Lewes to have some teeth pulled, they had their first experience of traveling under blackout conditions; approaching cars with their headlights shrouded like "small red eyes" cast a narrow ribbon of light at the center of the road—just enough so they could squeeze past each other, while everything, including the margins of the road, remained lost in darkness. Such scenes provided a fitting backdrop for Freud's works, which Virginia was avidly reading. She found his skepticism admirable, though disturbing, for if the unconscious governs our lives, if the human mind is a "whirlpool" of selfish instincts, then what are we to say about the ideals of civility and social progress? At any rate, she endorsed Freud's attack on religious authority. "His savagery against God good," she noted. "The falseness of loving one's neighbours. The conscience as censor."

The quality of her life had changed. The old rhythms created by work and social connections, by the alternations of city and country life, had been completely disrupted. She could hardly imagine peacetime London, with lights and traffic, ringing phones and a constant stream of visitors who never left her alone. The memory of her walks through "little alleys with the brass bound curtains & the river smell & the old woman reading" evoked whatever shreds of patriotism she had in her. Winding up the urban part of her life and moving to the country was a far greater break, she concluded, than any change of houses. And what a relief to exchange London for open space and solitude. The country offered constant small discoveries, like the sight of "a cormorant and kingfisher together on the river in a storm" or a hidden hollow in the downs where she took shelter from the high winds. Very likely she would never live in the city again, she wrote Vita. But all the time the feelings of helplessness induced by the war took their toll. One bitter January evening she noted in her diary that she intended to sit by the fire, reading "some severe classic," and forget about the high rent they were paying for the London house they couldn't live in, and her other anxieties. Earlier that day she had noticed that the wintry landscape, whose beauty gave her intense pleasure, also seemed barren and indifferent, echoing her own divided state.

> [Virginia's diary, January 20, 1940]
> I walked on the bank & home over the marsh. The beauty was ethereal, unreal, empty. A June day. 10 degrees of frost. All silent, as if offered from another world. No birds, no carts, men shooting. This specimen against the war. This heartless & perfect beauty. The willows ruby red, no rust red; plumed; soft . . . & the hills white. But some emptiness in me—in my life—because L. said the rent was so high. And then the silence, the pure disembodied silence, in which the perfect specimen was presented; seemed to correspond to my own vacancy, walking muffled with the sun in my eyes, & nothing pressing urging only this iron hard, ground, all painted. The men were waiting for widgeon. . . . We sat in the sun on the bank. All looked very distant, & picked out—the little stems of smoke—the wild duck—the horses huddled & still. No thoughts populated; I was somehow held in a pair of pincers, & came home to cook crumpets to revise my article; & all the words seem bodiless too. So what about a severe classic?

A dissociated episode: thoughts absent, words "bodiless," Virginia feeling "somehow held in a pair of pincers," which was the insidious grip of the war, emptying everything—her self, her writing, her favorite landscapes—displaying a purple background that had become almost invisible while it colored the whole vista, its cruelty underlined by the hunters waiting to shoot the quick freshwater birds. But she rallied, reminding herself not to brood on her own failure. This was a time to build her strength, a time "for living: unless one's to blow out; which I entirely refuse to do." The statement again reveals her impulsive haggling with disaster, simultaneously suggesting that she might die silently and effortlessly as a flame goes out, or she might be blown away like a leaf in the wind, or torn from life with explosive force.

Coming home after wading through the marsh in rubbers and greatcoat on a windy February day, Virginia noted that the spring, though dormant, was not far off, and it would be cruel, for they were all "being led to the altar this spring: its flowers will I suppose nod & yellow & redden the garden with the bombs falling."

She sent off the completed manuscript of Roger's biography to Margery Fry on February 23, feeling like a small child handing in a school exercise, and promptly came down with a sore throat and a fever that lingered in one form or another for five weeks. The first verdict on *Roger Fry* came on March 10, when she was up and about but still running a temperature. Leonard had read half the book and thought it flawed, as he told her during a walk through the watermeadows—very outspoken, almost angry, in his criticism. The book was merely analysis "not history," he said, that is, it lacked a point of view. Her method of presenting the themes in Roger's own words, without providing clear interpretive cues for the reader, could only work if the subject himself were a "seer" with a message that stood on its own, which Roger was not. The reader needed direction, and she had hobbled her imagination by using a style of "austere repression," which made the book "dull to the outsider. All those dead quotations." Leonard commented in his autobiography that Virginia had forced herself to write the biography against her natural bent, and *Roger Fry* therefore emerged in a "slightly broken-backed" condition. At the time, in 1940, he delivered his objections with such force that she was convinced she had failed, though one part of her remained skeptical, suspecting he had an unconscious motive—lack of sympathy with Roger, perhaps. She was not upset, however, since her ego was not seriously engaged, as it would have been with a novel—after all, the book was closer to "a piece of cabinet making" than a work of art. But the other readers were enthusiastic: Vanessa wrote that the biography brought Roger back to life for her, and Virginia should not change anything; Margery, too, found the portrait extremely lifelike, saying simply: "It's *him*"—which encouraged Virginia to publish it without major changes. Margery also provided a long list of small corrections and insertions, a form of torture that kept Virginia tinkering with the manuscript till April 9.

Meanwhile the birds clustered in the elms, carrying twigs for their nests, and Virginia allowed herself to hope for something resembling a normal spring, her first spring in the country since 1914, when she had been recovering from a nervous breakdown. They would peddle Hogarth Press books at shops round the coast, stop for tea and browse among antiques "& there'll be a lovely farmhouse—or a new lane—& flowers—& bowls with L"—these and many more pleasures beckoned: "May coming & asparagus, & butterflies." She was content not to think very much, but to rest in pure sensation, to have done with "future skirmishing or past regretting," and to relish the life of Monday or Tuesday, casting off her puritanical guilt. She had done her share for the human race by writing *Three Guineas* and owed "nobody nothing." Furthermore, she was being drawn into village life, actively participating in the social gatherings of the Rodmell Women's Institute, where she saw quarrels and intrigues whose ferocity equaled that of great nations. "The hatred for the parsons wife passes belief," Virginia wrote on April 6, adding that she and Leonard were regarded as "red hot revolutionaries because the Labour party meets in our dining room." Three days later the first major battle of the war began in the North Sea, when the Germans launched an invasion of Norway and Denmark.

16 *Weeping Willie*

Naval battles in the North Sea, British ships laying mines and landing troops on the coast of Norway to fight the German invaders. . . .
Virginia noted that "the first crunch of the war" had come. The moment had a perverse fascination; after months of anxious uncertainty,
she said, it gave "the old odd stretch to the back curtain of the mind."
Odd to meet this shadowy threat on a fine spring day when daffodils
were blooming along the terrace, to find her world divided between
two realities, with the flowers in front like a bright film over an obscure background where hostile forces tugged at the fabric of her self.
She heard the airplanes flying overhead, their shadows passing over
banks of violets, leaving her chilled in the sun.

She had spent this April morning writing a lecture for a working-
class audience in Brighton. She had promised to talk to the Workers'
Education Association about the young left-wing writers associated
with Auden, Isherwood and Spender. She suspected that their coherence as a group had ended in 1939: the war had scattered them and
changed their priorities; one could, perhaps, sum up their development now, though many of the issues that inspired them seemed oddly
remote. Virginia's lecture, "The Leaning Tower," which began with
a general account of class distinctions in English literature, described
the dilemma of the young writers who came of age around 1925 and
found themselves drawn into ideological battles for which their interests and education had not prepared them. They became socialists,
but bumped up against the awkward fact that as members of the
upper middle class, they sat "upon a tower raised above the rest of
us," a tower built on the privileges and money they had inherited

from their fathers. They could hardly shed their educations in public schools and elite universities, and these conferred other advantages they still enjoyed, in spite of feeling guilty about them. As a result their voices sounded strident, and their attacks on bourgeois society were both violent and halfhearted. Trapped on the tower, they could not admit the incongruity of their position. "They are profiting by a society which they abuse," Virginia commented. "They are flogging a dead or dying horse because a living horse, if flogged, would kick them off its back." Furthermore, the tower was no longer stable and upright; it was a leaning tower, threatening to cast its occupants to the ground, though for the time being it still offered a very fine view. It was inevitably a slanted view, a suspect view, that made them painfully self-conscious, sapping their creative strength; for a writer needs to become unconscious in order to create, needs a trancelike concentration, Virginia said, in which the "undermind works at top speed while the uppermind drowses," which was impossible in the leaning tower. Limited by these conditions, the young writers of the 1930s had spent a great deal of their energy on reporting rather than creating. Their best writing had been autobiographical; they had been "great egoists," she concluded, who had dared to tell the truth about themselves, and whose revelations might speed the arrival of a future classless society.

Virginia's relationship to her working-class audience contained its own contradictions. She had spoken of the typical young writer sitting "upon a tower raised above the rest of us," identifying herself as one of "us" rather than "them," taking her stand as an outsider who had never gone to a public school or a university. But socially she too sat upon the leaning tower; her iconoclasm did not cancel the advantages she had gained from being Sir Leslie Stephen's daughter. Though she used the first person plural, the gulf that separated her from the working class was immense, as she observed in a letter to Vita's son, Ben Nicolson. Commenting on the lecture, she asked how one could tell "people who left school at 14 and were earning their livings in shops and factories that they ought to enjoy Shakespeare?" For the moment these class differences were eclipsed by the shared dangers of the war. Referring to the war in her talk, she invoked feelings of solidarity with her audience that enabled her to say "we" without strain or apology.

§

The British fleet controlled the seas around Norway, but during April the Germans gained the initiative in ground and air combat, and on

May 6 Virginia reported the withdrawal of British troops from Norway. This "first defeat of the war" coincided with disturbing news about Angelica Bell. She had been having an affair with an old family friend, David Garnett, known as "Bunny," who was twenty-six years her senior. His first wife had recently died, and Virginia soon afterward asked Angelica whether she intended to marry him, implying that it would greatly distress Vanessa if she did. Angelica said she did not want to marry anyone. But on May 6 Virginia heard the news that Angelica and Bunny were on their way to Yorkshire, where they planned to spend the next two months together—an "explosion of love" that was particularly devastating for Vanessa. Years ago, during World War I, the bisexual Bunny had been Duncan Grant's lover, and had wanted to go to bed with Vanessa, who turned him down. When Vanessa gave birth to Duncan's child in 1918, Garnett had admired Angelica in her cradle and boasted that he would marry her someday. Now that threat to turn the tables on Vanessa seemed about to be carried out. Bunny had lured Angelica to come away for a tryst among the northern moors; Virginia imagined them "setting the supper in order & retiring to the couch," her puckish niece in the arms of "that rusty surly slow old dog with his amorous ways & primitive mind." The mismatch presented another sign of disorder, another disaster of the war—"Julian's death renewed," she said—as if the force that had killed the brother had struck again, condemning his sister to a life "without youth & laughter." The thought made Virginia feel old and empty, and she pictured herself drifting among indifferent tides that carried her out relentlessly "into the sea of old age," far away from "the land with its children."

Meanwhile, the new, violent phase of the war progressed rapidly. Following their success in Norway, the Germans launched an all-out offensive, beginning with a lightning invasion of Holland and Belgium on May 10, while at the same time their tanks penetrated the French defenses in the Ardennes, which were thought to be impassable and were only lightly defended. During these battles Virginia was correcting the galleys of the Fry biography, which she put in the mail on May 13, trying to preserve some sense of accomplishment in the midst of the general confusion; at that very moment the European armies were fighting "the greatest battle in history." No doubt it was shameful to think of her personal interests at such a time. Churchill, who had succeeded Chamberlain as prime minister on the day the Germans began their attack, had just made a famous appeal to the nation: "I have nothing to offer but blood, toil, tears and sweat," which the papers soon transformed into the more catchy "blood, sweat and tears." Speaking before Parliament, he urged the people to wage war with all their strength and to pursue "victory at all costs . . . in spite of all terrors," for that was the only way to ensure the survival of the empire and the civilization it stood for. He faced the future with "buoyancy and hope," he said, confident that "our cause will not be suffered to fail among men." Grand and slightly archaic language that evoked a long view of history, time measured in centuries or generations and personal lives reduced to invisibility. Virginia felt the great shifting masses on the Continent, the present upheavals connecting back to the Napoleonic wars, which were as fresh in memory as if they had just ended. And spring glowed on the margins of her mind as she thought of the great armies fighting.

> [Virginia's diary, May 13 and 14, 1940]
> The third day of the Battle of Waterloo. Apple blossom snowing the garden. A bowl lost in the pond. Churchill exhorting all men to stand together. . . . These vast formless shapes further circulate. They aren't substances; but they make everything else minute. Duncan saw an air battle over Charleston—a silver pencil & a puff of smoke. Percy has seen the wounded arriving in their boots. So my little moment of peace comes in a yawning hollow. But though L. says he has petrol in the garage for suicide shd. Hitler win, we go on. Its the vastness, & the smallness that makes this possible. So intense are my feelings (about Roger): yet the circumference (the war) seems to make a hoop round them. No, I cant get the odd incongruity of feeling intensely & at the same time knowing that there's no importance in that feeling. Or is there, as I sometimes think, more importance than ever? . . .
> Yes, we are being led up garlanded to the altar. A soldier with his rifle. The Dutch Govt & Court here. Warned of clergymen in parachutes. War war—a great battle—this hot day, with the blossom on the grass.

Reacting to Churchill's defiant rhetoric, Virginia envisioned the war as an impersonal mechanism, a system of "vast formless shapes" whose orbit marked the circumference of all their daily lives. The shapes were substanceless and yet had the power to make the silver pencil and puff of smoke materialize in the sky, fixing a visible intersection point between vastness and smallness. The vastness and the smallness made life possible because she was able to disconnect them; she could go on with the small tasks of writing, walking, and cooking dinner as if nothing had changed, though the petrol in the garage was a sign of how shaky the normal routines had become.

Her comment about the detachment that enabled her to go on implied the opposite as well—that a change in their lives, or in the intensity of the violence, might soon make it impossible to go on. She escaped the war when she could by living in the moment, enjoying the end of *Roger Fry*, ignoring the "yawning hollow" around that small sheltered spot, but the sense of incongruity that often assailed her revealed deep inner stresses.

On the Continent German tank columns advanced toward the English Channel, seeking to cut the Allied armies in France and Belgium in two. The battle raged so furiously, Virginia reported, that it could not go on much longer, and the outcome would be clear within ten days. The government appealed for civilians to man a Home Guard in case of landings by German paratroops. Eager to be actively engaged, Leonard said he would join, which caused Virginia to remark acidly that guns and uniforms are always slightly ridiculous. Their nerves were severely strained by the rumors about invasion and the consequences that would follow, for they might be left with no way out. On May 15, feeling a need to clear the air, they seriously discussed their options. As a Jew and a prominent socialist, Leonard would be singled out for particularly harsh treatment, and they agreed that suicide would be preferable to falling into Nazi hands. Virginia thought they should act at once if England was defeated. "What point in waiting? Better shut the garage doors." Having settled on a course of action she returned to her work in an easier frame of mind. No, she did not want to die—she was in the midst of writing a new novel and she hoped for another ten years of creative activity. But their ability to examine the dangers together, facing the future without romanticizing or evading the issues, calmed and freed her to be herself. She could view the war with some of her old defiant skepticism. Having assessed the latest disasters, she insisted that the patriotic appeals, and the war talk were all mere "bombast. . . . One old lady pinning on her cap has more reality." There was nothing admirable or noteworthy about using suicide to escape the Nazis—it would be more like a necessary chore. "So if one dies, it'll be a common sense, dull end—not comparable to a days walk, & then an evening reading over the fire." Her skepticism influenced Leonard, who gave up the idea of joining the Home Guard and settled on more mundane duties as a fire watcher. In his autobiography he commented on the limits of realism and the force of habit, even at desperate times: "When one is contemplating suicide by asphyxiation in a damp and dirty garage after breakfast, one continues to cook and eat one's eggs and bacon for breakfast."

❧

The war sharpened contradictions. As the allied armies suffered one defeat after another, Virginia felt the growing split, the separation between the realms of vastness and smallness. Much as she feared a German victory, she was also disgusted by English propaganda—the "cheery hero-making" on the radio and in the papers, the unctuous voices praising "the laughing, heroic, Tommy—how can we be worthy of such men?" Oh, the tedium of the speeches in which she knew the ending of every sentence—all the perorations delivered in "high-flown tense" voices. They did lift people's spirits, she conceded; they were the easiest things to write—she herself could "reel off patriotic speeches, by the dozen." Perhaps today's heroes would be tomorrow's derelicts, turning barrel organs in the streets for small coins. But if hearty patriotism was suspect, pacifism no longer served her either, and she had nothing to put in its place. Though it was hard to concentrate, she kept up her routine, writing short essays and reviews, shutting out the battle cries when possible. She had her own hard-headed way of reading the news, noticing the boundaries between fact and fantasy and resisting the lure of wishful thinking. The war had its particular immediacy in Rodmell: several village men whom she had known since they were children were fighting in Belgium. Her maid-of-all-work, Louie, had a brother at the front—not a mythical tommy but a live soldier whose adventures brought the gritty facts home to her.

The split was woven into their lives, which echoed with appeals for heroic sacrifice and were cramped by petty frustrations—shortages of sugar, meat or petrol; irregular bus and train schedules. On May 20 Virginia recorded her impressions of the philosopher G. E. Moore, who had come with her old Bloomsbury friend Desmond MacCarthy, to spend the weekend—a visit during which she had felt uneasily aware of housekeeping details. Moore's philosophy had inspired a whole generation of Cambridge intellectuals, and she remembered the youthful reverence with which she had once spoken a few words in his presence. Though he showed the same fine simplicity as ever, his stature had somehow diminished, and Virginia noted that now their reverence was "what one might call retrospective." They drank tea and discussed the influence he had wielded with his resounding silences, an example that had sometimes had the effect of silencing his followers. Detecting a reproach, Moore objected: "I didnt want to be silent. I couldnt think of anything to say." Then Virginia had given them an extravagant lunch of guinea fowl, and she observed that the great man attacked his food vigorously, as if compensating for short rations at home: "munches like a chaff cutter . . . takes a logical view of food; eats philosophically to the end: while Desmond sprinkles sugar & cream, also liberally but erratically." There was the war, insidiously lodged among the dishes on the table, distracting her with notions of economy. "So the housekeeper in me rises into being, in this miserable life of detail & bombast."

Virginia followed these domestic notes on May 25 with her reading of the latest news from the front, bursts of exasperation breaking through the cool, telegraphic style of her diary. The Germans, she wrote, had punched a twenty-five-mile-wide hole through which their tanks poured into the heart of France, while the Allied armies did nothing to stop them. The defenders' demoralized state made the outcome seem inevitable. "The feeling is we're outwitted. Theyre agile & fearless & up to any new dodge. The French forgot to blow up Bridges. The [Germans] seem youthful, fresh, inventive. We plod behind." Bad news kept coming in as the French armies in the north disintegrated, and the much smaller British Expeditionary Force, which was in danger of being cut off, retreated under fire to the beaches round Dunkirk. Between May 27 and June 4 nearly 340,000 men gathered at Dunkirk and were ferried across the Channel by a motley fleet of troop transports, fishing boats, and small pleasure craft, showing a resourcefulness that the Allied commanders on the Continent noticeably lacked. The evacuation saved the English regular army that would defend the island in case of invasion, while behind them the surviving French forces formed a new defensive line along the Somme River. These events riveted the attention of the Rodmell villagers, whose sons were engaged in the retreat, and whose houses were only a few miles from the sea. Dunkirk for them, Leonard wrote, was a "harrowing business. There was not merely the public catastrophe . . . in the village we were domestically on the beaches."

Virginia partly shared these feelings, having grown increasingly involved in village life. She was also repelled by the narrow-mindedness of the villagers. The experience of living among working-class people made her keenly aware of class differences and of her own identity as an educated man's daughter. She had been doing her civic duty by helping the Women's Institute with a play they were going to put on.

Its ready-made sentiments gave her a taste of the communal psychology, which she found degrading: "minds so cheap, compared with ours." A quite different "us" and "them" from the one she had invoked in her "Leaning Tower" lecture. She remarked that Margaret Llewelyn Davies had condemned the insolence of middle-class women, but the working people themselves were at fault for imitating the most cloying of middle-class manners. "Whats wrong is the conventionality—not the coarseness. So that its all lulled & dulled. The very opposite of 'common' or working class." Furthermore, the villagers had no discretion, circulating absurd rumors about German spies disguised as nuns and parachutists landing near Eastbourne. They, the common people, possessed "a surplus of unused imagination," and it was the job of the educated class to check it. Virginia was struck again by "the helplessness of the lower orders" and the weight of class distinctions when she heard that the duke of Northumberland had been killed in the war. The old class prejudices were still deeply ingrained, and she observed how they colored her reaction to the news. Her judgment echoed the harshness of previous generations. It went without saying that the duke's death made a special claim on one's sympathies. "I had a sense of a very heavy tree fallen," she wrote. "A young man so loaded with everything to be lopped. A kind of crash it seemed, for a duke to fall, compared with a Harry West." Harry West was her maid Louie's brother, then at Dunkirk.

As a stay against confusion Virginia started working on "Pointz Hall" again, noting that a part of her that had been dormant while she wrote *Roger Fry* came to life in the novel. She worked on it only for short intervals—it was a much greater strain than biography—but the first draft was almost complete. On May 31, while the action at Dunkirk was at its height, she reported that she had plotted the whole ending of the book in her head, and now only needed to fill it in on paper. The creative impulse had so completely absorbed her that she could hardly remember her walk, and whether she had come through the meadow or over the downs. What a relief to "tap that old river again," to taste the words and fit them to a voice. She added that such visions kept their radiance, even in spite of general disorder, and for brief moments it was possible to feel happy. She had felt very happy weeding, alone with Leonard on the terrace; the morning had breathed contentment—at least a passable imitation of contentment, except for the insidious thought at the back of her mind that it was all ephemeral—"theres no support in the fabric . . . theres no healthy tissue round the moment. It's blown out." An image of the fear flickering on the back curtain of her mind. The air was troubled by that thought, but she could still rest in the moment, the windblown freshness that enveloped her body: "wind, warm wind washing all the crevices . . . an air cleanliness, not a soap & water one."

France's ordeal came to a head on June 5, during one of the Woolfs' visits to London. On that day the Germans launched a new offensive, aimed at breaking through the line along the Somme and capturing Paris. The attackers deployed more than a hundred divisions against the sixty French divisions opposing them. The evening after this battle began, Virginia and Leonard sat in their drawing room at Mecklenburgh Square with Kingsley Martin and the novelist Rose Macaulay seriously debating the question of suicide. The darkness fell. They went on sitting—a hot evening, no one lit a lamp—while Kingsley Martin, "diffusing his soft charcoal gloom," and counting every likely setback with relish, laid out the chain of disasters that would follow the fall of France. Virginia boiled it down: "invasion here; [fifth column] active; a German pro-Consul; English Govt in Canada; we in concentration camps, or taking sleeping draughts." A grim prospect that lowered everyone else's spirits while inspiring the lugubrious Martin with some perverse kind of satisfaction. During his recital and the following conversation the darkness deepened and the stars came out. The visitors stayed on till after one. Resenting Martin's dependence on Leonard, his pleasure in predicting the worst, Virginia commented acidly to Ethel that he had "sucked every drop of lifeblood to feed his great purple vampire body."

Still, there were islands of normality where small pleasures and hurts persisted in the usual way. While the battle on the Continent raged, Virginia was fretting that Elizabeth Bowen had not answered two of her letters and must therefore intend to break off their friendship. She liked talking to Bowen about her craft, and the imagined slight rankled. Then Bowen's answer came, cordial as ever, and that cloud lifted, cheering Virginia—a happy day, until she heard the radio announce that Paris was almost surrounded. She felt a constant sense of incongruity. On June 9, while inserting the last corrections into the proofs of *Roger Fry*, she detected a corrosive edge in the summerlike heat, a rumor of concentration camps and poisonous fumes that made her recoil, declaring, "I dont want to go to bed at midday: this refers to the garage." The downs and meadows shivered in that distant fire, which she heard then as "a kind of growl behind the cuckoo & t'other birds: a furnace behind the sky." Her self was losing its center. "The writing 'I' has vanished. No audience. No echo. Thats part of one's death. Not altogether serious, for I correct [*Roger Fry*]." A recognition and denial of the apocalyptic moment—it was only "part of ones death . . . not altogether serious," though the flat, two-dimensional feeling, the disappearance of an echo, seemed to prove the opposite.

On June 14, the day Paris fell, the Woolfs toured Penshurst Place, an Elizabethan stately house not far from Sissinghurst, where Vita lived. She went with them and introduced them to Penshurst's owner, the half-blind Lord De L'Isle, a descendant of Sir Philip Sidney, installed in a drab apartment like a relic of the ancien régime, an urbane old man with whom they chatted politely, smiling at his risqué joke, as if the world were not in ruins.

Three mornings later, Harry West arrived in Rodmell and collapsed outside his sister's door, so disheveled and dirty that for a moment she didn't recognize him. He had been walking all night. Louie came to Virginia, bursting with Harry's experiences on the Belgian front, where the retreating English troops had been constantly strafed by German planes. Many were killed, and among the dead bodies he saw two men from the village, one of them his cousin. On the road to Dunkirk they approached a German pillbox. The officer told them to take their boots off and crawl around it; then he went himself with a grenade and blasted it. Later Harry was talking to a chap who showed him a silk handkerchief he had bought for his "joy lady." Just then a bomb fell, killing the man instantly, and Harry brought back the handkerchief, along with two gold watches he had scooped up in a jewelry store. Virginia transcribed some details in her diary, telling how Harry "hadnt boots off for 3 days; the beach at Dunkirk—the bombers as low as trees—the bullets like moth holes in his coat—how no English aeroplanes fought. . . . At Dunkirk many men shot themselves as the planes swooped. Harry swam off, a boat neared. Say Chum Can you row? Yes, he said, hauled in, rowed for 5 hours, saw England, landed—didnt know if it were day or night or what town—didnt ask . . . so was despatched to his regiment." She added that he had come back hating the French and dead set against the war, which she supposed was a more typical reaction than the BBC caricatures of the laughing, heroic tommy.

The old war hero Marshall Petain had just formed a new government in France, intending to ask the Germans for peace terms, a policy tantamount to surrender. On that day, June 17, Churchill spoke to the nation, declaring that with their navy controlling the sea and the home defense forces stronger than ever before, they could repel any likely invasion. England would go on fighting, no matter what happened. There was some grim comfort in the fact that there were no more allies to consider; they were fighting alone, backs to the wall. Virginia noted the speech and went on to quote Kingsley Martin, who as usual spread "charcoal gloom," predicting that they would be beaten within the next few weeks and would suffer the same fate the Poles had suffered when England abandoned them: poetic justice. He had his supply of morphine ready. Suicide was a frequent topic, almost a commonplace, among Virginia's friends. Vita and Harold Nicolson felt sure they would be arrested by the Germans, and Harold undertook to get poison for them both. "I am not in the least afraid of such an honourable death," he wrote her. "What I dread is being tortured and humiliated. . . . I shall ask my doctor friends." Vita replied that she did not want to live if he died; she promised not to do anything rash, but wanted to have a painless drug in her purse. The Woolfs decided to do the same, asking Virginia's psychiatrist brother, Adrian, for a lethal prescription.

Virginia felt a hollowing out of her self, the end of everything she cared about. Her mind was clear and yet unable to concentrate on any one thing, attuned to the menace in the crystalline air, thinking: if this was to be her last lap shouldn't she perform some appropriate gesture, read Shakespeare or finish writing "Pointz Hall." She couldn't settle to either of these things. "Oughtn't I to finish something by way of an end?" she reflected. "The end gives its vividness, even its gaiety & recklessness to the random daily life. This, I thought yesterday, may be my last walk." There was a certain freedom in having very little time, an occasion for defiance that also was a form of saying good-bye. The freedom carried her on to thoughts about poetry. She had been reading Shelley and Coleridge, whose purity and depth (how lightly their musical phrases shaded into deeper thought) made her want to respond in her own language, to invent a new kind of criticism based on anonymity that would address "the old problem: how to keep the flight of the mind, yet be exact"—a reflective note she had not sounded in months. Her agitation about the war remained, but for the moment she reduced it to a simple declarative sentence, recording the raids on the coast: "6, 3, 12 people killed nightly."

The emergency generated another kind of clarity about the limits of her self. She had invited Elizabeth Bowen to Rodmell on June 25 — a visit Virginia had looked forward to, but the war fractured social relations, and talk with Bowen was halting, even at the best of times. She had a bad stammer; it often took her several painful tries before she could get a word out, which made her seem to flutter "like a moth buzzing round a flower." The strain of talking round her impediment for two days left Virginia feeling jangled.

[Virginia's diary, June 27, 1940]
    How difficult to make oneself a centre after all the rings a visitor stirs in one. . . . How difficult to draw in from all those wide ripples & be at home, central. I tried to center by reading Freud. These rough rapid twinkling ripples spread out & out—for some hours after [Elizabeth Bowen] is in the train. . . . A high wind was blowing; Mabel & Louie picking currants & gooseberries. Then a visit to Charleston. Threw another stone into the pond. And at the moment, with ["Pointz Hall"] only to fix upon, I'm loosely anchored. Further, the war—our waiting while the knives sharpen for the operation—has taken away the outer wall of security. No echo comes back. I have no surroundings. I have so little sense of a public that I forget about Roger coming or not coming out. Those familiar circumvolutions—those standards—which have for so many years given back an echo & so thickened my identity are all wide & wild as the desert now. I mean, there is no "autumn" no winter. We pour to the edge of a precipice . . . & then? I cant conceive that there will be a 27th June 1941. This cuts away something even at tea at Charleston. We drop another afternoon into the millrace. . . . Then Bunny as bluff & burly & beefy as a Farmer lurches in with Angelica. A clock ticks somewhere. Nothing said.

Virginia's feeling of emptiness, of being dispersed like ripples flowing outward till they are gone, with no echo or reflection, nothing to contain and send them back toward the center, blends almost casually with the millrace and the flood pouring toward an abyss. The passage combines the two forms of violent death that appear most often in her writing, images of drowning and of falling off a mountain or other great height. She was drawn to water always and identified with it, a fluid being whose life depended on the limits set by her artistic identity. She had once described "a perfect dwelling-place" created by musicians, a structure of which one could say, "Very little is left outside." There was no shelter now, no "outer wall of security," though she continued to write from force of habit. The war had broken the circle of her readers and left her alone on alien ground, "wild and wide as the desert."

The trouble at Charleston underscored her sense of isolation. Vanessa and Duncan's anger that Bunny had been making love to their daughter hung in the air, but as believers in personal freedom, they could not object and try to separate Angelica from her manipulative lover. There was no center. The ticking clock accentuated the silence.

✤

German raiders regularly flew over Rodmell, and Virginia observed how quickly one learned to take the air traffic and occasional explosions in one's stride. During the day heavy trucks rumbled through the countryside, and the banks of the river where she walked swarmed with men placing sandbags, pouring concrete for gun emplacements, camouflaging their work with boughs, making ready for an invasion within the next few weeks. Virginia kept an attentive eye on village activities and people. Attending a first-aid training program, she was impressed by a cast of local characters performing new roles. Miss Emery, their dog-breeding neighbor, showed great tact and resourcefulness as an instructor, portraying "English country spinsterhood at its best . . . everything spaced, brief & clear. . . . All about the Water Co & the tap & the Rectory scullery." After another meeting, this one all about poison gas, sixty-year-old Miss Green took off her cloak and demonstrated how to escape a burning house by letting herself down in blue shorts, "hanging by her toenails & descending with a jump," from the rectory window, whereupon Mr. Hanna, captain of the Local Defence Volunteers, said he didn't dare jump even from a bus, let alone a window—his bones were like glass. Virginia took note, making deadpan entries in her diary. She was struck at night by the beauty of searchlights feeling for German airplanes, the broad stalks of light rising all over the meadow "in extreme antennal vibration," while a high drone like a dentist's drill buzzed in her ear.

The Hogarth Press published *Roger Fry* on July 25, and in spite of the war Virginia found herself worrying about what the papers would say. The public echo, the sense of an audience, was gone, but the old familiar questions—would they dismiss her work, would they ignore it?—survived. The reviews were generally favorable, the *Times Literary Supplement* rating *Roger Fry* among the best of biographies. The book's emphasis on art and sensibility reminded people of happier times, and it sold briskly, almost immediately going into second and third printings, though sales fell off after a fierce air raid on London.

Virginia worried about how friends who had known Roger well would receive her work, and she was relieved when Desmond Mac-Carthy praised the fidelity of the portrait in the Sunday *Times*. Two of the reviewers disturbed her by suggesting the present irrelevance of the old artistic debates. The first, E. M. Forster, wrote that the biography was both sad and sustaining: sad because Fry's kind of humanism had been so brutally devalued since his death; sustaining because his integrity and endurance could inspire others to keep on resisting the barbarians. He declared that Fry was lucky to die when he did, in 1934, adding that one's thankfulness for Fry's death was "a measure for our present insecurity." Forster's fatalism left Virginia feeling vaguely depressed, in spite of his approval of her work. The art critic Herbert Read, on the other hand, enraged her by attacking Fry and Bloomsbury for cultivating their private sensibilities and failing to help build "a new order of society." Fry's work had been fatally compromised, Read objected, by "the prettiness and the protectiveness of the Ivory Tower"—a charge that Virginia dismissed, along with the reviewer, whom she thought "venomous and malignant."

At the same time she received a stream of private letters about the book, one of which, from Vita's son, Ben Nicolson, who was serving in an anti-aircraft battery, moved her particularly—an impulsive letter, written during an air raid and launched against a background of chattering guns and bomb blasts. Ben, the art historian, blamed Fry and his friends for having lived in a fool's paradise, shutting out "all disagreeable actualities" and allowing Nazism to grow without doing anything to stop it. These urbane intellectuals had spent their lives visiting art galleries, Ben said; they had sat around in armchairs, discussing Spinoza. Now the young had to suffer because people like Roger had found politics too much of a bore to bother about. Their indifference had led to these planes overhead dropping bombs. His charges were fueled by a sense of personal betrayal that Virginia could not dismiss. She wrote an elaborate reply, taking his letter apart sentence by sentence. What could Ben be thinking of? she declared—Roger's life had never been easy. As a young man he had "faced insanity, death and every sort of disagreeable." He had opposed his family's wishes, lived hand to mouth from lecturing and journalism, and only received the recognition of a Slade Professorship shortly before his death. This in comparison to Ben's own privileged career: school at Eton and Oxford and then a posh job assisting Kenneth Clark as keeper of the king's pictures. Far from being indifferent to "humanity in the mass," Roger had tried constantly to open their eyes to the value of artistic form, a kind of engagement that fitted his gifts and disposition. He had taught people to see more clearly, heightening their awareness, "and wasn't that the best way of checking Nazism?" Ben wrote again, clarifying his views: he had no quarrel with art criticism as such, but he believed that Bloomsbury had given up on trying to educate the masses and concentrated instead on cultivating highbrow tastes that could never appeal to ordinary people. Oh, but Ben took Bloomsbury too seriously, Virginia volleyed back (she had first written a reply deploring his use of the label "Bloomsbury" but scrapped it)—he should consider, she said, that even artists like Keats, Shelley, and Wordsworth had failed to influence the politics of the last century. How could the less gifted Bloomsbury artists hope to succeed? Still, it was worth trying, and perhaps he himself would one day show them how to do better. She ended by reporting that they were in the midst of an air raid at Rodmell. They were all under fire— and she knew he was in the thick of the battle.

The fire came closer and closer. On August 16, while Virginia and Leonard were in the garden, enemy planes suddenly swooped down on them. They lay under a tree, flat on their faces with their hands behind their heads, hearing a sound "like someone sawing in the air just above us." A bomb exploded somewhere, shaking the windows of Virginia's lodge, which she thought for a moment was going to fall on them—an empty feeling mixed with a little fear, thoughts "of nothingness—flatness, my mood being flat." Planes buzzed and sawed around them, and they heard the thunder of guns.

She felt a different kind of shock when Vita phoned on August 30 saying she could not come for a visit that day because they were having an air raid and she was on call as an ambulance driver. Bombs were exploding around Vita's house as they talked. The voice of her friend—she "might be killed any moment," Virginia thought—made the danger more real than the actual enemy planes had done. Now she felt it completely—"we are in the war"—as if her imagination needed that distance in order to grasp the violence. She dashed off a note to Vita saying she had just put flowers in the guest room before the phone rang. Rodmell was perfectly peaceful; they were playing bowls. "What can one say—except that I love you and I've got to live through this strange quiet evening thinking of you sitting there alone." A brimming message ending with a confession such as one makes before a death: "You have given me such happiness."

❧

The end of civilization arrived in stages. In September the air war reached a new level of ferocity, which was apparent in the skies above

Rodmell with a great increase in the number of daylight raids. They came over with a roar, flying low and fast, and were gone before one could think. At night the traffic of German bombers on their way to London made so much noise, Virginia said, it was like "buses and drays. . . . We might be in the Strand, here at night." The siren grew intimately familiar; the papers dubbed it Weeping Willie, and Virginia remarked that it wailed every day, "punctual as the vespers. We've not had our raid yet, we say." The explosions came closer as the Germans attacked nearby coastal defenses, railway lines, and power stations. Blasts sounded close as a slammed door and knocked the pen out of Virginia's hand as she wrote. The anti-aircraft guns on nearby Itford Hill would join in, going pop pop pop, and sometimes a plane disappeared over the ridge trailing smoke. Twice while she was playing bowls, RAF fighter planes shot down a raider in full view. Virginia saw first "a scuffle; a swerve; then a plunge; & a burst of thick black smoke." Except for the closest hits, the air raids faded into the background and she learned to go on writing her letter, without bothering to get up and look out the window. "Only a German bomber? Oh thats all." It all struck her, she said, as "a very dreary game of hide and seek played by grown ups. . . . Why do people think that whats unpleasant is therefore real?" She was aware that their survival depended on the outcome of these games, since the Germans could not invade England unless they controlled the skies, and to do that they had to destroy the Royal Air Force, which stayed alive all through September by downing twice as many German planes as they themselves lost.

While the battle of Britain raged, Virginia suffered her own private shock, the destruction of her London home, which also happened in stages. The Woolfs drove up to London for the day on September 10 and found that the house directly opposite 37 Mecklenburgh Square had been hit by a bomb and reduced to a pile of smoking bricks. Their house was undamaged, but a delayed-action bomb had landed in a flower bed, where it remained, unexploded, forcing the police to cordon off the square. Virginia observed how calmly the residents took the destruction. Two Hogarth Press employees stood at the barricade, their faces serene and "tough as leather." Mr. Pritchard, the solicitor who shared their building, was outraged by German impertinence. There was nothing for the Woolfs to do but turn around and drive back to Rodmell. They stopped to view some of the devastated areas around Holborn: heaps of broken glass everywhere; a large shop reduced to rubble; the gutted structure of a hotel; a wine shop with its

Figure 21. Milk delivery amid the ruins.

windows blown out and people standing inside with drinks. Leaving the center, they drove past miles and miles of untouched houses—like the empty streets of a dead city. Virginia wrote Ethel that she was distressed by the thought of the old women who kept lodging houses in back streets, "all dirty after the raid, and preparing to sit out another." She added: "We, after all, have at least been to Italy and read Shakespeare. They havent: dear me, I'm turning democrat." In spite of the strained irony, she felt unexpected admiration, not only for the ordinary chars and shopkeepers, but also for "tweed wearing sterling dull women" and even politicians—Churchill, at least. She confided to Ethel that while picking blackberries for dinner she had conceived a new book about English literature and "Common History," and intended to ride out the war in her own freewheeling style: "I think I can weather—I mean weather cock—I mean brain spin—another ten years if Hitler doesnt drop a splinter into my machine."

Since the bomb at Mecklenburgh Square had brought the Hogarth Press to a standstill, the Woolfs arranged with John Lehmann to move their offices to safer quarters in Letchworth. The square stayed closed for a week till finally the bomb went off, severely damaging their house—ripping doors off their hinges, bringing down ceilings and smashing Virginia's china. Subsequently a land mine explosion at the rear made the house completely uninhabitable. Their books lay in huge piles among mounds of rubble, and you could stand on the ground floor and look up through the holes in three floors to the roof. So the destruction she had imagined slowly undermining the summer house in the "Time Passes" section of *To the Lighthouse*, leaving it open to sun and rain, had been translated into a different harsh reality. The loss of Mecklenburgh Square permanently changed the balance Virginia had always preserved between urban and country regimes. She cursed that it had happened just after they had made the new flat livable, but they were lucky to have Monk's House, and she did not let rancor disrupt her daily stint of writing on "Pointz Hall."

Marooned on their "desert island," she found life tolerable, and even pleasant from time to time. It was vital to protect oneself, she told Ethel, by letting down a "safety curtain—a heavy iron drop over ones own scene." Temporary relief, but she used it, content to rest in the small acts of her daily life—days that began lazily with breakfast in bed, a bath and orders for dinner, then a cigarette followed by a morning of writing in the garden lodge. Her afternoons and evenings were divided among chores and diversions, which she listed in her diary, packing the bare facts in so densely that not a note of discord could slip in. "Walk to Southease. Back 3. Gather & arrange apples. Tea. Write a letter. Bowls. Type ["Pointz Hall"] again. Read Michelet & write here. Cook dinner. Music. Embroidery. 9.30 read . . . till 11.30. Bed." Keeping her thoughts steadfastly off the war, she concentrated on village life, which she pictured as admirably "free & disengaged—a life that rings from one simple melody to another." A suspicious kind of simplicity, though, that depended on isolation and could only be secured behind an artificial "iron drop."

In mid-September a small unpleasant episode revealed how low Virginia's flash point was. Helen Anrep, Roger Fry's companion, had rented a cottage in Rodmell, and Virginia had angry visions of meeting her and her two oafish children constantly—they would be dropping in; she would not be able to step outside to post a letter without "seeing a face like a codfish in embryo." It was all Vanessa's fault for telling them about the cottage and actually arranging it. In a rage about being invaded, Virginia lashed out at her silent sister—the worst tantrum she had had in years. Afterward she was baffled when Vanessa wrote coolly that the Anreps intended to stay only a week. She had thought they were staying indefinitely. The misunderstanding annoyed Virginia doubly because, as she admitted, it was "an ignoble fret." Relations between her and Vanessa were strained for a while, but soon mended when Vanessa's and Duncan's studios at Fitzroy Square were both hit by bombs and their contents, including a hundred paintings, destroyed. The only things they managed to salvage were a Frigidaire and a statue.

The war broke down the remaining walls of security. Virginia still enjoyed the quiet hour around sunset before the bombers came. From her lodge she could see a haystack glowing in the marsh and a plume of smoke rising from a distant train. The air was slightly brittle. Remembering a line from Gray's Elegy—"And all the air a solemn stillness holds"—she thought, yes, until "the cadaverous twanging" of the planes strikes up at eight-thirty. Incongruity seemed to haunt the landscape itself.

[Virginia's diary, October 2, 1940]

Cows feeding. The elm tree sprinkling its little leaves against the sky. Our pear tree swagged with pears; & the weathercock above the triangular church tower above it. Why try again to make the familiar catalogue, from which something escapes. Should I think of death? Last night a great heavy plunge of bomb under the window. So near we both started. A plane had passed

Figure 22. St. Paul's Cathedral survives the Blitz.

dropping this fruit. We went onto the terrace. Trinkets of stars sprinkled & glittering. All quiet. The bombs dropped on Itford Hill. There are two by the river, marked with white wooden crosses, still unburst. I said to L.: I dont want to die yet. The chances are against it. But theyre aiming at the railway & the power works. They get closer every time. . . .

[Her thoughts turn to Lady Oxford, widow of the former prime minister, whom she asked to intercede for Robert Spira, a Jewish refugee interned as an enemy alien. Asquith's widow writes saying she has got him out and asking Virginia to send "a long letter all about yourself & what you believe."] What do I? Cant at the moment remember. Oh I try to imagine how one's killed by a bomb. I've got it fairly vivid—the sensation: but cant see anything but suffocating nonentity following after. I shall think—oh I wanted another 10 years—not this—& shant, for once, be able to describe it. It—I mean death; no, the scrunching & scrambling, the crushing of my bone shade in on my very active eye & brain: the process of putting out the light,—painful? Yes. Terrifying. I suppose so—Then a swoon; a drum; two or three gulps attempting consciousness—& then, dot dot dot.

So consciousness spirals in on itself and its confused end. The familiar downs and church tower, which gave her pleasure and solace in the past, have been reduced to a dull "catalogue," and she can only register her awareness that "something escapes." She observes the richness of nature, which she is no longer free to enjoy. "Should I think of death?" she asks and shortly afterward does just that, fixing her thoughts on the last moments of expiring consciousness. She thinks of death too in the sense of considering its claims and reminding herself she does not want to die yet.

17 *Oblivion and Water*

It was a beautiful fall—apples and pears ripening in the crisp, bright atmosphere, but stormy weather was coming and the invasion season was over for the year. The Germans scaled back their raids on coastal defenses, which meant fewer bombs bursting around Rodmell, though the enemy planes still flew overhead in the evenings on their way to London. Over all an ominous calm, like the eye of the storm—no doubt the invasion would come in the spring, a warning that made Virginia cling to the passing moment. She watched the colors of marsh and hillside, the fringe of late flowers and the mists rising from the downs like changing scenes in a theater; the display was so enchanting, she said, she couldn't stop looking.

The war restricted travel, making it hard to see friends, who were all "isolated over winter fires," but it sometimes had the reverse effect of bringing people closer together. Virginia's attachment to Vita was stronger than it had been in years. On October 10, after spending the day with her old friend, she declared how glad she was that their love had "weathered so well." Though Vita had grown somewhat slack and blowsy, Virginia said, she had such a vivid personality, she was so affectionate and direct—"wholly without the little artists back kitchen smell"—that she felt charmed and invigorated. Afterward, in an expansive mood, Virginia let herself savor the moment, burying any thought of the war. "How free, how peaceful we are," she wrote without perceptible irony. "No one coming. No servant. Dine when we like. Living near to the bone." Two days later she embroidered on the same theme: "If it were not treasonable to say so, a day like this is almost too—I wont say happy: but amenable. The tune varies, from one nice melody to another. . . . Breakfast, writing, walking, tea, bowls, reading, sweets, bed." A pleasant domestic routine, but the illicit quiet was disturbed by a letter from Rose Macaulay, whose account of life in London, contrasting with the relative ease of Virginia's days, almost punctured her carefully constructed detachment. She did not let it. "The globe rounds again," she wrote, and added: "Behind it—oh yes."

The following day she wrote a section of "A Sketch of the Past" describing the "mutilation" she had suffered after her mother died, the shock at the age of thirteen of discovering "the insecurity of life," remembering something gone, a lesson that was reinforced two years later by the death of her half sister, Stella. Not only a mutilation, but perhaps a sign that the gods had singled out her family for special treatment, had used that sacrifice to endow them with more insight and sensitivity than was given to most people. After her brother Thoby's death in 1906 she had an image of herself suspended between two great grindstones, subject to the whim of blind forces. At another point, shifting the metaphor, she declared that if life presented this challenge, if it staged such fits of wild kicking and rearing, then it was "a thing to be ridden . . . something of extreme reality." The thought enhanced her sense of her own importance, her role in the scheme of things, since the gods had respected her enough to sentence her to the ordeal of being "ground between grindstones." The sufferings of her youth had a special meaning now in the midst of a war that administered frequent doses of "extreme reality." Then she feared that isolation would deaden her sensibilities; she was "terrified of passive acquiescence," she said. Without the bustle of the London streets, she had to create another kind of intensity by concentrating still more on her writing, hoping the effort would not stir up a "rough wave"— best not to think about it. "Pointz Hall" still absorbed most of her time: she had "never had a better writing season"; and she had started taking notes for the next book, "Reading at Random," a commentary on the evolution of English life and literature, beginning with the minstrel-like Anon. Her present life, with few visitors or other distractions, she said too blandly, gave her just the space she needed for her work—long uninterrupted hours on their "lovely free autumn island."

It was a perfect Indian summer day, she noted on October 17, with a red admiral butterfly alighting on a rotten apple in the grass, but there was still the refrain of bombers flying to London every night, the wailing sirens, the bitter dialogues with herself: "Who'll be killed tonight? Not us, I suppose." Another fact it did no good to think about. She denied its importance, except as a "quickener," a wave that stained the soft evening air with "a very faint shade of bodily risk." Aside from that slight disturbance, the war was "almost forgettable." Forgetting took work, though, and she applied herself, boasting that she had "mastered the iron curtain for my brain. Down I shut when I'm tied tight. No reading no writing. No claims, no 'must.' " She made herself immune. The news that 52 Tavistock Square had been destroyed by a bomb hardly moved her, except with relief that they would no longer have to pay rent for the empty house. On their next day-trip to London she visited the pile of rubble where the house had stood, finding nothing recognizable there but a battered wicker chair and a signboard, and concluded that their luck had turned: by moving to Mecklenburgh Square they had avoided losing all their possessions. On the other hand, the idea of losing possessions and starting life over, almost bare, was highly attractive when she considered the loads of furniture and books that would have to be rescued from the fallen plaster at Mecklenburgh Square (another bomb had burst nearby) and transported to Rodmell.

Leonard in his autobiography remembered this as a relatively untroubled time. His account of that Indian summer emphasizes the positive rhythm of their lives. On the whole Virginia seemed content to live quietly, concentrating on the end of "Pointz Hall," reading and doing her household tasks while they waited for "the next catastrophe." The atmosphere, as she said, was almost too amenable, discouraging much reflection or self-analysis. Describing that stillness in the eye of the storm, Leonard concluded that "the last months of 1940 passed away for Virginia in a real—and yet false—tranquility." The final oxymoronic phrases suggest that Virginia's iron curtain gave her only limited protection and ultimately shut nothing out.

On November 2 the banks of the tidal Ouse River, which had been ruptured by bombs earlier in the year, burst again, admitting a cascade of white water so that gulls floated where the farmers had planted their crops. When the heavy rain and high winds subsided, sheets of water covered the fields right up to the back gate of Virginia's garden. From her writing table she saw the sea outlining "yellow islands: leafless trees: red cottage roofs"—a vista of great beauty. The road she often walked to the downs was under water, and she came back home dripping wet one day, having slipped into a deep hole while exploring the flooded fields. She loved this "savage medieval" state of nature—"all floating tree trunks and flocks of birds and a man in an old punt, and myself so eliminated of human feature you might take me for a stake walking." A great solace to lose herself in the subtle play of shifting reflections. Like the unlit London streets, the Sussex meadows had reverted to an earlier state belonging to a more primitive world. She wished the flood would last forever, washing away all signs of human presence and leaving the world "as it was in the beginning."

The human landscape, too, grew increasingly "medieval." While Leonard was down with the flu at the beginning of November Virginia took over the job of blacking out the windows at night, and she accidentally let some chinks of light show through the curtains, bringing down on herself the wrath of the local constable, who complained that she had been delinquent for several nights running and threatened to fine or arrest her if it happened again. She tried to soften his indignation, aiming her "lady battery" at him and putting the blame on Leonard's illness, but with no success. He liked to lord it over a lady—one of those pugnacious working-class men who alternate between servility and boorishness, having "no 'manners' to fall back on." His rudeness, she said, was the sign of a rupture in the social order, a "breach in the bank of class manners," which was worth noting, since it gave a useful glimpse of the anger below the surface.

❧

Isolation increased Virginia's dependence on her work. She grew obsessed with the final scenes of "Pointz Hall," and the book's rhythm seemed to color all her thoughts, invading every moment of the day. Writing, she had said, is nothing but "putting words on the backs of rhythm"; it was the rhythm that gave her writing its character, but the rhythm could also become destructive by running obsessively in one's head. At such times, she wrote, the rhythm "winds one into a ball: & so jades one." Aiming to give her head a rest, she took a two-day break from fiction to dash off several pages of "A Sketch of the Past." The looser style of memoir writing had a "rather profound" liberating effect.

She had never seen the abuses of her youth as clearly as she saw them now against the background of the war. Recording some memories of her father, she applied that disillusioned awareness to the contradictions she had observed in late Victorian society. All during her early years she had been aware of a split between the intellectual interests she shared with her father and the effects of the patriarchal system, which distorted every aspect of family life. So her father, who was known by his friends as a liberal and fair-minded man, used shameless emotional blackmail against his daughters—fits of rage and mawkish self-pity—such as he would never have permitted himself in the company of men. Vanessa had become the family housekeeper after her mother died, and she endured constant tantrums and demands for sympathy "because she was then (though gilt with an angelic surface) the slave." His histrionic displays were as cruel, Virginia thought, as if he had given her an actual whipping. Stephen's blindness to his daughter's pain was a sign that in spite of his powers as a thinker, his imaginative faculties had remained stunted. When it came to human motives and feelings, his views were "so crude, so elementary, so conventional that a child with a box of chalks could make a more subtle portrait."

Her father's self-indulgence left Virginia with a lasting awareness "that nothing is so much to be dreaded as egotism. Nothing so cruelly hurts the person himself; nothing so wounds those who are forced into contact with it."

George Duckworth gave an even more vicious example of the Victorian double standard, demanding that his young half sisters observe all the fine points of upper-class decorum in public while he sexually abused them in private. Reviving these memories, Virginia connected the deceptive standards of the past to the deadly contradictions of the present. "The division in our lives was curious," she wrote of her youth. "There were so many different worlds: but they were distant from me. I could not make them cohere; nor feel myself in touch with them." Early in life she had learned to avoid shocks by assuming the role of spectator, a method she used now to insulate herself from the war. The attitude imposed its own dangers, but it relieved her to trace the pattern, observing how naturally the traumas of the past dovetailed with the present, and having done so she turned back to "Pointz Hall" with renewed energy.

She finished it on November 23. The moment passed without much fanfare, merely a slight jog in the daily progress from breakfast to bed; it passed in a deceptive calm, as if her isolation—she had lost the sense of her audience—had dulled the lure of completion. "Pointz Hall" shared the spotlight with a small domestic experiment. The previous day the Woolfs had bought a cream separator, a sievelike device for making butter, and that morning Louie suddenly appeared carrying a jar of milk with an actual pat of butter floating in it. Virginia left her writing to witness the skimming off of the milk and they brought the rich residue to Leonard in triumph. In her diary she lightly paired these two successes, the butter and the completion of her book. In "Pointz Hall" she had separated out an essential deposit of ideas. The novel, she wrote, with butter still in mind, was "an interesting attempt in a new method . . . more quintessential than the others. More milk skimmed off. A richer pat, certainly a fresher than that misery *The Years*. I've enjoyed writing almost every page." She did not allow a moment for the usual anxieties about her work to creep in. On the same day she began writing the first pages, a brief preliminary sketch, of her commentary "Reading at Random." The new book, about the stages of English literature, a subject that drew on a lifetime of reading, would keep her well occupied, supplying her with a regular allotment of "daily drudgery"—a reassuring prospect. Perhaps she would pair it with a short novel beginning on the top of a mountain, a vision she had first recorded in June 1937 of "a dream story . . . about lying in the snow; about rings of colour; silence . . . & the solitude"—imagery suggesting withdrawal from the world and a return to the subjective mode she had not attempted since *The Waves*. But she had the job of getting "Pointz Hall" ready for publication, and that novel, with its sharp satire of an English village on the eve of the war, was a reminder of how effectively her present life in Rodmell with all its dull mediocrity broke up the path to her visionary mountaintop. In any case, there were weeks of drudgery ahead, beginning with the task of copying the manuscript—the text was rough in places, and she would refine and revise constantly as she retyped it. And there were interruptions: a trip to London, followed by the arrival in Rodmell of all the remaining contents of the Mecklenburgh Square flat—books, papers, and furnishings—which were deposited in rented space and in every available nook and cranny of Monk's House; then two weeks spent preparing and writing an essay on the actress Ellen Terry, the heroine of the farcical *Freshwater*; but by December 24 she was immersed in the revisions, declaring that she was "word drugged" again. The phrase suggests her flight from a reality that became harder and harder to ignore.

※

"Pointz Hall" registers several kinds of incongruity. It is about being detached and involved, about the failure of feeling and its unchecked growth. It plays lightly on the decline and fall of a civilization, spoofing as the darkness falls. Behind the satire, coloring the fictional setting, lie the realities of Virginia's life in Rodmell and her reactions to the war.

Her working title derives from the country house where the parish church is holding an annual benefit. A group of village shopkeepers and laborers, under the direction of the slightly disreputable Miss La Trobe, perform a pageant about England's history, presenting scenes in various styles from Elizabethan times to the present day. The action alternates between scenes from the play, which occupy about a third of the text, and a frame story about Isabella, who is unhappily married to Giles Oliver, the inheritor of Pointz Hall, with major asides to the dramatist La Trobe and to several members of the audience. There is no plot—just the ebb and flow of the social gathering, punctuated by episodes of the pageant, as the Olivers and their guests negotiate the day's random and predictable events.

Miss La Trobe's amateur theatrical disturbs both husband and wife by reminding them that they spend most of their lives acting parts they dislike and wearing masks to hide their true feelings. Isabella's life as a proper upper-middle-class matron, ordering fish for dinner, taking care of a house and servants and two children, thwarts her desire for artistic expression. Lines of poetry chime obsessively in her head and she jots them into an account book, but the results are abortive. She imagines having an affair with a neighboring gentleman farmer, but this passionate impulse alternates with a wish for oblivion. The village play intensifies Isabella's detachment and confirms her dislike of social conventions. Watching a particularly operatic recognition scene, she concludes that the plot is "only there to beget emotion," and there are only three emotions. "Love. Hate. Peace. Three emotions made the ply of human life." Amplifying these ideas, the narrator suggests that our words, and often our feelings, are prescribed for us by tradition and cultural heritage, further underlining the analogy between the actions onstage and the roles we play in our daily lives.

Though less self-aware than Isabella, Giles shares his wife's dissatisfaction with the role assigned to him. He is stuck in his job as a stockbroker in London, while every day the paper reports new atrocities on the Continent. The present day's festivities increase Giles's frustration by reminding him that he is only a spectator here, a passive member of the audience, obliged to make polite conversation. He is sexually attracted to one of his guests, the ample, good-natured Mrs. Manresa, and enraged by the companion she has brought with her, a homosexual poet, William Dodge, who triggers all his homophobic prejudices. Walking along the path during the interval, he kicks savagely at a stone and remembers a childhood game. "He played it alone. The gate was a goal; to be reached in ten. The first kick was Manresa (lust). The second Dodge (perversion). The third, himself (coward). And the fourth and the fifth and all the others were the same." Absorbed in this mood, he finds an omen under his feet in the form of a green snake with a toad stuck in its throat. "The snake was unable to swallow; the toad was unable to die. A spasm made the ribs contract; blood oozed." The scene derives from an incident Virginia recorded in 1935, though the oozing blood is an embellishment, perhaps to suggest a parallel between predatory nature and the bloody slaughter on the battlefield. Giles heightens this effect with his own violent move. "It was birth the wrong way round—a monstrous inversion. So, raising his foot, he stamped on them. The mass crushed and slithered. The white canvas on his tennis shoes was bloodstained and sticky. But it was action. Action relieved him."

The snake and toad carried disturbing associations. In her 1935 diary Virginia had coupled their death agony with a dream about suicide in which she glimpsed a "body shooting through the water." "Pointz Hall" implies a similar emotional equation. Giles's act is followed by a scene in the ancient barn where members of the audience are taking tea. Standing among them, Isabella shrinks from the hard, glazed faces around her, concentrating on oblivion and water, imagining a cool, quiet place in the woods where there is a wishing well under whose water she might find relief—a baptismal scene, but not of this world. Would she mind, she asks herself, elaborating the fantasy, would she mind "not again to hear on the trembling spray the thrush sing, or to see, dipping diving as if he skimmed waves in the air, the yellow woodpecker?" Such worn scraps of language run through her mind all day. Strolling round the grounds during a later interval, she picks up the refrain. "'Where do I wander?' she mused. 'Down what draughty tunnels? Where the eyeless wind blows? And there grows nothing for the eye. No rose. To issue where? In some harvestless dim field where no evening lets fall her mantle; nor sun rises. All's equal there.'" Isa's thoughts generally sound like this. They form a pastiche, a shimmering surface, like a tempting pool with a muddy bottom. Her inner monologues, distributed throughout the novel, could almost be parodies. They are as quaintly rhetorical as any of Miss La Trobe's lines, but they lack the dramatist's satirical edge. They are often merely obfuscating—lines like "no evening lets fall her mantle," reaching into the poetic past to sanitize the idea of death. Isa deploys them in the same way Virginia used her iron curtain—they form a verbal fabric that dissolves harsh realities into vague apparitions. In Isa's numbed state, political ideas move to the same rhythm. "Always I hear corrupt murmurs; the chink of gold and metal. Mad music. . . . On, little donkey, patiently stumble. Hear not the frantic cries of the leaders who in that they seek to lead desert us." While conveying her submerged anxiety, the language also muffles her feelings, leaving readers to decipher what they can through the rhetorical fog.

Like Isabella, Miss La Trobe (a troubadour, an anonymous artist?), is in trouble. She is an outsider with a small "o," ostracized by respectable society for her lesbianism, though they are willing to exploit her talents. La Trobe's despair over every glitch in her play provides a comic foil to Isa's obsessive anxiety. When the whole performance seems about to disintegrate because she has introduced ten minutes of present-time "reality," that is, left the audience to stare at an empty stage, La Trobe's despair grows beyond all bounds. The dose of pure reality added by indifferent cows in the meadow and swallows overhead has destroyed the audience's focus. "'Reality too strong,' she muttered. . . . Her little game had gone wrong. . . . Panic seized her. Blood seemed to pour from her shoes. This is death, death, death, she noted in the margin of her mind; when illusion fails." The mock horror is part of La Trobe's "little game," an instinctive act that coincides with her cool habit of making notes "in the margin of her mind." A typical artist's vanity, the narrator implies—thinking the world will come to an end because a scene has fallen flat. Then a brief rain shower falls, diverting the restless audience till a recorded nursery rhyme catches their attention again. "The King is in his counting house," sings the voice from the gramophone. In the audience Isabella answers with her own silent refrain: "'O that my life could here have ending.' . . . Readily would she endow this voice with all her treasure if so be tears could be ended." Isa blankets the pain with phrases, her stilted language again suggesting that reality is too strong for her.

❦

Parody not only dominates Miss La Trobe's play, with its satires on Elizabethan drama, Restoration comedy, and Victorian romance, but crops up in the frame story, which is studded with sly echoes of newspapers, histories, and guidebooks. The narrator's remarks at the outset about the house's location set the satiric tone. "It was a pity that the man who had built Pointz Hall had pitched the house in a hollow, when beyond the flower garden and the vegetables there was this stretch of high ground. Nature had provided a site for a house; man had built his house in a hollow." Here human folly feeds into the mock solemnity of the last words. The novel's language sometimes grows archly melodramatic, as if subtly comparing that childish excess to the absurdity of the current bloodshed. Giles in his rage feels he has been manacled to a rock (polite society, the pageant) "and forced passively to behold indescribable horror." William Dodge admits his self-hatred in an unspoken confession with fascist overtones: "At school they held me under a bucket of dirty water, Mrs. Swithin; when I looked up, the world was dirty. . . . I'm a half-man, Mrs. Swithin; a flickering, mind-divided little snake in the grass." Isabella too slips into unconscious parody, echoing popular romances in her account of the gentleman farmer in whose "ravaged face" she detects mystery and silent passion. She never encounters him after the opening scene, but keeps glimpsing the man in gray in the distance, an elusive, slightly sinister figure.

Parody in itself invites a critical and detached frame of mind, but the parodies in "Pointz Hall" are embedded in other kinds of writing. Two important female characters thread their way and spread their influence among the audience, giving their own personal accents to the basic emotions. While Isabella and La Trobe are haunted by failure, Mrs. Swithin and Mrs. Manresa belong to a genial race of life-affirming spirits with the gift of charming those around them. To the skeptical Isa and William, Mrs. Swithin, who grew up during the reign of Queen Victoria, provides a reminder of how far they have strayed from the attitudes of their parents. Her natural piety, symbolized by the cross on a chain round her neck, is a reassuring relic of that earlier age. They draw a droll picture of the old woman's "circular tour," affectionately describing her faith that "sheep, cows, grass, trees, ourselves—all are one. If discordant, producing harmony—if not to us, to a gigantic ear attached to a gigantic head." The old lady seems almost weightless, up in the clouds and touching "ground now and then with a shock of surprise." Her comic foil is Mrs. Manresa, a thoroughly good sort, whose ample figure and vitality make her seem "goddess-like" to her admirers, a vision of fertility and sexual ease. Two maternal guests at the gathering, with some of the same mythic powers Virginia ascribed to her own mother, whom she remembered from childhood mainly as "a general presence, rather than a particular person," but a radiant presence, lighting up the world for those around her. "All lives directly she crossed them seemed to form themselves into a pattern."

By blending parody and myth Virginia was able to present her complex themes in deceptively simple and concise terms, since the hybrid form conveys several layers of meaning at once. The central pageant illustrates the failure of art to capture ordinary random existence and by analogy, the failure of all authorized histories to convey the fullness of being between the recorded acts. The pageant's meaning is ambiguous, implying ironic detachment, as parodies do, and at the same time reminding the audience of their English identity, their collective debt to the past. It presents national myths and political leaders with childlike naiveté and so invites skepticism, implicitly asking readers to reject the mystique of power and examine the human faces behind it. The pageant reinforces the point by casting familiar village characters as historical figures. Within Queen Elizabeth's elaborate costume lurks Eliza Clark, who keeps the village shop and can easily haul a flitch of bacon or tub of oil. Her gown adorned with sixpenny brooches and metallic scouring pads, she becomes larger than life for a moment, evoking "the [Elizabethan] age in person." Then a pretty village girl wearing a flowing bedspread advances to portray the Age of Reason and the local pub-keeper in the cape and helmet of a Victorian policeman delivers a moralizing lecture. The debunking effect of these scenes culminates in Mrs. Swithin's remark that there is no such thing as history. There never were such people as "the Victorians . . . only you and me and William dressed differently."

"Pointz Hall" invokes communal rituals, as well as the benign influence of Swithin and Manresa, to defuse the current preoccupation with bombs and bloodshed. The grave laughter that pervades Woolf's account is heightened by the bumbling speaker who rises as the final applause for the village pageant dies down. The audience sees, "as waters withdrawing leave visible a tramp's old boot, a man in a clergyman's collar surreptitiously mounting a soap-box." He is their neighbor and spokesman—there to say a few concluding words and slightly embarrassed by the task. Mr. Streatfield comes from the old school; he is "a piece of traditional church furniture; a corner cupboard . . . fashioned by generations of village carpenters after some lost-in-the-mists-of-antiquity model." Inept and sincere, he comically reverses the sense of a familiar proverb—"Am I treading, like angels, where as a fool I should absent myself?"—but gets the spirit right. His homily presents no doctrines or authoritative opinions, but bits of traditional wisdom, awkwardly expressed. "We are members one of another. Each is part of the whole." The clergyman's simplicity redeems or humanizes the drone of conventional piety. "There he stood their representative spokesman; their symbol; themselves; a butt, a clod, laughed at by looking-glasses; ignored by the cows. . . . 'May we not hold,'" asks the diffident speaker, "'that there is a spirit that inspires, pervades?'" He declines to go beyond that question. "'I am not here to explain. That role has not been assigned to me.'" Reaching a full stop, he shifts to an appeal for money, which is briefly interrupted by airplanes flying in formation overhead; then, to the discomfort of some spectators, the collection box is passed around by jibbering Albert, the village idiot.

Going beyond such humorous excursions, the novel ends with a vision of eternal recurrence. Miss La Trobe receives an unexpected illumination after her play is over. Feeling severely let down by the performance, convinced that her work is a failure, she is distracted by a flock of starlings swooping into the tree under which she stands; they make a humming, buzzing cacophony that proclaims the fecundity of nature, all the "branches, leaves, birds syllabling discordantly life, life, life, without measure." The hum of life inspires Miss La Trobe to conceive the opening of a new play. She imagines two figures facing each other on "high ground at midnight" and so anticipates the novel's final scene, acting as a medium, because her art links her to an underlying force that also shapes the real-life action.

The final scene is set in the drawing room where Isabella and Giles face each other at the end of the day, but the narrator adjusts the focus to bring in a view of the surrounding countryside, which is reverting to wilderness. Her enhanced vision, which might be called "mythicomedy," abolishes the distinction between inside and outside, past and present, allowing us to glimpse an elemental drama just beginning as the novel ends. Consumed by hatred and love, husband and wife approach a silent reckoning.

> Before they slept, they must fight; after they had fought, they would embrace. From that embrace another life might be born. But first they must fight, as the dog fox fights with the vixen, in the heart of darkness, in the fields of night.
> Isa let her sewing drop. The great hooded chairs had become enormous. And Giles too. And Isa too against the window. The window was all sky without colour. The house had lost its shelter. It was night before roads were made, or houses. It was the night that dwellers in caves had watched from some high place among rocks.
> Then the curtain rose. They spoke.

Like Isabella, though without her archaic tone, the narrator uses poetic language to reveal and conceal her inner life. All is artifice and at the same time deeply personal. The passionate quarrel between Isabella and Giles is laced with echoes of Conrad's *Heart of Darkness* and the Bible. Literature is the iron curtain sectioning off Virginia's emotional life, her last defense against feeling. In the finale, when the curtain rises, myth, drama, and naturalistic narrative fuse into a single substance, a tissue of lived poetry, where the words and the acts are one.

⚘

In spite of her celebration of village life in "Pointz Hall," Virginia was increasingly disenchanted with Rodmell and critical of her neighbors. Her diaries and letters throughout December 1940 and January 1941 expressed frequent boredom and irritation. As treasurer of the Women's Institute she sat through tedious meetings and went about collecting sixpences from the members. Rodmell society relentlessly embraced her—aside from Vanessa and her family, she rarely saw anyone other than the villagers—and she felt obliged to be civil. Neighbors dropped in unexpectedly, interrupting her at her writing; she was stuck for an hour listening to an old doctor's widow who came to ask advice about growing tomatoes and lingered on, prodding the lawn with her stick, talking about nothing in particular. Virginia detected no echo in the village, "only waste air." Even the children were dull and spiritless in comparison to London children. The pettiness of her daily life was underscored by the winter cold, which made it hard to ignore physical discomforts. On December 19 she drew up a list of inconveniences that dispelled any hint of holiday cheer, even though the war for the moment seemed far away. The tiny allowance of petrol made visiting impractical and the scarcity of butter, milk, and eggs curtailed hospitality if visitors did come. "So little fat to cook with. And so much shopping to do. And one has to weigh and measure." The deterioration of the mail service further complicated social life. All these were minor inconveniences—no one was going hungry or freezing yet—but the small constraints darkened her mood, making her feel more than usually suspicious of the people she met in Rodmell. Human foibles she might have noticed with interest in the past irritated her intensely. The villagers exploited her and Leonard, she complained, extracting their ideas and feeding on their vitality. They were preyed on by "vampires. Leeches. Anyone with 500 a year & education, is at once sucked by the leeches. Put L and me into Rodmell pool & we are sucked—sucked—sucked. . . . We've exchanged the clever for the simple. The simple envy us our life"—and she might have added, they tried to drag her down to their own

level. Leonard discussed this outburst in his autobiography, acknowledging that it showed signs of imbalance, but he added that she might
have experienced such a "short sharp spasm" at any time in her life,
and he could not connect it, except in hindsight, to anything more
serious.

Meanwhile, the authorities warned that a German invasion was no
more than a month or two away; the crisis would come before Easter. Virginia hated this slack, dead time of inactivity and described it
as "the worst stage of the war." Leonard, the fatalist, found a grim
satisfaction in awaiting the catastrophe—it almost buoyed him up—
but she only felt stifled by it. Queer, she said, living "without a future . . . with our noses pressed to a closed door."

Thoughts of death made her recover feelings she hardly knew she
still had. On December 22 she noted that she had been going through
old papers, reading her father's memoirs and love letters to her
mother, seeing them afresh with a "child's vision." Those glimpses of
her parents inspired very tender feelings, though she resisted nostalgia, knowing how oppressive those days had often been. Her father's
voice seemed to rise from the page, silencing her judgment of him.
The tenderness was simply another fact; it did not undo the harm he
had done, but while it lasted, her anger receded into the background.
She described her feelings in language that echoed devotional ca-
dences. "How beautiful they were, those old people . . . how simple,
how clear, how untroubled. . . . He loved her—oh & was so candid
& reasonable & transparent—& had such a fastidious delicate mind,
educated, & transparent. How serene & gay even their life reads to
me: no mud; no whirlpools. And so human—with the children & the
little hum & song of the nursery." A domestic psalm, reaching beyond the disorder and complexity of the real world—only a step away
from the broken, inarticulate cries and endearments she had once invoked in *The Waves*, searching for "a little language such as lovers
use, words of one syllable such as children speak when they come into
the room and find their mother sewing and pick up some scrap of
bright wool." She wished to hold the feeling, not to infect it with her
aging skepticism. It was already tarnished, already fading, and she
tried to slow the process, reminding herself to admit "nothing turbulent; nothing involved; no introspection." A resolve that subtly seems
to admit introspection in the act of banning it.

❧

A new friend entered Virginia's life toward the end of the year. Octavia Wilberforce sometimes stopped in to see the Woolfs when her

medical rounds took her in the direction of Rodmell. They had first met Octavia in 1937 through Elizabeth Robins, the actress and novelist, with whom Octavia shared a house in Brighton. Virginia and Octavia had a distant family connection—Virginia's great-grandfather had married the sister of William Wilberforce, the antislavery crusader who was Octavia's great-grandfather. Virginia described her as "a very fresh coloured healthy minded doctor, in black, with loops of silver chain, good teeth & a candid kind smile." To Leonard she gave the impression of being "large, strong . . . completely reliable, like an English oak," with strong roots in the Sussex countryside. She was the eighth of nine children (therefore Octavia) in a prosperous upper-middle-class family. As a young woman she had been expected either to marry or to stay idly at home, but she had become a doctor in spite of her family's opposition. Medical training, only recently opened to women, was an obstacle course; with the encouragement of her older friend Elizabeth Robins, whom she looked up to as a surrogate mother, she persevered, eventually building a pioneering and successful practice in Brighton.

During her occasional visits, "cousin" Octavia noticed that Virginia had lost weight and was thin as a rail. To her clinical eye both Woolfs looked frail and in need of fattening up. When she came to Monk's House early in December, Octavia brought with her a supply of milk and cream from a farm where she managed a small herd of dairy cattle. She reported the details of the visit in a long letter to Elizabeth Robins, who had returned to her native America for the duration of the war. They had talked a great deal about Robins herself, and a book she had written about backstage life in the 1890's. A delicate moment came when Octavia repeated her opinion that Virginia was "probably the greatest living writer of English prose." Virginia received the praise bashfully, as if tasting forbidden sweets. Octavia preserved the absurdity of the moment in a few awkward phrases. "This [her greatness] she showed disbelief at but did, I think, finally accept simply and rather touchingly." Before leaving, Octavia invoked her privileges as a doctor by urging them both to pay more attention to their diets, and to let her send Devonshire cream as a small return for the pleasure she had received from Virginia's books. Subsequently she made the "business proposition" to send them weekly supplies of milk and cream in exchange for a copy of Virginia's next book. To Elizabeth Robins she wrote: "They both look thin and half-starved and if anybody ought to benefit from my herd it should be those waifs. Waifs I'm sure they are about food." Virginia accepted

Figure 23. Octavia Wilberforce in her medical student days.

the offer, but insisted that it should take the form of a trade. Though they had nothing to equal the precious cream, they had large quantities of apples from their orchard to give her. As for her writing—she was still transcribing and revising "Pointz Hall"—it was absurd, she said, to equate Octavia's bounty with "an unborn and as far as I can tell completely worthless book. I've lost all power over words, cant do a thing with them." This provoked a friendly debate about the relative merits of books as against cream. Octavia explained in one of her letters that she spent most of her time feeling humiliated by her inability to help her patients, and the chance to actually do something constructive, "the illusion that with enough extra milk you might both go ahead and . . . write your greatest masterpieces," lifted her spirits. As for Virginia's complaint that she had lost her power over words, Octavia argued that "every true genius has to lie fallow for a time," a form of benign neglect that would lead eventually to a richer harvest. Virginia ignored these attempts to reassure her and stuck to the main point, replying that "nothing we both ever to the end write can outweigh your milk and cream at this bitter and barren moment." So Octavia sent the products of her dairy twice a week, also dropping in from time to time, though she was careful not to impose by coming too often.

Though generous and well-meaning, Octavia had no feeling for nuances and lightly brushed aside Virginia's bleak words. Her gifts of milk and cream, her insistence that Virginia should gain weight, tied in with a history she knew nothing about. Virginia had spent several periods in a nursing home, where her "neurasthenia" was treated with enforced bed rest and a rich milk diet. She had never lost her hatred of those treatments and her dislike of doctor's orders. Her attitude toward food, Leonard remarked, was colored by a deep sense of guilt. "It was always extremely difficult to induce her to eat enough food to keep her well. Every doctor whom we consulted told her to eat well and drink two or three glasses of milk every day. . . . But I do not think that she ever accepted it. Left to herself, she ate extraordinarily little and it was with the greatest difficulty that she could be induced to drink a glass of milk regularly every day. . . . Our quarrels and arguments were rare and almost always about eating or resting." Octavia's gifts, kindly offered, carried their own special freight.

❧

Virginia assumed that the Nazi invasion, which the authorities still expected in the spring, perhaps as early as March, would be closely followed by her own death, and she sometimes spoke as if the two events were interchangeable. Reflecting that she might be seeing the downs and meadows for the last time, she tried again to fix their contours in her memory. On January 9, 1941, she described the snow-covered slope of Asheham down—"red, purple, dove blue grey" in the setting sun, a brilliant expanse, against which rose the dark little cross of the neighboring church. The enchantment of the scene, with its pinkish highlights and the marsh "like an opaque emerald," was heightened by her sense of an ending. In her diary the visual beauty alternated with reminders of death. Today they were burying her maid Louie's aunt, who had been killed when a bomb fell on her house. Outside Virginia's window the downs glowed rose and purple. She felt the two notes—the woman's death and the snowy landscape—sounding in unison and remembered Faust's bargain, which she had reversed by vowing to cling to the imperfect moment. "Are these the things that are interesting? . . . that say Stop you are so fair? Well, all life is so fair, at my age. I mean, without much more of it I suppose to follow. And t'other side of the hill there'll be no rosy blue red snow."

She was reading Elizabethan drama in preparation for her next book while she finished revising "Pointz Hall," and literary allusions, like her reference to Goethe's *Faust*, acted as a distancing device, enabling her to treat death with some detachment. Like Isabella in "Pointz Hall," she used elegiac phrases and bits of poetry to blot out her anxiety. Luckily she had inherited a taste for reading, she told Ethel on February 1, and so could always concentrate her mind by remembering that she had "only 3 months to read Ben Jonson, Milton, Donne, and all the rest!" She had arranged a last scene for herself, she said; she would be reading Shakespeare in the midst of an air attack, having forgotten her gas mask, and so "fade far away and quite forget . . ." The truncated line from the "Ode to a Nightingale" gave Virginia a kind of immunity—Keats's words were so familiar there was no need to explain or justify them, no need, amid the general disaster, to examine her own assumptions.

During the first two months of 1941 Leonard grew worried about her health and began consulting Octavia Wilberforce, who in effect became her doctor as well as her friend. Virginia felt she had reached a creative limbo and wrote now merely out of habit. She was still getting letters about *Roger Fry* and found some of the readers' comments upsetting. She had offended one lady by describing an incident during Fry's school days, when a boy soiled himself and also soiled the schoolmaster who was whipping him. Another reader was indignant about Fry's unflattering picture of Pierpont Morgan and Americans in general. Stung by these comments, Virginia ironically dismissed all praise and absorbed the blame. "I never like or respect my admirers," she wrote, "always my detractors." Observing her fragility, Octavia did her best to reassure Virginia about the value of her next book, "Reading at Random." Such a disinterested critical commentary, she said, was just what many readers wanted to help take their minds off the war. In a letter to Elizabeth Robins on January 31, she stressed how much she liked those rather high-minded citizens, the Woolfs, adding that Virginia was looking thinner and thinner. Her energy seemed depleted, "she can't work long at a stretch, never after tea — and often breaks off when rather desperate and goes and makes a pudding or something. If you ask me I think she is a thoroughly frail creature."

On the other hand, Elizabeth Bowen, who came to Monk's House for a three-day visit on February 13, found Virginia in good spirits — curious as always about other people's lives, the details of which made her laugh immoderately. She remembered Virginia kneeling on the floor — they were tacking up a torn curtain that needed to be mended — and "she sat back on her heels and put her head back in a patch of sun, early spring sun. Then she laughed in this consuming, choking, delightful, hooting way." That boisterous moment set the tone of the visit. Bowen's departure was followed closely by the arrival of Vita, whom Virginia had invited to spend the night at Monk's House and give a talk to the Rodmell Women's Institute. The whole week, which had begun with a hectic trip north to visit the Hogarth Press in Letchworth, gave Virginia some relief from her isolation, but it was no substitute for the "higher life," which increasingly seemed to elude her.

That became painfully clear after she finished revising "Pointz Hall." On February 26 she reported transcribing the last scene of the novel, having finally hit on the title *Between the Acts*, which referred not only to the inner play, but to political and domestic acts as well. The act of giving the manuscript to Leonard left her feeling more threadbare and vacant than she had felt in years. Since she had lost the sense of her audience, it was hard for her to imagine writing another major work, though she needed her daily dose of drudgery more than ever. But no, she was stunned by the mediocrity of village life, preoccupied with bare necessities, and so obsessed with food that she would not give away even a spice bun. In the same diary entry she drew an acid sketch of a pasty-faced couple she had seen gorging themselves on cakes in a Brighton restaurant. "Where does the money come to feed these fat white slugs?" She could still escape the general inanity by working on "Reading at Random," but criticism did not sustain her like fiction. The possibility of using her work, as she had always done, to preserve her sanity and stability, seemed increasingly remote, and she asked herself: "Shall I ever write again one of those sentences that gives me intense pleasure?"

In order to take her mind off herself Virginia had the idea of making a "living portrait" or picture in words of one of her friends. On February 28, two days after finishing *Between the Acts*, she offered to do a sketch of Octavia—she already had a vivid picture of her childhood in that country house with the beautiful name, Lavington—and if that succeeded perhaps Octavia would sit for a full-scale portrait. The doctor tried to hide behind her profession, objecting that if the piece were published she would be accused of advertising. She hemmed and hawed and finally conceded that it might be fun to try. She had felt threatened, Octavia said later, but soon began to feel flattered, realizing what a marvelous chance it would be for her, with her "unanalytical mind . . . to talk to a born clarifier." Virginia thought her a highly "paintable" subject because of her self-possession and practicality: "the reticence, the quiet, the power . . . she's healing the sick by day, and controlling the fires by night"—a reference to Octavia's fire-watching duties in Brighton. For her part, Octavia thought it came down to the attraction of opposites. The hypersensitive Virginia was fascinated by Octavia's active temperament, her physical toughness and love of games and the outdoors. Drawing Octavia's portrait would encourage Virginia to focus on those practical interests and that outgoing character, helping her to live in the moment without spiraling downward into self-analysis and depression.

Still, Virginia's awareness that they had no future colored the most commonplace events. She went to hear Leonard lecture on history to the Workers' Education Association in Brighton, and afterward noticed the signs of approaching spring—someone wearing a colorful hat and rouged, overdressed old women in the tea shop and the waitress in a checked cotton uniform—clear and distinct shapes seen through a transparent film that clouded over as she reminded herself to stay calm and keep her attention fixed on external objects.

[Virginia's diary, March 8, 1941]

No: I intend no introspection. I mark Henry James's sentence: Observe perpetually. Observe the oncome of age. Observe greed. Observe my own despondency. By that means it becomes serviceable. Or so I hope. I insist upon spending this time to the best advantage. I will go down with my colors flying. This I see verges on introspection; but doesn't quite fall in. Suppose, I bought a ticket at the Museum; biked in daily & read history. Suppose I selected one dominant figure in every age & wrote round & about. Occupation is essential. And now with some pleasure I find that its seven; & must cook dinner. Haddock & sausage meat. I think it is true that one gains a certain hold on sausage & haddock by writing them down. . . .

[She has written to T. S. Eliot and Stephen Spender and will invite herself to stay with Ethel.] This to make up for the sight of Oxford Street & Piccadilly [in ruins] which haunt me. Oh dear yes, I shall conquer this mood. Its a question of being open sleepy, wide eyed at present—letting things come one after another. Now to cook the haddock.

"Open sleepy," that is, to live in the present, seeing every pebble under one's feet in minute detail, but approaching ruins and rubble in a state of dreamy detachment. Being awake, then, to the passing moment, but immune to the general horror—an attempt to deploy the old fire curtain, which no longer protects her. She will not think about herself, she says, "no introspection," even as she lists her own morbid symptoms. Henry James's advice to observe perpetually offers a variation on De Maupassant's remark that writers never simply live, but use their most intimate moments to furnish their art. But Virginia is beyond such reflections. Perhaps she will go down with her colors flying; perhaps haddock and sausage will lure her back into the swing of domestic life.

18 *Time Passes*

Octavia Wilberforce arrived at Monk's House on March 12 for her first portrait session, and found Virginia in a very fragile state, which quite made her forget her own stage fright. Virginia confided that she had just finished her novel and was feeling "depressed to the lowest depths," as often happened after a major work. She felt so useless—the village would not even let her do her share as a fire watcher, and she envied Octavia for leading such an active, committed life. Oh, but what Virginia did was unique, Octavia said—no one else could write her books. Octavia talked about her childhood, describing her happy early years on a country estate in Sussex. Again Virginia responded with recollections of her own youth, especially the time after her mother died, when her father went to pieces and "threw himself too much upon us . . . made too great emotional claims upon us," an affliction, she said, that "accounted for many of the wrong things in my life. I never remember any enjoyment of my body." Virginia said the burden of her father's grief had condemned her to live in an intellectual and emotional hothouse. She had no chance as a girl to play games or tramp through the woods, and so she had formed the habit of turning inward, which had become second nature to her. Leonard often urged her to think less about herself and more about "outside things." After the session Octavia speculated that Virginia feared breaking down again and had seized on the verbal portrait and the experiment of using her as a model because the contact with her "bucolic and hefty" personality had a tranquilizing effect.

Octavia was content to play that role and, incidentally, to send detailed reports on their meetings to Elizabeth Robins, who admired

Virginia so much. Unfortunately, Octavia's skills as a psychological observer and writer did not match her good intentions. Her letters provide valuable information, but they ignore variations in tone and offer dubious renditions of Virginia's speech. No doubt she reported the content accurately, but the clumsy phrasing—"made too great emotional claims upon us . . . accounted for many of the wrong things in my life"—sounds suspiciously like Octavia's own.

Virginia was under a cloud again on March 14, when the Woolfs went to London for the day in order to discuss Hogarth Press business with John Lehmann. He was very excited by the news that she had finished *Between the Acts*, but she tried to damp his enthusiasm, pointing out that she and Leonard disagreed about the book's merits. She grew agitated, her hands trembling, as she insisted that the "so-called novel" was a failure and did not deserve to be published—"much too slight and sketchy," as she later informed Lehmann. Leonard thought otherwise, gently protesting that she herself knew very well "it was one of the best things she had written." Virginia agreed to let Lehmann read the manuscript and cast a tie-breaking vote, but her depression increased. On March 18 she came home from one of her long walks in the rain, drenched to the skin, "looking ill and shaken," and said she had slipped into a ditch. Her disheveled state and something about the look on her face made Leonard terribly uneasy, but he feared that she might break down completely if he spoke too bluntly. Virginia continued to lose weight, eating very little and refusing to take the usual precautions of bed rest and a fattening diet; she insisted that there was nothing at all wrong with her. In a quandary, Leonard asked Vanessa to give her sister a firm talking-to about the need to build herself up, but Vanessa's appeals had no more effect than Leonard's.

At a second "seance" on March 21, Octavia confessed how hard it had been for her to defy her family by becoming a doctor, what a moral coward she was, how she'd "always lied to save my skin as a child." She was shy about discussing these subjects, but Virginia's impersonal attitude—she sat looking off into space, keeping her profile to Octavia and only occasionally turning to ask a question—made it easy to confide in her. At one point Virginia said she had been considering what method to use in doing this portrait. Her two previous attempts at biography, *Orlando* and *Roger Fry*, had been failures, and now, buried in the country, without "the stimulation of seeing people," she felt completely blocked. She summed up the situation with bleak finality. "I can't write. I've lost the art." The sound of Virginia's voice put Octavia on the alert. She took this confession more seriously than previous ones. Speaking as a doctor, she urged Virginia to try positive thinking—praised the virtues of fresh air and a stiff upper lip, chided her for giving in and "making the war an excuse." She must stop it at once, and buck up, settle down, put her nose to the grindstone, because her writing was by far the most important consideration. Furthermore, she must stop brooding about the past—forget her family's troubles, all that "blood thicker than water balderdash." Virginia replied that she had "taken to scrubbing floors when she couldn't write"—it helped take her mind off her problems. Summing up her impressions afterward, Octavia wrote that Virginia was too preoccupied "with her own mind and its reactions. It would do *her* a world of good to harrow a field or play a game." These well-meaning sentiments are perilously close to the views of Dr. Holmes in *Mrs. Dalloway,* the obtuse doctor who advised the suicidal Septimus Smith that "health is largely a matter in our own control. Throw yourself into outside interests; take up some hobby. . . . Try to think as little about yourself as possible."

On the same day Virginia received a letter from Vanessa urging her to be sensible and follow her loved ones' advice, since she was in a confused state in which "one never admits what's the matter." She should be resting, building up her strength rather than scrubbing floors that could just as well stay unscrubbed forever. Vanessa made no bones about the dangers ahead. "What shall we do when we're invaded if you are a helpless invalid—what should I have done all these last 3 years if you hadn't been able to keep me alive and cheerful. You don't know how much I depend on you." The harsh first clause is offset by Vanessa's reminder of their close and loving relations. Her severity did not offend Virginia—on the contrary, she found the schoolmarmish tone ("you *must* be sensible") endearing, a typical display of Vanessa's formidable character. She wrote a reply beginning: "You can't think how I loved your letter." An astonishing opening, considering what followed, which was a suicide note. It was true—she loved the stern, maternal voice, invoking old ties; she also wanted to make it unmistakably clear that the letter had not distressed her in any way. But she went on to say that she had "gone too far this time to come back again. I am certain now that I am going mad. . . . I am always hearing voices, and I know I shant get over it now." She insisted that Leonard had been entirely good, no one could have done more, but he would be better off without her. "I can hardly think clearly any more," she wrote. "I have fought against it, but I cant any longer." A deceptively plain last sentence that leaves a large ambiguity: Fought against what?—against mental illness or the wish to die? Which was stronger, fear or desire? Or were they equally blended? "I have fought against it"—words one speaks at a moment of self-abandonment, implying surrender to temptation or necessity, looking forward to the moment of release.

⚶

Virginia wrote her letter to Vanessa on Sunday, March 23. She did not send it. Around that time, either the Tuesday before or after, she wrote another suicide note, addressed to Leonard, and kept that too in reserve for future use. The process of putting down her thoughts on paper may have given her some breathing space. On Monday, March 24, Leonard noted that she was slightly better. She felt well enough to record the day's events in her diary: an evocative entry, like so many others, though a shade bleaker than most. They had visited Mrs. Chavasse in the village, a dressmaker sitting in a red and brown room, her knitting in hand; she told them, almost at once, that two of her sons had been killed in the war. "This, one felt, was to her credit." On that note the conversation foundered. Virginia offered a few feeble comments, but her words "perished in the icy sea between us. And then there was nothing." A windy day, she reported, bringing gusts of sea air from the English Channel. Vanessa was spending the day in seaside Brighton, and Virginia, feeling attached, imagined "how it wd be if we could infuse souls." She might divert herself now by planning her portrait of Octavia. She added a note about the present moment. "Two long letters from Shena & O. I cant tackle them, yet enjoy having them." \And last, a hint of spring. "L is doing the rhododendrons . . ."

Nothing had changed—Virginia was eating very little and refusing to rest. By Wednesday Leonard was more alarmed than ever. Later he recalled thinking that her state was "very dangerous. Desperate depression . . . her thoughts raced beyond her control; she was terrified of madness. One knew that at any moment she might kill herself." Again he had to decide whether to sit tight or take action and run the risk of making Virginia still more desperate; any wrong word or misstep could drive her over the edge. He was haunted by the memory of her previous suicide attempt in 1913, when she had swallowed an overdose of Veronal immediately after a visit to her doctor. Then too she had insisted there was nothing at all the matter with her. Leonard decided he had to take the risk of getting professional help.

On Thursday morning he called Octavia, who was in bed recovering from the flu and not sure her legs would carry her, but she agreed to see Virginia in her Brighton office that afternoon if he could persuade her to come. Virginia said no, she didn't need a doctor, but Leonard persisted and she allowed herself to be persuaded. Once in the examining room, she grew restive again, as if she had detected something in the air that confirmed her suspicions.

[Octavia to Elizabeth Robins, March 27, 1941]
  Oh but it was rocky going . . . a battle of—not wits but *minds*. "*Quite* unnecessary to have come" [Virginia said]. Wouldn't answer my questions frankly (though I asked rather few, for me) and was generally resistive. I met each phase patiently. "All you have to do is to reassure Leonard." Finally, after I gently and firmly told her that I knew her answer wasn't true [and explained the facts about her condition] . . . she began in her sleep-walking way at my request to get undressed. Stopped. "Will you promise if I do this not to order me a rest cure." *Blast* say I to myself. I look her confidently in the eye: "What I promise you is that I won't order you anything you won't think it reasonable to do. Is that fair?" She agreed. And we went on with the exam—she protesting at each stage like a petulant child!
  Well, at the end we start off again and talk. And then she does confess her fears. That the past will recur—that she won't be able to work again and so on. Tragic. God knows if I did her a penn'orth of good. . . . "*Because* you'd had trouble and come through it, shouldn't this be a reassurance to you that if you'll take things easy now . . ." [Octavia's ellipsis; she offered all the predictable arguments.] Oh I expect I did no real good. But I threw in somewhere, putting out my hand and clasping her icy cold one, "If you'll collaborate I know I can help you, and there's nobody in England I'd like, *adore* more to help." She looked a little less strained and perhaps a trifle detachedly pleased!! But the *poignancy* of it all. And *can* I help?

Still debilitated by the flu and alarmed by Virginia's appearance, Octavia fell back on the familiar doctor-patient protocols, patiently allowing Virginia's "phases" to run their course. She looked into Virginia's eyes with a look meant to convey her good faith and also to bring the patient into line—bright and manipulative. If Virginia would only trust her and collaborate . . . there was nobody in England she'd rather help . . . subtly shifting ground, and with just a hint of self-aggrandizement, but nothing excessive, adopting Virginia's problem as her own—and in the process growing impersonal, sinking her private self in her professional role. If Octavia humored her patient as one humors a "petulant child," Virginia knew it, and knew she had fallen into a trap, for her resistance confirmed what they had all been saying—that she was not fit to decide for herself and must rely on some authority. Such mortifying thoughts increased her inner defiance, while providing further proof, if any were needed, of her deterioration. Octavia remained unaware that the examination evoked some of Virginia's worst experiences with doctors.

Virginia feared that Octavia might order her to take a rest cure, that is, send her to a sanatorium, as her doctor had done in 1913, shortly after her marriage. The anger she felt at that time had inspired her portrayal of Sir William Bradshaw, the sadistic doctor in *Mrs. Dalloway*. Armed with the authority to stamp out "unsocial impulses," Bradshaw took pleasure in imposing his will on defenseless patients like Septimus, whom he planned to send to a home "where we will teach you to rest." Bradshaw was pitiless—"he swooped; he devoured. He shut people up." And in her account of Septimus, the shell-shocked young man with the hawklike nose, Virginia described her own horror of falling into the hands of strangers just when she felt most naked and defenseless. Recoiling from that misery, Septimus learned the sublime code of abjectness, the luxury of feeling oneself "condemned, deserted, as those who are about to die are alone," and so discovering "a freedom which the attached can never know." His dissociation provided a refuge, a feeling of invulnerability, like that of a castaway "who gazed back at the inhabited regions, who lay like a drowned sailor, on the shore of the world."

The drowned sailor, the shell-shocked soldier, were Virginia's doubles, her secret sharers. She too inhabited a watery realm and heard the bird songs coming through the waves, like Septimus, who lay "on a cliff with the gulls screaming over him." Her accounts of depression often present such twofold visions—of the sufferer standing on a high, rocky place and then of falling, plunging into the sea. As Septimus knew, "once you fall . . . human nature is on you. Holmes and Bradshaw are on you." Those shadowy tormentors now closed in again, superimposing themselves on Octavia, obscuring her past kindnesses, bringing back memories of obtuse doctors and insidious appeals to authority: "I know I can help you." Ironically, Octavia fixed on the idea that Virginia was "haunted by her father," but she was blind to the way her own methods raised the ghosts of authoritarian elders.

After the examination Octavia conferred privately with Leonard and decided it was not safe to make any drastic changes—things should go on as before, at least for the next few days, but, if possible, he should persuade Virginia to give up all intellectual work—no writing and criticism for a month. She lived too much in the abstract realm of books and ideas, Octavia said. "Let her be rationed, and then she'll come good again." While they were talking a low-flying German bomber passed directly overhead—a deafening roar, followed by the chatter of machine guns and then an explosion in the distance. Afterward Leonard remembered the impact, but at the time they were so involved in their conversation they hardly noticed it. And that too was ironic, since it was the nightmarish atmosphere—the air raids, the isolation and loss of an audience, the paranoia caused by fear of invasion—that had brought Virginia to the verge of a breakdown.

The encounter made Octavia uneasy, and after the Woolfs left she wrote to Virginia, intending to include the letter with her next milk delivery. She urged Virginia again to restrict herself to light housework, "watch the birds, do a bit of embroidery, design a new chair cover for ½ hour—eat a little more—specially carbohydrates." And then, when she recovered, perhaps she might turn around "and write the greatest masterpiece of this century." Her tone grew increasingly hearty and avuncular, promising that Virginia would get well if only she would cooperate: "So is that agreed?" Octavia approached her patient with great affection and wrote as a friend, not just a doctor, inviting Virginia to call her up at any time, day or night, if she needed someone to talk to. But Virginia never saw the letter.

She took care of some unfinished business later that day. John Lehmann had given a favorable verdict on *Between the Acts*, sending her a telegram and a letter to express his admiration. The novel pushed prose "to the extreme limits of the communicable," he declared, and was "filled with a poetry more disturbing than anything she had written before." Virginia had made up her mind, however, and she wrote asking him to withdraw the book, which was "too silly and trivial" to be published. She apologized for giving him so much trouble, but she had written it at odd intervals, when her brain was "half asleep," and had not realized how bad it was till after sending it to him. Leonard deposited her letter in the mail that evening, and he took the unusual step of enclosing with it a note of his own, explaining that Virginia was "on the verge of a complete nervous breakdown," a state that had been coming on for some time. There was no chance of publishing *Between the Acts* for the moment—it would have to be put off indefinitely. He added that the whole thing was a nightmare and warned Lehmann not to acknowledge his letter.

Three months earlier Virginia had called *Roger Fry* "an experiment in self-suppression," and the same terms could be applied to the books immediately preceding it, *The Years* and *Three Guineas*, with their elaborately orchestrated "facts." All through the 1930s, and with greater insistence as the war approached, she had charted her own form of inner exile, vowing that she would indulge in no introspection. She had a need, as Leonard suggested, to write against her natural grain, renouncing the subjectivity of her earlier fiction, thereby bending herself out of shape, as if doing penance for the world's sins. In *Between the Acts* she had changed her direction again, trying to fashion parody and caricature into instruments capable of sounding a note of prophetic intensity. Her description of the novel as "trivial and silly" drastically overstated the case—the book contains luminous writing and rich satirical moments—but it does have some weaknesses in its unfinished form: the failure to take the portrayal of the central character, Isabella, beyond the level of self-parody and the thinness of some parts of the pageant, such as the Victorian episodes. Ironically, artistic failure is one of its themes. Miss La Trobe's village play illustrates the inevitable conflict between the artist's conception and the shabby means she has for its realization—a satirical point that resonated with Virginia's own judgment that her artistic powers had deteriorated. In eroding her ties to her audience, the war had also undermined her faith that she had anything left to say. She had told Octavia she could no longer write, she had lost her power over words—a complaint that Octavia dismissed as merely fanciful, thus ignoring Virginia's very real fear that she would never again enter the visionary state in which she had written *To the Lighthouse* and *The Waves*.

❧

On the morning after her unsettling consultation with Octavia, Virginia's condition was worse. Trying to follow the doctor's orders, Leonard arranged for her to do some housework to take her mind off herself. Louie Everest described the morning's events. She was tidying Leonard's study when the Woolfs came in and he asked her to give Virginia a duster so that she could help clean the room. Louie did so, "but it seemed very strange. I had never known her want to do any housework with me before. After a while Mrs. Woolf put the duster down and went away."

Alarmed by Virginia's state, Leonard had spent some time talking to her in her bedroom early that morning, but he felt he couldn't keep her under constant surveillance, which she would have found intolerable; in any case, it was impossible to do so without hiring trained nurses. The comings and goings around the house followed the usual rule of order and randomness. Leonard spent the morning working at his desk and in the garden; Virginia divided her time between her writing lodge and the upstairs sitting room. At one point Leonard went into the lodge and found her writing on a tablet, and she got up and came into the house with him. Later on Louie saw her put on her coat, take her walking stick and walk quickly through the garden toward the river.

A crisp, clear spring day. The path shone, muddy under her gum boots. Time passing. . . . She had dispensed with hours, but there were still minutes and seconds, which subdivided, inviting her to number every bud on the tree, and divided again, a never-ending stream of motes. Her sensations had been reduced by the same process, growing narrow and acute as they approached the vanishing point. She stumbled into bushes, tripped over stones. She picked up a stone and fitted it into her jacket pocket; then another. She waded into the water carrying her stick and let it go . . .

At one o'clock, when Louie rang the bell for lunch, Leonard came in, found two letters on the mantelpiece, opened the one addressed to him, and saw at a glance that something terrible had happened. He ran frantically out the back gate across the water-meadows to the river, where he saw footprints leading into the water and found Virginia's walking stick drifted up against the riverbank. No other trace of her. Louie had gone to get help, and they searched all day and on into the evening, tramping to Virginia's favorite haunts, until it grew too dark to continue.

⚜

Virginia's death was not caused by any sudden dementia or wild aberration. She had thought it through and written her letters to Leonard and Vanessa in advance. In a sense, she had prepared for this all her life. But it was not predetermined, either—she chose the time on the spur of the moment, and was making plans shortly before her death to revise *Between the Acts* as well as to see her friends in April. Her last few days were colored by this incongruity, this permeable skin between two realities, since she had already decided to kill herself, and still went on as if she had an indefinite amount of time ahead of her. Then the warning signs—disorientation, voices—coupled with the hopelessness she felt in Octavia's office, carried her over a threshold. At that point she put her plan into action, leaving the two letters she had prepared, and scribbling a third that Leonard later found on her writing tablet, in which she said another good-bye and added a hasty response to Octavia's arguments. "I know that I shall never get over this. . . . Nothing anyone says can persuade me." The last sentence expressed her defiance of all professional advice and claimed the right to judge for herself, regardless of the cost.

Two letters for Leonard, then—both written under great stress, but they were readable and clear enough in their intent—first to shield him from guilt by assuring him that he had done all for her that was humanly possible, and then to justify herself by explaining that she had compelling reasons for doing what she did.

[Virginia to Leonard, March 18(?) 1941]
Tuesday
Dearest,

I feel certain that I am going mad again: I feel we cant go through another of those terrible times. And I shant recover this time. I begin to hear voices, and cant concentrate. So I am doing what seems the best thing to do. You have given me the greatest possible happiness. You have been in every way all that anyone could be. I dont think two people could have been happier till this terrible disease came. I cant fight it any longer, I know that I am spoiling your life, that without me you could work. And you will I know. You see I cant even write this properly. I cant read. What I want to say is that I owe all the happiness of my life to you. You have been entirely patient with me and incredibly good. I want to say that—everybody knows it. If anybody could have saved me it would have been you. Everything has gone from me but the certainty of your goodness. I cant go on spoiling your life any longer.

I dont think two people could have been happier than we have been. V.

[The second note, which Virginia left on a writing block in her garden lodge, was probably what she had been writing when Leonard came to fetch her on the morning of March 28, 1941.]

Dearest,

I want to tell you that you have given me complete happiness. No one could have done more than you have done. Please believe that.

But I know that I shall never get over this: and I am wasting your life. It is this madness. Nothing anyone says can persuade me. You can work, and you will be much better without me. You see I cant write this even, which shows I am right. All I want to say is that until this disease came on we were perfectly happy, It was all due to you. No one could have been so good as you have been, from the very first day till now. Everyone knows that. V.

You will find Roger's letters to the Maurons in the writing table drawer in the Lodge. Will you destroy all my papers.

Knowing how much Leonard must be suffering, and haunted by her own failure to help, Octavia called and went over to see him. They discussed Virginia's medical history, agreeing that the war had revived her fears of having another breakdown like the one she had suffered before and during World War I—there was little anyone could have done to save her. On her way out, Octavia turned to offer some consolation. Speaking as a doctor, she said, she believed Leonard's care of Virginia had been "Heaven inspired. . . . Nobody else could have kept her going so long." She stood at the bottom of the stair and he, standing above her, held out a hand, averting his face, which was puckered up and just breaking into tears. Afterward he set down his thoughts in an undated note, rendering a bitter judgment on his own human fallibility.

> It is a strange fact that a terrible pain in the heart can be interrupted by a little pain in the fourth toe of the right foot.
> I know that V. will not come across the garden from the lodge, & yet I look in that direction for her. I know that she is drowned & yet I listen for her to come in at the door. I know that it is the last page & yet I turn it over. There is no limit to one's stupidity & selfishness.

As for Vanessa, who had always been reticent, her letters expressed surprise and bewilderment more than any other emotion. "I think nothing could have prevented the possibility just then," she wrote to Vita on April 2—"only I wish I had realised it, but I didn't at all." To Jane Bussy, a family friend, she wrote that Virginia had seemed perfectly normal; "of course I didn't see her often enough really to judge. But I think she must have got very much worse rather suddenly at the end. . . . Only the day before I had rung her up and said I was coming to tea and she had seemed pleased."

The police dragged the river, but Virginia's body did not surface till almost three weeks later when some teenage cyclists came upon it, washed up against the riverbank near where Leonard had retrieved her stick. A policeman knocked at the door to relay the news and Louie described her feelings on hearing it. "He said that there were heavy stones in the pockets of her jacket, and she must have put them there and then walked straight down into the river. And that was terrible. It was the most terrible thing I have known."

Perhaps not so for Virginia? . . .

She had written of death as temptation and violation, invented fables of its extreme reality, but what did any scene in a book have to do with the simple act of walking into the water? Did mere imagery dictate the means she chose? Surely art and life follow their own separate courses. And yet her literary themes anticipated the event, closing the logical circuit between thought and action; on the other hand, the physical act of drowning seemed separate and unrelated to anything outside itself. She had once imagined leaving a "simple and profound paper upon suicide" for her friends. Her last letters were too restricted to give that testimony, but she had distributed its contents throughout her writings. Hints of it were contained in the recurring motifs she used to map the submerged side of life. "If I werent so miserable I could not be happy," she said, and her metaphors echoed that motif; responding to unfriendly reviewers, she focused on the happy fall, the delight of being exploded, the pleasure of being abused, and many variations reflecting her fear of exposure and lust for fame. She felt the joy of anonymity, and the horror (now the war had dispersed her audience) of being invisible.

Two impulses ran through her writing, yielding complementary images of an immersion in the depths and a plunge from the heights. She pictured drowning as a merciful end, a dreamlike sinking toward darkness, softened by the rippling of water and the rhythm of the waves, which must surely be benign, she suggested, its murmurings bringing rest to the weary sailor. Sometimes the waters grew monstrous, sucking one down into whirlpools or sweeping one over frightful precipices. But here the image interlocked with the equally obsessive image of falling off a mountain or jumping out a window. She had imagined how Septimus leaped to his death—the ground flashing up,

Figure 24. Looking toward Godrevy Lighthouse from the room that was Virginia's nursery at Talland House, St. Ives; photographed in 1984 by the author.

the rusty spikes running through him, the body thrashing there "with a thud, thud, thud in his brain and then a suffocation of blackness." Countering these visions, the testimony of the stones in Virginia's pockets offered a reminder that drowning, too, is hard, that one does not sink easily. The body wants to swim and needs some ballast, some dense object (and the help of heavy boots) to drag it to the bottom.

At some obscure moment Virginia had passed a point of no return, gone too far to come back again. Step by step, refusing to eat, refusing to rest, she had divested herself, renouncing the natural world.

Most people find it easier to hold on to sorrow than joy, to nurse injuries than admit favors, but Virginia had the gift of sustaining joy, which is why her friends found her a most delightful companion. Her novels are humorous and elegiac, radiantly clear in the midst of sorrow. Through her fictional alter ego in *The Waves*, she pictured her own dissolution set on a soft Mediterranean evening in Spain. Rhoda, with her tour party, approaches the top of a high hill that offers a view across the sea to Africa. In a detached and dreamlike state she imagines that the summit is the end; she is riding a mule and she is on her deathbed, feeling her spirit reach out toward distant realms, looking down from the height, but weightless and disembodied, as if the waves are rising to enfold her, as if she has launched out over the edge of the precipice into space, high above "the lights of the herring fleet. The cliffs vanish. Rippling small, rippling grey, innumerable waves spread beneath us. I touch nothing. I see nothing. We may sink and settle on the waves. The sea will drum in my ears. The white petals will be darkened with sea water. They will float for a moment and then sink. Rolling me over the waves will shoulder me under. Everything falls in a tremendous shower, dissolving me."

Appendix: The Wilberforce Letters

Following is Octavia Wilberforce's record of her meetings with Virginia and Leonard Woolf.

Elizabeth Robins, to whom most of Wilberforce's letters were addressed, had played leading roles in Ibsen's plays on the London stage during the 1890s. Herself a successful popular novelist, Robins had known Virginia's parents and was a great admirer of her work. I have restored a few passages that Wilberforce omitted when she transcribed the letters in her autobiography and omitted passages unrelated to Virginia Woolf.

[Octavia to Elizabeth Robins, December 1940]

I went to tea with the Woolfs and I found them apologizing for untidiness, that is to say books and wine bottles and cases in process of being unpacked as the result of their having to salvage some of what was left of their London quarters, and most friendly. She told me she had written to you, but was scared lest her saying anything to you about your writing should enrage (that was her term), as "authors are very queer people." I assured her that I knew there was no one who would have so much influence upon you as she. This she did not accept, but said, well anyhow if her letter did enrage you, the blood would be on my head. I cheerfully accepted this responsibility. In subsequent talk, she said that she hated to be written to about her work, as people often annoyed her, by for instance saying, "When are you going to give us more criticism?" which to her sensitiveness meant they did not want any more novels.

[The Woolfs] said of course how much they liked you and recalled when they had first met you, she as a child when you were
acting Ibsen I gather, and then not again she said until the "awful occasion when I was given a prize, and the awful things that
were said about my work on a very hot afternoon. It was a cheque
for £40 and anyhow did help us to have a holiday abroad. But
there were there the queerest collection of second rate people."
Here Leonard interrupted and said, "Do you remember that appalling woman whose reputation Baldwin made?" (I suggest
Mary Webb [best-selling author of *Precious Bane*]) "Yes, that's
her name who came and tackled me about some reviewing. I, on
The Nation at the time, had given her a book to do, and it was
so atrociously done that I did not give her any more and she
made a dead set at me on this occasion to find out why, which
was very embarrassing." Then Virginia went on "and when Miss
Robins came up and said such sensitive understanding things to
me, and I think mentioned my mother, I longed to talk to her,
and I was immediately impressed by her personality and quite
overwhelmed. After that we wrote and asked her to do something for the Hogarth Press." She then asked how long I had
known you, and had been much impressed by your modesty,
had thought it so extraordinary that you should have valued so
much her view of Vol. 1 [of Robins's memoirs], as she felt that
you were so great that her view should not have mattered to you.
I recalled how she had said to you that she would like to discuss
the art of writing with you, and that when we had got into the
car you had made me realize how you looked upon her as probably the greatest living writer of English prose. This she showed
disbelief at, but did, I think, finally accept simply and rather
touchingly. . . .

I also said that as a doctor I felt that prevention was much the
most important side of Medicine, and that if I might be allowed
to send her some more Devonshire cream as a small return for
the pleasure she had given me by her books, I would feel myself
privileged.

He asked whether you ever really relaxed, you were always so
perfect when they'd seen you, he couldn't imagine your doing
so. . . . She went through your "Both Sides [of the Curtain]" and
the parts she had been impressed by. How fascinating you must
have been that all these people, the best of the '90's, should have
gone out of their way to help you. Why didn't you, since you
were so successful, stay on the stage? . . . I liked them so much in

their appreciation of you. They were so simple and unaffected about it all. There's no doubt she regards you with no little awe. She talked a lot about [Robins's] "Theatre and Friendship" and how enormously she had loved that. . . . "I know nothing and have always wanted to know about the stage, so was thrilled by it," she said.

f

[Octavia to Elizabeth Robins, December 23, 1940]

At 4 went over with Devonshire cream to the Woolfs. I thought having done my duty all around I'd give myself a treat. Moreover, if Hitler is going to invade or be nasty I'd a feeling I'd get all I could done before Xmas Eve. . . . I marched up the path and greet Leonard and dog and he takes basket with cream and says he'll fill it with apples in return for cream. A barter scheme which entirely suits me. Find Virginia inside with hands worse than icicles. I say how truly grateful I am to her and report your cable saying, "Virginia's letter sets me to work again." She turns her back on me rather shyly and hearing the end turns round with a beaming and delightful smile. "Say it again!" I obey. And to hide her extreme pleasure she makes for kitchen to get the teapot. When she returns I say, "So you see I was right and I know any-how what helps one author." "Yes, but tell me again the exact words." Again I obey. Then she branches off: "I've had such an upsetting afternoon—do you know Lady Oxford?" I said I'd seen her. "Well, she sent me down a statue of Voltaire which she wished me to have after her death. You see she sent for me as she wanted me to write her obituary, so I went. And of course she knew Vanessa and me as children walking in my father's garden."

"Oh, any truth in it?"—[that she knew them as children]. "Not the least. And she said that we had been life-long friends ever since and she writes to me now every day. But what am I to do with Voltaire? You must see it. She is a queer woman." And [Lady Oxford] described how her house having been bombed she sleeps in a tunnel (I think at the Savoy) garbed in a sort of tea gown "designed by Virginia" says Lady Oxford and when she enters it at night so cheerfully arrayed in almost Eastern attire all the other drab and dowdy ones are greatly heartened. . . . She apparently has been trying to reform Virginia's clothes for her. Tells her she looks dowdy.

"Do you know somebody at Henfield, [Virginia asked], she

has often written to me . . . her name is. . . ." I produce Rachel Sharp. "*Yes*, do you know her? She wrote me a furious letter saying I had no business to put in anything so perfectly repulsive and dreadful as what Roger said about his school. . . . I must be a *sensual* horrid creature, quite the reverse from anything she had felt about me before." I don't remember exactly what she said in reply. But to me she said that Margery [Fry] had wanted much more of Roger's frank account put in as she felt it ought to be more generally known what does (or can) happen at boys' schools. And she thought Rachel must have read very little if this was the worst she had read. . . .

We went upstairs to the little, warmer, room and examined a bronze statue of Voltaire seated in a chair. "Do you like Roger Fry?" I'd said I was reading it slowly in homeopathic doses and loving it. "Most interested in it"—I'm beginning to say, "No," interrupted Virginia "do you like him as a man?" I say yes and rather wonder what I ought to hand out that would hit the right note—as truth to tell I am greatly interested in the book and the way she has done it but have never thought, and don't know now, how much as a man I like him! So I retrieve myself from the edge of the precipice of inadequacy and say, "But *I've* got a quarrel with you too," and laugh. She looks up almost scared. (There's something birdlike about her quick sensitive reactions, don't you think?) "You say about doctors," and I go on with a reassuring grin, "that they have no imagination nor spirit of initiative." "Did I?" She leaps in all seriousness to the charge. "Roger was so queer about his health, etc." She excuses herself quite ardently. . . . She had been sorting papers, love letters from her father to her mother. Had been swept away by them. "Poor Leonard is tired out by my interest in my family and all it brings back." I say how I'd stayed with Mrs. Yates Thompson and how much I'd gathered they liked [Leslie] Stephen. . . .

P.S. She so actively both loved and hated at the same time her father. Thought it a contribution that psychologists had explained that this was possible.

≫

[Octavia to Elizabeth Robins, no date]

I *like* to see the Woolfs and be intellectually roused by them.

I rang up Leonard to ask would they like some cream and may I bring it over after Out Patients? I've had a thumping success in taking Devonshire cream made by Maud to Leonard and Virginia. And I'm so glad. They both look thin and half-starved and if ever anybody ought to benefit from my herd it should be those waifs. Waifs I'm sure they are about food. Anyhow, pro tem I've arranged to barter my dairy produce in exchange for apples and, say I cheerfully, a copy of Virginia's next book. At the moment she says she has no power over words and can't write. (N.B. I think our dear friend loves to exaggerate, etc.) ([Air raid] All Clear gone, that's nice and early). And then [Virginia asked], "What shall I do? A novel, another biography, criticism?" O.W.: "Well you don't expect me to say as you have lots in your head. And in any case" . . . I was going on to say she had herself told me that she was enraged by people wanting this or that and inferring they didn't like t'other, when she chipped in "Yes I've lots of ideas germinating but I want to know what the public wants. You're one of my public." I, of course, with complete inadequacy plus native caution said nothing!!

ᵍ⁄ꝑ

[Octavia to Virginia, January 3, 1941]

If you try to weigh things on a balance it would take a sea of milk before I got even with you. My greatest joy in life has always been reading and you have given me untold delight and helped me at many a difficult moment. You have stimulated and helped E.R. as no one else can or could. And moreover please let me have a hand in being *constructive*. You see my job is nearly all either patching or regretting that God hadn't asked my advice! Much of practice is therefore spent in being humiliated by one's limitations. Now, to cherish an illusion that with enough extra milk you might both go ahead and feel you must write your greatest masterpieces is a great and cheering thought. I'm so glad you feel you've "lost all power over words." Go on and abandon yourself to that feeling, every true genius has to lie fallow for a time while the seed germinates—as you know perfectly well. So I'm quite unmoved, instead merely reassured as to the certainty about my part of the bargain and what the book will be like.

As to Roger Fry I can imagine no more really expert biographer. Have you been thinking of writing your father's life? I expect that's cheek and I grovel in advance! You said authors are touchy and I'm suddenly brought up against that warning and am not sure where I've got to as I really know you very little. Or is it that the remote cousinship makes an illusion that I feel I know you . . . well, *better* than I know my near cousins?

❧

[Octavia to Elizabeth Robins, January 15, 1941]

I have hoped that my visits to the Woolfs would stimulate and stir you. Do they? I can't quite be sure of my own diagnosis yet. But I'm pretty sure of certain things. That physically they're both frail.

But to go on about Virginia. And at first I felt she'd exaggerate and overstate to make any sort of amusing story, yes, I think she still would—but about her craft, your writing, any good writing and her own efforts I don't feel she's the same person. That's the side I like and admire. The respect for words, the constructive artist, the builder and architect passionately concerned that each brick is well and truly laid—nay, is perfectly placed in the one and only perfect position . . . that's the Virginia that makes me feel I'm a nitwit and makes one want to start afresh and stretch one's brain.

❧

[Octavia to Virginia, January 26, 1941]

About this new book ["Reading at Random"] I'm inclined to think its just what is most needed now, and after the War. I come across a lot of people who are starving for good books. . . . I feel that unless we all get back to some sort of settled good reading we'll lose our sense of proportion and thought (if any). It will mean we'll be so standardized in our minds by newspapers and wireless as most of the world is in its uniformed clothes now. And Hitler & Co have played on just that note—its a great simplification of life to be told what to wear, do, think, even eat! and it appeals to the lazy side of man so that existence becomes almost as low a job as any other form of animal life. . . .

Monday . . . And now your kind letter has come. I'm relieved to know you can still eat. I'm quite unperturbed that you say you can't write. The longer you feel like that the better you'll write when you do get really going. So just don't try. Pot Pourri [milk cow] and her descendants are standing up to all claims with complete confidence so there's plenty of cream to come.

❧

[Octavia to Elizabeth Robins, January 31, 1941]

I went over to W's today. Took them some calycanthus since

L. is such a great gardener. He was *thrilled* by it—so was she only she's a vaguer less expressive person. . . .

Well anyhow those two citizens—that is their role—are *nice* folk. She looks thinner and thinner, says she's teaching herself to cook in order to be ready for anything. "After the war we certainly shan't get anybody to do for us and at any moment we may have to do for ourselves." This not on financial but general grounds. And I gave her various recipes. . . .

And I suddenly felt how deep and solid her affection is for him—how real and rooted. . . .

She affected to be worried over an American letter. From a woman in Boston about Roger [Fry]. About five type-written pages accusing her of worsening the international relationship between the two countries because she had said frankly what R. thought of some Americans and specially Pierpont [Morgan]. It was no end abusive. Really idiotic. And as Virginia rather sadly said, after all he ran down the English just as much, the only people he thought anything of were the French. So I cheered her on to write shortly, saying that. And also, her own idea, that we were all fighting together for freedom—and if you couldn't faithfully report a man's views without being called over the coals where are you? She was genuinely perturbed at being so violently attacked. There's no doubt they're both a highly sensitive couple. And she takes life hard. I've a suspicion that they both quite like to see me for my comparative stolidity. She also told me a little of her, mainly past, worries. Headaches etc. And I gather even now she can't work long at a stretch, never after tea—and often breaks off when rather desperate and goes and makes a pudding or something. If you ask me I think she is a thoroughly frail creature and I wish we could do something to binge her up. . . .

I told her on Friday that I was very unobservant and didn't notice environments often—or what people wore or even if they were or were not good looking. She looked a little surprised and then said: "No, but you look for their character." I *didn't* say I, as a reflex, absorbed their physical fitness and disabilities to a large extent. And then she said she was glad I didn't notice as their room was so untidy, etc. etc. whereas "I remember at Montpelier Crescent I noticed that you had pots on mats and were very tidy." I laughed and said that was a special effort since she was coming I had to try and make a good impression.

✔

[Octavia to Elizabeth Robins, February 28, 1941]

Today I went over to Virginia and Leonard's.

They'd "had visitors." Quentin, the nephew who had devoured all Leonard's marmalade! Also Vita. Not I gather at the same moment. She had brought them butter. But I can't say I think *my* milk ministrations are doing much good. She, Virginia, looks a better colour but is still as thin as a razor.

I honestly think they like to see me. They most affectionately ask after you. Full of a kind solicitude. We'd a long discussion on *Three Guineas*. She said that work had brought more letters and fury than any book she'd ever written. Did *I* think it overstated and shrill? Indeed no. . . . V.W. [had] been asked to be the one woman on the London Library and she was writing to refuse. She doesn't hold with all these honorary degrees or titles etc. . . .

Then, as I got up to go she looks at me gravely in that detached way and says, "I think I'd like to do a sketch of you, would you mind?" She'd been talking about Roger F. just before and for a moment I took this literally i.e. paints! but got there before too late, making some idiotic remark about there not being enough to do it on and she knew nothing about me. "Yes I've already a picture of you as a child at Lavington, beautiful name, and you could talk to me. You see, I think it would be rather fun to do portraits of living people—anonymously of course." I say, hunting round in my embarrassment and not being sure whether to be flattered or annoyed and feeling frankly bewildered wondering what she was "getting at." I say, "But if it were good—er— it would be recognized and the—er—in my profession I should be had up for advertising," and I appeal to Leonard. He non-committal but considers in his judicial way there might be something in that. She then says: "Oh then you wouldn't like it." At which I think of you and how *you'd* perhaps like it and say: "Oh I think I'm really immensely flattered and I think it might be rather . . . fun," lamely. "Well I might try and send it you to see what you think?" And I make off feeling I'd better hurriedly escape . . . and *longing* for your guidance in the matter. . . .

Oh, I've remembered V. said this phase of the war is rather like waiting in the ante room of a Dr. or dentist's. Shall one pick up and read Punch, or isn't there time or attention enough—not a bad description, eh?

ℐ

[Octavia to Elizabeth Robins, March 14, 1941]

And you approve of Virginia's idea? Bless me. I nearly turned it down. That was my first instinct. Then I began to feel a bit flattered that *her* mind should want to tackle me as a subject. Then I thought how you'd be pleased. Then she wrote the letter I sent you. To which I replied should I come over on Wednesday and collect two pots of gooseberries (barter for milk) and as to "torture to sit" [for her portrait]—I had an unanalytical mind and it would be marvellous to talk to a born clarifier. She rang up and I went over after nearly a whole night out fire watching and a heavy Out Patients. Found them having tea. (Nearly ran away on the doorstep, with sudden stage fright!!) After tea, upstairs to little room where you sat and Leonard and Virginia talked. Presently Leonard says he'd better leave us to it. Virginia says something to hold him and he stays another ten minutes. (They *do* work well together.) Then he picks up some proofs, says he must get back to his work and will leave us to our "seance" and goes off. Virginia moves to his chair on side of fireplace and says tactfully (wily V!) she had been feeling desperate—depressed to the lowest depths, had just finished a story. Always felt like this—but specially useless just now. The Village wouldn't even allow her to fire watch—could do nothing—whereas *my* life. . . . *No* I say firmly and point out that only she could write as she does and so on. . . . "Leonard says I shouldn't think about myself so much and I should think more about outside things." I say how my job does too much of that, lames one too much and knocks out your concentration. "No, not when you're actually on a case." How did *she* know? "No," I agree, "not at the actual moment. But afterwards, reading, writing, anything, its all interruption. . . ." "Yes, but people *need* you. You're doing something worthwhile, practical." I agree that except at times immediately after a book is out and reviews are tumbling over themselves a writer hasn't the advantage of the stage where the audience pulls the best out of him. And then suddenly we talk of Lavington and my childhood. I can't remember when it was—ages ago—but I must have said something of Lavington garden as she says she sees the background and the beauty and peace. . . . "But had you no dark and depressing times?" Poor Virginia—thirteen when her mother died—her sister died at twenty five and both were irreparable blows. And her father rather went to pieces I think after her mother's death and "threw himself too much upon us. Was too emotional and took too much out of us, made too great emotional claims upon us and that I think has accounted for many of the wrong things in my life. I never remember any enjoyment of my body." I questioned what she meant. "You adored the woods and games—I never had that chance." It was all for her I gather intellectual and emotional—no healthy outdoor outlet.

And as we talked one thing became clear to me. Her interest in me I believe is because I'm the farthest possible opposite to her own build-up. Outside interests, physical toughness and game loving as against that narrowed introspective searching, restless rather hauntingly fearful but brilliant mind.

She said she envied me my touch with reality; did I never make notes of any of the interesting things that came my way. And, next minute, "drink in women. Was it curable?" She had a friend—gifted poetically—and a little more description, and I thought I knew whom she meant. [Probably Virginia herself.] You can guess, I'm sure. Very distressed about this.

Heaven knows what impression she got at the end of an hour. But I know I interested and surprised and took her out of herself. And isn't that an achievement in these grim days, for that rather unhappy haunted by the past, if I'm any judge, gifted genius? And I got a pretty shrewd picture of her en passant in the process. Her step brother George [Duckworth] she evidently adored. Did you know him?

Oh! and I told her at the start, that the basis of medicine, science, was to try to be truthful—whereas for her I inferred that it wasn't so important. But my immediate difficulty was to be sure of what *was* the truth. I might have added that I spent my time living ahead and not in the past. Again the reverse of that backward-looking spirit.

Sunday 16th. I've no idea of the dimensions of anything else she wants to do this job—nor I think has she entirely. I gathered she had attempted somebody else and not been pleased with it. . . . I didn't ask who it was though I wouldn't mind asking her about anything, she and L. are the frankest couple I've met on short acquaintance. But I feel she's the most highly sensitive, easily hurt person and I'd handle her as gently as I could. During part of the last war was when she lost hold and I've a feeling back of my head that she's a bit scared this may happen again. In which case anybody as bucolic and hefty and—what am I? tranquilizing perhaps—may help her somewhat.

❧

[Octavia to Elizabeth Robins, March 22, 1941]

Yesterday I went over to the Woolfs again. . . . Virginia by way of being down but looking rather better colour than often. Wanted to know more of my youth. What my first impressions of you were. But darling I'm so wordless talking to that quick, partly vague and partly genius of a mind. And anyhow . . . it's difficult. For my part what I seem to gain is, by bits and pieces, a picture of Virginia's earlier years or anyhow what she was like. She asked me yesterday if I'd ever read *Orlando*. "Oh yes," I say brightly—"What did you think of it?" "Immensely clever as far as I remember but it's so long since I read it that I don't remember anything about it except a vague picture of their skating on the Thames. I *never* remember books farther back than six months probably"—and I felt generally inadequate and uncomfortable.

"Well that was a fantastic biography and *Roger Fry* is the other I've attempted and both are failures . . . and I don't know exactly how I'd do you; probably more like Orlando—but I can't write. I've lost the art. . . . But you are doing more useful work, helping things on. . . ." So then I tell her how far more important her work is and try to buck her up. "Yes, but I'm buried down here—I've not the stimulation of seeing people. I can't settle to it." I say she's making that an excuse, making the war an excuse. And it's a difficult time to concentrate now. But she's got to do it and stick to it. Golly, what I wouldn't give to be able to write as she can.

I said I thought this family business was all nonsense, blood thicker than water balderdash. Surprised her anyway. I'm sure *she* thinks far too much of it!

She said she had taken to scrubbing floors when she couldn't write—it "took her mind off." She's too taken up with her own mind and its reaction. It would do *her* the world of good to harrow a field or play a game.

Drink and smoking we also went into. Before Leonard. He very sound. I do *like* L. And I'm sorry for V. I feel she's her worst enemy.

❧

[Octavia to Elizabeth Robins, March 27, 1941]

I've been under the weather about a week . . . with flu I suppose. Felt most sickly. However after bed and a temperature and general feeling of unable to crawl round I'm lying in bed at 11 A.M. (first day of temp. down) when telephone rings. *Leonard.* Wants my professional help. About her. And then he pours out his difficulties and fears, and *her* fears. She had said she wouldn't see me but, he sounded desperate, things were getting too bad and he felt he must have help. I'm in a cleft stick. *Can* I help. Can I get to her as regards my own legs?

But one knows what the stimulation of an urgent appeal is and I conceal my bedbound state and finally arrange that he brings her here at 3.15 unless she jibs. I feel that I can do more to impress her professionally in my own surroundings; easier to get across when I'm in charge of the environment.

So, later, he rang up to confirm appointment.

And they came.

Oh but it was rocky going. I forgot to cough and entirely lost my own sensations of weakness in a battle of—not wits but *minds.* "*Quite* unnecessary to have come," [Virginia said]. Wouldn't answer my questions frankly (though I asked rather few, for me) and was generally resistive. I met each phase patiently. "All you have to do is to reassure Leonard." Finally, after I gently and firmly told her that I knew her answer wasn't true, [and explained the facts about her condition] . . . she began in her sleep-walking way at my request to get undressed. Stopped. "Will you promise if I do this not to order me a rest cure." *Blast* say I to myself. I look her confidently in the eye: "What I promise you is that I won't order you anything you won't think it reasonable to do. Is that fair?" She agreed. And we went on with the exam—she protesting at each stage like a petulant child!

Well, at the end we start off again and talk. And then she does confess her fears. That the past will recur—that she won't be able to work again and so on. Tragic. God knows if I did her a penn'orth of good. But . . . I had some inspirations. "*Because* you'd had trouble and come through it, shouldn't this be a reassurance to you that if you'll take things easy now . . ." etc. [Octavia's ellipsis]. "If you have an appendix operation it leaves a scar on your body but thats all and you forget about it—if you have a mental illness it leaves a scar on your memory perhaps but thats all. Its only if you think about these things that it matters." Oh I expect I did no real good. But I threw in somewhere, putting out my hand and clasping her icy cold one, "If you'll collaborate I know I can help you, and there's nobody in England I'd like, *adore* more to help." She looked a little less strained and perhaps a trifle detachedly pleased!! But the *poignancy* of it all. And *can* I help?

At one moment I'd almost a thought of Backset for her [a rest home for professional women, founded by Robins] but the risk is great I feel. However, if *ever* we took any risk it must be with her, I feel you'd say as regards Backset's good name, eh?

Anyhow, I'm very busy at the minute and she's the sort of case that needs time. Oh dear!

Well, I'm going back to bed soon to get rid of the aches and gird myself anew for the next trial. . . .

In the midst of my talk after with Leonard machine gunning followed by a crump. I hope something brought down. But we neither felt it of interest or importance by comparison with the matter in hand. I continued to drive home my points. "No writing or criticism for a month." She has been too much nurtured on books. She never gets away from them. "Let her be rationed and then she'll come good again. *If* she'll collaborate . . ."

⁂

[Octavia to Elizabeth Robins, March 28, 1941]

Was it only last night I wrote to you? I'm still pretty weak after the 'flu and only saw Davy of all my patients today. But early I wrote and sent by the milk what I hoped might be a reassuring gentle, friendly note to Virginia (who could not have got it). Just after lunch about two I rang up. No reply. Troubled, a little haunted by a look I surprised yesterday I rang again at 6:30. Leonard answers: "A dreadful catastrophe has happened. . . ." Poor distraught unhappy people. She slipped off about 12—leaving a note behind—they dragged the river, he had found her stick at the edge. I'm greatly shocked and most unhappy. Rang up Ryle [colleague] told him all I'd discovered yesterday. He, bless him, comforting, reassuring. Said . . . that if it hadn't been today it would inevitably have been sooner or later whatever any of us had done. And that if I'd taken drastic steps yesterday and suggested a nursing home, etc. it would only have precipitated it last night. And I did right in giving her a chance. Isn't it all tragic? I so much wish now that I had gone over more often and tried to get hold of her more as a friend. But, as you know, I'm shy and I always felt her aloofness and I had a horror of possibly boring that highly intellectual cultivated mind so I consciously rationed myself of visits. Though I believe they always did like me to go. And since she had this portrait idea it gave me an excuse—but no, it would not have helped. She was desperate and scared . . . and, my belief is, haunted by her father. I said this to Leonard and he agreed. "We've been so happy together," she said to me yesterday of their marriage. She also felt acutely not being able to do anything about the War . . . and I had thought I was clever in quoting what she herself had said about Jane Austen and the Napoleonic Wars [that they occurred during Austen's life and she never once referred to them in her work], getting on with her job all the time. She had smiled quite naturally and been pleased about my throwing back her own words at her. Oh *damn*. I did so hope I could help.

⁂

[Octavia to Elizabeth Robins, March 29, 1941]

To continue. Still no news. They are still dragging the river and until they are successful there can be no inquest I believe. I talk to Leonard on 'phone. Finally, after lunch am so *haunted* by Virginia and my own failure to help and thinking round in circles that I feel, "If I'm like this what is Leonard going through?" So I ring up: would he like me to go over for a short while. Very much, says he. I go and we discuss her whole life medically and what specialist she had seen etc. How when Leonard married her he knew nothing of her affliction. Its recurring nature—the many advices. Her happy nature. His completely truthful direct way of dealing with her condition to her. Finally I think we agreed that it was the association of the 1914 War and her worst phase that had haunted her mind now and convinced her a similar happening in this War was likely to happen. He asked if when I talked to her I felt she was paying attention etc. I said frankly that I'd gathered from what she said from time to time that she was depressed and needing distraction—and I had had an odd feeling that I *did* distract and bring her a certain amount of—*peace*. He looked relieved and said he had hoped that might be so.

When I came away picking my way down the narrow stairs I say over my shoulder, "As a Doctor one thing strikes me very forcibly that you were Heaven inspired in the care you took of her and literally nobody else could have kept her going so long." I reach the bottom, turn and find his hand held out and his face all puckered just breaking into tears. I shake it hurriedly—make off and call back that I'll wait to hear from him as to news. (I'll have to give medical evidence.)

In one of my letters I believe I said I felt V. insincere. In the light of greater knowledge let me take this back with both hands. Amazing sense of truth, but occasional lapses of vagueness due to the Devil who took possession.

[Octavia to Elizabeth Robins, March 30, 1941]

Slept like a rock for the first time since I had 'flu till 5.45. Am so thankful I took courage in both hands and went over to see Leonard yesterday. After a night of absorption of facts—the only way my slow brain works—I am now sure that as long as War was on I don't think it would have been possible to hold Virginia's mind. Without War I'm sure I could have helped and completely saved her. Tragic. Anyhow I'm also feeling today that I'm *amazingly* lucky to have had even that small amount of closeness to such a mind. But I do regret that I was not myself more warm and *expressive*, shall I say? But I never am—however I may feel, as you well know. Am afraid of it, I suppose? The last day we sat in that little room and I told her about my difficulties and about wanting to do Medicine, my moral cowardice and not daring to have it out with my family—about how I'd always lied to save my skin as a child, what it meant to meet you with your high standards, how you had made me feel so differently about Truth and so on. She sitting and interjecting helpful questions, sitting close to and hugging the fire—behind her that large window which overlooks the wide expanse of field and valley, flat and green, through which runs that evil river which a week later was to clutch that free spirit (yes *indeed*, free if ever there was one when the devil did not take possession) and which now is being dragged and wont give up its jealously held treasure.

To go back to my visit. I have a patient waiting this end at 6.15; the siren goes in the distance. It strikes me as remote and wholly of another world. Where that keen mind presided, Hitler, Luftwaffe and all the rest just did not exist. But my eye catches the clock. Its 6.10. "Golly, I've a patient at 6.15." "Yes," she looks up, her habit was to leave me her profile and only occasionally face me with a direct question; I'd taken this as her sensitiveness to my shyness in talking lamely about myself. "Yes, but its far more important for you to sit and talk to me," and with a note of appeal: "Don't go yet." You will remember that when we went over together she always begged you not to go so soon. As I see it now true contact with another and especially outside minds was a handrail that helped her. So I stay put divided and tortured as usual between two loyalties—longing to stay and knowing the patient would be waiting. And in the interval (I dont recollect how it came out) but I say, looking out the South window on my right, "You have no idea how much I enjoy coming over, how it helps talking to an—er—outsize mind" and then feeling desperate at my inability to find words. "Oh I cant say what I want," and with my 'flu starting and a head of wool I subside sulkily into silence and wish for you as spokesman. She stirs and alters her position and says quietly: "Oh but do try—I want to know. You dont know how much I need it" and eyes me gravely and steadily. I (again as usual) feel she is doing this to try to help my inadequacy with words. I had already told her that nothing [that] ever happened to me or was said to me sank in at the time and was only absorbed afterwards at its true value and she had been most understanding as to this. An *easy* person to talk with and a heavenly agility of mind which returned, as a first class tennis player does, the most erratic or difficult ball. And now I realize I might have helped her—perhaps—quite considerably if I'd had the key to her need. As we went downstairs she says, "Isn't there anything I can do for you? Can't I catalogue your books?" I say something grateful and in my own mind discard this idea as wholly improvident—would one employ a diamond cutter to hew coal? But if I'd known—it might have helped to give her such a manual job to keep the Beast at bay. . . . Anyhow did I tell you that in my reassurance to her on Thursday I'd said, "There's nobody in England I want more to help than you." And Leonard said that that evening after her visit here she was cheerful and quite different. Next day alas! came the voices—the thing she had had before which always presaged disaster—well apart from my sense of being asked to get at it too late I do feel now that short of end of War I'd no hope of success.

N.B. Let us be realistic. If I'd had her here to do books and thought I was succeeding and then . . . this. Wouldn't it have been even worse?

ℱ

[Octavia to Elizabeth Robins, April 19, 1941]

On Thursday night I dreamed so vividly that Virginia had turned up again, alive. So when I woke I was quite disappointed to know it was a dream. While I was out at Backset that P.M. Leonard rang . . . to say they'd at last recovered the body and the inquest was yesterday. The Coroner apparently didn't need me. I'm glad it is now all over. One goes on regretting the waste. And quite plainly she *was writing her very best*. What tricks the mind was playing her. Also, how impossible it must be for a writer to judge his own work. Wasn't it odd that I'd dreamed of her like that? There's a lot we don't understand in this world.

Sources

References to Virginia Woolf's diaries and letters are given by volume number, page, and date (month/day/year). When more than one passage from a single diary entry or letter appears on a page, the first reference in the notes identifies the source of all.

Abbreviations

BA: *Between the Acts*
BEGINNING: Leonard Woolf, *Beginning Again*
BELL: Quentin Bell, *Virginia Woolf: A Biography*, 2 vols.
BERG: The Henry W. and Albert A. Berg Collection at the New York Public Library
D1–5: *The Diary of Virginia Woolf*, 5 vols.
DECEIVED: Angelica Garnett, *Deceived with Kindness*
DM: *The Death of the Moth*
DOWNHILL: Leonard Woolf, *Downhill All the Way*
JOURNEY: Leonard Woolf, *The Journey Not the Arrival Matters*
L1–6: *The Letters of Virginia Woolf*, 6 vols.
MB: *Moments of Being*, 2d ed.
MD: *Mrs. Dalloway*
ME: *The Moment and Other Essays*
OW: Octavia Wilberforce, "The Eighth Child"
RECOLL: Joan Russell Noble, ed., *Recollections of Virginia Woolf*
RF: *Roger Fry*
TG: *Three Guineas*

TL: *To the Lighthouse*
TW: *The Waves*
TY: *The Years*

⚶

Prelude: The Shapes a Mind Holds

1   "*They are at our mercy.*" TL, 260
2   "*serenely absent-present.*" D4, 219, 5/9/34
3   "*in a biography all is different.*" "'I am Christina Rossetti,'" *The Second Common Reader*, 214–15
5   "*she was pure.*" DM, 237
    "*a real relationship between men and women was then unattainable.*" Virginia Woolf, *The Pargiters*, xxx
    I acted in self-defense." DM, 237–38
6   "*writing of them was a necessary act.*" D3, 208, 11/28/28
    "*harder to kill a phantom than a reality.*" DM, 238
7   "The Waves *is my first work in my own style!*" D4, 53, 11/16/31
    "*became a different person in her fifties.*" Heilbrun, *Hamlet's Mother*, 90
    "*They should all be killed.*" D1, 13, 1/9/15
    "*there's some meaning [in] it.*" D1, 91, 12/13/17
8   "*flowers she could bear to see cut.*" MD, 182
    "*layers that do not interpenetrate.*" Zwerdling, *Virginia Woolf and the Real World*, 139
    "*history has a word to say about it.*" A Room of One's Own, 93
    "*the lady with the pug dog.*" Ibid., 92
9   "*a guerrilla fighter in a Victorian skirt.*" Marcus, *New Feminist Essays*, 1, 5
10 "*background [measuring] rods or conceptions,*" MB, 73
    ancient civilizations, Egypt, Greece and Rome. The Waves: The Two Holograph Drafts, 7
    "*I am writing to a rhythm and not to a plot.*" L4, 204, 8/28/30
    "*nothing but putting words on the backs of rhythm.*" L4, 303, 4/7/31
11 *an interest in* "*anthropological truth.*" Stape, ed., *Virginia Woolf: Interviews and Recollections*, 143
12 *had never been said before.* L4, 151, 3/15/30; 3/17/30

One. Human Nature Undressed

13 "*O & the servants.*" D4, 12, 2/17/31
    total population of 45 million. "The Disappearance of the Governing Class," *Political Quarterly* 1, no. 1 (1930): 105

14 *"reflection in which we both swim about."* D3, 219, 3/28/29
   "rather lonely & painful." D3, 219, 3/28/29

15 *tapped loudly at her window one night.* Vanessa Bell, *Selected Letters*,
   314, 3/5/27
   "put practically everything in; yet to saturate." D3, 210, 11/29/28
   "so quick, in some ways so desperate." D3, 219, 3/28/29
   decided there and then to acquire these things. D3, 212, 12/18/28
   "& poverty has ceased." D3, 219, 3/28/29

16 *seven distinct, idiosyncratic personalities.* D3, 221, 4/13/29
   "To walk alone in London is the greatest rest." D3, 298, 3/28/30
   "more pleasure than those dozens of grosses." D3, 300, 4/11/30
   Virginia's diary, D3, 301

18 *"invited other friends to stay."* Branson and Heinemann, *Britain in the*
   1930's, 156–57

19 *"the most faithful and enraging of her kind."* L4, 224, 10/3/30
   "something in the universe that one's left with." D3, 113, 9/30/26
   "our reconciliations." D3, 274, 12/15/29
   a "funny rather mulish face," D4, 206, 3/27/34

20 *"one of us would call an upset inside."* D2, 52–53, 7/13/20
   "For 3 years I've been ill." D3, 333, 11/12/30
   never, never to believe her again." D3, 75, 4/18/26
   "she doesn't care for me, or for anything." D3, 240, 8/8/29
   "worse than operations for cancer." L4, 227, 10/8/30

21 *"it is all over & calm & settled."* D3, 240, 8/10/29
   the greatest compliment possible. D3, 75, 4/18/26
   "impressive because of its undress." D3, 241, 8/10/29
   harder than she had expected it to be. D3, 241, 8/10/29

22 *"eating rice pudding by the baby's cradle"* D3, 236, 6/23/29
   in return for doing their housework on a regular basis. D3, 255, 9/21/29;
   D3, 258, 10/2/29
   a cabinet minister's salary. D3, 237, 6/30/29
   "pilchards from a net." L4, 176, 6/8/30
   about £150. Branson and Heinemann, *Britain in the 1930's,* 135
   "such a disease as the poor are." L4, 230, 10/16/30

23 *"I've only a few years to live I hope."* D3, 110, 9/15/26
   ultimately called The Waves. D3, 113, 9/30/26
   "Yes, even having children would be useless." D3, 235, 6/23/29

24 *her summer holiday in July.* D3, 235, 6/23/29
   "tight into a ball," D4, 28, 5/30/31
   "gloom and horror open round me" L4, 422, 12/29/31
   "excellent reason for dying." Camus, *The Myth of Sisyphus,* 4
   "to know herself by." TL, 60

"as I have almost constantly" D1, 298, 9/13/19

25 *"a creature of laughter and movement,"* RECOLL, 49

"far out to sea and alone" MD, 11

Two. A Taste of Salt

26 *"I belong to the crowd,"* she told Virginia. D3, 292, 2/21/30

27 *"the glory of a flaming pedigree."* Smyth, *Impressions that Remained*, 6

"the glare of the arena." Edward Sackville-West in St. John, *Ethel Smyth*, 246

"Bacchic frenzy with a toothbrush." St. John, *Ethel Smyth*, 155

purple, white, and green tie. Ibid., 153

" 'just human nature.' " BA, 102

29 *"Bloomsbury village"* in the midst of the city. DOWNHILL, 121

"the doings of other people." RECOLL, 86

"worn beauty of a hare's paw." Ibid., 84

driving her mad. Smyth, *Impressions that Remained*, 476

a *"bluff military old woman,"* D3, 290, 2/21/30

30 *"nothing but seeing you for ten days."* D3, 291, 292, 2/21/30

"Let me stand alone." St. John, *Ethel Smyth*, 72

31 *"a large worm, in her temple which swells."* D3, 291, 2/21/30

"old char in her white alpaca coat." D3, 306, 6/16/30

"delicious ease." D3, 308, 7/6/30

32 *"opening and shutting in the twilight."* L4, 205, 8/28/30

"I don't like other women being fond of you" D3, 314, 8/25/30

her *"last barren years"* had been fructified. D3, 326, 10/23/30

"doctor what she thinks to be the truth." St. John, *Ethel Smyth*, 223, 222

33 *Virginia to Ethel,* L4, 422

34 *"narrow, ascetic, puritanical breed."* L4, 155, 4/6/30

35 *"intimate details of sexual life."* L4, 159, 4/22/30

Leonard planted hollyhocks in the garden. L4, 160, 4/22/30

"off at the shadow of a leaf." L4, 159, 4/22/30

36 *"when I saw it, under the sea."* L4, 223, 9/28/30

"shaded by weeds." L4, 196, 8/2/30

"a tropical fish swimming in a submerged forest." L5, 129, 11/24/32

"dimly green like a fish-pond." RECOLL, 87

"translucent underwater world." David Garnett, *Great Friends*, 120

"leaving behind it a taste of salt." RECOLL, 87

"Woolf in a jungle." L4, 180, 6/22/30

37 *living on top of a "volcano."* L4, 422, 12/29/31

voices telling her to do "all kinds of wild things," L1, 142, 9/22?/04

"a tremendous sense of life beginning." L4, 78, 8/15/29; D3, 287, 2/16/30

38   *"as usual I am romancing,"* L4, 203, 8/19/30
     "different from the ordinary human being," L4, 168, 5/14/30
     "give her things to play with, like a child." L4, 203, 8/19/30
     "all of the spiritual, intellectual, emotional kind." L4, 200, 8/15/30

39   *"incongruous and almost indecent in the idea."* Nigel Nicolson, ed., *Vita and Harold: The Letters of Vita Sackville-West and Harold Nicolson,* 159
     "kisses from the inner wrist to the elbow." DECEIVED, 107
     "contact with either male or female body." L4, 200, 8/15/30
     "walked over Mountains with Counts." L4, 180, 6/22/30
     "a flat fish with eyes not in the usual place." L4, 172, 5/26/30
     an alligator or a whale. L4, 194–95, 8/2/30; L4, 151, 3/15/30
     Virginia to Ethel, L4, 231

40   *"the Polar region of Cambridge."* L4, 230, 10/16/30
     "I say the crowd is right." D3, 292, 2/21/30
     a fortnight's writing in the confusion. D3, 304, 5/18/30

41   *"occasionally sublime"* D3, 312, 8/20/30
     "steady as a cab horse." L4, 183, 7/1/30
     poetry that made all other writing unnecessary. D3, 313, 8/20/30
     "the first horror of feeling out of control." D3, 314, 8/28/30
     fainted again trying to go upstairs. D3, 315, 9/2/30

42   *"blown into the first puddle and drown."* L4, 203, 8/19/30
     "to have another life, & live it in action." D3, 317, 9/8/30
     "the movement of one's own bowels." L4, 244, 11/2/30; L4, 240, 10/30/30

Three. Lady Rosebery's Party

43   her mystical *"playpoem,"* D3, 203, 11/7/28
     by the time she finished her second draft in February, *1931.* Branson and Heinemann, *Britain in the 1930's,* 20; Taylor, *English History,* 358
     "the most remarkable happening in British political history," Sidney Webb, "What Happened in *1931"*
     "sensational rumours," D4, 39, 8/15/31

44   *"the hills lay low, in cloud."* D4, 39, 8/15/31
     "taken a vow of silence for ever." L4, 408, 11/22/31
     "rollicking" stories about her musical career. D4, 7, 1/23/31

45   *"about the sexual life of women."* D4, 6, 1/20/31
     "The Open Door" or *"Opening the Door."* D4, 6, 1/23/31; D4, 7, 1/26/31
     "people up there with her." RECOLL, 155
     "voices that used to fly ahead." D4, 10, 2/7/31

46 *"until the whole has been first understood."* Schopenhauer, *The World as Will and Representation*, 1:xii–xiii

"wave after wave, endlessly sinking and falling." The Waves: The Two Holograph Drafts, 7

47 *"where the swallow dips her wings."* TW, 105

"poor little Ginny," D4, 79, 2/29/32

48 *foretelling the children she would bear.* TW, 98–99

"made of six lives." TW, 229

"but at the same time, cannot forget." TW, 277

"You seem so foreign," she had told him. L1, 496, 5/1/12

50 *"red pitchers to the banks of the Nile."* TW, 95, 66

"very, very dangerous to live even one day." MD, 11

"It stamps and stamps." TW, 58

"we are bound, as bodies to wild horses." TW, 64

"nothing but their blind stupefied hearts." Yeats, "Ego Dominus Tuus," *Collected Poems*, 159

"hunt us to death like bloodhounds." TW, 159

"on the back of something that will carry us on." TW, 162

51 *"this is our consolation."* TW, 163

"savagely into the sticky mixture." TW, 75

"she had killed herself." TW, 281

52 *"the wind of her flight when she leapt."* TW, 288–89

"fluttering like a leaf in a gale." L4, 291, 2/16/31

"among empty bottles and bits of toilet paper." D4, 12, 2/17/31

a "volcanic eruption" DOWNHILL, 54

53 *"symptoms threatening a breakdown."* DOWNHILL, 55

"if one doesn't make a fool of oneself?" L4, 294, 2/21/31

"sensibility verging on insanity." D4, 43, 9/15/31

54 *"If I werent so miserable I could not be happy."* D4, 12, 2/17/31

her social standing as an artist. D4, 14, 3/19/31

"flames and ruin about her ears." DOWNHILL, 98–99

"betrayed and made to smile at our damnation." L4, 298, 3/11/31

55 *"I should kill myself—so much do I suffer."* L4, 302, 3/29/31

"by my own struggle with The Waves." L4, 298, 3/11/31

Virginia to Ethel, L4, 297–98

56 *"out of touch with reality than I have been in years."* L4, 298, 3/11/31

"Her strength of feeling is her power over one." D4, 13, 3/16/31

"So I was glad of what you said." L4, 305, 4/8/31

57 *"take offense at unintentional rudeness."* Beatrice Webb, *Diary*, 243, 4/1/31

"instant dismemberment by wild horses." L4, 302, 4/1/31

Once she had owned a white tailless cat, L4, 329, 5/12/31

58 *"worn into deep waves, up to the tower."* L4, 321, 4/24/31

"a visionary coinciding with the right moment." D4, 23, 4/27/31
"I who am not reticent." D4, 18, 4/30?/31
things that anchored one to earth. D4, 36, 8/7/31

59   *Virginia found their way of life "almost divine."* L4, 335, 5/23/31
in order to calm herself. L4, 303, 4/7/31
"her persecution for the past 50 years." L4, 334, 5/23/31
"This is happiness." D4, 27, 5/28/31
a "refreshing purity" DECEIVED, 53, 108–9

60   *an "infinitely young and unprotected soul."* TW, 219
"his thin, flea-ridden body." Gordon, *Virginia Woolf,* 142

61   *"the Hambantota District in Ceylon."* DECEIVED, 109
turning their idyll into a "nightmare." BEGINNING, 156
in the head, you know," she wrote to a friend. L1, 488, 2/7/12
"in an instant, without any reason." BELL, 1:185
from summer 1913 to autumn 1915. BEGINNING, 160

62   *"He did not hate her; he hated himself."* Leonard Woolf, *The Wise Virgins,* 227

Four. God's Fist

63   *compare the present emergency to that of 1914.* Colin Bell, *National Government 1931,* 4
the "rule of old men," Joad, "Prolegomena to Fascism"
this extremely personal, difficult book. D4, 36, 7/17/31
She should "simplify and clarify a little" L4, 357, 7/19/31

64   *an "instinct to double-cross."* BEGINNING, 223
"jokes of British political life." Beatrice Webb, *Diary,* 244, 4/1/31
"you felt you had got inside a mental maze." BEGINNING, 221

65   *putting their country ahead of their own political interests.* Colin Bell, *National Government 1931,* 76
"the loyalty of a follower of wisdom." Ibid., 78
"is apparently not wasteful expenditure." Beatrice Webb, *Diary,* 249, 8/4/31

66   *creating a "Party Dictatorship."* Jennings, "The Constitution Under Strain"
"gloom that settled on all our circle" Lee, ed., Introduction to *Hogarth Letters,* x

67   *"the political menaces under which we all lived,"* DOWNHILL, 27
ancestral memories of oppression. D4, 51, 10/23/31
could only have been written at the present moment. Forster, *Goldsworthy Lowes Dickinson,* 230

68   *"'doing his bit' for the dear old country."* Ibid., 232
"the other waves have their life too" Ibid., 231

"The six characters were supposed to be one." L4, 397, 10/27/31

"dumb rage" that Thoby was not there L4, 391, 10/15/31

69 "my old friend Fight fight." D4, 43, 9/15/31

thinned the walls between the novel and poetry D4, 44, 9/16/31

"the exact shapes my brain holds." D4, 53, 11/16/31

a "dust dance," L4, 400, 11/1/31

"to give pain for pleasure." L4, 372, 9/2/31

"like people in a war." D4, 45, 9/21/31

if people abandoned all doctrines and causes. L4, 392, 10/18/31

"the pound would be smashed and the poor starve," Colin Bell, National Government 1931, 180–81

70 loss of savings deposited in the Post Office Savings Bank. Ibid., 189

"To spread the idiot tangle they have made." Roberts, ed., New Signatures, 47

"both went into fits of laughter." L4, 412, 12/10/31

journey to Malaga and might be away for months. L4, 412, has probable misreading, "Malaya"—Holroyd, Lytton Strachey, 1060; Carrington, Carrington, 493

71 one of the six intimate friends, D3, 48, 11/27/25

There was no one, she said, except Leonard, that she cared for more. L4, 415, 12/19/31

72 "survival of barbaric grandeur," Holroyd, Lytton Strachey, 140–41

"take the next boat home" Gordon, Virginia Woolf, 137; Holroyd, Lytton Strachey, 406

73 the crushing single-mindedness of the past week. D4, 57, 12/29/31

"being laid out like a mist between the people she knew best." MD, 12

"tossed his poems into the waste-paper basket." DM, 225

"how can he get better?" D4, 64, 1/18/32

the family, though worn down, felt hopeful again. L5, 5, 1/14/32

74 which made Rodmell seem almost suburban. D4, 64, 1/18/32

"happier than any person could be." Carrington, Carrington, 175, 178

and at once fell deeply in love. Holroyd, Lytton Strachey, 634–35

75 the "dangerous complexity" of their ménage. Ibid., 882

"Oh, It's his knees." Ibid., 647

"who will commit suicide they think." D4, 61, 1/1/32

76 "Lytton died yesterday morning." D4, 64, 1/21/32

Virginia to Carrington, L5, 11–12

Five. Ghosts: The Empty Room

77 "continue that wild flight." Virginia Woolf, "Old Mrs. Grey," DM, 17

walking alone in the country. L4, 380, 9/16/31

grounded her in England. D4, 124, 9/16/32

"the English brought together accidentally." D5, 72, 3/27/37

"assuage one's misery." BEGINNING, 48

78   *"vegetative dilation and expansion."* Quoted by Roger Coleman, *Down-land*, 12

"float a whole population in happiness," D5, 72, 3/27/37

"words on the backs of rhythm." L4, 303, 4/7/31

"sheet of perfect calm happiness." D4, 246, 10/2/34

"wings sweeping up & up." D4, 124, 9/16/32

79   *"St. Paul's and Westminster Abbey."* L5, 39, 4/1/32

"I generally like buggers:" L5, 10, 1/29/32

"Lytton dead & those factories building." D4, 74, 2/8/32

80   *"Suicide seems to me quite sensible."* D4, 66, 1/30/32

"I cry in an empty room." Carrington, *Carrington*, 489, 495

intuitive connection between them. D4, 74, 2/8/32

81   *"a great harm to myself."* Carrington, *Carrington*, 490

"Carrington: A Study of a Modern Witch," in Partridge, *Julia*, 119

found herself overcome by tears. Carrington, *Carrington*, 491

appreciated or loved him enough. Ibid., 466, 467

82   *"some very singular books, if I live."* D4, 53, 11/16/31

"everything was something else." Flush, 28

"venomous snakes coiled." Ibid., 109

"the yellow dog—it did not matter which." Ibid., 127

"lost his coat but is free from fleas." Ibid., 144

83   *We have to live and be ourselves,"* L5, 28, 3/2/32

"and let us bless you for it." L5, 8, 1/21/32

"This is no help to you now," L5, 12, 1/31/32

the bond between them remained constant. L5, 25, 2/28?/32

"Hunt in Pegg's Cunt." L5, 27, 2/29/32

"sticking in the Mount of Venus." L5, 22, 2/23/32

84   *"best part of his life still goes on."* L5, 28, 3/2/32

"devilish though it is for you." L5, 31, 3/10/32

"because you understand." Carrington, *Carrington*, 492

she refused to lecture. L5, 27, 2/29/32

"compliment he would have liked." D4, 79, 2/29/32

85   *hoped to bury Lytton's ashes.* Partridge, *Love in Bloomsbury*, 201

"I find that unbelievable." Ibid., 203

"to give her some interruption." L5, 34, 3/15/32

"in the money bags these 50 years," D4, 80, 3/10/32

"one of the most painful days" DOWNHILL, 251

86   *"He taught me everything I know."* D4, 82, 3/12/32

"that she could not go on much longer." L5, 34, 3/15/32

"thought of Lytton's death." D4, 82, 3/12/32
"a child who has been scolded." D4, 83, 3/12/32

87　*"who would do anything if she could."* L5, 32, 3/10/32
　　"graveyard" she had cleared under the ilex. Holroyd, *Lytton Strachey,*
　　　　1078; Carrington, *Carrington,* 494
　　"something terrifying: unreason." D4, 103, 5/25/32
　　Advice to Oneself, Carrington, *Carrington,* 499

Six. Ghosts: From the Acropolis

89　*"I couldn't lie to her."* L5, 38, 3/21/32
　　"made her kill herself." D4, 83, 3/17/32
　　"never see Lytton again. This is unreal." D4, 83, 3/17/32
90　*"changed by what one hears of them."* D4, 83, 3/17/32
　　last hour with Carrington had made a difference. L5, 38, 3/21/32
　　"Carrington killed herself & put an end to all this." D4, 85, 3/24/32
　　"squander a moment on repetition." D4, 85, 3/24/32
　　the friends who remained. D4, 88, 4/11/32
　　brothers and sisters approached as high adventure. BELL, 1:107
91　*"a highly respectable museum."* L5, 37, 3/20/32
　　"because I hate my own face in the looking glass." L5, 38, 3/21/32
　　"Such caper cutting about folly they are." L5, 40, 4/1/32
　　"emphatic and useless about Greece." D4, 88, 3/29/32
　　"That chinless man to suggest to me. Pah!" D4, 88, 3/29/32
　　and handed him the sandwich. L5, 45, 4/11/32
92　*"his sensibility to correct his brain."* Virginia Woolf, "Roger Fry," ME, 85
　　the earth would be inherited by the birds. BEGINNING, 96–97
94　*"to guard against the bites of sharks."* Lewis Carroll, *Alice in Wonder-*
　　　　land, 273
　　dangled from brass chains wrapped around his body. L4, 128–29,
　　　　1/18/30
　　"intensity behind gold-rimmed spectacles." DECEIVED, 101
　　an "elderly yak." L5, 50, 4/19/32
　　too much in love with her brother to accept anyone else. Vanessa Bell,
　　　　letter, BERG, 4/19/32
95　*"girl of 23, with all her life to come."* D4, 90, 4/21/32
　　the gaiety of her accounts of Greece. D4, 91, 4/21/32
96　*"tortoise crosses the road—sometimes a lizard."* L5, 54, 5/1/32
　　"she's fearfully humble." L5, 50, 4/19/32
　　"who exist by virtue of their white petals." D4, 90, 4/18/32
　　"like wandering in the fields of the moon" D4, 94, 5/2/32
　　"a fine sample of Fry tenacity." L5, 57, 5/2/32

97   *"punctured a tire and run over a serpent."* L5, 57, 5/2/32

    "as sweet as nuts and soft as silk." L5, 49, 4/19/32

    "I must make a note of that." "Roger Fry," ME, 86

    Roger had done about twenty pictures. L5, 56, 5/2/32

    "pleasure from just having experiences." Fry, *Letters*, 2:670, 5/4/32

98   *"youth at its spring."* L5, 56, 5/2/32

    "no power of dissociation." L5, 56, 5/2/32

    "best admirer of life and art I've ever travelled with." L5, 59, 5/4/32

    "vindictive" Christ, L5, 60, 5/4/32; Spalding, *Roger Fry*, 280

    the one at Sunium built on exactly the same plan. D4, 92, 4/24/32

    a cart horse and a thoroughbred stallion. L5, 59–60, 5/4/32

    "waves on the grey hillside." L5, 60, 5/4/32

    Virginia to Vita Sackville-West, L5, 61–62

99   *conceal it from her at all costs.* BELL, 1:110

100   *"creep down and up with tremendous jars."* Fry, *Letters*, 2:688

    the best holiday they had had in many years. D4, 95, 5/8/32

    English tightness and respectablity. L5, 62, 5/8/32

    "once loved Cornwall as a child." D4, 97, 5/8/32

    "philanthropise for ever instead." L5, 56, 5/2/32

101   *she had made a mistake.* L5, 56, 5/2/32

    present in his work as an impurity. D4, 95, 5/2/32

Seven. Anonymity and Rhythm

102   *"philosophy of anonymity,"* D4, 186, 10/29/33

    "climaxes of despair," L5, 67, 5/26/32

103   *"too silly even for me."* L5, 66, 5/25/32

    "full Sunday dress immersed in cold water." D4, 102, 5/23/32

104   *"he seemed the rat and the detail the dog."* Lehmann, *In My Own Time*, 110

106   *"the immense responsibility that rests on him."* D4, 102, 5/25/32

    "things generally wrong in the universe." D4, 102–3, 5/25/32

    "bringing order & speed again into my world." D4, 103, 5/25/32

107   *use her critical faculties more fully.* D4, 103, 5/26/32

    "We are back again in 1914." Lord Ponsonby, "The Future of the Labour Party," *Political Quarterly* 4 (1933): 33

    "This conference was no exception." Taylor, *English History*, 451

    "He doesnt much notice who's there." D4, 107, 6/3/32

108   *"One would say we must."* D4, 107–8, 6/3/32

    "on the verge of a precipice." D4, 108, 6/4/32

    that most journalists did in one. L5, 68, 6/5/32

"steadily and in advance of the time-table." Lehmann, *Thrown to the Woolfs*, 33

"more malleable, & less pernickety," D4, 110, 6/18/32

"Mirsky and his prostitute." L5, 71, 6/22/32

109   from material reality *"to a world of esthetics."* Mirsky, *The Intelligentsia of Great Britain*, 117, 118

    "that didnt lubricate our tea." D4, 112, 6/28/32

    "some I never see at all." L5, 74, 7/1/32

    "the absolute delight of dark & bed." D4, 114, 7/8/32

110   *"Why do a single thing one doesn't want to do?"* D4, 115, 7/13/32

    "one person's happy at any rate." D4, 116, 7/13/32

    "refuse aspirants to interviews." L5, 77–78, 7/14/32

    "in a rose coloured tea gown, signing autographs" L5, 78, 7/14/32

    threatening to exit on this tragic note. D4, 119, 7/22/32

    "dramatising herself instead of being anything." D4, 119, 7/22/32

111   *"not only by you—by myself also."* L5, 81, 82, 7/28/32

    the sun would go out for her. Smyth, letter, BERG, 7/30/32

    nudge each other and laugh. BEGINNING, 29

    "I lie awake at night longing for rest." D4, 118, 7/21/32

    "capable of dying," D4, 120, 8/5/32

112   *"then I think what about bed."* L5, 88–89, 8/9?/32

    "break through the usual suddenly and so violently." L5, 94, 8/18/32

    "the galloping horses got wild in my head." D4, 121, 8/17/32

113   *"to fetch mice from the marsh."* D4, 121, 8/17/32

    "pounding must must must break something," L5, 94, 8/18/32

    "splintered fragments of my body." D4, 121, 8/17/32

    "profound and primitive of instincts." DM, 221

    horseman riding forth to defy Death. TW, 83, 79, 297

114   *"rethink them into uncultivated land again."* D4, 120, 8/5/32

    "even an ugly race horse, is beautiful." L5, 100, 9/7/32

    "a strange rhythmical chant" "Leslie Stephen," *The Captain's Death Bed*, 68

    "easy indolent writing." D4, 123, 9/2/32

    declined to send any answer. Leonard Woolf, *Letters of Leonard Woolf*, 311

115   *"Now I can roam about the basement unperturbed."* D4, 123, 9/2/32

    "a plain dowdy old woman." D4, 124, 9/16/32

    "This will go on after I'm dead." D4, 124, 9/16/32

116   *"human ingenuity in torture."* D4, 125, 9/16/32

    "even with a nail through it." "Old Mrs. Grey," DM, 19

    "Yes, my thighs now begin to run smooth." D4, 124, 9/16/32

    "backed" by the downs. D4, 125, 10/2/32

117   *finding an artistic form to connect them.* "Notes on D. H. Lawrence,"
      ME, 80

      "*I dont escape when I read him.*" D4, 126, 10/2/32

      any attempt to get a finger into her mind. L4, 333, 5/18/31

118   "*a system that did not shut out.*" D4, 127, 10/2/32

      "*from 1880 to here & now.*" D4, 129, 11/2/32

      "*the whole of human life.*" D4, 134, 12/31/32

      "*Don't be caught looking.*" The Pargiters, 18

119   "*do anything towards attaining that end.*" The Pargiters, 158; Elizabeth
      Mary Wright, *The Life of Joseph Wright*, 311

      see only the people she wanted to see. D4, 129, 11/2/32

      illness sound worse than it really was. L5, 108, 10/6/32

      "*or hale me off to them on theirs.*" D4, 133, 12/19/32

120   "*Death I defy you &c.*" D4, 129, 11/2/32

      "*come and laugh at me*" L5, 120, 11/6/32

      "*if he were a fish, stink, to put it plainly.*" L5, 139, 12/26/32

121   "*like a chamois across precipices.*" D4, 129, 11/2/32

      she hardly knew where she was. D4, 133, 12/19/32

      talk, which "*I always want to go on with.*" L5, 129, 11/25?/32

      Virginia's diary, D4, 134–35

122   "*Time stand still here.*" D4, 102, 5/25/32

      "*And time come to an end for me.*" Goethe, *Faust*, part 1, lines 1692–
      1706—my translation, with help from Eric Marder.

123   "*the verge of total extinction*" D4, 132, 12/19/39

Eight. The Firing of Nelly Boxall

124   *bought with their literary earnings.* D4, 125–26, 10/2/32

      the sky seemed hung with "*silver shields.*" D4, 143, 1/15/33

125   "*not a money car.*" D4, 143, 1/15/33

      a tigress gliding along Bond Street and Piccadilly. L5, 157, 2/14/33

      "*cruise*" *at fifty miles an hour.* L5, 146, 1/6/33

126   "*We want to be barbarians.*" Bullock, *Hitler*, 276

      "*Arnold Bennett life in the form of art?*" D4, 161, 5/31/33

127   "*honour worship? Mumbo Jumbo!*" L5, 172, 3/26/33

      instinctive distrust of such publicity. D4, 148, 3/25/33

      "*citizen of the World rather than an Englishman.*" "Oliver Goldsmith,"
      The Captain's Death Bed, 11

128   *aboriginal people to whom it had belonged* Ibid., 12–13

      "*not by fighting them; by ignoring them.*" D4, 153, 4/29/33

      making up scenes of "*The Pargiters*" D4, 159, 5/21/33

129   *"the best death bed place I've ever seen."* L5, 187, 5/18/33
love of Italy and hatred of Fascism. L5, 187, 5/18/33
"highly pictorial, composed, legs in particular," D4, 160, 5/23/33
"nothing makes a whole unless I am writing," D4, 161, 5/31/33
"yes: the proportion is right." D4, 162, 6/8/33

130   *"I can see the day whole, proportioned."* D4, 232, 7/28/34
"Their attitude to life much our own." D4, 116, 7/13/32
"the details will dovetail in." Elizabeth Mary Wright, *The Life of Joseph Wright*, 307
"not lay too much stress on what does not matter." Ibid., 303–4

131   *"gaseous, with elementary emotions."* D4, 165, 6/20/33
"I have a dread of 'seeing' people." D4, 172, 8/12/33
"wakes me, if I leave the curtain open." D4, 174, 8/24/33
regrouted and digging a new one. D4, 176, 9/2/33

132   *"here and now" while presenting universal themes.* D4, 199n, 1/16/34
"the press of daily normal life continuing." D4, 152, 4/25/33
"of looking at the new pond, of playing bowls." D4, 181, 9/26/33
low motives for her friends' innocent acts. Sencourt, *T. S. Eliot*, 61
"full-blown paranoia with delusions," Matthews, *Great Tom*, 104n

134   *Virginia dreaded seeing her again.* L5, 71, 6/22/32
come after them with a carving knife L5, 207, 7/26/33
"thinks she puts it on; tries to take herself in." D4, 178, 9/10/33
"Eliot is at Harvard. But why? Come back soon." L5, 151, 1/15/33
Virginia's diary, D4, 178–79

135   *there are finer ways to impress the world* L5, 83, 7/31/32
"mercilessly, again and again, demanding sympathy." TL, 59

136   *"one in a page is enough to colour a chapter."* L5, 193, 6/6/33
galloping "over turf as springy as a race horse." L5, 249, 11/19/33
minor distractions, mere "rain drops." D4, 186, 10/29/33

137   *"find its dimensions, not be impeded."* D4, 186–87, 10/29/33
"one must be aware of oneself." L5, 239, 10/29/33
"a straw horse & its not me at all." D4, 191, 11/29/33
outside or beyond the common wavelength. D4, 191, 11/29/33

138   *"break his mould callously,"* D4, 5/14/33
"breaking the mould made by The Waves*."* D4, 233, 7/28/34
"Everyone I most honour is silent." L4, 422, 12/29/31

139   *"takes a slow run, circles & rises."* D4, 187, 11/12/33
"extinction" becomes desirable. ME, 188
carrying the dead on their last journey. D4, 187, 11/12/33

140   *Vanessa would never, never fly again.* L5, 244, 11/10/33
"how I hate caring for people!" L5, 243, 11/8/33
"didn't like the flavour of the Jew." L5, 258, 12/12/33

"the porter, the policeman and the bootmaker?" L5, 262, 12/21/33

141   *"what a Christmas tree is to a child."* L5, 255, 12/3/33

"small; but not evil." D4, 191, 12/4/33

"like a butler used to the best families." D4, 192, 12/4/33

"lain on cushions and shied roses at them." L5, 254, 12/3/33

"officials so noble but so chilly?" L5, 255, 12/3/33

142   embedded *"in a rich porous earth."* D4, 193, 12/17/33

A *"fairly specimen day."* D4, 195, 12/21/33

a luster, *"like lichen on roofs."* D4, 150, 4/13/33

143   *fire Nelly once and for all by Easter.* D4, 202, 2/16/34

garrulous Nelly was always with her. L4, 422, 12/29/31

"repeat one thing over & over." D2, 162–63, 2/14/22

clue she often looked for in diaries. D3, 274, 12/15/29

John Lehmann, who had coolly dropped in D4, 202, 2/18/34

"What Angelica will live to see boggles me." L5, 277, 2/15/34

144   *"gay & garrulous as a lark."* D4, 204, 3/14/34

"you dont treat me like a maid." D4, 205, 3/19/34

care Virginia found hard to resist. L5, 285–86, 3/29/34

suspecting he would try to dissuade her. D4, 205, 3/19/34

145   *"till I almost died of it."* L5, 285, 3/29/34

"executioner & the executed in one." D4, 206, 3/26/34

"This has to be lived I say to myself." D4, 206, 3/26/34

"foolish mulish face puckered up." D4, 206, 3/27/34

leaving her cook in possession of the house. L5, 285, 3/29/34

"appeals and maniacal threats." L5, 285, 3/29/34

they would blame her for being let go. D4, 207, 4/11/34

"No I really couldn't Sir." D4, 207, 4/11/34

146   *Virginia replied firmly: "Ah but you must."* L5, 285, 3/29/34

I felt a thousand times reassured." L5, 285, 3/29/34

a luxurious calm descended on her. D4, 207, 4/11/34

Leonard found irritating but tolerated D4, 221, 5/18/34

"came straight up to the bed and cuddled me up." Nelly Boxall in "A Portrait of Virginia Woolf by Her Friends," BBC Home Service, August 29, 1956

she was an admirable cook. Lanchester, *Charles Laughton and I*, 191

Nine. Acts in a Play

147   *the preceding chronicle of "facts."* D4, 221, 5/22/34

all the July apples on the grass." D4, 232, 7/28/34

148   *"I am breaking the mould made by The Waves."* D4, 233, 7/28/34

without the narrator's intervention. D4, 207, 4/17/34

"*the different strata of being,*" D4, 258, 11/1/34
"*corpses of drowned men.*" L5, 291, 4/13/34

149 "*how deeply rooted they are.*" L5, 296, 4/27/34
"*how well they drink it!*" L5, 296–97, 4/27/34
"*What shall I say to the conger eels*" L5, 297, 4/27/34

150 "*ramshackle & half squalid.*" D4, 210, 4/30/34
"*sense of time shifting & life becoming unreal,*" D4, 211, 5/1/34
George's influence on their young lives L5, 299, 5/4/34
"*sent turtle soup to the invalids.*" MB, 166

151 "*sobbing loudly, but continuing to eat.*" MB, 167
"*and took me into his arms.*" MB, 177
"*Go and tear it up.*" MB, 151
"*and the grave I suppose nearer.*" L5, 302, 5/10/34

152 "*People gathering sea weed & heaping carts.*" D4, 214, 5/4/34
"*that seems to amount to marriage.*" D4, 217, 5/8/34
"*the famous interview with the blue eyes,*" D4, 217, 5/8/34
"*her life was ended.*" "Swift's Journal to Stella," *The Second Common
    Reader*, 66

153 Swift's "*egotistic attachments.*" Stephen, *Swift*, 136
"*half responsible for her being.*" "Swift's Journal to Stella," *The Second
    Common Reader*, 62
"*the dregs of London.*" D4, 215, 5/6/34
"*this hate—it does nobody any good.*" D4, 218, 5/8/34
"*dont mind poverty so much.*" D4, 214, 5/4/34
"*these dwellers in the very heart of the land.*" D4, 218, 5/8/34

154 "*this vast illumination.*" D4, 219, 5/9/34
"*the rage & storm of thought.*" D4, 219, 5/9/34

155 "*& is still there, in Stratford.*" D4, 220, 5/9/34
"*the soft subconscious world become populous.*" D4, 221, 5/22/34

156 "*the crude delusions of a savage.*" Leonard Woolf, *Quack, Quack*, 19
"*the heart of a gorilla or savage*" Ibid., 24–25
Virginia's diary, D4, 223–24

158 "*the ideal of human life!*" L5, 313, 7/2/34
"*no Treasury control of the soldiers.*" D4, 236, 8/7/34

159 "*if there's no future for our civilization.*" D4, 241, 9/2/34
"*one little book, and then another little book,*" TY, 390
"*Why is Christianity so insistent and so sad?*" L5, 319, 7/29/34
"*How can you belong to such a canting creed?*" L5, 320, 7/29/34
if she had not married an atheist like Leonard. Smyth, BERG, 8/2/34

160 "*an empty white waistcoat.*" L5, 321, 8/8/34
"*my Jew has more religion in one toe nail*" L5, 321, 8/8/34
deplored his hostility to religious faith. Smyth, BERG, 8/12/34

"the race that wrote the Bible." Smyth, BERG, 8/17/34

161 *"bawled, about God and Dulwich."* D4, 239, 8/26/34

"It rained. All ugliness was dissolved." D4, 241, 8/30/34

Ten. On Being Despised

162 *"we are the music."* MB, 92

163 *"We sat on the seat there for a time."* D4, 242, 9/12/34

"I was not feeling enough. So now." D4, 242, 9/12/34

164 *and come to the same conclusion.* MB, 92

"It was like a scene in a play." TY, 47

"the two walls held themselves apart," TY, 46

"something I could not catch; distraught." MB, 91

165 *"equally, evenly, with indefatigable fingers."* TL, 192

"his arms, though stretched out, remained empty.]" TL, 194

"the conventions of sorrow," MB, 95

166 *"this magnificent blaze of color."* MB, 93

"peace & breadth, I hope." D4, 245, 9/30/34

"And I feel it through Nessa." D4, 253, 10/17/34

167 *"obscurity is also pleasant & salutary."* D4, 252, 10/14/34

"shoots into nothingness" opening to engulf her. D4, 260, 11/2/34

the blind concentration of a mole. D4, 260, 11/2/34

in fact had found it a great relief. D4, 261, 11/15/34

168 *"the dews on the lawn,"* Freshwater, 29

"green ice, smooth ice." L5, 362, 1/8/35

169 *"filling up a blank in my knowledge of the world."* D4, 274, 1/11/35

"doubt, conceit, desire for . . . intimacy." D4, 277, 2/5/35

described as "a dear old ass." D4, 263, 11/21/34

"yellow, riven & constricted." D4, 262–63, 11/21/34

"a vast sorrow at the back of life this winter." D4, 277, 2/5/35

"that blasted Chapter . . . that d——d chapter." D4, 290, 3/22/35, 3/25/35

"hated & despised & ridiculed." D4, 289, 3/18/35

170 *a "heroic" tour.* D4, 298, 4/12/35

"a great flaming Goddess" L5, 383, 4/3/35

"its the person's own edge that counts." D4, 282, 2/26/35

women incapable of advanced research. D4, 283, 3/1/35

the lord mayor of London's ceremonials, D4, 300, 4/14/35; D4, 307, 4/27/35

171 *"where we shot & tortured & imprisoned."* D4, 292, 3/27/35

"No no no, ladies are quite impossible." D4, 297, 4/9/35

Virginia's diary, D4, 298

172 *imminent war after every committee meeting.* D4, 303, 4/20/35
173 *"Leonard's nose is so long and hooked."* L5, 385, 4/18/35
"unjustifiable risk with Virginia's nerves." BELL, 2:189
"hesitate to enter a European country." DOWNHILL, 185
"if a flower could look very unhappy." D4, 304, 4/22/35
174 *"Germany will get her colonies."* D4, 304, 4/22/35
"since our Jewishness is said to be a danger" L5, 386, 4/26/35
rejecting Bloomsbury's pacifist ideals. Spalding, *Vanessa Bell*, 273
175 *"when human nature is so crippled?"* D4, 307, 4/28/35
skimmed along "in flocks like starlings." D4, 309, 5/6/35
complacency remarkable even by English standards. L5, 391, 5/8/35;
D4, 310, 5/8/35
this haven of beauty and bad taste DOWNHILL, 188
176 *"the first stoop in our back."* D4, 311, 5/9/35
178 *"unending procession of enthusiastic Nazis."* DOWNHILL, 191
"There is no place for Jews in— —." D4, 311, 5/9/35
"all processions and marching and drilling." DOWNHILL, 192
179 *"such a 'dear little thing' could be a Jew."* DOWNHILL, 193
"a stupid mass feeling," D4, 311, 5/9/35
"I have forgotten 2 days of truth." D4, 311, 5/12/35
"protect [them] from the native savages." DOWNHILL, 194
180 *to advertise one's social or artistic standing.* L5, 396, 6/2/35
"glass varied from gloomy to transcendent." D4, 316–17, 5/29/35
buried part of their private play life in the orchard. D4, 318, 6/1/35
"this cursed dry hard empty chapter." D4, 319, 6/5/35
"radiance through the green grey haze." L5, 399, 6/6/35
181 *"a round of great pillars to set up."* D4, 321, 6/13/35

Eleven. Slow Motion: *The Years*

190 *"every sort of grinding mill."* L5, 408, 6/25/35
a sequel to A Room of One's Own L5, 405, 6/21/35
191 *"absolutely wild, like being harnessed to a shark."* D4, 348, 10/27/35
ones that sprang "fresh from the mind." D4, 286, 3/11/35
kept receding toward the horizon. D4, 334, 8/16/35
applying the standards of her youth. D4, 326, 6/25/35
192 *"the world is to their liking."* D4, 332, 7/19/35
"science has helped them to electric toasters." D4, 332–33, 7/19/35
"wild retyping" D4, 332, 7/17/35; D4, 334, 8/16/35
had spent last night in the open. D4, 335, 8/21/35
193 *"the body shooting through the water."* D4, 338, 9/4/35
"threatening, advancing & retreating at Geneva." D4, 339, 9/6/35

194   *"lachrymose, self-righteous Lansbury."* DOWNHILL, 244–45
      fascinating to watch, "as good as any play," D4, 345, 10/2/35; L5, 432,
      10/14/35
      "hawking their consciences about," L5, 432, 10/14/35
      "Had he been born a duke—" D4, 345, 10/2/35
      did not make her like the victim any better. L5, 432, 10/14/35
      "beef & beer—which she must cook?" D4, 345, 10/2/35
195   *"politics ought to be separate from art."* D4, 346, 10/2/35
      dashing off a chapter of "The Next War" D4, 346, 10/15/35
      "neighbours talk politics, politics." L5, 428, 10/4/35
196   *pressure on her to finish the novel quickly.* D4, 347, 10/15/35
      "its difficult to go on, very slowly." D4, 348, 10/27/35
      "terrible fluctuation between the 2 worlds." D4, 350, 11/1/35
      "absurdities, that make up one's life." BELL, 2:190
197   *London basked in pleasantly mild November weather.* D4, 351, 11/5/35
      "precisely like a statue in a street." L5, 441, 11/9/35
      loved Tom in her "spasmodic fashion." L5, 442, 11/13/35
      "worship of the decay and skeleton." L5, 448, 12/1/35
198   *"outer to inner & inhabit eternity."* D4, 355, 11/27/35
      "even attempt to ask if its worth while." D4, 360, 12/28/35
      "Never did I enjoy writing a book more, I think," D4, 361, 12/29/35
      "& read some remote book." D4, 361, 12/30/35
199   *relief of writing fresh sentences again.* D5, 14, 3/4/36
      "such feeble twaddle—such twilight gossip" D5, 8, 1/16/36
      left "to moulder in ones own dung." L6, 18–19, 3/11/36
      "after an hour, the line began to taughten." D5, 17, 3/16/36
      facade of ordinary Mondays and Tuesdays. D5, 17, 3/13/36
      "Whats your opinion, Leonard, of whats-his-name?" L6, 19, 3/11/36
200   *Italians rallying round Mussolini.* D5, 17n, 3/13/36
      say to outsiders, "You can't come in." L6, 20, 3/11/36
      "And she may live 20 years. . . . What a system." D5, 19, 3/20/36
      Virginia to Ethel, L6, 17–18
201   *delayed that moment as long as possible.* BELL, 2:194
202   *"after congestion suffocation."* D5, 22, 4/9/36
      "look at a starling in the rain." L6, 27, 4/20/36
203   *"the end of civilization,"* L6, 37, 5/11/36
      "Showers of gravel fly, but there they are." L6, 38, 5/11/36
      Virginia to Ethel, L6, 39
204   *doppelgänger looking back at her.* DOWNHILL, 154
      time "when I couldn't control myself." L6, 44, 6/6/36
      "close to a suicidal state," D5, 24, 6/11/36
      set off the headache and depression. D5, 24, 6/21/36

"My brain is like a scale: one grain pulls it down." D5, 25, 6/23/36

"like the iron clasp of a statue on a horse's reins." L6, 47, 6/18/36

206 *"I dont want to go into it."* L6, 57, 7/20/36

"remote strange places, lying in bed." L6, 70, 9/4/36

"enraged rats gnawing the nape of my neck." L6, 76, 10/9/36

"& always with the certainty of failure." D5, 31–32, 11/10/36

207 *"all vanities are less than the slug on the Zinnia."* L6, 58, 7/22/36

did more than enough for them both. L6, 60, 7/25/36

208 *grooves on either side of her nose.* MB, 217

"too long exposed to artificial light to do without it." D5, 28, 10/30/36

"it must not be emphasized or prolonged." D5, 27, 10/30/36

throw it on the fire. D5, 29, 11/3/36

would bring on a major breakdown. DOWNHILL, 155

"very tired. Very old." D5, 29, 11/3/36

209 *as if the blood had stopped flowing to her brain.* D5, 30, 11/3/36

"it must be published." D5, 30, 11/5/36

"I have never had such an experience before." D5, 30, 11/5/36

"I'm so sick of it I can't judge." L6, 84, 11/14/36

210 *"increases his sensibility."* "The Artist and Politics," ME, 182

"Dine with Adrian tonight." D5, 32, 11/10/36

Twelve. An Inch of the Pattern: *The Years*

211 *"its uncropped, unpruned, natural state."* MB, 208

"plump for the Prince without hesitation." MB, 208

212 *going through her second divorce.* D5, 37–38, 11/27/36

"Let him marry whom he likes." D5, 39, 12/7/36

"moralities—will never be the same again." D5, 39–40, 12/7/36

"in the nursery, trying to make up his mind." D5, 40, 12/7/36

desire to marry an American divorcée. Quoted in Donaldson, *Edward VIII*, 400n

"'Ought to be ashamed of himself,'" D5, 40, 12/10/36

213 *"till they both cooled: no one objected."* D5, 41, 12/10/36

"Its dreadful, dreadful, she kept saying." D5, 42, 12/10/36

"No one could ever tell him a thing he disliked." D5, 43, 12/10/36

214 *"a set pigheaded steely mind."* D5, 43, 12/10/36

one man addressing the world. Quoted in Donaldson, *Edward VIII*, 412

"like a tree shaking off a load." D5, 44, 12/30/36

fear of falling apart. "No emptiness." D5, 44, 12/30/36

"a good many externals in its time." D4, 274, 1/11/35

216 *"Time had ceased."* TY, 278

"because we do not know ourselves" TY, 282

"'immune?' Was that what she meant?" TY, 293–94

217 *"speaking in another language."* TY, 299–300
218 *"myself and the world together."* TY, 410
 "two people out of all those millions are 'happy.'" TY, 388
 "this fractured world." TY, 390
 "another little book" instead of "living differently." TY 390–91
219 *"difficult: to combine the two."* D4, 353–54, 11/21/35
 "an incessant shower of innumerable atoms." "Modern Fiction," *The Common Reader*, 154
 seeming to move in random paths. TY, 366–67
220 *"half remembered, half forseen,"* TY, 369
 "She could not finish her thought." TY, 369
 "immunity from other feelings." TY, 370–71
 "another inch of the pattern." TY, 370
 "broken sentences, single words." TY, 411
 "knots in the middle of the forehead." TY, 414
221 *"little holes from which spokes radiated."* TY, 367
 "The blinds were white." TY, 428
222 a *"damned . . . bully."* TY, 330
 her cheeks burned and her hands trembled. D4, 241, 9/2/34
 "the only fine thing that was said in the war." TY, 336
223 *hardly fits the racist stereotypes.* TY, 340
 "ourselves small; a tumult outside." D4, 103, 5/25/32
 "seminal images" that inspired Woolf, Radin, *Virginia Woolf's* The Years, 88
 "What apes and cats we are." Ibid., galley 231
 "but all was tumbling to ruin." Ibid., galley 233
224 *self-mutilation, which she later regretted.* D5, 69, 3/15/37
 "happy tumultuous dream" D5, 52, 1/28/37
 "a piece of green linoleum." D5, 52, 1/23/37
 "a viper's nest of malodorous feelings." L6, 105, 2/10/37
225 *"killed her with their wild idiocy."* L6, 104–5, 1/27/37; L6, 107, 2/14/37
 only person singing was the undertaker's man. D5, 51, 1/23/37
 "she had been a kitten or a puppy." D5, 52, 1/23/37
 "But I must fight, thats my instinct." D5, 54, 2/12/37
 the "psychology of vanity." D5, 57, 2/18/37
 "keep dancing on hot bricks." D5, 55, 2/12/37
226 *"a prim prudish bourgeois mind."* D5, 58, 2/20/37
 "badness of my books affects the world." D5, 56, 2/18/37
 "dwelling is in the dark at the depths." L6, 111, 3/1/37
 "It affects the thighs chiefly." D5, 63, 3/1/37
227 *"held up to scorn & ridicule,"* D5, 64, 3/2/37
 "& that its failure is deliberate." D5, 65, 3/7/37
 "of course we actors are ignorant." L6, 116, 4/7/37

"Its the thing we do in the dark that is more real." L6, 122, 4/30/37

228   *"given a jump like a shot hare."* D5, 70, 3/19/37

addressing serious social issues. D5, 68, 3/14/37

an unimaginable future. Majumdar and McLaurin, *Virginia Woolf*, 372

"No one has yet seen the point," D5, 70, 3/17/37

"Its all very bad, but well meant—morally." L6, 113, 3/17/37

"cold and artificial and mainly external." Majumdar and McLaurin, *Virginia Woolf*, 387

229   *"originality of Miss Compton Burnett."* D5, 75, 4/2/37

"set on my own feet, a fighter." D5, 75, 4/2/37

"altogether muffed the proportions." L6, 116, 4/7/37

"those nights at Monks House." D5, 78, 4/9/37

"at the same time the most illuminating." D5, 67, 3/14/37

230   *Steinbeck's* Of Mice and Men. D5, 91, 6/1/37; Willis, *Leonard and Virginia Woolf as Publishers*, 290

Thirteen: Antigone's Daughters

231   *"whole population in happiness, if only they wd. look."* D5, 72, 3/27/37

over her skin and wanting to crush it, D5, 73, 3/28/37

232   *"a hole for a mouth."* BELL, 2:253

crushed on some lodging house wall. BELL, 2:254

"is to be pitied for tis surely blind." D5, 78, 4/9/37

233   *"the lovely sulky look of a half tame creature."* Julian Bell, *Essays, Poems, and Letters*, 3

"Something to me tragic in the sadness now." D5, 68, 3/14/37

with the zest of amateur tacticians. D5, 79–80, 4/15/37

"keeping something up his sleeve." D5, 79, 4/15/37

"hope to avoid complete extinguishing disaster." Julian Bell, "The Proletariat and Poetry: An Open Letter to C. Day Lewis," *Essays, Poems, and Letters*, 324

234   *discussions seem silly and self-indulgent.* Ibid., 373

endangered humanist values and artistic life. Ibid., 388, 384

"finish off with a decent fight." Ibid., 166, 157

235   *"Goodbye until this time next year."* BELL, 2:256

"I have decided never to analyze." BELL, 2:256

protected her from external shocks. D5, 101, 7/11/37

"9 months gloom & despair I suppose." D5, 102, 7/12/37

"Botten calling with the milk in the morning." D5, 99, 6/28/37

236   *broken a passenger's nose against the windshield.* Julian Bell, *Essays, Poems, and Letters*, 193, 190

"entertaining and very satisfactory." Ibid., 192

"go to Holland & look at birds." D5, 76, 4/2/37

"*Some mystic survival. The young wanting it.*" D5, 76, 4/2/37

237 *made any other memorial seem redundant.* D5, 102–3, 7/19/37
"*a part of the fictitious, not of the real life.*" D5, 103, 7/19/37
in order to keep from howling. D5, 104, 7/19/37

238 "*when otherwise it would have stopped.*" Vanessa Bell, *Selected Letters*, 475
"*the spectator's attitude in being wanted.*" D5, 104–5, 8/6/37
Virginia's diary, D5, 104–6

239 *only point in the day she had looked forward to.* BELL, 2:203; Vanessa Bell, *Selected Letters*, 475
"*like a dilapidated fish.*" D5, 106, 8/11/37

240 "*the colour of lions*" *in the heat.* L6, 153, 8/5/37
"*could never love another woman as he loved her.*" D5, 108, 8/17/37
"*the quality of the smile on her face.*" DECEIVED, 119
"*a genteel form of suicide.*" Stansky and Abrahams, *Journey to the Frontier*, 50
"*without if possible hurting his mother.*" DECEIVED, 119
stimulant or antidote to counter her influence. Julian Bell, *Essays, Poems, and Letters*, 157
"*not too strong a word for either of us.*" BELL, 2:257

241 "*find you sitting there. Roger felt the same.*" L6, 159, 8/17/37
"*ever since I can remember.*" Stansky and Abrahams, *Journey to the Frontier*, 195
"*I wouldn't mind losing a few years for one.*" Julian Bell, *Essays, Poems, and Letters*, 198, 196
"*going phut in a lethal chamber.*" Ibid., 157
"*stayed in England & faced drudgery.*" D5, 108, 8/17/37
"*one must control feeling with reason.*" Stansky and Abrahams, *Journey to the Frontier*, 399
"*like a motor in the head over the downs.*" D5, 111, 9/26/37

242 "*comment on his education & our teaching.*" D5, 126, 2/3/37
"*Shut my mind to anything but work & bowls.*" D5, 111–12, 9/26/37
"*you will be able to tell her it's true.*" Vita Sackville-West, *Letters to Virginia Woolf*, 403
message "*meant something I cant speak of.*" L6, 175, 10/1/37

243 "*Whats odd is I cant notice or describe.*" D5, 113, 10/12/37
"*like a physical volcano.*" D5, 112, 10/12/37
"*And our marriage so complete.*" D5, 115, 10/22/37

244 "*great spray fountain bursting*" D5, 116, 10/25/37
"*a queer animal rhapsody, restrained by L.*" L6, 185, 10/26/37
would not pass without inflicting new torments. D5, 121, 12/18/37

245 "*then the time passes.*" D5, 125, 1/9/38
announcing her "*amazing relief.*" L6, 208, 1/14/38

she wished she could help her sister. L6, 211, 2/3/38
felt very grateful, though she couldn't show it. Vanessa Bell, BERG, 2/4/38
"extremely clear analysis." D5, 127, 2/4/38
246 "a good piece of donkeywork." D5, 127, 2/4/38
blend into a new compound. TG, 97–98
247 "derision and freedom from unreal loyalties." TG, 142
silence and noncooperation. TG, 194
"As a woman my country is the whole world." TG, 197
thinking of him as she wrote. D5, 148, 6/3/38
mulberry, whose leaves they devour. TG, 135
lose their sense of proportion. TG, 129
248 "Only a cripple in a cave." TG, 131–32
"dead children killed by bombs." L6, 85, 11/14/36
"crush him in our own country." TG, 98
"armful of dead leaves upon the blaze." TG, 65
"will laugh from their graves." TG, 151–52
"a match to the paper. Look, how it burns!" TG, 184–85
249 "but are ourselves that figure." TG, 258
"and there will be no more horses." TG, 302
"sermons are not preached." TG, 63–64
actual facts in the real world. TG, 177
250 "sharpness takes some time to be felt." D5, 84, 4/30/37
country has always treated her as a slave. TG, 191, 197
"like drops of dirty water mixing." D5, 129, 3/12/38
emigrating "from our doomed Europe." D5, 134, 4/12/38
251 "Aeroplanes droning over the house." D5, 131, 3/22/38
"to see the daffodils; the old beggar woman—the swans." D5, 131,
    3/22/38
"has digested his dinner he will pounce again." D5, 132, 3/26/38
"afraid of nothing. Can do anything I like." D5, 136, 4/28/38
"on my own forever." D5, 136–37, 4/28/38
"pack may howl but it shall never catch me." D5, 141, 5/20/38
252 "like a moth dancing over a bonfire." D5, 142, 5/24/38
"a sweat stain, a tear stain, a gash" L6, 216, 2/24/38

Fourteen. A Purple Background

253 "autobiography in public"—a mode she hated. D5, 141, 5/20/38
"refusing to be stamped & stereotyped." D4, 187, 10/29/33
marked a "spiritual conversion." D5, 137, 4/29/38; D5, 141, 5/20/38
insulated her against the impact of surface events. D5, 133, 3/31/38;
    D5, 133, 4/12/38

254 *"sober drudgery"* to distract her and steady her nerves. D5, 133, 4/12/38

255 meet the original Virginia again. Monk's House Papers, University of
Sussex Library, 2/6/38

"(He's grey: so am I)." L6, 214, 2/14/38

a shy and stoical woman. "Lady Ottoline Morrell," D5, appendix 2, 365

256 *"doing well out of Ottoline."* D5, 140, 5/12/38

Virginia's diary, D5, 135

257 *"to the time of sneer enthusiasm enthusiasm sneer."* D5, 145–46,
5/28/38

the sneers had very little sting. D5, 148, 6/5/38

"too fair-minded and sincere to want to trip her readers up." D5, 148n,
6/3/38

"the beauty of her gospel." Majumdar and McLaurin, *Virginia Woolf*,
405

"our mad, armament ridden world." Majumdar and McLaurin, *Virginia Woolf*, 402

258 ignoring the radical content of her proposals. Ibid., 401

"generally kind, rather surprised, & its over." D5, 149, 6/11/38

"enlarge the imaginative, and take stock of the emotion." L6, 235,
6/7/38

"propellor invisibly quick and unconscious." D5, 151, 6/16/38

259 *"also it is oneself—the real Virginia or Ethel?"* L6, 246, 6/26/38

"with the gentleman's technique, you win." Sackville-West, *Letters to
Virginia Woolf*, 412–13

"more pains to get up the facts and state them plainly" L6, 243, 6/19/38

"And the porridge is a dream. Only I loathe porridge." L6, 249, 6/28/38

260 *"sicklied me over with praise of charm and wit."* L6, 256, 7/22/38

"bellicose and urge their men to fight?" Sackville-West, *Letters to Virginia Woolf*, 415

"idiotic games for which I pay." D5, 160, 8/7/38

261 *"turned queer"* since her son died. D5, 161, 8/17/38

"What else can a gnat on a blade of grass do?" D5, 162, 8/17/38

"in sober prose, with dates attached?" L6, 267, 8/29/38

bowls, which was their "mania." They picked dahlias. D5, 164, 8/28/38

"Any news? What d'you think?" D5, 166, 9/5/38

the Prime Minister cares one straw about. D5, 166, 9/5/38

262 "Yet nobody must tell the truth. So one forgets." D5, 167, 9/10/38

"1914 but without even the illusion of 1914." D5, 170, 9/14/38

"the [Labour Party] counters Hitler." L6, 270, 9/11/38

"One in which mice & matchboxes are collected." D5, 168, 9/10/38

"only my inviolable center: L. to wit." D5, 183, 10/30/38

263 "What'll he gobble next." D5, 173, 9/22/38

the week beginning Monday, September 26. L6, 275, 10/1/38

"Go and fit your gas masks." L6, 275, 10/1/38

"hinting that he meant to kill himself." L6, 276, 10/1/38

264   "howling like wild beasts" in response to the Führer. L6, 276, 10/1/38

"get some solidity into my mind." D5, 174–75, 9/28/38

"a general feeling of flight and hurry." L6, 277, 10/1/38

"London ravaged by cobras & tigers." D5, 178, 10/2/38

265   Chamberlain's "sensational announcement." D5, 175–76, 9/29/38

"he appeared ten years younger and triumphant." Harold Nicolson, Diaries and Letters, 1930–1939, 370

"like coming out of a dark room." D5, 176, 9/29/38

"believe it is peace for our time." L6, 280, 10/3/38; Taylor, English History, 526

attack when he grew stronger and they were unable to resist. L6, 280, 10/3/38

"unreality that clouded all distinct feeling." D5, 176, 9/30/38

266   "soberly & truly life after death." D5, 177, 9/30/38

"weather symbols—roping everything in." D5, 178, 10/1/38

"peace without honour for six months." L6, 278, 10/1/38

"damnable servility . . . the worst failure imaginable." L6, 294, 10/24/38

"So we dont think of death." D5, 190, 12/11/38

267   "intolerably airy and off the point," L6, 289, 10/13/38

surrounded by little statues of Egyptian gods. D5, 202, 1/29/39; D5, 202, 1/30/39

268   "to supply sympathy to sympathy addicts." D5, 191, 12/11/38

too much attention to her own personality was worth at least £150. D5, 200, 1/18/39

"Oh she'll never repay you"—Virginia ground her teeth. D5, 206, 2/28/39

outlined the main events of Roger's life. D5, 207, 3/11/39

"not in the spirit of the Munich meeting." D5, 208, 3/16/39

"There's always our dear old war." D5, 215, 4/15/39

This "purple background" clouded their Easter D5, 213, 4/11/39

"Never felt it so strong before." D5, 215, 4/15/39

drawing room chair or a silver sugar caster. L6, 262, 8/7/38

269   "yet 'life in common' is an immense reality." D5, 216, 4/28/39

Virginia's diary, D5, 216

Fifteen. To the Altar

270   that "great peaceful garden." D5, 219, 5/25/39

"great mistresses of the art of speech." "Madame de Sévigné," DM, 54

271 *grays and whites, suggested natural refinement.* L6, 338, 6/13/39
youngsters danced and cavorted through the night. L6, 341, 6/18/39
to "get the right proportions." D5, 220, 6/23/39
"compared to the integrity of painting." MB, 85
"his pertinacity would bore holes in granite." D2, 150, 12/18/21
pronounced it "a great advance." D5, 221, 6/26/39

272 *"it was awful—like wild beasts."* Woodeson, *Mark Gertler*, 326–27
"better than through any painted shade of mine." L6, 417, 8/16/39
"poetise" and impose her own personality. D5, 200, 1/18/39
"iron pattern" of realistic chronology. JOURNEY, 40
"it is drudgery & must be; & I must go through with it." D5, 217, 5/1/39
"abstracting it into themes." L6, 426, 9/4/40

273 *breaking waves and splashing water.* MB, 64
personal yardsticks, one used to measure all events. MB, 73
"burst its green case and unfold its immense cup of red." RF, 16
retiring to his studio to contemplate Giotto. RF, 214

274 *"Madness declared itself."* RF, 103
"but it cannot be exaggerated." RF, 103
"tragedy when I married, added a fearful delight." Spalding, *Roger Fry*,
61; RF, 94–95

275 *"I hope you won't mind making us all blush,"* Vanessa Bell, *Selected
Letters*, 450
a special "quality of 'reality.'" RF, 229
"the immortal apples, the eternal eggs." RF, 215

276 *"they aim not at illusion but at reality."* Quoted in RF, 177–78
exposing them, Virginia said, to "the shock of reality." RF, 178
"the most abused, of all living art critics." RF, 160
"of all the religions that have afflicted man." RF, 231
detachment provided by the aesthetic emotion. RF, 232
"majesty of mountains and the melody of music." RF, 285
"break the rhythm before it gets quite fixed." RF, 283

277 *"invests them with a peculiar reality."* RF, 296
"by asking nothing for oneself." RF, 215
"broke the rhythm before it got quite fixed." RF, 295–96

278 *"sucked drop by drop for years to come."* D5, 222, 6/28/39
"such a bore to visit. Still she was somebody." D5, 223, 7/3/39
revering the memory of their dead father. Leonard Woolf, *Sowing*,
32–33
"& yet demands more life, more life." D3, 231, 5/31/29
"paper upon suicide which I see myself leaving for my friends?" D3,
231, 5/31/29

279 *"The Poles vibrating in my room."* D5, 225, 7/11/39

in order not to freeze in her tracks. D5, 225, 7/12/39

"I said, You must decide. So he sent them away." D5, 227, 7/28/39

"his peach tree—to be pulled down because of me." D5, 227, 7/28/39

280 *"The most beautiful of women."* D5, 228, 7/28/39

"Jackmanna again. How my eye feels rested." D5, 229, 7/31/39

"human voices wake us & we drown." D5, 228, 7/30/39

two London houses, neither one livable. L6, 350, 8/19/39

"I suspect some desire to 'get on with it.'" D5, 231, 8/25/39

"What can you do against fate?" D5, 230, 8/25/39

282 *"playing bowls. No feeling of patriotism."* D5, 231, 8/28/39

"I have my old spurs & my old flanks." D5, 232, 8/28/39

"May flies buzz. I am sleeveless in the heat." D5, 232, 8/28/39

283 *"a mere surface for gangsters."* D5, 233, 9/3/39

revising a sentence of "Roger Fry." D5, 233, 9/3/39

"any idea is more real than any amount of war misery." D5, 235, 9/6/39

284 *her garden, where the apples shone in the sun.* D5, 233, 9/3/39

"lots of small bothers & arrangements." D5, 235, 9/6/39

"cold & torpid. Endless interruptions." D5, 234, 9/6/39

just been beaten and robbed. D5, 236, 9/11/39

feeling as if she had been knocked on the head. L6, 358, 9/12/39 or
    9/13/39

285 *"So my reasons are half in half."* D5, 236, 9/11/39

a purpose around which to order her days. D5, 237, 9/23/39

"love interest is supplied chiefly by frogs." "White's Selborne," *The
    Captain's Death Bed,* 20

"everyone humped with a gas mask." D5, 242, 10/22/39

"People grope their way to each others lairs." D5, 242–43, 10/22/39

the mood of "barren horror." D5, 243, 10/22/39

286 *"rats in caves live as we do."* L6, 364, 10/16/39

"drawing the curtains and finding it a fine day." L6, 366, 10/25/39

"the only happiness thats secure." D5, 248, 12/2/39

"Always take on new things. Break the rhythm." D5, 248, 12/2/39

287 *"sit over our logs this bitter winter night."* D5, 251, 12/17/39

margins of the road, remained lost in darkness. D5, 250, 12/9/39

"The conscience as censor." D5, 250, 12/9/39

whatever shreds of patriotism she had in her. D5, 263, 2/2/40

288 *she took shelter from the high winds.* L6, 373, 12/3/39

Virginia's diary, D5, 259–60

"to blow out; which I entirely refuse to do." D5, 260, 1/20/40

289 *"the garden with the bombs falling."* D5, 265, 2/8/40

"All those dead quotations." D5, 271, 3/20/40

"slightly broken-backed" condition. JOURNEY, 42

"a piece of cabinet making" than a work of art. L6, 381, 2/1/40

encouraged Virginia to publish it without major changes. D5, 272,
3/20/40

290 *"May coming & asparagus, & butterflies."* D5, 276, 3/29/40
"the Labour party meets in our dining room." L6, 391, 4/6/40

Sixteen. Weeping Willie

291 *"stretch to the back curtain of the mind."* D5, 279, 4/13/40
inherited from their fathers. "The Leaning Tower," ME, 112
292 *"if flogged, would kick them off its back."* Ibid., 118
it still offered a very fine view. Ibid., 115
"top speed while the uppermind drowses," Ibid., 110, 109
"they ought to enjoy Shakespeare?" L6, 421, 8/24/40
293 *disturbing news about Angelica Bell.* D5, 282–83, 5/6/40
"amorous ways & primitive mind." D5, 283, 282, 5/6/40
far away from "the land with its children." D5, 283, 5/6/40
"the greatest battle in history." D5, 284, 5/13/40
"nothing to offer but blood, toil, tears and sweat." Churchill, *Their Finest Hour,* 25
294 *"not be suffered to fail among men."* Ibid., 26
Virginia's diary, D5, 284
295 *"Better shut the garage doors."* D5, 284, 5/15/40
"an evening reading over the fire." D5, 285, 5/15/40
"cook and eat one's eggs and bacon for breakfast." JOURNEY, 46–47
296 *"how can we be worthy of such men?"* D5, 292, 6/3/40
perorations delivered in "highflown tense" *voices.* D5, 290, 5/30/40
"reel off patriotic speeches, by the dozen." D5, 288, 5/29/40
"what one might call retrospective." D5, 286, 5/20/40
297 *"in this miserable life of detail & bombast."* D5, 286, 5/20/40
"[Germans] seem youthful, fresh, inventive." D5, 287, 5/25/40
"we were domestically on the beaches." JOURNEY, 54
298 *"minds so cheap, compared with ours."* D5, 288, 5/29/40
"The very opposite of 'common' or working class." D5, 289, 5/29/40
the job of the educated class to check it. D5, 290–91, 5/31/40
the duke of Northumberland had been killed in the war. D5, 291, 6/3/40
to "tap that old river again," D5, 291, 5/31/40
299 *"an air cleanliness, not a soap & water one."* D5, 290, 5/30/40
"concentration camps, or taking sleeping draughts." D5, 292, 6/7/40
"his great purple vampire body." L6, 402, 6/9/40
"bed at midday: this refers to the garage." D5, 293, 6/9/40
300 *"No audience. No echo. Thats part of one's death."* D5, 293, 6/9/40
"was despatched to his regiment." D5, 297, 6/20/40
BBC caricatures of the laughing, heroic tommy. D5, 298, 6/22/40

301 *"I shall ask my doctor friends."* Harold Nicolson, *Diaries and Letters*, 90
"This, I thought yesterday, may be my last walk." D5, 298, 6/22/40
"6, 3, 12 people killed nightly." D5, 298, 6/22/40

302 *Virginia's diary*, D5, 299
"Very little is left outside." TW, 163

303 *"Water Co & the tap & the Rectory scullery."* D5, 288, 5/29/40
let alone a window—his bones were like glass. D5, 302, 7/12/40
a dentist's drill buzzed in her ear. D5, 290, 5/31/40

304 *"a measure for our present insecurity."* Majumdar and McLaurin, *Virginia Woolf*, 423
help build "a new order of society." Ibid., 421
reviewer, whom she thought "venomous and malignant." Ibid., 422;
L6, 410, 8/6/40
Nazism to grow without doing anything to stop it. L6, 413, 8/13/40
engagement that fitted his gifts and disposition. L6, 420, 8/24/40

305 *"and wasn't that the best way of checking Nazism?"* L6, 414, 8/13/40
"sawing in the air just above us." D5, 311, 8/16/40
more real than the actual enemy planes had done. D5, 313–14, 8/31/40
"quiet evening thinking of you sitting there alone." L6, 424, 8/30/40

306 *"We might be in the Strand, here at night."* L6, 431, 9/12/40
"We've not had our raid yet, we say." D5, 313, 8/28/40
"a plunge; & a burst of thick black smoke." D5, 318, 9/11/40
"Only a German bomber? Oh thats all." D5, 325, 9/26/40
"Why do people think that whats unpleasant is therefore real?" L6,
431–32, 15/9/40
faces serene and "tough as leather." L6, 430, 9/12/40

308 *"dear me, I'm turning democrat."* L6, 431, 9/12/40
even politicians—Churchill, at least. L6, 434, 9/25/40
"if Hitler doesnt drop a splinter into my machine." L6, 430–31, 9/12/40
through the holes in three floors to the roof. JOURNEY, 63
"a heavy iron drop over ones own scene." L6, 433, 9/20/40

309 *"that rings from one simple melody to another."* D5, 325, 9/29/40
"seeing a face like a codfish in embryo." L6, 436, 10/1/40
admitted, it was "an ignoble fret." L6, 434, 9/25/40
Virginia's diary, D5, 326–27

Seventeen. Oblivion and Water

312 *their love had "weathered so well."* D5, 328, 10/10/40
"Living near to the bone." D5, 328, 10/10/40

313 *"tea, bowls, reading, sweets, bed."* D5, 328–29, 10/12/40
"The globe rounds again," she wrote," D5, 329, 10/12/40
the death of her half sister, Stella. MB, 137

"terrified of passive acquiescence," she said. D5, 329, 10/12/40
beginning with the minstrel-like Anon. D5, 327, 10/6/40
on their "lovely free autumn island." D5, 329, 10/12/40

314 *"No reading no writing. No claims, no 'must.'"* D5, 330, 10/17/40
waited for "the next catastrophe." JOURNEY, 69
"a real—and yet false—tranquility." JOURNEY, 75
"red cottage roofs"—a vista of great beauty. D5, 336, 11/5/40

315 *"you might take me for a stake walking."* L6, 444, 11/14/40
leaving the world "as it was in the beginning." D5, 336, 11/5/40
glimpse of the anger below the surface. D5, 336, 11/3/40
"winds one into a ball: & so jades one." D5, 339, 11/17/40

316 *"(though gilt with an angelic surface) the slave."* MB, 145
"a child with a box of chalks could make a more subtle portrait."
 MB, 146
"those who are forced into contact with it." MB, 146–47
"nor feel myself in touch with them." MB, 157, 158–59
brought the rich residue to Leonard in triumph. D5, 340, 11/23/40

317 *"I've enjoyed writing almost every page."* D5, 340, 11/23/40
mode she had not attempted since The Waves. D5, 95, 6/22/37; D5,
 341, 11/23/40

318 *"Three emotions made the ply of human life."* BA, 90, 92
"the fifth and all the others were the same." BA, 99

319 *"A spasm made the ribs contract; blood oozed."* BA, 99
a "body shooting through the water." D4, 338, 9/4/35
a baptismal scene, but not of this world. BA, 104
"skimmed waves in the air, the yellow woodpecker?" BA, 104
"nor sun rises. All's equal there." BA, 154–55

320 *"leaders who in that they seek to lead desert us."* BA, 156
"noted in the margin of her mind; when illusion fails." BA, 179–80
"with all her treasure if so be tears could be ended." BA, 181

321 *"man had built his house in a hollow."* BA, 10
"passively to behold indescribable horror." BA, 60
"mind-divided little snake in the grass." BA, 73
"gigantic ear attached to a gigantic head." BA, 175
"ground now and then with a shock of surprise." BA, 116
fertility and sexual ease. BA, 119
"seemed to form themselves into a pattern." MB, 83, 35

322 *fullness of being between the recorded acts.* MB, 70
"the [Elizabethan] age in person." BA, 83
"you and me and William dressed differently." BA, 174–75
"surreptitiously mounting a soap-box." BA, 189
"some lost-in-the-mists-of-antiquity model." BA, 190
"Each is part of the whole." BA, 192

323 "That role has not been assigned to me." BA, 192
"life, without measure." BA, 209
"Then the curtain rose. They spoke." BA, 219

324 talking about nothing in particular. L6, 475, 3/1/41
no echo in the village, "only waste air." D5, 357, 2/26/41
"And one has to weigh and measure." D5, 343, 12/16/40
tried to drag her down to their own level. D5, 342, 11/29/40

325 "short sharp spasm" at any time in her life, JOURNEY, 77
the crisis would come before Easter. D5, 355n, 1/26/41
"the worst stage of the war." L6, 475, 3/1/41
"with our noses pressed to a closed door." D5, 355, 1/26/41
"the little hum & song of the nursery." D5, 345, 12/22/40
"pick up some scrap of bright wool." TW, 295
"nothing turbulent; nothing involved; no introspection." D5, 345,
    12/22/40

326 "good teeth & a candid kind smile." D5, 49, 1/10/37
with strong roots in the Sussex countryside. JOURNEY, 80
"finally accept simply and rather touchingly." OW, 351
"Waifs I'm sure they are about food." OW, 356

328 "lost all power over words, cant do a thing with them." L6, 456,
    12/31/40
lead eventually to a richer harvest. OW, 357
"milk and cream at this bitter and barren moment." L6, 458, 1/9/41
"a glass of milk regularly every day." BEGINNING, 79–80

329 cross of the neighboring church. D5, 351, 1/9/41
"there'll be no rosy blue red snow." D5, 352, 1/9/41
"Milton, Donne, and all the rest!" L6, 466, 2/1/41

330 "always my detractors." D5, 352, 1/9/41
"she is a thoroughly frail creature." OW, 363
"choking, delightful, hooting way." RECOLL, 50

331 "these fat white slugs?" D5, 357, 2/26/41
"sentences that gives me intense pleasure?" D5, 357, 2/26/41
"to talk to a born clarifier." OW, 368
Octavia's fire-watching duties in Brighton. L6, 479, 3/13/41
toughness and love of games and the outdoors. OW, 368
Virginia's diary, D5, 357–58

Eighteen: Time Passes

333 happened after a major work. OW, 368
"I never remember any enjoyment of my body." OW, 369
think less about herself and more about "outside things." OW, 368

"bucolic and hefty" personality had a tranquilizing effect. OW, 370

334   *"much too slight and sketchy,"* L6, 482, 3/20/41

   "it was one of the best things she had written." Lehmann, *I Am My Brother*, 112

   said she had slipped into a ditch. JOURNEY, 91

   "always lied to save my skin as a child." OW, 376

   "I can't write. I've lost the art." OW, 371

335   *"a world of good to harrow a field or play a game."* OW, 371–72

   "think as little about yourself as possible." MD, 138, 149

   "how much I depend on you." Vanessa Bell, *Selected Letters*, 473–74

   "how I loved your letter." L6, 485, 3/23?/41

336   *"L is doing the rhododendrons . . ."* D5, 359, 3/24/41

   "at any moment she might kill herself." JOURNEY, 91

337   *Octavia to Elizabeth Robins,* OW, 372–73

338   *"He shut people up."* MD, 147, 154

   "a drowned sailor, on the shore of the world." MD, 140

   "on a cliff with the gulls screaming over him." MD, 213

   "Holmes and Bradshaw are on you." MD, 148

339   *"and then she'll come good again."* OW, 373

   "the greatest masterpiece of this century." Notes included with letter to Leonard Woolf, 3/29/41, Leonard Woolf Papers, University of Sussex Library

   "more disturbing than anything she had written before." Lehmann, *I Am My Brother*, 113

   "too silly and trivial" to be published. L6, 486, 3/27?/41

340   *warned Lehmann not to acknowledge his letter.* Leonard Woolf, *Letters*, 250

341   *"Mrs. Woolf put the duster down and went away."* RECOLL, 160

342   *Virginia to Leonard,* L6, 486

343   *"Nobody else could have kept her going so long."* OW, 375

   one's stupidity & selfishness. Leonard Woolf, *Letters*, 165

   "wish I had realised it, but I didn't at all." Vanessa Bell, *Selected Letters*, 475

344   *"she had seemed pleased."* Vanessa Bell, *Selected Letters*, 478

   "the most terrible thing I have known." RECOLL, 161

   "simple and profound paper upon suicide" for her friends. D3, 231, 5/31/29

346   *"then a suffocation of blackness."* MD, 280

   "a tremendous shower, dissolving me." TW, 206

Bibliography

Alvarez, A. *The Savage God: A Study of Suicide*. New York: Norton, 1990.

Annan, Noel. *Leslie Stephen: The Godless Victorian*. Chicago: University of Chicago Press, 1986.

Bell, Colin. *National Government 1931: Extracts from* The Times, *January to October 1931*. London: Times Books, 1975.

Bell, Julian. *Essays, Poems, and Letters*. Edited by Quentin Bell. London: Hogarth Press, 1938.

Bell, Quentin. *Bloomsbury Recalled*. New York: Columbia University Press, 1995.

———. *Virginia Woolf: A Biography*. 2 vols. New York: Harcourt Brace Jovanovich, 1972.

Bell, Vanessa. *Selected Letters of Vanessa Bell*. Edited by Regina Marler. New York: Pantheon, 1993.

Blythe, Ronald. *The Age of Illusion: England in the Twenties*. London: Hamish Hamilton, 1963.

Bowlby, Rachel, ed. *Virginia Woolf*. London: Longman, 1992.

Boxall, Nelly. "A Portrait of Virginia Woolf by her Friends." Cassette tape. BBC Home Service, August 29, 1956.

Branson, Noreen, and Margo Heinemann. *Britain in the 1930's*. New York: Praeger, 1971.

Brenan, Gerald. *Personal Record: 1920–1972*. New York: Knopf, 1975.

———. *South from Granada*. New York: Farrar Straus, 1957.

Bullock, Alan. *Hitler: A Study in Tyranny*. Rev. ed. New York: Harper and Row, 1964.

Camus, Albert. *The Myth of Sisyphus*. Translated by Justin O'Brien. New York: Vintage, 1955.

Caramagno, Thomas C. *The Flight of the Mind: Virginia Woolf's Art and Manic-Depressive Illness*. Berkeley: University of California Press, 1992.

———. "Manic-Depressive Psychosis and Critical Approaches to Virginia Woolf's Life and Work." *PMLA* 103 (January 1988): 10–23.

Carrington, Dora. *Carrington: Letters and Extracts from Her Diaries*. Edited by David Garnett. London: Jonathan Cape, 1970.

Carroll, Lewis. *Alice in Wonderland, Through the Looking Glass, The Hunting of the Snark*. New York: Modern Library.

Chapman, Wayne K., and Janet M. Manson, eds. *Women in the Milieu of Leonard and Virginia Woolf: Peace, Politics, and Education*. New York: Pace University Press, 1998.

Churchill, Winston. *The Gathering Storm*. Boston: Houghton Mifflin, 1948.

———. *Their Finest Hour*. Boston: Houghton Mifflin, 1948.

Coleman, Roger. *Downland: A Farm and a Village*. New York: Viking, 1981.

Colt, George Howe. *The Enigma of Suicide*. New York: Summit Books, 1991.

Cunningham, Valentine. *British Writers of the Thirties*. Oxford: Oxford University Press, 1988.

Darroch, Sandra Jobson. *Ottoline: The Life of Lady Ottoline Morrell*. New York: Coward, McCann, and Geoghan, 1975.

Davies, Margaret Llewelyn, ed. *Life as We Have Known It, by Co-operative Working Women, with an Introductory Letter by Virginia Woolf*. New York: Norton, 1975.

Delany, Paul. *The Neo-Pagans: Rupert Brooke and the Ordeal of Youth*. New York: Free Press, 1987.

De Salvo, Louise. *Virginia Woolf: The Impact of Childhood Sexual Abuse on Her Life and Work*. Boston: Beacon, 1989.

DiBattista, Maria. *Virginia Woolf's Major Novels: The Fables of Anon*. New Haven: Yale University Press, 1980.

Donaldson, Frances. *Edward VIII*. New York: Ballantine, 1980.

Dunn, Jane. *A Very Close Conspiracy: Vanessa Bell and Virginia Woolf*. Boston: Little, Brown, 1990.

Forster, E. M. *Goldsworthy Lowes Dickinson*. New York: Harcourt Brace Jovanovich, 1973.

Fry, Roger. *Cézanne: A Study of His Development*. New York: Macmillan, 1927.

———. *Letters*. Edited by Denys Sutton. 2 vols. New York: Random House, 1972.

———. *Vision and Design*. New York: Meridian, 1956.

Furbank, P. N. *E. M. Forster: A Life*. New York: Harcourt Brace Jovanovich, 1981.

Garnett, Angelica. *Deceived with Kindness: A Bloomsbury Childhood*. San Diego: Harcourt Brace Jovanovich, 1984.

Garnett, David. *Great Friends*. London: Macmillan, 1979.

Gillespie, Diane Filby. *The Sisters' Arts: The Writing and Painting of Virginia Woolf and Vanessa Bell.* Syracuse: Syracuse University Press, 1988.

Glendenning, Victoria. *Vita: The Life of Vita Sackville-West.* New York: Knopf, 1983.

Goethe, *Faust.* Vol. 1, *The First Part.* Edited by Calvin Thomas. Boston: D. C. Heath, 1892.

Gordon, Lyndall. *Virginia Woolf: A Writer's Life.* New York: Norton, 1984.

Graves, Robert, and Alan Hodge. *The Long Week-end: A Social History of Great Britain, 1918–1939.* New York: Norton, 1963.

Heilbrun, Carolyn. *Hamlet's Mother and Other Women.* New York: Ballantine, 1990.

———, ed. *Lady Ottoline's Album.* New York: Knopf, 1976.

Holroyd, Michael. *Lytton Strachey: A Biography.* Harmondsworth: Penguin, 1971.

Hussey, Mark, *The Singing of the Real World: The Philosophy of Virginia Woolf's Fiction.* Columbus: Ohio State University Press, 1986.

———, ed. *Virginia Woolf and War: Fiction, Reality, and Myth.* Syracuse: Syracuse University Press, 1992.

Isherwood, Christopher. *Mr. Norris Changes Trains.* London: Hogarth Press, 1935.

Jamison, Kay Redfield. *Touched with Fire: Manic-Depressive Illness and the Artistic Temperament.* New York: Free Press, 1993.

Jennings, W. Ivor. "The Constitution Under Strain." *Political Quarterly* 2 (1931): 204.

Joad, C. E. M. "Prolegomena to Fascism." *Political Quarterly* 2, no. 1 (1931): 82–99.

Kennedy, Richard. *A Boy at the Hogarth Press.* Harmondsworth: Penguin, 1978.

Kiely, Robert, ed. *Modernism Reconsidered.* Cambridge: Harvard University Press, 1983.

King, James. *Virginia Woolf.* London: Hamish Hamilton, 1994.

Lanchester, Elsa. *Charles Laughton and I.* New York: Harcourt Brace, 1938.

Leaska, Mitchell. *Granite and Rainbow: The Hidden Life of Virginia Woolf.* New York: Farrar Straus Giroux, 1998.

Lee, Hermione. *Virginia Woolf.* London: Chatto and Windus, 1996.

———, ed. *The Hogarth Letters.* London: Chatto and Windus, 1985.

Lehmann, John. *I Am My Brother: Autobiography II.* London: Longmans, 1960.

———. *In My Own Time: Memoirs of a Literary Life.* Boston: Little, Brown, 1969.

———. *Thrown to the Woolfs.* New York: Holt, Rinehart, and Winston, 1978.

———. *The Whispering Gallery: Autobiography I.* London: Longmans, Green, 1955.

Majumdar, Robin, and Allen McLaurin. *Virginia Woolf: The Critical Heritage*. London: Routledge and Kegan Paul, 1975.

Marcus, Jane. *Art and Anger: Reading Like a Woman*. Columbus: Ohio State University Press, 1988.

———, ed. *New Feminist Essays on Virginia Woolf*. Lincoln: University, of Nebraska Press, 1981.

———, ed. *Virginia Woolf: A Feminist Slant*. Lincoln: University of Nebraska Press, 1983.

Marder, Herbert. "Alienation Effects: Dramatic Satire in *Between the Acts*." *Papers on Language and Literature* 24, no. 4 (Fall 1988): 423–35.

———. "Beyond the Lighthouse: *The Years*." In *Makers of the Twentieth Century Novel*, edited by Harry Garvin, 62–69. Lewisburg: Bucknell University Press, 1978.

———. *Feminism and Art: A Study of Virginia Woolf*. Chicago: University of Chicago Press, 1968.

———. "The Mark on the Wall." In *Reference Guide to Short Fiction*, edited by Noelle Watson. Detroit: St. James Press, 1994.

———. Review of *Leonard and Virginia Woolf as Publishers: The Hogarth Press, 1917–41*, by J. H. Willis, Jr. *JEGP* 93, no. 1 (January 1994): 131–34.

———. Review of *Virginia Woolf and London: The Sexual Politics of the City*, by Susan Squier; *Unifying Strategies in Virginia Woolf's Experimental Fiction*, by Adrian Velicu, and *New Feminist Essays on Virginia Woolf*, edited by Jane Marcus. *Modern Language Review* 83, pt. 3 (1988): 705–7.

———. "Split Perspective: Types of Incongruity in *Mrs. Dalloway*." *Papers on Language and Literature* 22, no. 1 (Winter 1986): 51–69.

———. "Virginia Woolf's 'Conversion': *Three Guineas*, 'Pointz Hall,' and *Between the Acts*." *Journal of Modern Literature* 14, no. 4 (Spring 1988): 465–80.

———. "Virginia Woolf's 'System That Did Not Shut Out.'" *Papers on Language and Literature* 4, no. 1 (Winter 1968): 106–11.

Matthews, T. S. *Great Tom: Notes Towards the Definition of T. S. Eliot*. New York: Harper and Row, 1973.

McHenry, Dean E. *His Majesty's Opposition: Structure and Problems of the British Labour Party, 1931–1938*. Berkeley: University of California Press, 1940.

Mepham, John. *Virginia Woolf: A Literary Life*. New York: St. Martin's, 1991.

Mirsky, Dmitri. *The Intelligentsia of Great Britain*. London: Gollancz, 1935.

Morrell, Ottoline. *Memoirs of Lady Ottoline Morrell: A Study in Friendship*. Edited by Robert Gathorne-Hardy. New York: Knopf, 1964.

Muggeridge, Malcolm. *The Thirties: 1930–1940 in Great Britain*. London: Hamish Hamilton, 1940.

Nicolson, Harold. *Diaries and Letters, 1930–1939*. Edited by Nigel Nicolson. New York: Atheneum, 1966.

Nicolson, Nigel. *Portrait of a Marriage*. New York: Atheneum, 1973.

————, ed. *Vita and Harold: The Letters of Vita Sackville-West and Harold Nicolson*. New York: G. P. Putnam's Sons, 1992.

Noble, Joan Russell, ed. *Recollections of Virginia Woolf*. New York: Morrow, 1972.

Partridge, Frances. *Julia: A Portrait of Julia Strachey by Herself and Frances Partridge*. Boston: Little, Brown, 1983.

————. *Love in Bloomsbury: Memories*. Boston: Little, Brown, 1981.

Political Quarterly. Edited by Leonard Woolf and W. A. Robson. Vols. 1–12. London: Macmillan, 1930–1941.

Poole, Roger. *The Unknown Virginia Woolf*. Atlantic Highlands, N.J.: Humanities Press, 1982.

Radin, Grace. *Virginia Woolf's* The Years: *The Evolution of a Novel*. Knoxville: University of Tennessee Press, 1981.

Raitt, Suzanne. *Vita and Virginia: The Work and Friendship of V. Sackville-West and Virginia Woolf*. Oxford: Clarendon, 1993.

Reid, Panthea. *Art and Affection: A Life of Virginia Woolf*. New York: Oxford University Press, 1996.

Richardson, Elizabeth P. *A Bloomsbury Iconography*. Winchester: St. Paul's Bibliographies, 1989.

Roberts, Michael, ed. *New Signatures: Poems by Several Hands*. London: Hogarth Press, 1932.

Robson, W. A. *Political Quarterly in the Thirties*. London: Allen Lane, 1971.

Rose, Phyllis. *Woman of Letters: A Life of Virginia Woolf*. New York: Oxford University Press, 1979.

Ruotolo, Lucio. *The Interrupted Moment: A View of Virginia Woolf's Novels*. Stanford: Stanford University Press, 1986.

————. *Six Existential Heroes: The Politics of Faith*. Cambridge: Harvard University Press, 1973.

Sackville-West, Vita. *The Letters of Vita Sackville-West to Virginia Woolf*. Edited by Louise De Salvo and Mitchell A. Leaska. New York: William Morrow, 1985.

Schopenhauer, Arthur. *The World as Will and Representation*. Vol. 1. Translated by E. F. J. Payne. New York: Dover, 1969.

Sencourt, Robert. *T. S. Eliot: A Memoir*. New York: Dodd, Mead, 1971.

Seymour, Miranda. *Ottoline Morrell: Life on the Grand Scale*. London: Hodder and Stoughton, 1992.

Shone, Richard. *Bloomsbury Portraits: Vanessa Bell, Duncan Grant, and Their Circle*. Oxford: Phaidon, 1976.

Silver, Brenda. *Virginia Woolf's Reading Notebooks*. Princeton: Princeton University Press, 1983.

Smyth, Ethel. *Impressions That Remained: Memoirs*. New York: Knopf, 1946.

————. *The Memoirs of Ethel Smyth*. Abridged by Ronald Crichton. Harmondsworth: Viking, 1987.

Spalding, Frances. *Roger Fry: Art and Life*. Berkeley: University of California, 1980.

———. *Vanessa Bell*. San Diego: Harcourt Brace Jovanovich, 1983.

Spater, George, and Ian Parsons. *A Marriage of True Minds: An Intimate Portrait of Leonard and Virginia Woolf*. New York: Harcourt Brace Jovanovich, 1977.

Spender, Stephen. *Vienna*. New York: Random House, 1935.

———. *World Within World: The Autobiography of Stephen Spender*. London: Faber and Faber, 1977.

Spilka, Mark. *Virginia Woolf's Quarrel with Grieving*. Lincoln: University of Nebraska Press, 1980.

St. John, Christopher. *Ethel Smyth: A Biography*. New York: Longmans, Green, 1959.

Stansky, Peter, and William Abrahams. *Journey to the Frontier: Two Roads to the Spanish Civil War*. Boston: Little, Brown, 1966.

Stape, J. H., ed. *Virginia Woolf: Interviews and Recollections*. Iowa City: University of Iowa Press, 1995.

Stephen, Leslie. *Sir Leslie Stephen's Mausoleum Book*. Oxford: Clarendon, 1977.

———. *Swift*. New York: Harper and Brothers, 1901.

Symons, Julian. *The Thirties: A Dream Revolved*. London: Cresset, 1960.

Taylor, A. J. P. *English History 1914–1945*. Harmondsworth: Penguin, 1979.

Tremper, Ellen. *Who Lived at Alfoxton: Virginia Woolf and English Romanticism*. Lewisburg: Bucknell University Press, 1998.

Trombley, Stephen. *All That Summer She Was Mad: Virginia Woolf: Female Victim of Male Medicine*. New York: Continuum, 1982.

Walter, Bruno. *Theme and Variations: An Autobiography*. New York: Knopf, 1966.

Webb, Beatrice. *The Diary of Beatrice Webb*. Edited by Norman and Jeanne MacKenzie. Cambridge: Harvard University Press, 1982.

Webb, Sidney. "What Happened in 1931: A Record." *Political Quarterly* 3, no. 1 (1932): 1–17.

Wilberforce, Octavia."The Eighth Child." Typescript, Fawcett Library, London.

Willis, J. H. *Leonard and Virginia Woolf as Publishers: The Hogarth Press, 1917–1941*. Charlottesville: University Press of Virginia, 1992.

Wilson, Duncan. *Leonard Woolf: A Political Biography*. New York: St. Martin's, 1978.

Wilson, Jean Moorcroft. *Virginia Woolf and Anti-Semitism*. London: Cecil Woolf, 1995.

———. *Virginia Woolf: Life and London: A Biography of Place*. London: Cecil Woolf, 1987.

Woodeson, J. *Mark Gertler: Biography of a Painter*. Toronto: University of Toronto Press, 1973.

Woolf, Leonard. *Barbarians at the Gate*. London: Victor Gollancz, 1939.

——. *Beginning Again: An Autobiography of the Years 1911 to 1918*. New York: Harcourt Brace Jovanovich, 1964.

——. *Downhill All the Way: An Autobiography of the Years 1919 to 1939*. San Diego: Harcourt Brace Jovanovich, 1975.

——. *Growing: An Autobiography of the Years 1904 to 1911*. San Diego: Harcourt Brace Jovanovich, 1975.

——. *The Journey Not the Arrival Matters: An Autobiography of the Years 1939 to 1969*. San Diego: Harcourt Brace Jovanovich, 1975.

——. *Letters of Leonard Woolf*. Edited by Frederic Spotts. San Diego: Harcourt Brace Jovanovich, 1989.

——. *Quack, Quack*. New York: Harcourt Brace, 1935.

——. *Sowing: An Autobiography of the Years 1880 to 1904*. San Diego: Harcourt Brace Jovanovich, 1975.

——. *The Wise Virgins: A Story of Words, Opinions, and a Few Emotions*. New York: Harcourt Brace Jovanovich, 1979.

Woolf, Virginia. *Between the Acts*. New York: Harcourt, Brace, and World, 1941.

——. *The Captain's Death Bed and Other Essays*. London: Hogarth Press, 1950.

——. *The Common Reader: First Series*. New York: Harcourt, Brace, and World, 1953.

——. *The Complete Shorter Fiction of Virginia Woolf*. Edited by Susan Dick. 2d ed. San Diego: Harcourt Brace Jovanovich, 1989.

——. *The Death of the Moth and Other Essays*. San Diego: Harcourt Brace Jovanovich, 1970.

——. *The Diary of Virginia Woolf*. Edited by Anne Olivier Bell, assisted by Andrew McNeillie. 5 vols. New York: Harcourt Brace Jovanovich, 1976–1984.

——. *Flush: A Biography*. New York: Harcourt, Brace, 1933.

——. *Freshwater: A Comedy*. Edited by Lucio P. Ruotolo. New York: Harcourt Brace Jovanovich, 1985.

——. *The Letters of Virginia Woolf*. Edited by Nigel Nicolson and Joanne Trautmann. 6 vols. New York: Harcourt Brace Jovanovich, 1975–1980.

——. *The Moment and Other Essays*. London: Hogarth Press, 1952.

——. *Moments of Being*. Edited by Jeanne Schulkind. 2d ed. San Diego: Harcourt Brace Jovanovich, 1985.

——. *Mrs. Dalloway*. New York: Harcourt, Brace, and World, 1953.

——. *Pointz Hall: The Earlier and Later Typescripts of* Between the Acts. Edited by Mitcheall A. Leaska. New York: University Publications, 1983.

——. *The Pargiters: The Novel-Essay Portion of* The Years. Edited by Mitchell A. Leaska. New York: Harcourt Brace Jovanovich, 1978.

———. *A Room of One's Own*. San Diego: Harcourt Brace Jovanovich, 1989.

———. *The Second Common Reader*. New York: Harcourt, Brace, and World, 1960.

———. *Three Guineas*. London: Hogarth Press, 1952.

———. *To the Lighthouse*. New York: Harcourt, Brace, and World, 1955.

———. *The Waves*. New York: Harcourt, Brace, 1931.

———. *The Waves: The Two Holograph Drafts*. Edited by J. W. Graham. Toronto: University of Toronto Press, 1976.

———. *The Years*. New York: Harcourt, Brace, 1937.

Wright, Elizabeth Mary. *The Life of Joseph Wright*. London: Oxford University Press, 1932.

Yeats, W. B. *Collected Poems*. London: Macmillan, 1969.

Zwerdling, Alex. *Virginia Woolf and the Real World*. Berkeley: University of California Press, 1986.

Acknowledgments

My thanks are due to old and new friends. More than three decades ago, Joyce Warshow suggested that I write my first study of Virginia Woolf; Berenice Carroll later proposed a radical interpretation of Woolf's work that led me to focus on the years leading up to World War II. I am indebted to the many biographers, scholars, and critics who have provided the essential foundation for a study of Woolf, especially the editors of the diaries, Anne Olivier Bell, assisted by Andrew McNeillie, and the editors of the letters, Nigel Nicolson and Joanne Trautmann, without whose work a book like this one could hardly have been written. I am indebted to Quentin Bell and Angelica Garnett, whose biographical writings convey the Bloomsbury ethos in a voice of their own. To the late Quentin Bell, who read a draft of the opening of this book, I am indebted for advice and encouragement.

I am grateful to Nina Baym, George Dimock, Carolyn Heilbrun, and Ellen Rosenman, who read the manuscript in its entirety and made suggestions that significantly influenced the final shape of the book. Carolyn Heilbrun very generously read both preliminary and final drafts.

My old friend and colleague Gary Adelman, with whom I discussed the work at every stage, has given me the full benefit of his critical insight and subversive wit. I have benefited from the constructive comments and thoughtful attention of Tom Bassett, Bernard Cesarone, Ina Gabler, Philip Graham, Kelly Knowles, Johanne Rivest, Carol Spindel, and Ryan Szpiech.

The University of Illinois granted me a sabbatical and released time from regular teaching duties so that I could work on this book. I am grateful to the University Research Board, the Office of International Programs, and the Department of English for providing funds for research and travel.

I have received valuable assistance from those in charge of archives and documents. Mabel Smith kindly permitted me to reproduce Octavia Wilberforce's letters and to quote from an unpublished note; she also graciously provided photographs of Dr. Wilberforce. I received assistance and advice from William Brockman and the staff of the University of Illinois English Library, Stephen Crook at the Berg Collection, David Doughan of the Fawcett Library, Cathy Henderson of the Harry Ransom Humanities Research Center, and Bet Inglis of the University of Sussex Library Manuscripts Section.

Heather Ahlstrom of the Harvard Theatre Collection and Jonathan Thristan of the Tate Gallery Archive were unfailingly helpful in the search for photographs. I am also indebted to Barbara Blumenthal of the Mortimer Rare Book Room, John Delany of London's Imperial War Museum, Sheila Taylor of the London Transport Museum, and Leslie Swift of the U.S. Holocaust Memorial Museum.

Special thanks go to my daughter-in-law, Simone Leigh, for taking on the task of doing photo research and for giving me the pleasure of working with her. Harriet Price provided a wealth of information on literary matters and helped me obtain permissions with grace and efficiency. Bernhard Kendler of Cornell University Press smoothed the publication process with humor and great editorial acumen.

Four members of my family have helped me in material and spiritual ways over the years. My brother, Eric, and my sons, Michael and Yuri, gave me their loving attention and provided notes on the style and substance of this book. My wife, Norma, read and commented on each chapter as it was completed, read my revisions, and then made detailed suggestions on the final draft. Her presence reminds me every day that truth in art and in life can go hand in hand.

❧

I acknowledge with thanks the following permissions to quote from copyrighted sources. The Executors of the Virginia Woolf Estate for quotations from *The Diary of Virginia Woolf*, vols. 3–5, published by the Hogarth Press, and from *The Letters of Virginia Woolf*, vols. 4–6, published by the Hogarth Press; Jonathan Cape and A. P. Watt Ltd. on behalf of Sophie Partridge and the Executor of the Estate of David Garnett for "Advice to Oneself" from *Carrington: Letters and*

Extracts, edited by David Garnett; the trustees of Backsettown, and the Royal United Kingdom Beneficent Association for the letters of Octavia Wilberforce; and Harcourt, Inc., and the Estate of Leonard Woolf, for a passage from *The Letters of Leonard Woolf*.

Credits for permission to reproduce photographs are due to the Nina Beskow Agency for figure 16; The Harvard Theatre Collection, Houghton Library, Frederic Woodbridge Wilson, Curator, for figures 3, 4, 7, 8, 9, 11, 12, 14, 15, 18, 19, and 20; the trustees of the Imperial War Museum for figures 21 and 22 (IWM references KY 5863^A, Hu 36155); the London Transport Museum for figure 2; Mortimer Rare Book Room, Smith College, for figure 1; Mabel Smith for figure 23; the Tate Gallery Archive for figures 5, 6, 13, and 17 (Tate references AI19, Q37, Q38); Richard Freimark, courtesy of the U.S. Holocaust Memorial Museum Photo Archives, for figure 10.

Two sections of the "Prelude" first appeared, in somewhat different form, in an essay, "The Biographer and the Angel," in *The American Scholar* 62, no. 2 (Spring 1993): 221–31, copyright © by Herbert Marder.

Index

Entries under Woolf's name are grouped as Events, Motifs and Themes, and Works. Abbreviations used in the Index are JB: Julian Bell, VB: Vanessa Bell, OW: Octavia Wilberforce, LW: Leonard Woolf, VW: Virginia Woolf.

	DATE DUE		